SETTLING THE SCORE

Michael Oliver is a freelance writer and broadcaster on music. For many years he presented BBC Radio 3's *Music Weekly* programme, and for a long period regular editions of Radio 4's *Kaleidoscope*, subsequently writing and presenting the documentary series *Soundings* for three years. Among hundreds of other programmes he wrote radio biographies of Verdi and Puccini. He has been writing for *Gramophone* magazine for thirty years, and has contributed to every issue of *Classic CD*, as well as to numerous other periodicals: he is the founding editor of *International Opera Collector*. He has contributed to books on various aspects of music and has published biographies of Igor Stravinsky and Benjamin Britten. He lives in London and Italy.

Settling the Score

*A Journey through
the Music of the Twentieth Century*

EDITED BY MICHAEL OLIVER

*Based on the Radio 3 Programmes
by arrangement with the BBC*

faber and faber

First published in 1999
by Faber and Faber Limited
3 Queen Square London WC1N 3AU

Photoset by Agnesi Text, Hadleigh
Printed in England by Clays Ltd, St Ives plc

Michael Oliver and the BBC are hereby identified as author of this
work in accordance with Section 77 of the Copyright,
Designs and Patents Act 1988

A CIP record for this book
is available from the British Library

ISBN 0-571-19580-6

2 4 6 8 10 9 7 5 3 1

Contents

Foreword

BBC Radio 3's *Sounding the Century* was one of the largest and most ambitious projects the network has undertaken; there were live concerts around the country from February 1997 to July 1999 and many other broadcasts continuing until the end of 1999. We devoted many hours of broadcasting to twentieth-century music and directed much of the network's resources towards new performances of the modern orchestral repertoire, at a time when we could have provided much easier and less demanding fare.

Why did we do it? *Sounding the Century* grew out of a fundamental belief that the last hundred years have produced some of the most thrilling, important and moving music ever written, and that it was about time we recognized the fact.

Following the success of the network's year-long season of British music, *Fairest Isle*, in 1995, it was clear that an attempt to provide a rich cultural context for twentieth-century music could succeed in broadcasting terms; and there was only one absolutely right moment, as the end of the century approached, to attempt this; it was now or never.

Music was at its heart, planned with artistic consultant George Benjamin and realized with administrator Lucy de Castro in collaboration with all the orchestras around this country. But, as this book demonstrates, the project was also more than music. Throughout *Sounding the Century* the attempt was made to explain and illuminate the music with its social context – part of this, of course, provided by broadcasting itself, which had accumulated a rich archive of material and interviews with some of the leading musical figures of our time.

Settling the Score, the series that forms the basis of this book, was a most ambitious series of documentaries produced during that time under Edward Blakeman's expert direction, surveying all the main themes of the century's musical experience using fascinating BBC material. I am delighted that in publishing this book with Michael Oliver's new narrative, Faber are giving permanence to a valuable project in a medium which, to radio listeners as well as radio producers, can often seem frustratingly impermanent. I hope this exploration of the music of the twentieth century will provide thought-provoking stimulation for those who will create and hear the music of the twenty-first century.

Nicholas Kenyon

Nicholas Kenyon was Controller, BBC Radio 3, from 1992 to 1998 and originated the *Sounding the Century* project. He has been Director of the BBC Proms since the 1996 season.

Preface

The art of music has changed more radically and more rapidly in the twentieth than in any previous century. The changes have been numerous and complex, and their effects have varied widely from place to place. As the century has proceeded, the difficulty of writing a history of its music has become ever more apparent. Attempts have been made, by tracing influences, trying to isolate principal lines of development, etc., but to regard (say) Schoenberg and his followers as crucial and therefore to dismiss Shostakovich as irrelevant in so far as he seemed to ignore Schoenberg is clearly a hopelessly narrow and inadequate way of describing the phenomenon. Schoenberg, it can now be seen, was proposing radical and important solutions to a problem affecting the Austro-German tradition, from Haydn and Mozart through Beethoven, Schubert, Brahms and Bruckner, to Wagner, Mahler and beyond. Composers who felt no particular affinity with that tradition – Russian composers, for example, who had been striving for generations to find a national alternative to that tradition – would not necessarily find Schoenberg's proposals relevant to them, but Shostakovich was not therefore a marginal figure.

Far from one school or technique attaining primacy, the tendency in the final third of the century especially has been towards a multiplicity of styles. Although one of these styles, minimalism, can be seen as a reaction against the dogmatic post-Schoenbergian modernism that prevailed in many quarters in the 1950s and 1960s, the styles that have arisen since then are on the whole neither dogmatic nor combative. Indeed a variety of musical idioms can often be perceived even within the work of a single composer. Thus Alfred Schnittke referred, often ironically, sometimes with a sense of almost nihilistic despair, to a wide range of styles and periods, while in some of his recent compositions György Ligeti combines techniques drawn from African music, the works for mechanical piano of Conlon Nancarrow, and aspects of minimalist or 'systems' music in a style that remains intensely personal.

As well as a multiplication of styles, the sheer amount of music being composed at the turn of the twentieth/twenty-first century is unprecedented, and there has never been a larger number of musicians for whom composing is their central activity, even if the overwhelming

ix

majority of them have to do other work in order to live. Whereas a critic prepared to travel fairly extensively around 1900 could have been reasonably certain of attending every European première that was then perceived as of major consequence, such a feat would not be possible now. Important premières now take place in many countries – including throughout the Americas and the Far East – that either had very little concert activity or were not perceived as musically important a century ago. If the critic cannot keep up with this bewilderingly varied plethora of new music, what chance is there for the listener?

The abundance of new music is matched by a vast increase in the amount of music from the past that is now available to the concert-goer and especially to the collector of recordings. Music before Bach, for example, was little known and little studied in 1900. Now many ordinary listeners are familiar with the music attributed to Abbess Hildegard of Bingen, who was born six centuries before Bach, and many other once-forgotten composers, of many periods, have been rediscovered and have acquired popularity. This huge expansion of the repertoire makes it very easy for listeners to avoid anything that they expect to be difficult or unpleasant, and for many that is the reputation that modern music has acquired. In fact the variety of music currently being written, from the simplest to the most complex, has never been greater, and much of it is readily approachable.

Even those composers whose music does have an element of difficulty to it are often more accessible than much writing about them implies. Reading about the elaborate formal processes of Pierre Boulez's *Le marteau sans maître* or about his early attempts to write 'total serial' music, or indeed reading Boulez's own polemics about creative amnesia and the need for music to be in perpetual movement towards the future can be less helpful in appreciating *Le marteau* than sur-rendering to its elegantly glittering sound world, which is at times a great deal closer to Ravel's *Laideronnette, Impératrice des Pagodes* than perhaps Boulez would be ready to admit. The language of musical analysis has developed as fast as the art itself, but to enjoy a work by Elliott Carter it can be less useful to pore over tables of tempo relation-ships in his music than to recall the composer's own voice saying, with wonder and sheer delight, 'It's flying!'

Hence this book, which is an attempt to tell the story of twentieth-century music not in technical terms, nor by discussing chains of influence ('Schoenberg begat Webern; Webern begat Stockhausen') or national schools. Nor is there any attempt to isolate 'central' figures and ignore 'marginal' ones. Which of this century's composers will seem the most important in the year 2100 is a matter for those who will be alive then. The book surveys those influences – many of them not specifically musical – which have affected the music of the twentieth century; it examines the many functions of music, the way that the musical profession and the musical public have changed, and the effect on both of them of politics, technology, the media and a growing awareness that the history of music is not just the history of Western concert music. It also examines the raw materials of music – melody, rhythm and harmony – and the ways in which they have changed or developed over the course of the last century. It does these things by using the words of those who have made the century's music, and those who will be making it in the coming century, for it is impossible to look back over such a history without looking forward as well.

Settling the Score is based on a series of twenty documentary programmes, broadcast on BBC Radio 3 over a period of two years. Much of the material was drawn from the BBC's vast archives, but many musicians and others were interviewed especially for the series; those interviews themselves now form part of the BBC archives. Each programme was prepared by a writer and a producer, but to put as much emphasis on the archive 'witnesses' as possible the programmes were not presented by those who devised them; any necessary linking script was read by an actor, Samuel West. For the purposes of this book – which is essentially an oral history of twentieth-century music – the archive material has been transcribed very nearly intact to retain the immediacy and colour of the spoken word, and has been edited only minimally, for the sake of ease in reading. The introductions to each chapter are my own, as is the arrangement of the archive material.

Michael Oliver

Acknowledgements

As was said in the Preface, the introductory section of each chapter and the ordering of the subsequent material is mine. But the task of compiling the radio programmes upon which the chapters are based was carried out with great skill and imagination by a number of producers in the BBC Radio Classical Music Department, working in each case with an independent adviser or specialist (I myself performed that function on four of the programmes). I am indebted to them, and list their names here with gratitude. This book is in very large part their work, but they cannot, of course, be held responsible for opinions that I have expressed or for the reordering of the material that they collected. In each case the BBC producer's name is listed first, followed by that of the adviser or compiler. I owe a particular debt to Edward Blakeman, whose overall responsibility the series was; it and this book would have been much the poorer without his skill, unremitting hard work and unfailing good humour; and to Kate Heeley, who researched the programmes and co-ordinated the production of the material for this book.

Michael Oliver

The publishers and the BBC are grateful to the copyright holders of archive material reproduced in *Settling the Score*, as used in the BBC series. While every effort has been made to trace all those concerned, the publishers would be pleased to hear from anyone that we have inadvertently failed to contact.

The extract on pp. 155–6 from *The Piano Player* by Anthony Burgess is reproduced by permission of the Random House Group.

List of Contributors and
Sources Quoted

Many of those listed were interviewed especially for the BBC Radio 3 documentaries on which this book is based. Where dates are added after a name in the main text, the material quoted came from the BBC archives or from printed sources.

THOMAS ADÈS   composer and pianist
JULIAN ANDERSON   composer
LAURIE ANDERSON   American composer and performance artist
ERNEST ANSERMET (1883–1969)   Swiss conductor
FELIX APRAHAMIAN   critic and writer
KENNETH ARCHER   art historian and theatrical consultant
ARISTOXENUS (4th century BC)   Greek philosopher
SIR MALCOLM ARNOLD   composer, formerly orchestral trumpeter
DAVID ATHERTON   conductor; joint founder, London Sinfonietta
MILTON BABBITT   American composer and teacher
EVELYN BARBIROLLI (Evelyn Rothwell)   oboist, widow of Sir John Barbirolli
SIR JOHN BARBIROLLI (1899–1970)   conductor; began career as orchestral and solo cellist
HUGH BEAN   former leader, Philharmonia Orchestra
DAVID BEDFORD   composer
SIR THOMAS BEECHAM (1879–1961)   conductor; founder of the London Philharmonic and Royal Philharmonic Orchestras
LUDWIG VAN BEETHOVEN (1770–1827)   composer
SIR LEONARD BEHRENS (1891–1978)   former chairman, Hallé Orchestra
GEORGE BENJAMIN   composer; Artistic Consultant to BBC Radio 3's *Sounding the Century* series
SIR RICHARD RODNEY BENNETT   composer and jazz pianist
HECTOR BERLIOZ (1803–1869)   French composer
SIR HARRISON BIRTWISTLE   composer
SIR ARTHUR BLISS (1891–1975)   composer; Master of the Queen's Music 1953–75

JOHN BORLAND (1866–1937)   from 1909 Music Adviser, London County Council

GEORGINA BORN   Lecturer in the Sociology of Culture, Cambridge University

GIDI BOSS   Israeli record and radio producer

NADIA BOULANGER (1887–1979)   French teacher of composition

PIERRE BOULEZ   French composer and conductor; founder–director of IRCAM (Institut de Recherche et de Coordination Acoustique/Musique)

SIR ADRIAN BOULT (1889–1983)   first principal conductor of the BBC Symphony Orchestra (1930–50)

JOSE BOWEN   Director, Centre for the History and Analysis of Recorded Music, Southampton University

MARTYN BRABBINS   conductor

NEIL BRAND   pianist for silent films

ERNEST BRAVINGTON   trumpeter; former Chairman, London Philharmonic Orchestra

BERTOLT BRECHT (1898–1956)   German poet and playwright

BENJAMIN BRITTEN (Lord Britten of Aldeburgh; 1913–1976) composer and pianist

GAVIN BRYARS   composer

ANTHONY BURGESS (1917–1993)   novelist and composer

DIANA BURRELL   composer

FERRUCCIO BUSONI (1866–1924)   Italian–German composer and pianist

HENRI DE BUSSCHER   Belgian oboist; member of Queen's Hall Orchestra 1904–13

JOHN CAGE (1912–1992)   American composer

CORNELIUS CARDEW (1936–1981)   composer; founder of the Scratch Orchestra

SIR NEVILLE CARDUS (1888–1975)   critic and writer on music

BRENDAN CARROLL   biographer of Erich Wolfgang Korngold

ELLIOTT CARTER   American composer

AVRIL COLERIDGE-TAYLOR   composer and conductor; daughter of African–English composer Samuel Coleridge-Taylor (1875–1912)

STEVE CONNOR   Professor of Modern Literature and Theory, Birkbeck College, London University

NICHOLAS COOK   musicologist

MERVYN COOKE   Lecturer in Music, University of Nottingham

AARON COPLAND (1900–1990)   American composer

PAUL DANIEL   conductor; Music Director, English National Opera
MICHAEL DAUGHERTY   American composer
SIR PETER MAXWELL DAVIES   composer
SIR (HENRY) WALFORD DAVIES (1869–1941)   composer, organist and educationalist
CARL DAVIS   composer, especially of film music
SIR COLIN DAVIS   conductor
JOHN DEATHRIDGE   musicologist and critic
CLAUDE DEBUSSY (1862–1918)   French composer
NORMAN DEL MAR (1919–1994)   conductor and writer on music
NIKOLAI DEMIDENKO   Russian pianist
JENNY DOCTOR   Librarian, the Britten–Pears Library
JOHN DRINKWATER   composer
SIR JOHN DRUMMOND   formerly Director, Edinburgh Festival, and BBC Controller, Music, and Controller, Radio 3
ROGER DURSTON   Director of Music, Wells Cathedral School
HENRI DUTILLEUX   French composer
TERRY EDWARDS   choral conductor
CYRIL EHRLICH   social and economic historian
SIR EDWARD ELGAR (1857–1934)   composer; Master of the King's Music 1924–34
MISCHA ELMAN (1891–1967)   Russian-born American violinist
ANTHONY EVERITT   former Secretary-General, Arts Council of Great Britain; author of Gulbenkian Foundation report *Joining In*
MORTON FELDMAN (1926–1987)   American composer
BRIAN FERNEYHOUGH   composer
MICHAEL FINNISSY   composer
HENRY FOGEL   Manager, Chicago Symphony Orchestra
MICHAEL FORSYTH   writer on acoustics
SIMON FOSTER   formerly Managing Director, Virgin Records; Director of Concerts and Recordings, Royal Philharmonic Orchestra
CHRISTOPHER FOX   composer
SIMON FRITH   writer on popular music; Professor of English, Strathclyde University
JOSEF FROMMELT   Swiss music teacher; President, European Union of Music Schools
ANDREI GAVRILOV   Russian pianist
PHILIP GLASS   American composer
ALEXANDER GOEHR   composer; formerly Professor of Music, Cambridge University

SZYMON GOLDBERG (1909–1993)   Polish-born American violinist and conductor

MIKE GONZALEZ   Lecturer in Hispanic Studies, Glasgow University

SIDONIE GOOSSENS   harpist

PENELOPE GOUK   historian of medicine

LUCY GREEN   Head of Music and Drama Department, London University Institute of Education

SUSAN GREENFIELD   neurologist; Professor of Synaptic Pharmacology, Oxford University

VICKY GREGORY   Chief Executive, Bridgewater Hall, Manchester

PAUL GRIFFITHS   critic and writer on music

PETER GRILLI   Executive Director, Donald Keene Centre of Japanese Culture

RAYMOND GUBBAY   impresario and concert promoter

ERNEST GUIRAUD (1837–1892)   French composer and teacher

BERNARD HAITINK   Dutch conductor

CRISTÓBAL HALFFTER   Spanish composer and conductor

ARTHUR HAMMOND   former Musical Director, Carl Rosa Opera Company

JEAN HARVEY   formerly Chief Examiner, Associated Board of the Royal Schools of Music

JONATHAN HARVEY   composer

GAVIN HENDERSON   Director of Dartington Summer School of Music; Principal, Trinity College of Music

HANS WERNER HENZE   German composer

DAME MYRA HESS (1890–1965)   pianist; joint founder, wartime National Gallery concerts

SIR SEYMOUR HICKS (1871–1949)   stage entertainer and theatrical manager

DUNCAN HINNELLS   Historian of the Music Department of Oxford University Press

STEPHEN HINTON   musicologist

MILLICENT HODSON   American choreographer and dance historian

CHRISTOPHER HOGWOOD   conductor and harpsichordist; founder of the Academy of Ancient Music

ROBIN HOLLOWAY   composer

IMOGEN HOLST (1907–1984)   composer, teacher and writer on music; daughter of Gustav Holst

FRANK HOWES (1891–1974)   music critic of *The Times*, 1943–62

DAVID HUCKVALE   film-music historian

JOHN HUNTLEY   film-music historian

JOHN IRELAND (1879–1962)   composer and pianist
CHARLES IVES (1874–1954)   American composer
LEOŠ JANÁČEK (1854–1928)   Czech composer
STEPHEN JOHNSON   critic and writer on music
HERBERT VON KARAJAN (1908–1989)   German conductor
BERNARD KEEFFE   conductor and teacher
HANS KELLER (1919–1987)   Austrian-born musician and writer;
   former Chief Assistant, New Music, BBC
DAISY KENNEDY   Australian violinist
MICHAEL KENNEDY   critic and biographer
JOHN MAYNARD KEYNES (1883–1946)   economist; first Chairman,
   Arts Council of Great Britain
PETER KIVY   philosopher of music
ZOLTÁN KODÁLY (1882–1967)   Hungarian composer and music
   educationalist
RAFAEL KUBELIK   Czech conductor
JOHN KUCHMY   orchestral player
PIERRE LALO (1866–1943)   French critic and writer
CONSTANT LAMBERT (1905–1951)   conductor, composer and writer
REX LAWSON   writer on player-pianos and mechanical music
NORMAN LEBRECHT   arts journalist, author of *When the Music
   Stops . . .*
STEPHEN LEDBETTER   musicologist with Boston Symphony
   Orchestra
JENNIE LEE (Baroness Lee of Asheridge; 1904–1988)   Labour
   politician; first British Minister for the Arts
NICOLA LEFANU   composer; Professor of Music, York University
WALTER LEGGE (1906–1979)   record producer; founder of
   Philharmonia Orchestra
ERIK LEVI   writer and critic; author of *Music in the Third Reich*
NONA LIDDELL   violinist; founder member and leader, London
   Sinfonietta
GYORGY LIGETI   Hungarian-born composer
MAGNUS LINDBERG   Finnish composer
TASMIN LITTLE   violinist
GERARD MCBURNEY   composer and writer
JOANNA MACGREGOR   pianist
RICHARD MCNICOL   flautist; London Symphony Orchestra music
   animateur
FERGUS MCWILLIAM   horn player, Berlin Philharmonc Orchestra
SIR JOHN MANDUELL   formerly Principal, Royal Northern College
   of Music

WILLIAM MANN (1924–1989)   critic, writer and translator; music critic of *The Times* 1960–82

GUGLIELMO MARCONI (1874–1937)   Italian inventor of radio telegraphy

SIR NEVILLE MARRINER   conductor; founder of the Academy of St Martin in the Fields

PETER MARTIN   sociologist

ODALINE DE LA MARTINEZ   Cuban-born conductor

DIEGO MASSON   French conductor

MUIR MATHIESON (1911–1975)   conductor; Musical Director, London Films

COLIN MATTHEWS   composer

SIR ROBERT MAYER (1879–1985)   German-born patron of music; founder of Robert Mayer Orchestral Concerts for Children and of Youth and Music

WILFRID MELLERS   composer; former Professor of Music, York University

MELINA MERCOURI (1925–1994)   Greek actress, singer and politician

OLIVIER MESSIAEN (1908–1992)   French composer, organist and teacher

RODNEY MILNES   critic; editor *Opera* magazine

DONALD MITCHELL   critic and writer on music

GERALD MOORE (1899–1987)   acccompanist

GILLIAN MOORE   Artistic Director, London Sinfonietta

TOM MORRIS   Manager, Cleveland Orchestra

BRYCE MORRISON   critic and piano teacher

PETER PAUL NASH   composer

ERNEST NEWMAN (1868–1959)   critic and writer on music

IVOR NEWTON (1892–1981)   accompanist

FIAMMA NICOLODI   Italian musicologist; author of *Musica e musicisti nel ventennio Fascista*

SIR ROGER NORRINGTON   conductor

MICHAEL OLIVER   writer and broadcaster

JOSE ORTEGA Y GASSET (1883–1925)   Spanish writer and philosopher

DAVID OSMOND-SMITH   Professor of Music, Sussex University

JOHN PAYNTER   composer; former Professor of Music Education, University of York

SIR PETER PEARS (1910–1986)   tenor; creator of most of Benjamin Britten's tenor roles

FRITZ PEPPERMULLER   member of Berlin Philharmonic Orchestra under Wilhelm Furtwängler

JACK (JOHN F.) PFEIFFER (1920–1996)   American record producer
ROBERT PHILIP   critic and historian of recorded music
GREGOR PIATIGORSKY (1903–1976)   Russian-born cellist
PRINCESSE EDMOND DE POLIGNAC (1846–1942)   French
   (American-born) patroness of new music
ANDREW PORTER   musicologist, critic and translator
PETER PRESTON   biographer of General Franco
RUTH RAILTON   founder, National Youth Orchestra of Great Britain
DAME MARIE RAMBERT (Cyvia Rambam, Miriam Ramberg, 1888–
   1982)   Polish-born dancer, teacher and director; founder of
   Ballet Rambert
PETER READMAN   businessman; Chairman of the Chamber
   Orchestra of Europe
STEVE REICH   American composer
FREDERICK RIDDLE   former principal viola, Royal
   Philharmonic Orchestra
JANET RITTERMAN   Director, Royal College of Music
ALEC ROBERTSON (1892–1982)   critic and broadcaster
NIKOLAY ROERICH (1874–1947)   Russian painter and stage designer
NED ROREM   American composer and writer
GENNADI ROZHDESTVENSKY   Russian conductor
MIKLÓS RÓZSA (1907–1995)   Hungarian-born composer
ARTUR RUBINSTEIN (1887–1982)   Polish-born pianist
BERTRAND RUSSELL (3rd Earl Russell; 1872–1970)   philosopher
   and mathematician
KEN RUSSELL   film and television director
PAUL SACHER (1906–1999)   Swiss conductor, founder of Basle
   Chamber Orchestra
HARVEY SACHS   American writer and critic; author of *Music in
   Fascist Italy*
STANLEY SADIE   musicologist and critic; editor *The New Grove*
EDWARD SAID   cultural commentator
SIR MALCOLM SARGENT (1895–1967)   conductor
PADDY SCANNELL   Reader, Centre for Communication and
   Information Studies, University of Westminster
AUGUST WILHELM VON SCHLEGEL (1767–1845)   German poet
ARTUR SCHNABEL (1882–1951)   Austrian-born pianist and
   composer
GEORGE BERNARD SHAW (1856–1950)   Irish playwright and novelist;
   began career as music and drama critic
ROBERT SIMPSON (1921–1998)   composer

HOWARD SKEMPTON   composer

LEONARD SLATKIN   American conductor

JOHN SLOBODA   cognitive psychologist

LYDIA SOKOLOVA (Hilda Munnings, 1896–1974)   English-born ballerina, danced in corps de ballet in first performance of *The Rite of Spring* and took role of Chosen Virgin in 1920 revival

STEPHEN SONDHEIM   American composer of musicals

NEIL SORRELL   ethnomusicologist

ISAAC STERN   American (Russian-born) violinist

KARLHEINZ STOCKHAUSEN   German composer

LEOPOLD STOKOWSKI (1882–1977)   American (English-born) conductor

IGOR STRAVINSKY (1882–1971)   Russian composer (later naturalized French, then American)

TORU TAKEMITSU (1930–1996)   Japanese composer

RICHARD TARUSKIN   American musicologist; authority on Russian music

JOHN TAVENER   composer

MICHAEL TILSON THOMAS   American conductor and pianist

OLAV ANTON THOMMESEN   Norwegian composer

VIRGIL THOMSON (1896–1989)   American composer and critic

JUDITH TICK   Professor of Music, Northeastern University, Boston

SIR MICHAEL TIPPETT (1905–1998)   composer

SUSAN TOMES   pianist

MICHAEL TORKE   American composer

PAUL TORTELIER (1914–1990)   French cellist

SIR DONALD TOVEY (1875–1940)   composer, writer and educationalist

BASIL TSCHAIKOV   clarinettist

JULIA USHER   composer and music therapist

RALPH VAUGHAN WILLIAMS (1872–1958)   composer

FRIEDELIND WAGNER   teacher and stage director; granddaughter of Richard Wagner

STEPHEN WALSH   critic and writer on music

SIR WILLIAM WALTON (1902–1983)   composer

JULIAN LLOYD WEBBER   cellist

PAUL WEBSTER   pianist and teacher

KURT WEILL (1900–1950)   German-born composer

ELMAR WEINGARTEN   Intendant, Berlin Philharmonic Orchestra

JUDITH WEIR   composer; Director, Spitalfields Festival

ARNOLD WHITTALL   musicologist and writer

ELIZABETH WILSON   writer on music; author of *Shostakovich
Remembered*

JULIA WOLFE   composer

SIR HENRY WOOD (1869–1944)   conductor; founder of the
Promenade Concerts named after him

HUGH WOOD   composer and teacher

JAMES WOOD   composer, percussionist and conductor

LADY JESSIE WOOD   companion of Sir Henry Wood

JOSEPH WORTIS   colleague of Sigmund Freud

ROGER WRIGHT   Head of BBC Classical Music, now Controller,
Radio 3

CHARLES WUORINEN   American composer

IRINA ZARITSKAYA   Russian violin teacher; Professor at Royal
College of Music

Settling the Score

I 1900

A historian is a prophet who looks backward.
AUGUST WILHELM VON SCHLEGEL, 1798

T HE YEAR 1900 was the end of an old century as well as the beginning of a new one. The Habsburg Empire still ruled Austria, Hungary and much of Eastern Europe, the Romanov dynasty still reigned in Russia, the Ottoman Empire in the Near East. Victoria, Queen of the United Kingdom for sixty-three years and Empress of India for twenty-three, still ruled over an Empire upon which it seemed that the sun would never set. In English the popular books of the day were the 'Raffles' stories of E. W. Hornung, Somerville and Ross's *Some Experiences of an Irish R.M.* and Anthony Hope's tales of Ruritania; theatre-goers thronged to Sir Arthur Wing Pinero's *Trelawny of the 'Wells'*. Abroad, Georges Feydeau had another success in Paris with his *La dame de chez Maxim* and Arthur Schnitzler a scandalous one in Vienna with *Reigen*.

In the world of music Verdi was still alive, as was Dvořák (at work on *Rusalka*). Rimsky-Korsakov completed his opera *The Tsar's Bride*, begun thiry-five years earlier, and started work on *Tsar Saltan*. In Britain Edward Elgar was seen as a coming man following the success of his *Enigma Variations*; of his more established seniors Sir Hubert Parry was appointed Professor of Music at Oxford and Director of the Leeds Festival, while Sir Charles Stanford was at work both on his opera *Much Ado About Nothing* and his First Irish Rhapsody.

The deaths were reported of Sir Arthur Sullivan and Johann Strauss II.

In South Africa the Boer War, which had broken out in 1899, continued. The relieving of besieged Mafeking and Ladysmith saw the most widespread public rejoicing in London since the Queen's Jubilee three years earlier; to prevent Boer civilians from collaborating with the rebels they were rounded up into what were termed, in a newly coined phrase, 'concentration camps'. In Britain the General Federation of Trades Unions (later to become the Trades Union Congress) and the Labour Representation Committee (later the Labour Party) were established, in the USA the American Federation of Labour, in Russia the Socialist Revolutionary Party, which advocated terrorism. Vladimir Ilyich Ulyanov had just returned from three years' exile in Siberia for his part in the Union for the Struggle for the Liberation of the Working Classes. He would soon adopt the pseudonym Lenin.

The first International Congress of Women was held in London. The school leaving age in the United Kingdom was raised to fourteen (elementary education had been both free and compulsory since 1870). Max Planck advanced his quantum theory, London's underground railway was electrified and the escalator invented. Sigmund Freud published his treatise *The Interpretation of Dreams*, Albert Einstein was formulating his special theory of relativity and Bertrand Russell was working on his *Principles of Mathematics*.

In Vienna the association of artists and designers who chose *Ver Sacrum* as their motto had already built the Sezession building for their exhibitions in 1898; similarly in Russia the first major historical exhibition of Russian art, curated by Sergey Diaghilev, was mounted by his magazine *Mir Iskustva*. In Dublin Lady Gregory and W. B. Yeats founded the Irish Dramatic Movement and staged Yeats's play *The Countess Cathleen*. In Paris and Barcelona paintings by Pablo Picasso were seen by the public for the first time. Giacomo Puccini, in London for the local première of his *Tosca*, went to the theatre for a performance of the American David Belasco's play *Madame Butterfly*. At La Scala, Milan, a young tenor, Enrico Caruso, triumphed in Donizetti's *L'elisir d'amore*; meanwhile in Rome Pope Leo XIII still had a castrato, Alessandro Moreschi, singing in the Sistine Chapel choir. In Austria Gustav Mahler, during his summer holiday from directing Vienna's Imperial and Royal State Opera, began writing his Fourth Symphony. Though it was not to be performed for another three years, Arnold Schoenberg completed his string sextet *Verklärte Nacht* and began his vast *Gurrelieder*.

Mostly in local rather than in national papers, and little noticed except by the families and friends of those concerned, the births were announced of Georges Auric and Francis Poulenc, Vladimir Nabokov and Luis Buñuel, Aaron Copland and Kurt Weill, Duke Ellington and Marlene Dietrich.

But if, as Professor Ehrlich suggests below, the nineteenth century did not really end until the outbreak of the First World War, the last years of the 'long nineteenth century', as it has been called, also saw the death of Queen Victoria, and thus of the Victorian era (and the beginning of the Edwardian, until the succession of George V in 1910) and the coming to power in Britain of a Liberal government. President McKinley of the United States was assassinated and succeeded by Theodore Roosevelt. In Britain the Women's Social and Political Union was founded, with the slogan 'Votes for Women'. In Ireland the Sinn Fein party (its name the Irish Gaelic for 'We ourselves') was formed. In 1905 revolution broke out in Russia, Leon Trotsky heading the St Petersburg Soviet, but was soon and brutally suppressed. In France Captain Alfred Dreyfus, convicted of treason in 1894 and condemned to life imprisonment on Devil's Island, was declared innocent by a court of appeal in 1906. British Members of Parliament received a salary (of £500 a year) for the first time.

The same period saw the rise of gramophone recording, Enrico Caruso making his first records in 1902. In the following year Orville and Wilbur Wright made the first flight in a heavier-than-air machine. A scheme for a Channel tunnel was rejected by the British Parliament. The North and South Poles were both reached for the first time. The S.S. *Titanic* sank after collision with an iceberg off Cape Race. The London Symphony Orchestra was founded; cubism was defined in a statement by Pablo Picasso and Georges Braque: 'Paint not what you see, but what you know is there'; Sergey Diaghilev established his Ballets Russes; the words 'tango', 'blues' and 'jazz' came into widespread use.

*

At the turn of the century

JANUARY 1ST, 1900: I begin today a new year, full of anxiety and fear for what may be before us. I pray that God may spare me yet a short while to my children, friends and dear country, leaving me all my faculties and to a certain extent my eyesight. May he bless our arms and give our men strength to fulfil their arduous task. (Queen Victoria's Diary)

The Boer assault of Ladysmith

Details of the Fight – British Bayonets At Work

FOR THE SECOND TIME the Boers have made an attack on Ladysmith, and for the second time they have failed, with disastrous results . . . Major Miller-Wallnutt, of the Gordons, was directing the fire of his men with splendid effect, and exposed himself with almost reckless bravery. Again and again did the Boers try to shoot him down, without success. At length a huge Boer, with a long, flowing beard, leaped to his feet, and, with instant aim, shot the Major in the head with an express bullet. The missile was of the ordinary explosive sporting type, and the poor officer's head was almost shattered to pieces. His murderer – there is no other word suitable – was riddled with bullets before he could sink back to his place. (*Daily Telegraph*, 26 February 1900)

Seeds of change

WHEN I WAS BEING ANALYSED by Freud I was also studying neuro-anatomy, but Freud said to me, 'Young man, study biochemistry: that's where the future lies. We psycho-analysts,' he went on, 'we can observe and describe the path the mind takes as a mental disorder develops, but the force that pushes the mind along this path is hidden from our view. It is biochemical, and the next step will be to discover its nature.' (Joseph Wortis, 1965)

STRUCTURE IS WHAT is most significant in our knowledge of the physical world, and for ages structure had been conceived as depending upon two different manifolds, one of space, the other of time. Einstein showed that, for reasons partly experimental and partly logical, the two must be replaced by one, which he called space-time. (Bertrand Russell, 1954)

I CAME ACROSS RECENTLY a map of Europe in 1500 with rings marked on it to indicate how long it would take for an item of news to pass across Europe. And basically if Vesuvius had erupted and totally destroyed Naples London would have learned of this in three weeks, but probably longer. By the end of the nineteenth century, because of the train, because of telegraphy, news passed much more rapidly than it had ever done before. So a very fast-moving war like the Boer War would have been constantly discussed in the newspapers and constantly updated. People would have been able to follow the fortunes of battle in a way that was unprecedented, I think, until the late nineteenth century. (Michael Oliver)

1900 seen from 1999

IT SEEMS TO ME that our obsession with birthdays and centenaries and all that – all of these things were totally lacking in 1900; entering the new century was simply not a big deal. And I think that's right in historical terms too, because I think from an historian's point of view the nineteenth century, in so far as it ends at all, it ends in 1913, because so much of what we think of as the features of the late nineteenth century, of modernization and all that, continued to a height, to an apogee, in 1913. The Russian Revolution had not happened, there were no passports, so that it was truly an international economy and as far as musicians are concerned, they really did cross these frontiers; and of course the most recent frontier to have been crossed to be significant for this market was America. (Cyril Ehrlich)

THE POPULATION IN the United States went from about 40 million in 1870 to about 100 million in 1916, so we're in a period of tremendous growth. And the music profession itself went from (if you want statistics) about sixteen thousand employed in the profession in 1870 to about ninety-two thousand in 1900. That's an increase, a huge increase, of over 200 per cent. So that we have a burgeoning population; we have 25 million immigrants coming here in this period. There's an enormous growth in vaudeville, in theatre, and there were eighteen thousand bands in the United States around 1900. Even though the New York Philharmonic Orchestra, for example, had a hundred musicians in 1860 and went down to sixty musicians, a lot of those musicians could find work in New York – saloons or concert halls or cafés or theatre orchestras – you could make a living. It was a Cinderella profession, a rags to riches profession, to some extent, but it was also a reasonable profession for a young person to think about. (Judith Tick)

Opening of the Paris Exhibition

From Our Own Correspondent

YESTERDAY WAS FAVOURED with charming weather, and the light and soft spring air which flooded Paris contributed their part to the effort to make the inauguration ceremony more than an ordinary official function. Science and art and human labour, and activities less refined, solicit here the attention of the peoples. All punishments in the army and navy and State schools were cancelled yesterday in honour of the opening, and all sailors had a ration of wine. (*The Times*, 16 April 1900)

THE MOTOR CAR was becoming a regular social problem – some people called it worse things, as you can gather from this topical song I used to sing on the stage in 1906. And another rather interesting thing is that the chap who wrote that song was an unknown young American – fellow named Jerome Kern:

> Oh what is the thing that helps to keep the population small?
> What is it makes us run like hares and jump a six-foot wall?
> What is it makes us all turn pale and feel that life is flat,
> And murmur sadly, 'What's the use? I can't compete with that'?
> It is the motor car, it is the motor car!
> If you exceed the legal speed, you'll have to pay.
> You get on very well until you're blown to . . .
> And you motor down to Brighton for the day.

(Seymour Hicks, 1946)

Obituary

OUR BERLIN CORRESPONDENT telegraphed last night: the well-known author, Friedrich Wilhelm Nietzsche, died at Weimar yesterday morning. Nietzsche's fame rests upon his philosophy of the 'Superman', and he has been described as being in philosophy what Wagner was in music. His glorification of 'personal force' as the only power that ought to be allowed to rule in the universe was little to the taste of the time in which he lived, and his works were certainly not taken very seriously in England. (*The Times*, 27 August 1900)

BECAUSE OF THE SPEED with which news travelled by this period, people must have been aware of a climate of change. There was famine in India, there were rebellions in China, Japan was stirring, America was beginning to act like a great power, things were not quite right in Russia, so there was perceived instability, and one does find a sense of questioning. That is one of the things that Chekhov is about: his plays look at a vanished and irrecoverable past and look into a dubious future. Tolstoy, having written epics, is now much more concerned with the morality of society and how we shall build the future of this coming century. And, particularly in distinctly rigid societies like the Habsburg Austro-Hungarian Empire, like the Russian Empire, there was a quite widespread feeling that the *status quo* had become fossilized. And in both those societies you come across young artists and thinkers feeling, 'We cannot cope with this top-heavy, impossibly bureaucratic, impossibly authoritarian, rigidly conservative society any longer; and we need new organizations in which these arts can take place. The art that we are working in – painting, drama, music – hasn't begun to realize its boundaries yet.' (Michael Oliver)

A new musical century dawns

I THINK IT MUST HAVE BEEN a very interesting time in the first decade of this century. There was an optimism, a belief in science, that it could really transform the world and that it could lead us to paradise. That may be an exaggeration, but there's a saying of Debussy: 'I want to write a new music that will equal the era' – I think he said – 'of the Eiffel Tower and aeroplanes.' And there must have been a tremendous optimism and confidence in the future and that, with all its uncertainties, must have been very exciting to live through.

Several things: there is the close of the tonal system, an absolute rupture with Romanticism and what the nineteenth century represented; the rediscovery of older music and a different way of looking at the past – learning from the past in much greater and more profound ways than ever before and yet at the same time, partly as a reaction to that, an absolutely violent, at certain points complete rejection of the past, which had not happened for centuries. Beyond that, the thing that is really new about the twentieth century is constructivism, the idea of composers inventing their own laws and composing not in a well-known and much used vernacular tradition but inventing their own world, a world of sound and a world of laws and of techniques. I think that really is new, and it's a response to the great emphasis put on personal liberty in the twentieth century (sometimes of course shattered horrendously): the individual having the right if not the necessity to express his or her own individual thoughts and indeed inventing the idiom, from the smallest atom upwards, of their work. (George Benjamin)

M. DEBUSSY'S SCORE of *Pelléas and Mélisande* defies description, being such a refined concatenation of sounds that not the faintest impression is made on the ear. The composer's system is to ignore melody altogether; his personages do not sing, but talk in a sort of lilting voice to a vague musical accompaniment of the text. The effect is quite bewildering, almost amusing in its absurdity. (*The Era*, London, 2 May 1902)

Philharmonic Society. 77th season, 1889

Third Concert, Thursday April 11th, 1889, St. James's Hall

Conductor, Mr. Frederic H. Cowen
Doors open at half-past seven o'clock.
To commence at 8 o'clock precisely.
Part 1: Symphony in E flat, by Mozart
Air, 'Divinités du Styx' from Alceste, by Gluck,
sung by Miss Marguerite Hall (her first appearance at these concerts)
Concerto in B flat for Pianoforte and Orchestra, No. 1,
by Tchaikovsky, played by Monsieur Sapellnikoff,
conducted by the COMPOSER
Part 2: Orchestral Suite in D Opus 43, by Tchaikovsky,
first time in England, conducted by the COMPOSER
Songs, from Joshua by Handel and from The Tempest by Purcell,
sung by Mr. W. H. Brereton
Overture 'Lurline' by Wallace

The repertoire at the turn of the century

THIS IS DIFFICULT, actually; it's more difficult, I think, than people – including musicologists – allow. When people talk about concerts in the past they tend to talk about things like first performances, which by my book are really not very important. To really know you need the kind of statistical grasp – you need to do some counting – which is, after all, what we do nowadays when we talk about *Top of the Pops*. When we say that a record is in the top twenty or whatever these are quantitative measurements and they do at least have the merit that they're objective. I mean, provided you're not lying when you say this, they give you some sense of order of magnitude. Now, to push that back into the past is something that we have done very little of. We need to do much more empirical research. (Cyril Ehrlich)

YOU WOULD HAVE HEARD, around 1900, lots of mixed concerts, with vocal performances of opera as well as symphonies; Mendelssohn was very popular here, Mozart and Haydn less so. Strauss after 1900, a little bit of Debussy, Franck. They did play living composers: I'm thinking of Frederick Stock in Chicago, for example; he was a very prominent advocate of local talent. But certainly the notion of a historical repertoire was not in place in 1900. The repertoire was much more alive; I think it was more diverse also. If you look at

Sousa's concerts, he can have opera airs existing with two-steps and ragtime, so right up there with ragtime and marches and *Semper Fidelis* was a wonderful young soprano singing the latest air from a Wagner opera or a Verdi opera, adding a patina of culture to this otherwise very boisterous, optimistic kind of American music. (Judith Tick)

NOW WHEN I WAS quite a boy I went once to a play in the Midland Theatre, Manchester – they used to have a theatre in the Midland Hotel. And *hoi polloi* could get in, by paying a shilling, at the back. And they used to have orchestras in those days that played in the intervals, perhaps twenty players, and I heard for the first time in my life the 'Vilja' song from *The Merry Widow*. And that was the first time that music ever struck me in what I call an artistic way, because *The Merry Widow*, of course, on its plane, is just as great a work as *Figaro* on its plane. And it's what they call 'kitsch'. Now you can't define it in English: it's not vulgarity and it's not cheapness, it's a sort of consciousness that you're being sentimental and enjoying it. And you could go from Lehár and that 'Vilja' song and trace a direct line to Schubert and Mozart and the great music. (Neville Cardus, 1973)

BY THE FIRST DECADE of the twentieth century you had an enormous amount of music-making going on. You could go to a concert practically every night, even Sundays. Until quite recently there were no Sunday concerts, for example; you had Saturday afternoons and Sundays as the busiest parts of the week – and most people had a half-day holiday, which of course is linked to the growth of music-making. Most importantly for concert life the two best, most popular, concert venues that London has ever had got under way: the Bechstein Hall or Wigmore Hall and the Queen's Hall. Now all of this was taking place without any patronage at all. London was the richest city in the world but there was no patronage; the court was useless as far as music was concerned, and gave nothing. You had international concert agents articulating an international market, categorizing artists as top artists, middle artists, not-so-good artists, novices and so on, so that everything that took place depended absolutely on the financial acumen, the commercial risk-taking of entrepreneurs. That's why the great Newman of the Queen's Hall, Robert Newman, and his colleague Henry Wood were such a formidable team, because as well as putting on the best concerts in town, as it were, they also built the loyalty of an audience, which knew that it could depend upon them to get value for money at a modern, properly run, concert hall. The Queen's Hall was a totally new thing in concert experience. (Cyril Ehrlich)

Thursday 10th November 1910 at the Queen's Hall
Conductor, Sir Edward Elgar
To commence at 8 o'clock precisely
Part 1: National Anthem, scored by Elgar
Overture 'Naiades', by Sterndale Bennett
Violin Concerto, by Elgar: first performance, FRITZ KREISLER
Part 2: Symphony No. 1, by Elgar

IF YOU LOOK AT the travel diaries or travel engagements of great virtuosi of the period, you'll find that their lives were totally different from those of today. If a famous pianist comes to Britain once a year, he'll give a concert at the Festival Hall or the Wigmore Hall and go away again. Liszt played in forty, fifty different cities and towns, some of them quite small; Jenny Lind sang practically everywhere you can think of. The eagerness for musical experience at this time was huge, if one thinks perhaps of the prodigious activity of a network of choral societies, some of them, sure, giving *Messiah* at Christmas and *Elijah* at Easter and that was it, but some of them doing respectably big seasons, and many of them uniting for very large-scale choral festivals whose repertoire was often quite adventurous. (Michael Oliver)

The business of music

THE SONG OF HIAWATHA has been before the world both in Longfellow's original and numerous translations for nearly half a century, free to countless composers to exercise their ingenuity upon it. Yet not one has succeeded in producing music that lives as Mr. Coleridge-Taylor's will live. Coming now to the performance of the 22nd ultimo, let us say at once that the composer's triumph was complete. Rarely, if ever, has such a spontaneous outburst of genuine enthusiasm been witnessed in London at the production of a new work. The pent-up feeling of the deeply moved audience relieved itself in such cheers and shouts of approbation as must have warmed and gladdened the heart of the composer and, if we may incidentally say so, also of those who for some years past have hailed the young Anglo-African as the coming man in music. (*Musical Times*, 1 April 1900)

OF COURSE, AS YOU PERHAPS KNOW, he didn't get a penny from it. He sold the whole work outright for 115 guineas. Mind you, they acted as business people, they didn't know it was going to be so successful, obviously, but one begins to wonder if perhaps he couldn't have made it up some time later. I think my father knew the actual amount. He always used to laugh when he went into those wonderful premises in Wardour Street – deep carpet; he'd think, 'That was from *Hiawatha*!' (Avril Coleridge-Taylor, 1975)

COPYRIGHT WAS REALLY in a very difficult stage in 1900. The Geneva Convention and the various other international agreements on copyright were beginning to get under way but in England it isn't until the 1911 Copyright Act that you really get everything pulled together, that gives some real protection to the composer. The 1911 Copyright Act is a major step forward. The other step forward, expressly linked to that, is the formation of the Performing Right Society in England in 1914. From that time on any publisher and composer joining the Performing Right Society had the Society to represent them. Before 1914 this didn't exist for the English; what made it particularly galling was that it did exist for other countries, so that, for example, a French composer having some of his music played in London in 1910 or 1900 would be able to collect performing fees, simply because his works were represented by the French performing right society. Now all of this made for a very poor environment for composers and musicians generally to work in in England. (Cyril Ehrlich)

MUSIC EDUCATION in the public schools was well established, basically as a singing movement, and there were strong lobby groups of teachers in both public schools and private academies trying to work through a curriculum that would teach children how to sing. And by singing what we really mean back then was musical literacy – teaching them not only to sing but to read music. So that programme was in place in 1900, and certainly in the high schools there were ensembles, like bands and orchestras. I think there was a notion of democratizing the culture. One of Sousa's slogans was 'Music for the millions', and I think behind that was the idea that music should not be an élite product but should somehow be accessible; it should be a choice for an educated public. And certainly the notion of universal musical literacy reflects the progressive atmosphere of the period. (Judith Tick)

THE RANK-AND-FILE PROFESSIONAL MUSICIAN by 1900 was sweated labour. Very, very few could make a living from serious playing in concerts in the season. They would eke it out typically – and disastrously of course – by teaching. Virtually everyone who could play taught someone else to play, and inevitably this led to an excess of players. It was hazardous, because it was a very unhealthy trade, and of course there was virtually no insurance and certainly no health service or anything like that. TB was rife, etc. And there was a huge underworld, as it were, of shabby genteel: people who were festooned with diplomas had to look and dress respectably, which goes with the job, of course, but typically the shilling-a-lesson piano teacher is an example of that. And, for example, they would play not with the London Symphony Orchestra or the Queen's Hall Orchestra but in the local asylum – asylums provided employment for keepers who could also play an instrument. (Cyril Ehrlich)

The omnipresent piano and the growth of musical knowledge

ALMOST ALL ORCHESTRAL WORKS of the nineteenth century can be played wonderfully on the piano. Brahms symphonies: they sound fantastic on the piano, Beethoven symphonies too, and in many ways composers (like Schumann, for example) conceived orchestral works as piano-conceived works. Because the piano became a less central instrument to twentieth-century composers – the idea of transcribing a complex modern orchestral work for piano is absurd, it would just sound ghastly – it means a different attitude for composers, in some ways a more interesting attitude for composers. The slightly two-dimensional feeling of musical space that the piano imposes is a restriction, and it's been positive to get away from that. But for those people who learned music through the piano (as in the nineteenth century when hundreds of thousands of people played the piano to a high standard), I can understand that music conceived away from that medium is more difficult to perceive and also more difficult to assimilate because you can't take it home and play it. (George Benjamin)

IT WAS DIFFICULT to get through the day without hearing a piano. If you went into a public house there would be a piano; if you went to have tea there would be tea-shop music for the piano. At dances pianos were likely to be played. If you were entertaining at home you would sing around the piano. If you went to the music-hall, which was probably the most popular form of entertainment, you would hear songs and you would then buy the sheet music and you would sing it at the piano at home. And indeed most of the music publishing was based on that: it was dots on pages that music publishing was about, and the general ability to follow the dots on pages – either actually to be able to read the dots on pages or at least be familiar with the main tune of what they were going to hear when it's put on the page – that was very widespread. (Cyril Ehrlich)

Obituary

BY THE DEATH OF Sir George Grove, CB, which occurred at his residence in London last evening, the English musical world has lost not only one of its staunchest supporters but also one of its leading critics. For though he was not a musician by profession, yet his influence upon the best class of young native musicians was both widespread and beneficial. Perhaps for the very reason that he was an amateur and that, as a consequence, his enthusiasms were evidently disinterested, he acquired an influence in the world of music which was at least as great and as widespread as that of any professional musician. (*The Times*, 29 May 1900)

Signs and portents

IN DECEMBER 1901 I was able for the first time, by means of stations specially constructed for that purpose, to transmit and receive telegraphic signals right across the Atlantic Ocean from Poldhu in Cornwall to St John's, Newfoundland, a distance of about 1,800 miles. (Guglielmo Marconi, 1932)

SCOTT JOPLIN IS ONE OF THOSE interesting 'beyond-category' figures, and I use the phrase 'beyond-category' because that's Duke Ellington's phrase. Duke Ellington used to say, 'My music is beyond category: if it sounds good it is good.' And that's what Joplin was about; he saw ragtime not as a fast-driving, machine-age kind of sound that would capture this masculine energy of making railroads; but he saw it as an idiom that he could use to synthesize his understanding of African-American tradition with European-American tradition. That's the vision: it's extraordinary in 1900. And I found a replication of a concert, a programme that President William McKinley held in the White House in February 1901. And there in the White House they're not doing those wonderful quadrilles and square dances from Europe and those formal dances that had so dominated American musical life. They're doing the two-step: like everywhere else in the nation the White House was caught up in the great ragtime craze of the turn of the century. I think that's a very important point. So 1900 is the beginning of a kind of indigenous idiom that is going to become not only folk-based but commercial as well. And ragtime is the beginning of the miracle of jazz. (Judith Tick)

2 Music's Makers

I don't really understand what the problem about modern music is.
HARRISON BIRTWISTLE

NOTHING HAS CHANGED more in twentieth-century music than the role of the composer within society and the composer's relationship to the audience. When the century began the number of living serious composers who were well known to the public was small, the number of those who could make a living from composition very small indeed. Both of Britain's 'senior' composers, Parry and Stanford, held professorships of music (at Oxford and at Cambridge respectively) and important teaching positions in London. Elgar, their junior by only a few years, attempted to live by composing alone but achieved modest financial security only in middle age. Over the course of the century the amount of music performed has grown vastly, and the invention of radio, television and recording has revolutionized public access to music. But the public for new music has not grown commensurately.

Public subsidy of music in Britain was almost non-existent until the Second World War, when the Council for the Encouragement of Music and the Arts (subsequently renamed the Arts Council) began supporting concerts, partly as a means of maintaining public morale in wartime. It soon came to regard the fostering of new music as an important area of its work. The foundation of the BBC in 1922 was followed by its incorporation by Royal Charter in 1927, empowering it to draw its income from a licence fee paid by every owner of a radio.

This enabled the BBC to form the first full-time, salaried orchestra in Great Britain, and to become a powerful patron of new music. During the same period some publishers took the risk of promoting young living composers, sometimes paying them a retainer in the hope that their works would eventually prove a profitable long-term investment. Other sources of income for composers, apart from taking other and more remunerative work but thus composing only in their spare time, have included commission fees from artists, concert-giving bodies and festivals (often funded partly or wholly by the Arts Council or the Regional Arts Associations that it later created). Private sponsorship of the arts exists in Britain, but on a very small scale compared to the United States. The importance of corporate or business sponsorship has increased in recent years, but there are signs that it may not increase much further and in any case the total income drawn from this source amounts to only a fraction of the spending of the Arts Council or the BBC. This is especially true in the area of new music, where a business or corporate sponsor will be hoping to reach large audiences, which contemporary music does not always attract.

After the passing of the Copyright Act of 1911 and the foundation of the Performing Right Society in 1914, a composer of Elgar's generation received income directly from performing fees. In other words the greater part of his income depended upon the popularity of his music. Many of today's composers receive less income from the box office than from commission fees (ostensibly paid to ensure the right to a first performance but in fact a form of subsidy) or publishers' retainers: their income is dependent less on public popularity than on the favour of official or semi-official bodies or that of publishers.

A further difficulty for the living composer is that commissions come either from organizations specializing in contemporary music, and thus having a specialist and usually small audience, or, less often, from bodies such as orchestras, festivals or opera companies whose primary role is perceived to be the performance of the music of the past. A symphony orchestra, for example, will usually prefer a composer to write a work scored for its normal resources, programmable alongside the masterpieces of the established repertoire. It will generally be reluctant to consider a composer who is known to make much use of electronics or of unconventional instruments or groupings of instruments. Supported by public subsidy themselves, the established orchestras, opera companies and festivals are under strong financial pressure to maximize their audiences, and have on the whole performed very little new music. The average concert-goer, undeniably, is wary of modern music. Some composers are content, at least for the time being, to address a specialist audience; others are reluctant to enter a 'ghetto'. Some feel that those specialist organizations that have been set up to help in the promotion of new music can themselves, by catering to the established contemporary-music audience, hinder composers from finding and approaching a new public.

Elgar's successors, Ralph Vaughan Williams and Gustav Holst, attempted to build a new public by working with and writing music for amateurs and, in Holst's case, schoolchildren. Michael Tippett followed them, working as a young man with the unemployed and, later, organizing performances and musical education in the then depressed area of London surrounding Morley College. Benjamin Britten founded the English Opera Group, a chamber-opera company able to tour as widely as possible, and the Aldeburgh Festival, which involved the people of that small coastal town in the organization and performance of new music; he also wrote much music for children to perform. In all these he was attempting to build a new audience and, as he put it, 'to be useful – and to the living'. More recently Peter Maxwell Davies has built a successful music festival, with the enthusiastic participation of local people and children, at Kirkwall in Orkney. Some younger composers find work in the community not only a useful source of income but a potentially valuable way of breaking down the perceived barriers between the contemporary composer and the public.

It remains to be seen whether these new links will lead to a transformation of the way that new music is presented. In places other than concert halls? At times other than 7.30 in the evening? With amateur participation nearer the norm than the exception? With instruments more accessible to amateurs than violins or pianos? In many of these cases, and there may well be many others, a response will be demanded from the composer, and whatever that response may be will undoubtedly change the role of the composer in the twenty-first century.

*

The composer and the public

I LIKE TO LOOK ON the composer's vocation as the old troubadours or bards did. In those days it was no disgrace for a man to be turned on to step in front of an army and inspire them with a song. I know that there are a lot of people who like to celebrate events with music. To these people I have given tunes. Is that wrong? Why should I write a fugue or something that won't appeal to anyone when the people yearn for things which can stir them? (Edward Elgar, 1904)

AT THE BEGINNING of the century the composer, I think, was still able to identify himself as the cog in a mechanism of culture which was very much up and running and really saw no particular reason to doubt itself or to challenge itself. If you look at, say, Mahler working at the Vienna Opera, he knows who his audience is. In effect he gets feedback from them on all sorts of levels the whole time, and the people who go evidently feel that on many levels their lives are being made more full of interest and excitement. Going to the opera is a central moment of a confrontation with one's deepest self and one's deepest needs, so it's something that it's important to do regularly. It's rather like going to church in certain other social circumstances: it needs to be done quite often. The great problem now is that we still have these great institutions but the sense of excitement and of belonging to a specific social group whose lives really depend on them to a considerable degree has rather evaporated. (David Osmond-Smith)

I THINK EARLIER IN THIS CENTURY composers were much more tuned in to a local audience: there was a clear sense of contact. Now we don't know who we're contacting. And now we have institutions that take care of us – like the Arts Council and the BBC and business sponsorship of the arts – it's less direct than it was. On the other hand what I enjoy most are those old contacts that persist: working with musicians or a conductor and their feel for the type of musical world they live in and can interpret well. That's what I like: there there's real contact. (Jonathan Harvey)

MANY ATTEMPTS ARE MADE these days to create a community for the composer, and I think it's important to have a strong eye out for the bogusness of some of these claims. I think the true community that any composer has is a kind of personal community – it might be students, it might be a particular performing group that's played your work quite a lot, it could well be a particular summer school that you go back to year after year. One thing is that it won't be a community in the sense of a geographical community of twenty miles round where you live, as might have been the case with, say, Elgar. Given the condition at the end of the twentieth century we all know – the web, the CD and so on – 'community' is a completely different word now. So I think that feeling that the composer no longer has a community is wrong, and too pessimistic. (Judith Weir)

Patronage and the composer

WHAT WAS ALWAYS a much more direct and personalized relationship between composer and patron or patronizing institution – particular church, particular cathedral needs or whatever – has been radically displaced and mostly removed, I guess over the last hundred years, but with particular speed in the last probably seventy years. By the loss of this kind of direct relation, composers have to look to other sources to support and provide an economic basis for their existence and for their work. And the thing that arose was a series of different kinds of institution which have provided that kind of succour. (Georgina Born)

I THINK THE INSTITUTIONS that surround new music have changed, but I think there were as many institutions in the past. It's just that they've changed their shape and their colour as twentieth-century economics have changed the colour of the life we live in. I think one of the things that we currently in Britain are running the danger of losing sight of is the idea of a culture of patronage which the whole of the history of Western European civilization suggests is one of the bedrocks of that civilization. One has to have those things being done within a society that a large majority of people would not recognize the need for. I mean, I live in York, and the central building in York – the Minster – I'm sure was not the thing at the top of most people's minds in the twelfth or thirteenth centuries: 'We must have a Minster,' said all the peasants. But it's unthinkable to imagine the city without it or the cultural evolution of that part of the world without that building, and the same is true now, I think. We have to set aside money to create interesting things both for ourselves and for future generations. (Christopher Fox)

IN THE 1920s we had also the problem in America – I don't know now what it was like in England – but in America of course we had a different social situation; we had many wealthy people who supported contemporary art. When the income tax became higher and stronger and more important, all these people were no longer able to support contemporary art the way they had, so the whole musical scene had to be supported by many people rather than the few. Which meant that the contemporary world was not so well supported because obviously large numbers of people don't understand contemporary music very much and they're not particularly anxious: they want to hear Beethoven and Mozart, which is understandable. But they were before that time, in the 1920s, a very strong support. I remember myself as a boy going to hear Berg's *Wozzeck*, I think for the first time – it was either the first or second year after it had been performed in Vienna – played in New York at the Metropolitan Opera House. They played the operas of Schoenberg, *Die glückliche Hand*. All those things were given, and it was because there were wealthy people who were willing to support contemporary music on a rather large scale. Mrs Thomas Edison was one of them, I remember. And when the social situation changed these people no longer were supporting, so it changed the entire world. Now I think that the basic problem of our particular field is that ours is more an educational than an entertainment field. And it should be supported as education is, as I see it anyhow, and in America it's considered as a field of entertainment and so it shouldn't be supported. (Elliott Carter)

Does society want composers?

FOR ME THE SOCIAL DIMENSION of what one does as a composer is actually very important. And I think it's perhaps because I'm at an age where for the large part of my career as a composer there have been people around – politicians, arts bureaucrats, journalists and even fellow composers – saying things like, 'Well, we have no right to write music which doesn't engage with an audience, because that's what music is: music is part of the entertainment industry, so music must entertain, and if you write music which is not immediate and accessible then you're not doing your job, and you're being irresponsible and you are living in an ivory tower.' It strikes me that in the long run that will be seen to have been a complete blind alley. (Christopher Fox)

IT'S A VERY DIFFICULT QUESTION to answer, the relationship of the artist to society. As society changes so the artist changes; everything changes. But ultimately of course we write music because we've got that kind of a kink. The trouble is that over the period of change that's taken place since the nineteenth century, when Romanticism got in the ascendant and the Industrial Revolution was taking place, things were changing very fast and at the same time artists were becoming more and more inclined to express their own personal feelings at the expense of everything else. This meant that artists were constantly trying to be different from each other. And when everybody's trying to be different from each other you know what happens: in the end they all seem the same. I don't blame audiences for not turning up when there's a new work in a concert, because bitter experience has taught them what they might possibly expect. The artists and the public are alienated from each other. (Robert Simpson, 1973)

AT THE PERFORMANCE mild protests against the music could be heard from the beginning. Then, when the curtain opened on a group of knock-kneed and long-braided Lolitas jumping up and down (*Danse des adolescentes*) the storm broke. Cries of 'Ta gueule!' came from behind me. I left the hall in a rage. I was sitting on the right near the orchestra, and I remember slamming the door. I have never again been that angry. (Igor Stravinsky, recalling in 1958 the première of *The Rite of Spring* in 1913)

A LOT OF MUSIC of this century is not I think made to be understood fully in that sense. It is socially very disruptive; a lot of it therefore has not entered the norm of the concert repertoire and cannot do, in a way, because it's challenging too many of society's preconceptions about what music should be. In that sense, no longer is it entertainment in the accepted sense of the word, or it's too disruptive to be viewed as entertainment. Having said that, I don't think there's anything wrong with being entertained. Some of the greatest art this century is hugely entertaining. I think Edmund White remarked of the Diaghilev circle that Diaghilev and Balanchine and Stravinsky all shared this understanding of how to put an artistic artefact to an audience in such a way that it would be dazzled or entertained, but at the same time be presented with a product of the highest quality. (Julian Anderson)

I DO FEEL VERY STRONGLY that music is a demonstration of integrity; and that is why it's valued, and that is why it's played such a great part in the twentieth century. I think it's been seen as a beacon of integrity during that time, and I think it's done a very good job. (Howard Skempton)

THINGS HAVE CHANGED in what people expect from creativity. Consequently we're now in a time where everything is expected to be there immediately – I mean the understanding of it. And if it doesn't do that, then it's not the problem of the audience, it's the problem of the person making the music. I mean, the ridiculous thing about my *Panic* at the Proms – that really wasn't about my piece. That was about the fact that it was a modern piece of music in that context; and I think that any piece of modern music in that context would have created that sort of response. But more than that, I think that there was an audience there that didn't even know what modern music is. (Harrison Birtwistle)

Finding a new role for the composer

THE NEXT TWENTY OR THIRTY YEARS are going to be a time for the self-definition – possibly re-self-definition – of democracy as far as cultural production is concerned. It is inevitably the case that if you have created a social and political system that depends on a wide-scale consensus, there are going to be consistent pressures in effect to find the highest common factor at all levels with which everybody feels reasonably comfortable and with which they can identify. So deciding what sort of work we need to do, what sort of pieces we need to write, and so on and so forth, actually becomes under these amorphous but, if you like, ideologically necessary circumstances extremely difficult. One of the things that people tend to do therefore is to keep repeating old rituals: the big piece for the concert hall, the major opera, and so on. And therefore we put pressure on individual artists and composers to be enterprising, to be inventive, to produce something new, to astonish the world. Because in effect we haven't got a social structure that says, 'Why don't you play that game? We enjoy playing that game. We will play it with you.' It is a dreadful pressure, actually, to put on composers of any age, but particularly and obviously young ones. (David Osmond-Smith)

ONE OF THE PROBLEMS with art music today is that it still preserves the theatrical baggage of nineteenth-century music-making. That's one of the reasons why I have no intention of ever writing an orchestral piece for the nineteenth-century/early twentieth-century orchestra, because I don't want to have anything to do with that theatrical framework – the idea that the leader comes on and the people clap. *Why?* That the conductor comes on and people clap a bit more. Again, *why?* It doesn't happen in any other form of entertainment. Equally, in a lot of the grander forms of chamber music, there's a similar accumulation of ritual. Ritual is great, ritual is fine, but it should be reviving itself; it should be changing itself far more often than it does. Again, I think the example of popular music is telling, in that there are lots of rituals associated with it, but they change generation by generation. (Christopher Fox)

COMPOSERS IN THEMSELVES change, I think, far less than the world around them. J. S. Bach, for example: he's a composer whose preoccupations, I'm sure, were inside himself very similar to mine. He was interested in structure; he was interested in self-expression; he was interested in making statements about the world in its entirety – and

23

that's very much what interests me. The demands on him were in some ways the same, and In some ways very different. They were the same in that he had to make a living, he had to do other things beside composing in order to do so, he had to fit in to his professional pecking order, his professional world, and he also had to deal with the various people who would be coming up with the money to pay him, such as various aristocrats or various kinds of local government, for example. In some ways that's not so very different from what happens now, but basically I think the composers really still want the same thing, which is independence, the ability to express themselves (because that happens best – at least certainly for me, but I think for most people – in an independent framework). But at the same time the things that go against that independence are the need to make yourself prominent, especially in a professional context, the need to fit in the framework for which you're going to get paid for your work, and nowadays that's by a process known as commissioning – a rather strange process by which a cultural commissar says in advance, 'You, you, you, you are selected to write music and you will write, and you'll get your money a bit first and then the rest afterwards.' So it's a kind of battle of these things inside yourself and those things outside yourself. Sometimes they're in sync; other times they're not. (Peter Paul Nash)

Finding a new platform for the composer

THE CONVENTIONAL CONCERT-HALL situation is very much a class thing, and it's something that we really shouldn't have to tolerate now. Our reaction to the past is bound to be ambivalent. I think as composers – and I've said this before and I've no reason to change my mind – part of the reason we're composers is because we want to demonstrate our commitment to music. We have a passion for music, we have a love of music, and this probably includes Bach – perhaps most composers. But, on the other hand, we can't expect to bath in the same water, as somebody once put it, or repeat the old tricks – certainly I can't. I don't think in that way. I think much more about structure, about form, about texture, about colour, and I think one of the exciting things about contemporary music is that it does exploit colour and texture in a way that would have been unthinkable in the nineteenth century, and therefore has the potential for tenderness and so on that is rather special. There is a dialogue with the past, a dialogue with tradition; somehow we've got to preserve that dialogue. (Howard Skempton)

A CERTAIN REVERENCE AND RESPECT for what is being done is part of the thing that makes communication possible. Informality is a deeply wonderful thing and there were times when musicians in the modern music world concerned themselves with removing the gap between the places where the audience sit and the stage and increasing communication – I don't know whether we were meant to have a string quartet on our laps or what. I think this is nonsense. I'm not John Cage, I don't think this bleeds out into the world. I go to hear a string quartet that lasts twenty minutes and I have to make an intense effort, just as I do if I go to the National Gallery and look at the Van Eycks which are currently on show there. I've got to prepare myself inwardly if I want to get anything out of it. Of course I can walk round it, but nothing will happen. And if you want anything to happen from music a certain formality – expressed in penguin outfits and dressing up and all those things that are so scorned as being middle class and superficial – is in fact most helpful. (Alexander Goehr)

IF PEOPLE PLANNED concerts more, as it were from the music upwards rather than from the concert downwards, we'd see a very different sort of concert. We would see them differently performed, differently programmed, differently dressed, differently lit. The fact is that the concert is a fantastically dramatic event – it has to be – but most of the concerts you go to you'd never guess: the drama is played down about as far as it possibly could be, to the most drab level. And if these things were considered more from the point of view of the music, we would get a very different and far more enlivening event. On the other hand, if you're going to go on commissioning music to fill empty spaces in concerts, I don't know how you could do this. If you don't know what you're going to get in advance, how on earth can you proceed other than have 'Oh, gosh, this is a "This Ensemble"-type concert, and there's this blank space and, gosh, there's a new piece fitted in there, and clap the composer and goodbye, and let's have some Mozart.'

But when you look around at the more imaginative concert planners around the country very often they turn out to be composers as well. I mean, for example, the composer-directed festivals at Aldeburgh and Cheltenham. And you nearly always find in this situation that the composers are fantastically unselfish, given what they could get away with in their position. (Peter Paul Nash)

Changing musical institutions

INSTITUTIONS HAVE A VERY particular function. Their role really is to purify, to be the gate-keeper, to make those judgements of value and therefore to mediate and reproduce a particular view of what constitutes important music in our day. (Georgina Born)

THE CULTURAL-COMMISSAR FIGURE can get between the composer and the audience. This is a feeling I often have and I'm sure many other composers also have. The reason for this is not because they necessarily want to attract all the stage-lighting, you might say, to themselves (although that has happened in the past). The reason is quite simply that they have certain structures that lumber on in their tremendously ponderous way because of the finance involved, because of the sheer mechanics involved, and they sometimes forget that these structures can certainly get in the way of the composer, and also get in the way of the audience. The trouble is that any organization of this kind is going to regard itself as the centre of events, whereas the composers of course are going to regard themselves as the centre of events. (The only people who don't regard themselves as the centre of events are the audience, but that's really because they don't want to: they're not there to provide the entertainment, they're there to roll up and sit in the seats and have themselves enriched in one way or another.) I think there is, because of the increasing power given to cultural controllers, too much taken away from composers. They don't listen to composers enough. (Peter Paul Nash)

THERE ARE COMPOSERS who think the world owes them a living, that when they leave music college, within a few years, they will have a publisher, and the publisher will look after them, and the publisher will do all the work promoting their works. The BBC will phone them up and say, 'Here's your Prom commission for next year; hope that'll keep you in clean socks until the following year.' And there are people who simply expect that the world will take care of them. If you work for the institutions that provide cultural environments, and hope that that will take care of you, then frankly you've narrowed down your horizons enormously. And I think people who develop the ability to survive without those are in a far healthier situation. (Gavin Bryars)

THE GOOD POINT about institutions is that there's an onus on them to be more reflexive than you or I or the old patron about what judgement they're making and why. Institutions are usually under some pressure to provide arguments as to the basis of their judgements and who they choose to give money to and to commission and so on. Now we might say that that's usually very imperfect. I think it is. I think that the institutions' roles become very self-reproducing. In fact they become the focus; they come to be believed; their judgements and their legitimations become unquestioned. And that is a major problem. (Georgina Born)

THERE IS ACTUALLY rather less of the kind of institutionalized patronage of new music now than there was when I was beginning my career thirty years ago. Because then there was certainly a real nourishing of the composer as an individual by the Arts Council, for example, with all kinds of commission schemes and bursary schemes and so on. And that has very largely been whittled away or disappeared. Policies have changed; priorities have changed; the coming of the National Lottery means that enormous projects and building-based projects often have favour over individual projects. Obviously the BBC has a very different role now in relation to living composers than it had thirty years ago. And so I think that in some ways we're in a curious flux in this country because we haven't yet moved to, say, the tradition of perhaps individual philanthropy in the United States, where a patron will commission a work, rather like an eighteenth-century European patron. That's come to a certain extent in this country, but not so much. (Nicola LeFanu)

FINDING A WAY of artificially re-creating a game between the cultural patrons of society – still, whether you like it or not, the middle classes – and individual working musicians is very hard. I don't know whether it can be done artificially. Maybe you've just to grit your teeth and wait for history to do a few more rotations and provide a set of circumstances in which that interaction is possible once more, and there'll have to be a great deal of general crossing of fingers on the part of those who are the organizers and promoters of culture that somehow things will come right. Because if they don't, well, we have really the composer as dinosaur. (David Osmond-Smith)

IT IS INCUMBENT upon the institutions to be flexible and to keep up to date without becoming slaves to fashion. I think, though, that one thing that is changing is the view that I would say British society has (even the musical part of it) as to what composers should do as a norm, and what kind of people they should be. I note that it is very common for a young composer nowadays to get involved in some type of musical education work, quite often involving children or young people, or to go into prisons or whatever. And there seems to be a change of attitude away from what one might characterize as the extreme idealism of the 1960s and 1970s, when I think that with one or two exceptions like Peter Maxwell Davies, it was very unusual for young composers to expect and to wish to go into that kind of educational work. But nowadays it's actually expected of them, and indeed it's a way that many of them can actually earn a decent living. (Julian Anderson)

Finding and creating a new public

I SUPPOSE, TO OVER-GENERALIZE wickedly, one could look at the last two hundred years as a period of increasing specialization with the composer – and this is a ridiculous caricature – making black marks on white sheets of paper in a silent room, which he then hands to some players who, having spent their lives developing technical virtuosity, then do a precise account of what the composer has written. Now there is a clear development of practice, where composers are saying, 'Look, I can best work if I begin in some sort of community setting.' The obvious kind of classical example would be Peter Maxwell Davies up in the Orkney Islands, and indeed the whole group of younger com-posers – James MacMillan and so forth – around him, for whom this really is the way to work. (Anthony Everitt)

IN ENGLAND OUR MUSICIANS are often too much the gifted amateur, and when they really get down to business they fumble and lose their way. In this country our young composers have not those practical opportunities of learning their job as *répétiteurs*, stage conductors and general assistants in the opera houses and concert rooms. Holst realized this, and partly of course from necessity but largely from choice he refused to view the world from the dignified eminence of the organ loft, but rushed into the mêlée of life armed with his trombone. (Ralph Vaughan Williams, 1954)

I THINK THAT the field of amateurs, or people working in a different way, with music as part of their lives, is going to get bigger and bigger. But I think there's still a need for expert help there, and I can certainly see the professional composer as one of those people. I think backward to the examples of people like Gustav Holst and Gerald Finzi, who almost killed themselves, both of them, in the effort that it takes both to be a professional composer and yet to gather amateurs together, to write music specially for them. But that is ever more, I think, a fertile area; it's something that has a big tradition in this country. (Judith Weir)

WHEN I WAS, say, in my twenties, at the beginning of my career as a composer, I believed passionately in the idea that the composer must serve the community, and I would use that word, 'serve'. I believed that because I'd been brought up in England, where we have this wonderful tradition that there is no great divide between professional and amateur, and the models were Holst, Vaughan Williams, Tippett, Britten – people who worked with amateur musicians and professional musicians alike, and made their own very best music for those people. I think there's nothing that can be more worthwhile than bringing the highest standards into the music-making of people whose technical proficiency may not be great, whether they're children or whether they're adult amateurs, and at the same time opening out the professional world so that we now have a very exciting kind of what's called the 'new musician', somebody whose skills are much more flexible. (Nicola LeFanu)

I BELIEVE THAT AN ARTIST should be part of his community, should work for it and be used by it. Over the last hundred years this has become rarer and rarer, and the artists and community have both suffered as a result. (Benjamin Britten, 1962)

THERE HAS BEEN A REVIVAL of the notion of the community school or the community college. I came across a number of examples, sometimes supported by the National Lottery, where schools or colleges created performing centres, which not only were useful for the school or the college students but, Janus-like, looked to the community as well. And so they were a kind of *entrepôt*, they were a kind of crossroads, where people from the community, professionals but also amateurs, and people in the school or the college were able to use the same facilities, exchange ideas, exchange experiences and so forth. Now the development of music resource centres within the reach of most people I think would be (a) a very good thing in itself but (b) it would lock the development of the teaching of music to life at large in the world, that's to say the social meanings of music to the intrinsic meanings of music. (Anthony Everitt)

ÉLITISM IS A VERY CURIOUS WORD, because as England is still such a socially divided country, such a class-ridden society, there's this strange phenomenon whereby a lot of money is put into institutions that are socially élite: only wealthy, rich people can afford to go to them. Now I think that is appalling, but nevertheless it is the policy of this country. However, an intellectual élite, or an élite of musical excellence – let's say a special school for young musicians – that kind of élite is open to anyone because there's no saying what genetics will allow a child to be born with an extraordinary talent. And yet that kind of élitism is frowned on. Somebody who dares to stand up, for example, for serious, intellectually challenging music, is accused of being snobbish: 'What field do you work in?' 'Well, I work in contemporary music; I'm what's called a serious classical composer.' 'Oh, how élitist!' Now I find it very sad that that confusion is made between two kinds of élitism, because it would be a sad country that didn't cherish the idea of some kind of intellectual excellence, which inevitably is going to be a small group of people, but not an exclusive group in the sense that they try to keep other people out, not that kind of clubbishness which, alas, has very often been the downfall of bits of English culture. (Nicola LeFanu)

I MIGHT SAY THAT, as we approach the end of this century, even compared to fifteen years ago, audiences have changed beyond all recognition. And they've changed an awful lot more than the composers and very, very much more than the cultural commissars. The mood, the sophistication of audiences now isn't anything like what it was in 1985 even. People have on many different levels all kinds of connections – maybe often unconscious or very partial – but nevertheless to all the main cultural streams of the century. They may not know the names, they may not know the time signatures, they may not know the sharps and flats, but somehow these influences are getting through. And basically a wide, multi-cultural society is better than a narrow society that's dominated, whether politically or through the market, by one particular strain. (Peter Paul Nash)

PEOPLE'S CHOICE IS EVERYTHING. I don't believe any more that any particular cultural activity belongs to a particular class. My own view is that people just have to pursue their true personal taste. They have to question what they're given as being the best available. Luckily, now, so much is available on CD, and I think it's up to every individual listener or player or musician to become an explorer, perhaps to be their own controller of their own network, shall we say, not to accept given taste, critical consensus. And the cheering thing is that they are in a position to do so and I think may be more so in the future. (Judith Weir)

THIS SORT OF NOTION that modern music is a problem, and that it doesn't communicate: I don't agree with that at all. I think music at the moment – the works being written and that have been written this century – is absolutely fantastic, is really quite exciting and interesting – maybe it's never been more interesting. I don't really understand what the problem about modern music is. (Harrison Birtwistle)

3 Music and Monuments

We were better at acoustics before we had acousticians.
JOHN DRUMMOND

FOR MANY PEOPLE the experience of concert-going is central to their experience of music, and the concert hall itself – its appearance, acoustic and atmosphere – is a crucial part of that experience. Although music is very ancient, public concerts are a relatively modern development, and halls built specifically for music still more so. In London the first regular concert series, promoted by Thomas Britton, 'the musical small-coals-man', began only in 1678. Britton's concerts were given in a low-ceilinged room above his warehouse in Clerkenwell and the audience, some of whom took part in the music-making as well, cannot have numbered more than a hundred or so, if that. Handel attended Britton's concerts, but by the time of his arrival in London in 1710 concerts on a larger scale were being given in the York Buildings, on the north bank of the River Thames, at the foot of Villiers Street off the Strand. It was immediately opposite the point where the Royal Festival Hall now stands, but seated fewer than a tenth as many – about three hundred.

Such was the growing appetite for public entertainment, including music-making, that larger halls were soon built; when Leopold Mozart brought his talented children Wolfgang Amadeus and Maria Anna to London in 1765 as part of their European tour, the two halls at which they appeared both had room for around six hundred people. For one of his concerts, at Spring Gardens, Leopold hoped for a capacity audience but, many members of the aristocracy being out of London, he was not disappointed with the profit he made by selling only two hundred tickets.

As the nineteenth century proceeded and cities, audiences and orchestras all grew larger, concert halls also grew. Many adopted one or other of the obvious models for a hall intended for large numbers: either the medieval guildhall or town hall or the eighteenth-century assembly room or ballroom, all of which tended to be rectangular, with perhaps shallow galleries on the side and rear walls, most of the audience being accommodated on the floor of the hall. Others took theatres as a model (most of Handel's oratorio performances were given in theatres), with one or more balconies.

Although some of the great nineteenth-century concert halls have survived (among the finest are the Grosse Musikvereinssaal – the 'Golden Hall' – in Vienna and the Concertgebouw in Amsterdam), many were destroyed during the Second World War, including the Queen's Hall in London and the Gewandhaus in Leipzig, both cele-brated for their acoustics. E. M. Forster's narrator in *Howards End* (published in 1910) reacted against the 'dreary' appearance of the Queen's Hall (its predominant colour was originally grey, its architect having dead mice hung in the painters' shop so that they could mix their colours to match the precise shade of a London mouse's belly) and the fact that even this hall had areas where the acoustic was less than perfect. To replace such halls as these and to cater for the still expanding but also changing concert public, many new halls were built in the decades after the war. Modern materials and building methods enabled new forms for concert halls to be investigated, but the science of acoustics was until recently imperfectly understood, and many modern halls have disappointed musicians and concert-goers; some have had to be expensively redesigned or equipped with 'assisted resonance'.

In many Western countries opera has also increased its audience greatly in recent decades. Opera is a vastly more expensive art form than the symphony concert or the solo recital, but the obvious economic solution to this problem, the building of extremely large theatres (a solution made perfectly feasible by modern structural engineering), exacerbates the acoustical problems as well as ensuring that in a theatre seating much more than three thousand many members of the audience are bound to be very far from the stage. Most of the great opera houses of the nineteenth century, with seating modified to suit modern standards of safety and comfort, can accommodate an audi-ence of fewer than two thousand.

As concert halls and opera houses have changed in form and grown larger in response to economic necessity and an expanding audience, that audience itself has changed. George Bernard Shaw, writing music criticism in the late nineteenth century, sometimes reviewed concerts given in private salons in the afternoon, concerts not accessible to the vast majority. And even the socialist Shaw, an advocate of 'rational dress', was obliged to wear either a stiff shirt and tailcoat or morning dress to many musical events – he would not have been admitted otherwise. The effect of broadcasting, recording and (in the United Kingdom only after the Second World War) public subsidy of the arts was to 'democratize' music, a move that had already begun with Henry Wood's Promenade Concerts at the Queen's Hall (with standing room available very cheaply) and, even earlier, with weekend 'popular concerts' at the Crystal Palace and elsewhere drawing large audiences, many of them from the 'tradesmen class'. There were similar developments in the United States.

Concerts themselves have changed less than one might expect to accommodate this new audience. Musicians at evening concerts mostly still wear a formalized version of the clothes that were obligatory in 'polite' society during the mid-nineteenth century. Most concerts are still given at a time originally fixed to allow members of the leisured classes to dress before an evening entertainment and to dine after it. Attempts to build a new audience with concerts specifically aimed at children have met with some success, but even in societies such as those of Britain or the United States – multi-racial and with increasing prosperity among working people – concert audiences remain predominantly white, middle-aged and middle class.

Orchestras themselves remain in many ways very conservative institutions. In most orchestras women account for only a very small minority of players (despite the fact that more women study music at conservatoires than men). The BBC Symphony Orchestra in the 1930s and the reformed Hallé Orchestra in the 1940s were the first British orchestras to recruit women as a matter of course, other than as harpists. In London most orchestras (save those of the BBC and the opera houses) are self-governing and their musicians self-employed. They are obliged because their subsidies are so low to take on as much work as they can find. Freelance orchestral musicians are still paid, as they were at the turn of the century, 'per session', a session representing either a concert or a three-hour rehearsal or recording. For a concert, the standard payment is still for two sessions, on the turn-of-the-century assumption that a single rehearsal will be ample. Because of the opportunities for commercial work in London (recording, film music, backing for pop groups) many musicians prefer to work freelance.

Because of this, London musicians have become famous for the speed with which they can produce a concert or recording with minimal rehearsal. The efficiency and virtuosity of such specialist contemporary groups as the London Sinfonietta owe something to this, and many composers have been indebted to them for it. However, although more concert music has been written since 1900 than in any previous century – perhaps more than in all previous centuries combined – the taste of concert-goers is still overwhelmingly for the familiar music of the more or less distant past. Contemporary composers have often expressed dissatisfaction with the traditional public concert and have tried to present their music in new ways, less formally and in buildings other than concert halls built to enshrine the established repertoire.

The number of concert-goers, though, has grown prodigiously. In 1937 *The Concert Goer's Annual* estimated that approximately ten thousand people in Britain had been to a public concert that year; some of them, of course, would have attended several. Within twenty years that figure had risen sixfold (both these figures seem under-estimates), and in a survey during the 1990s around $5\frac{1}{2}$ million people said that they had attended a concert of classical music during the previous year. This rise has been made possible partly by an increase in the number of publicly subsidized orchestras, but it is an increase all the more remarkable for being fuelled by influences that it was feared would have precisely the opposite effect. Indeed, it was confidently predicted that recording, then radio, then television would bring about the death of live music-making. The reverse was true, but the significance of another consequence of technological progress is still controversial: the fact that for many, perhaps most, music-lovers the public concert is no longer the central or most important part of their musical experience.

This fact has often been deplored, and it is true that when concerts were relatively infrequent and radio and recording as yet unknown, a performance of, say, Beethoven's Ninth Symphony would in many cities have been the first for several years and the last for an unpredictable period. In such circumstances most music-lovers would have looked forward to the event with keen anticipation; many would have prepared themselves by reading about the work or studying the score, and at the performance itself they would have listened more intently than many a modern concert-goer, with recordings of the work readily available and performances of it much more frequent. But the advent of modern media for the dissemination of music has also meant that the available repertoire has expanded hugely. Paradoxically, works that are very risky at the concert-hall box office are often available in numerous rival recordings, selling sufficient copies worldwide to satisfy the recording companies.

Some have wondered whether recording and radio will eventually become the primary media for spreading knowledge of new music. Were this to happen, the public concert would indeed become a museum event, and the symphony concert a particularly limited one, since even now much contemporary music is the preserve of specialist groups and many concert-goers now prefer to hear music of the eighteenth century and earlier played by period-instrument groups. Many such groups realize that to perform Bach with an orchestra of authentic size in a hall seating three thousand and designed for the orchestral repertoire of the nineteenth century is absurd, but they are often obliged to do so for economic reasons. Many contemporary groups, likewise, know that to draw an audience of a thousand for a new work by a fine but as yet unfamiliar composer is a success, not a failure, but in a hall seating three thousand it will look like a failure and in terms of box-office income it will compare most unfavourably with the sort of symphony concert for which the hall was designed. The financing of new music is the subject of a later chapter, but concert-hall design, which contributes so much to the enjoyment and excitement of the concert-going experience, which indeed helps to make people want to go to concerts, could make a contribution to the solving of this problem.

*

The concert hall – more than a container for music

DOESN'T LOOK TO ME as though there's any hope of rain coming from anywhere – it's a pretty clear sky and a moment ago there was almost a full moon looking straight at me across this blaze of smoke and ruins. Looking into it you can see twisted girders and some of those pillars that a lot of us knew when we went to visit the Crystal Palace; the organ, the whole business, the whole of that central hall is on the ground now, smouldering and burning and an occasional bit of wind catching it and making the flames fly up again. Smoke's going right away from me so I can see the whole length of this blazing mess . . . (Live radio commentary on the destruction of Crystal Palace, 1936)

CARNEGIE [HALL] HAD BEEN a part of my consciousness earlier than I am conscious of it. It was simply always there; it was the place one went to hear Kreisler, to hear Toscanini, to hear Rakhmaninov, to hear Schnabel, to hear the New York Philharmonic, to hear great cellists –

it was where you sanctified your belonging to the world of music. (Isaac Stern, 1991)

The Queen's Hall – 'dreary' and 'beloved'

IT WILL BE GENERALLY ADMITTED that Beethoven's Fifth Symphony is the most sublime noise that has ever penetrated into the ear of Man. The passion of your life becomes more vivid, and you are bound to admit that such a noise is cheap at two shillings. It is cheap even if you hear it in the Queen's Hall – dreariest music room in London, though not as dreary as the Free Trade Hall, Manchester – and even if you sit on the extreme left of that hall, so that the brass bumps at you before the rest of the orchestra arrives, it is still cheap. (E. M. Forster, *Howards End*, 1910)

IT WAS BEAUTIFUL, beautiful. It was a great large circle and everybody used to meet in the corridor behind the dress circle, which was level with the street. It was the most beloved of all concert halls – not only the audience but the artists, everybody adored it. The acoustics were perfect. (Ivor Newton, 1972)

IT WAS LOVELY to play in, marvellous to listen to, because it was big, but it had a feeling of intimacy always. And it was easy – I mean, if you were playing chamber music in there you could hear everybody else. You know, so often in these modern halls you can't hear anybody but yourself. It was an ideal hall; it was really a major tragedy that that went. (Evelyn Barbirolli)

I WAS ONE OF THE LAST to leave the hall on the Saturday and when I turned up for the morning rehearsal on the Sunday the place was smouldering. I remember Cedric Sharp was there, getting pieces of his famous cello from the orchestra room. I remember I picked up a mud-bespattered poster of what was in fact the last concert at Queen's Hall. (Felix Aprahamian, 1972)

The presence of sound

A HALL LIKE THE MUSIKVEREINSSAAL in Vienna or the Concertgebouw in Amsterdam is a very beautiful building, and you are very conscious of the gold and the bulging balconies and the statuary and all the rest of it. But what really makes it exciting is the presence of sound. I've been known to say in the past that we were better at acoustics before we had acousticians. (John Drummond)

THE LARGEST AUDIENCE was in the largest theatre where we performed, which was the Colón [Buenos Aires], and there in this great
early twentieth-century theatre we had, I must say, one of the most
exciting concerts that I can remember. (Benjamin Britten, 1967)

IT WAS VERY EXCITING because at the very first phrase in this enormous
theatre one was perfectly clear that one's voice was going right to the back
of it and was in fact living there, do you know? – you can feel it alive. I
had been told about this before; people had always said the acoustic in
the Colón Theatre . . . is the best in the world. (Peter Pears, 1967)

IT WAS ALWAYS A JOY to play in the Wigmore Hall because it's so
gemütlich, as they say in German – it's so comfortable, and actually
flattering to the performer, whether the performer's a singer or a string
player. (Gerald Moore, 1976)

Acoustical problems: the Royal Festival Hall

NINETEENTH-CENTURY CONCERT HALLS were built to a basic rectangular
shape. It was structurally simple. They were derived from the idea of
the palace ballroom with simple spans. They were tall and narrow,
because it was easier to build that way. But in the twentieth century
what happened was that architects were forced to provide more seats,
so they pushed the side walls apart and this created the fan-shaped
hall. Now that meant that the side walls and the galleries that wrapped
around the side walls no longer became the principal sound-reflecting
surfaces in the hall. As the walls were pushed apart, the ceiling had to
be lowered, and it was the ceiling that became the sound-reflecting
element. This had two effects. One was that the reverberation time of
the hall became very low, and the other effect was that the sound came
from overhead. Now it was only in the late 1960s that it was discovered that laterally reflected sound – sound being reflected from the
side – is very important in our perception of sound and in our spatial
perception. And it was only after that that the problems that had been
caused by these fan-shaped halls began to be tackled. (Michael Forsyth)

LONDON HADN'T HAD a really good concert hall since the Queen's Hall
was destroyed by bombs in 1941. The Royal Albert Hall, which has
had to house all the major concerts in the past ten years, is far too large
for many types of music and has never been good acoustically. But now,
once again, London possesses a fine medium-sized concert hall. It seats
something over three thousand people. It's a hall to which imaginative
minds have brought a combination of modern ideas on architecture, on

decoration, on seating and, perhaps most important of all, on acoustics. This hall forms the centrepiece of the Festival of Britain site on the south bank of the Thames, and it was indeed a happy inspiration of His Majesty the King to suggest that, in honour of the occasion for which it was built, it should be called the Royal Festival Hall. (Live radio commentary on opening of the Royal Festival Hall, 1951)

AREAS OF THE WALLS were covered in sound-absorptive material, whereas in the nineteenth century they would have been clad in thick plaster or masonry. There was a great myth that arose in the twentieth century among acousticians, musicians – it was completely universal – that thin wood panelling resonates rather like a violin, and this myth was very much current during the design of the Royal Festival Hall. So the Royal Festival Hall ended up much more dry than expected and of course the contrast with the Royal Albert Hall was quite dramatic and the public generally hated it, although, as one newspaper critic said, it tidied up London's string-playing overnight.

By the 1960s, the so-called technique of assisted resonance was invented and massive amounts of reverberance were added to the Royal Festival Hall artificially, and to this day most people don't realize that they are actually listening to an artificial acoustic rather than the natural acoustic of the hall. (Michael Forsyth)

Later attempts:

Barbican Hall

IT SEATS 2,026 PEOPLE in three curved, raked tiers. There are no boxes. Sightlines are good and a great deal of wood has been used for the décor. The acoustics have had a good deal of attention paid to them – there are various baffles . . . (Live radio commentary on opening of Barbican Hall, 1982)

Belfast Waterfront Hall

A SENSE OF PASSAGE from one age of Belfast to another was palpable when the city's sparkling new £32 million concert hall opened with a gala show on Friday evening. The Waterfront Hall rises on the banks of the River Lagan in a part of the city where the skyline was formerly dominated by Belfast's most eloquent monuments – the stern, mustard, ship-building cranes marked H&W. Now, however, the new optimistically glassy-domed oval building stands as the city's most imposing work of architecture – the structure that will inevitably become the symbol for Belfast in the next century. (*The Times*, 10 January 1997)

Bridgewater Hall, Manchester

THE HALLÉ MEMBERS said they were very happy with the acoustics of their new home, which seats 2,400 and has taken three years to build. A pioneering feature is the springs it sits on, designed to eliminate noise from Metrolink trams. With concert-hall acoustics such a contentious issue, Arup Acoustics (who worked on the Bridgewater) sought to achieve a mix of the two classic types of auditorium: the shoebox and the vineyard. (*The Times*, 13 September 1996)

Symphony Hall, Birmingham

THIS MONTH, SIMON RATTLE collects all £28 million worth of Birmingham's new Symphony Hall, which survived the early interest of Prince Charles, who called the projected building an unmitigated disaster, to materialize as the world's most sophisticated example of contemporary acoustic design. (*Independent on Sunday*, 7 April 1991)

THE NEW HALLS are many of them very lacking in presence and atmosphere and sort of flavour. I like the Doelen in Rotterdam very much – I think it's an extremely good post-war building. But, you see, Avery Fisher in New York was a disaster; the Sydney Opera House concert hall is not bad but not wonderful; Roy Thomson in Toronto is a disappointing hall; Symphony Hall in San Francisco is a disappointing hall. For me the greatest hall in Europe at the moment is the Philharmonie in Berlin: the most original and strange layout, but it has such a presence of sound – and that is what brings it home to you. (John Drummond)

WITH THE INVENTION of recordings and the availability of excellently recorded sound in the living room, the architect Hans Scharoun wanted to provide a new experience. He placed the orchestra in the centre and the audience was wrapped around the orchestra, so that even though the balance was by no means ideal, the audience did have a visually very exciting experience of going to the concert hall. (Michael Forsyth)

I THINK IT WAS, amazingly at that time in 1963, a democratic solution for the question which is really intriguing and hard to solve: how can one hear music together – from the first row it's wonderful, and from the eleventh also, but from the thirtieth it's a problem. I think the success really is due to this arrangement of the blocks around the stage. (Elmar Weingarten)

THE NEXT BIG TURNING POINT, I think, was the Dallas Symphony

Hall, which was the first hall that fully understood the principles of nineteenth-century concert-hall design and went back to these, and it's a very successful synthesis of acoustics and architecture.

A very good example of a hall that is modelled on the nineteenth-century shoebox hall and which does get it right is the recently built National Concert Hall in Taipei, in Taiwan. (Michael Forsyth)

New opera houses

OPERA IS INCREDIBLY POPULAR in Japan, and they've now got their own Japanese opera house, opened just a few months ago. In Scandinavia there are new opera houses in Gothenburg, Helsinki, and there's about to be one in Oslo. There's the brand-new opera house in Amsterdam. There's the Bastille in Paris, which nobody wanted – they'd already got four opera houses in Paris and it doesn't work in any sort of way, acoustically or visually. There's the new Met in New York – a huge building that by all the rules shouldn't work but does.

A lot of people involved in the opera world looked very enviously at Europe, where there was a far longer tradition of opera-going, and where the opera audience came from all levels of society. Opera was part of the way of life in Italy and Germany, and has been, I think, ever since it started. It's not like that yet here. It was getting to be in the 1960s, in that golden age of arts funding under Jennie Lee. (Rodney Milnes)

I WAS BROUGHT UP in an atmosphere of opera. It was Carl Rosa, it was D'Oyly Carte, but the excitement of those audiences in mining villages in Scotland when they were coming around I now find in my constituency – which is again industrial, in the heart of Cannock in Staffordshire. I challenge you straight away if you say that there is only a very small élitist public for opera or ballet or fine theatre. (Jennie Lee, 1970)

THERE'S NO DOUBT about the fact that opera and ballet and concert music and theatre were helped by an age of austerity. Munitions factory workers breaking off for their lunch hour to hear Adrian Boult conducting the LPO with Eileen Joyce wearing a pretty dress playing the Grieg Piano Concerto was something that a lot of people were turned on to music by. (John Drummond)

The changing audience

I HAVE ALWAYS WATCHED the people who fill the stalls when serious musical business is in hand with certain misgivings as to their sincerity. I have asked myself, is it love of music that brings them here, or merely social pressure – like that which forces little children into church to listen to sermons that they cannot possibly understand. (George Bernard Shaw, 1892)

WE HAD CONCERTS on Friday afternoons and the ladies live out in the country and they come into town and they do shopping on Friday afternoon, and they have all these bags with fruits in it and vegetables and all kind, cheese and so forth, and they even used to come and put those bags up on the stage. I noticed another thing, that at a certain time there was a certain train going out in the country and they all wanted to catch that train – they would leave before the concert end and make very great disturbance. (Leopold Stokowski, 1969)

WHEN I WENT THERE IN 1918, afternoon concerts were fashionable. You never had a concert on Saturday evening and it was unthinkable to have one on Sunday afternoon or Sunday evening because most of the leisurely rich were away at that time in their country houses. (Manager, Wigmore Hall, 1976)

THE HIGHEST PLANE of musical enjoyment during the concert was attained in Beethoven's Pianoforte Sonata in A♭. Unfortunately this plane is a select one; it is not everyone who feels at home on it. The audience held out for a while in silent misery, then they began to cough. It remains a matter for regret that the attendants did not remove them and treat their ailment by gently passing a warm steam-roller over their chests. (George Bernard Shaw, 1889)

FOR MY ADMISSION to the Promenade, I paid one shilling and six-pence. Smoking was allowed, excepting in one part of the grand circle where non-smokers could sit in comfort. And on the platform there was a large notice which said: 'Patrons are requested to refrain from striking matches during the music.' (Arthur Hammond, 1979)

AT TEN MINUTES TO ONE (the concerts were from one to two) Sir Kenneth Clark came in and said, 'There are a thousand people on the pavement.' And so we forgot the Home Office and let in over eight hundred, and so they started – and so they went on for six and a half years. (Myra Hess, 1962)

I JOINED THE QUEEN'S HALL at sixteen. The Proms at that time were sort of midway between the old Proms of cornet solos and things and what they are today. And of course every concert (because they lasted at least three hours and a half in those days) had to have three or four soloists – two singers, male and female, who in the second half had to sing what were known as the Boosey Ballads. And the subscription was a guinea – about fourpence a concert. (John Barbirolli, 1965)

YOU KNOW, TOO OFTEN have I heard, and read, that the Promenader is uncritical, fanatical, hysterical, uneducated musically, lacking in discrimination – all these awful things. But, you know, I'm not worried. I have seen hundreds of people queuing for hours, then standing for hours at a concert, then shouting and cheering their acclamations. (Malcolm Sargent, 1952)

WHAT THE PROMMERS have always contributed, the most important thing, is the sense that concert-going can be fun – not po-faced religious observance sitting in dark suits in serried rows not looking round you, but going to a hall whereby as a result of the architecture of the hall you can see other members of the audience and therefore the audience has a way of affecting each other, whether in its cheerfulness or its silences. (John Drummond)

THE SUCCESS OF your Henry Woods and your Charles Hallés is because they do manage to convince people of the power of the music, of the value of the works, and that they do everything they can to encourage and proselytize for what you might describe as an ideology of serious music. And this appeals to people from a very broad social spectrum. (Peter Martin)

I WAS THE FIRST oboe player in the Queen's Hall Orchestra from 1904 to 1913, under the able direction of Sir Henry Wood. The growth of musical appreciation in those years was amazing. Sir Henry educated audiences to know and like both classical and modern music. (Henri de Busscher, 1969)

HE [HENRY WOOD] would walk on with his little trotty steps, you know, and smile, and you seemed to feel he was embracing the audience and they all seemed his children. Of course, often and often I've seen him come down from the first overture or whatever started the Proms, he would come down with the tears running down his cheeks, and he would say, 'You know, they are all young people again – isn't it lovely!' (Jessie Wood, 1969)

marginal costs remain the same even if you sit in the cheap seats. You take a hall like the Barbican or the South Bank charging thirty-odd pounds now. They say, 'Oh you don't have to pay that; you can sit in a perfectly good seat for nine pounds.' OK, I'm sure you can, but the fact is that the bus fare is still the same, the tube fare is still the same, the car-parking is the same, the price of the programme, the price of the coffee. So you look at the associated figures and you find that concert life is currently being priced out of its core audience. (John Drummond)

AUDIENCES NOW ARE asking the impossible. They want a sound that replicates a CD sound – what I call the experience of sitting close to and far away from the orchestra at the same time, which of course is easy to achieve on a recording but difficult to achieve in the concert hall. As long as the traditional repertoire is there, people will continue to go to conventional concert halls, but there will be a constant search to provide something that the CD cannot provide within the living room. And as we go into the twenty-first century, in addition to understanding what makes good acoustics, the architect will continue to provide a new spatial experience for audiences, and this is the key to the future of concert-hall design. (Michael Forsyth)

THE AVAILABILITY OF RECORDED MUSIC makes the concert-going activity itself less essential to the experience of music. It is a particular way of experiencing music now, whereas in the past it was the only way. The experience of attending a concert in a large hall with hundreds or possibly thousands of others is itself the product of a particular time and place, and there is no reason whatsoever to imagine that this pattern of activity will continue unaltered into the twenty-first century. Concert-going is presented to us as one of the traditional mainstays of high culture in Western societies. But if you look at it historically speaking, it is relatively recent, and the conventions are relatively arbitrary; it's not been going all that long in the present form. And if it was to change its form or decline, well, we shouldn't really be surprised. (Peter Martin)

4 Music and the Media

They were trying to train people to be discerning.
JENNY DOCTOR

THE MUSIC-LOVER IN 1900 would have had access to far less music than his or her modern counterpart: concerts were much less frequent, and they included very little music more than two hundred years old. Music from outside Europe was almost unknown, and the music of Eastern Europe was very patchily represented in Western European concert programmes. On the other hand every 'serious' newspaper and quite a few popular ones (and, including provincial papers, weeklies and literary magazines, there were far more of them in 1900 than there are today) devoted considerable space to reporting and criticizing musical events. The number of musical magazines has increased slightly since 1900, but many of them now deal with such specialist fields as recording, opera, early and new music (all of them unthinkable as the subject for a specialist journal in Britain in 1900).

In every other area the amount of information available to the music-lover has increased vastly. Areas of music literally unknown at the beginning of the century now have books, copious learned papers and monthly or quarterly magazines devoted to them. The number of books that have been written about Monteverdi would astonish a reader of 1900, when his music was all but unknown; he would simply not be able to believe the number of recordings that are devoted to his works, many of which had not been available in print since the seventeenth century.

The overwhelming increase in the availability of recorded music, however, is a fairly recent phenomenon. The present author well remembers when copies of the standard catalogue of long-playing records, a smallish paperback volume, were commonly chained to the counter in record stores to prevent customers pocketing them. It would be wellnigh impossible unobtrusively to remove its current, telephone-directory-sized equivalent. For much of this century, however, the most potent influence in spreading musical knowledge was not recordings or printed matter but radio, and in Britain from the very earliest days the BBC perceived its role as an educational one. This involved not only the regular broadcasting of works from the accepted canon of great music but also expanding the repertoire, with an important place given to new music. Broadcast music was often introduced and analysed in radio talks by well-known scholars and writers. These were supplemented by articles in the Corporation's listings magazine, the *Radio Times*, and its now abandoned critical journal, *The Listener*, which also often reprinted the more important radio talks. By the 1940s the radio listener had access to a far wider repertoire than would be available at public concerts, except in the very largest cities.

The number of universities world-wide that offer degrees in music and in which research takes place has increased greatly over the last century, and this growth of musical scholarship has not only brought huge quantities of hitherto unknown music to light; it has also contributed widely to the knowledge of how this music should be performed. It can now be said, for example, with some precision what sort of harpsichord Bach would have expected for the performance of his keyboard concertos (well within living memory they were referred to in concert programmes as his 'piano concertos'), as well as the size of the orchestra, the precise instruments that made it up and the unwritten performing conventions of his time. In this way scholarship has profoundly affected the ways in which music is performed, and concert-goers and record buyers are far more aware of scholarship than ever before.

Scholarship and social trends together have contributed to a broadening of the scope of musicology. Very few scholars at the turn of the nineteenth/twentieth centuries would have concerned themselves with non-Western musics; such concepts as the sociology and economics of musical history would have scarcely been understood, while any suggestion that there would one day be scholars specializing in feminist musicology, gender studies in music or the analysis of Western demotic musics would have been regarded as fantasy. The result of all these developments has been a vast growth not only in the repertoire available for performance, listening and study, but in the amount that is known about that repertoire.

At the same time, the number of performed composers has grown substantially during the century, and although during its earlier years it was still possible to write a history of the century's music partly in a linear way, by considering the influences of seminal figures and works, and partly by classification or dividing composers into 'schools' centred around such figures, this has become more and more difficult as the century has approached its end. Styles have proliferated, as have individualist composers dependent on no style or school, making it very difficult even for a specialist to keep track of every composer who seems to be of some importance.

Inevitably this proliferation, of new composers and of rediscovered music from the past, has made the job of the critic both much more difficult and potentially much more important, if one of the critic's functions is that of a listener's or reader's guide through the labyrinth of available music. In newspapers, however, the space available for critical assessment and analysis has sharply diminished. When Alban Berg's *Wozzeck* had its first staged performances in London during the 1950s, the critic of *The Sunday Times*, Ernest Newman, devoted three successive weekly articles to the opera, each of them of over a thousand words. Nearly half a century later this would be unthinkable, not only because the number of significant performances during a week has greatly increased, but because the arts pages of most newspapers now have less space for reviews of 'classical' music, much more being devoted to rock and other popular musics, to interviews with and profiles of artists and to anticipatory previews rather than critical reviews of artistic events.

Detailed critical writing has retreated more and more to the specialist journals, whether dealing with new or early music, opera or recordings. A work perceived as major, by an established composer, will still receive some sort of coverage in the 'quality' newspapers, as will the arrival of an important new talent perceived as newsworthy. But for the general listener, not exposed to the full range of specialist journals, it is hard, perhaps even impossible, to obtain a balanced view of all that is happening in contemporary music. For anyone who believes that the art has never been richer or more varied, with fine music being written to satisfy all but the most conservative taste, this situation is a depressing one. It remains to be seen whether technical developments (for example the Internet or the ability of a compact disc to carry an analytical text, illustrations, even a full score, as well as the recorded music itself) will go some way to remedying it.

*

Radio – a new musical medium

THE MEDIUM DIDN'T EXIST, so they were creating it and they were
experimenting with what could happen. I think it's important to realize
that, at that stage, especially in the very early years, it was going alongside the music appreciation movement. The main speakers were Percy
Scholes and Walford Davies, and they were trying to introduce people
to musical concepts, so it was done on a music appreciation level. It
wasn't until later that they started talking in a more sophisticated way.
In the beginning it was definitely trying to educate the public, bringing
them culture; that was the whole purpose of the BBC. Another thing
that it's important to realize is that they were bringing a lot of people
music on a scale that had never been accomplished before, and development of culture meant development of what they defined as culture
and that included a lot of contemporary music. The BBC brought that
into the United Kingdom, really, so alongside Beethoven – much of
which had not been heard by many people around the country – they
were bringing them Schoenberg and Stravinsky and Bartók. There was
public reaction and they tried to use that to support what they were
doing, because the BBC actually wouldn't measure public reaction.
That didn't happen until the late 1930s. They refused to measure
public reaction because they felt that what they should be doing should
be despite public reaction; what they were doing was directing public
reaction. However, people wrote in quite a lot, and also a lot of the
things that they were doing were discussed in the general press – it
wasn't just the music press, it was actually discussed in the general
press. And what they would do is very cleverly choose letters that
balanced each other: people who hated Stravinsky were always paired
with people who loved it. And they always timed the publication of
these letters with an upcoming performance to show that people
should be fair. So it was all manipulation. There was a great public
outcry, though, and by the 1930s some of the policies start changing.
We start seeing them having to pay attention more to public reaction.
(Jenny Doctor)

NOW THIS MATTER of settling in a key as a dramatic event is a far
more important function of musical form than any question as to the
distribution and identity of themes. One of the most misleading of
terms, musical terms – more misleading in English than in other languages which have used a better terminology – is the word 'second
subject', which is applied in sonata movements to the main theme of
that group which is first established in a foreign key. I am often asked

which of many themes is the second subject of Brahms's Fourth Symphony or Beethoven's Seventh or of the 'Eroica' Symphony or of many other works, to which I am inclined to reply with a closely similar question: 'Who is the heroine of *David Copperfield*?' – a question to which the only intelligent answer must be 'Betsy Trotwood'. If you are going to search the first movement of the Seventh Symphony for a theme that looks on paper sufficiently distinct from the all-pervading anapaestic rhythm, you will come to no profitable conclusion and will probably hit upon the most dependent cause of the transition, because it's the only passage which looks on paper different from the rest. (Donald Tovey, broadcast talk, 1937)

CHOPIN, I THINK, in those preludes – those twenty-four preludes of his – will give you enormous guidance (a) as to the variety of texture which the modern piano can give you, (b) as to the importance of passing from textural enjoyment, if I can use that clumsy adjective, to thematic enjoyment. Now, the texture in No. 21 is very interesting. He starts with a chromatic texture like this – that's the idea in his head, that's what attracted him. And the tune, I'm sorry to say – I don't think it's wrong of me to say – I think it's an awfully cheap one. It goes like this, with a little crushed note. If anybody said to me, 'I think that's banal and it can't be by Chopin', I wouldn't be able to contradict him. We see that the tune of this would be nothing without the texture. Let's put it in that inoffensive way. Well, Chopin, who could write such sublime tunes, for the moment is not caring much about the tune. But the texture after sixteen bars, or even less – no, it's just sixteen – changes into an almost prehistoric texture, not chromatic at all, not even diatonic, but pentatonic. He uses those notes – I'm playing exactly what he's written and he's marked it *forte* – sounds dull, doesn't it? But it won't when I play the prelude; and then it dies down; now texture number three – I'm playing exactly what's there – and then back to the chromatic texture. And finally, with a few rather passing and unimportant melodic remarks, made three times, he brings an experimental piece of texture to an end. (Walford Davies, impromptu broadcast talk, 1937)

WALFORD DAVIES ASKED ME to prepare three or four programmes on plainsong. And I did this and, having got the first one ready, he asked me to come down for the weekend (I very often went down there, Cookham Dean) and do it to him and see what he thought, you see. Well, you can imagine, I took immense pains over this. I wrote out all the illustrations. Being plainsong I had to do them all on the piano just to show him the sort of thing it was. And I put my script up on the piano (he was sitting in an armchair behind me) and I began. And as I went I did what I always have done: I listened to myself. I thought, this is going well. And (he made no sound at all, you see) I came to the end of it, and I turned round beaming and I said to him, 'Well, Walford?' He said, 'It was wrong from beginning to end!' You can imagine what I felt like. I said, 'Why?' 'Because', he said, 'you were orating, you were giving an oration. I am one person in this room, and hundreds of people who will be listening to you, or one person, in a room, and it's to those you are talking, not to a great crowd of people. Go up to your room,' he said (I was over forty, you know, by this time, forty-six or so). 'Go up to your room,' he said. 'Think it all over again. In a hour's time come down and let's do it once more.' Well, I went up. I saw he was perfectly right. I read everything out up in my room there, every word, and I thought, no, that's not the right word, that's not a word I would use conversing to somebody, and I changed it all and I thought out the rhythm of it, and all the things I should have done before, had my imagination not failed me then. And I came down and I went through it once more and this time he said, 'Now, that's absolutely right. It's like a little miracle, and never forget it.' And I hope I haven't. (Alec Robertson, 1967)

I CAME OUT OF THE NAVY in 1946. I didn't go to university. I didn't ever know that music was going to be my job really; the criticism came later. But those years from 1946 to 1950-something, on the Third Programme, not just music but the talks by Bertrand Russell, Gilbert Murray and those sort of people – that was as good as being at an Oxford college, it really was. (Michael Kennedy)

'CAT, THE FRIEND of man.' What a splendid old phrase! One which I should like to see narrowed down occasionally to 'Cat, the friend of musician', for, with one or two noteworthy exceptions, I know of no composer, or executant, worth his salt who has not been devoted to the feline world. It is not without significance that the Egyptians, the most sophisticated of all the older civilizations, not only worshipped cats as goddesses (and, which is more important, gods) but had specially chosen singing cats yoked together to lend charm to their banquets. The whole history of Western music would have been different had it not been for the somewhat cynical discovery of the uses of catgut. (Constant Lambert, 1972)

Educating the listener

DURING THE WAR there was a huge rise in orchestral music and all of a sudden an unprecedented demand for concerts. But at the same time the number of pieces that people wanted to hear went down to about ten. They wanted to hear the same pieces over and over. So in a way the demand for culture had gone to the people in a way but it had actually narrowed what culture meant. That was why a lot of composers' groups began and many of the things that we now have. The Arts Council was trying to expand people's vocabulary but they didn't want that – they wanted something very specific. So in a way it backfired. One thing to remember is that before the war the wavelengths were not divided by topic, so you didn't have the equivalent of Radios 1, 2, 3 and 4. Everything was mixed up, so you would get a dance music programme followed by a very learned talk followed by jazz. There was talk of streaming but they refused to do that. And there were also campaigns for good listening, which were published all the time in the *Radio Times* and in the various BBC publications; they didn't want you to turn on the radio and have it as wallpaper music. They wanted you to choose what you were going to listen to, to sit in your armchair and to listen to it carefully. That was part of it; they were trying to train people to be discerning. Also they were trying to get more people to speak about a greater variety of things. The BBC, from even before it became very popular, was into old music, new music. They were trying to give a greater variety of information about all types of music. Especially just after the war, there was a great interest in older music, and there was a large project: 'The History in Sound of European Music'. They invited many people to come in and resurrect music that had probably not been performed in centuries. (Jenny Doctor)

The expansion of musical knowledge (I)

IT'S WORTH NOTING that the first edition of *Grove's Dictionary*, which was prepared in the last decades of the nineteenth century, didn't deal with any music before the year 1450 and it didn't deal with any non-European music to speak of – very little American, for example. In the 1910 edition it went back a little further; there were some important articles added on plainsong in particular, by a group of eminent plainsong scholars. But now, of course, we go back to what everyone reckons is 'the beginning', so that anything and the world is our parish; any ethnic group anywhere in the world we look at as impartially as we can, and European music is just one part – it is still an extremely prominent part – of the total picture. The scholars who wrote *Grove's Dictionary* were only a very few of them (mainly the Germans), professional musicologists. Nowadays there is scarcely anyone who would write for *Grove* who hasn't, as it were, done a Ph.D. in the subject on which he is writing. There's a new kind of professionalism. That was already coming in in Europe, in Central Europe, in the pre-war years. Then it became a massively large movement in the United States and in Britain, mostly post Second World War. Of course, with the change in the intellectual atmosphere, everything is changing in terms of what kinds of subject area you look into. Nobody thought, when I was working on the 1980 *Grove* edition, of having an article on feminism or on gender studies. Now it's a central topic, it's got to be considered and at some length, because it's become a topic of very great interest. (Stanley Sadie)

IT LEADS TO A new way of looking at history. In music, I think it's interesting: it's not just about women; it has to do with looking at repertoires of music that have sort of been written out of music history. A good example of this is what's called the British musical renaissance, something that started being written about at the very beginning of this century. You can follow it all the way through: there are still books being written that are called 'The British Musical Renaissance'. It deals with a very specific time, the growth of British music as it's seen, and it's defined by very specific repertoires that happen to be usually written by men, because of various opportunities that men had that women wouldn't have had, and it ignores other repertoires that actually would have allowed women's music to be recognized. Music that is performed in certain places, in the concert hall or in the opera house, music that is studied or taught within conservatoires, within very Establishment institutions, is emphasized and music that might have occurred in the home or actually been selling in droves in sheet publications is completely ignored. Certain women, especially British composers, who were writing at the same time as Stanford and Parry and were probably far better known – you see their music being performed on the BBC right up to the wartime, all the time, weekly. Liza Lehmann and Maud Valerie White are two that come to mind immediately. They were so popular yet they're not included in the studies of the so-called British music renaissance because their music doesn't come into what was defined as important in these music histories. (Jenny Doctor)

IF YOU LOOK AT the repertoire available on CD these days compared with the recorded repertoire of fifty years ago, it's burgeoned hugely, and this is partly the product of scholarly work. People, instead of dismissing operas by, say, Paisiello or Salieri, have actually gone and looked at them and found there's an awful lot of good, entertaining music in them. They've done proper editions of them and performed them. And then of course there's the original-instrument question, which has changed greatly because of musicological work. The study of how instruments were constructed has opened up new vistas in ways of listening to music. And there's a minimalist, as it were, generation of composers, the generation of Tavener and Pärt and Górecki, who have drawn on medieval music and plainsong, and that couldn't have happened without the influence of scholarship. (Stanley Sadie)

Scholarship and criticism

IT WAS IN BRONISLAW HUBERMAN'S time that the official myth of the allegedly authentic glissando-less pre-classical style was born. It's still alive and kicking, this myth, notwithstanding the historical fact that the chin-rest was introduced by Louis Spohr, probably because he had a long neck, and that therefore inaudible changes of position were impossible in pre-Romantic times, when the left hand alone had to hold the violin. Glissando, or (to give it its proper name) portamento, was ineluctably part and parcel of the violinist's position-changing technique and hence, like the singer's breath, part and parcel of the composer's own means of expression and articulation. Now, has anybody ever made as intense, exciting and melodically logical sense in Bach's A minor Concerto as Huberman, with his portamentos in the very places where Bach had intended them and not, therefore, merely in the slow movement? I suggest that this was how he played his own A minor Concerto – not the castrated way we nowadays hear it in sundry delusions of authenticity. (Hans Keller, 1983)

The expansion of musical knowledge (II)

SIR GEORGE'S OWN EDITION [of Grove], of course, is very much weighted towards the present, as it was then, i.e. the nineteenth century, and the big articles are the ones on Schubert and Mendelssohn, and, well, it would have been Brahms too, except by the time of the first edition he'd composed only his first two symphonies. Well, the next edition's really an elaboration and expansion of the first edition and it adds articles on some subjects to do with earlier music and broadens out a little. The third edition is in a way a classic. It's the 1927 edition, by H. C. Colles, and the 1940 edition is a simple modification and updating of that, although it's called the fourth edition. The 1927 edition is quite remarkably up to date with new developments: there's even a not unsympathetic discussion of the Second Viennese School, as early as that, which you might not have expected in conservative England. And then the circumstances of the Second World War have an enormous effect on the 1954 edition. International communications weren't good during its preparation in the late 1940s and consequently it's rather more British-based and British in outlook. It's not yet fully awakened to the needs of scholarship and what's beginning to go on in the scholarly world. And that's why we had to have rather a long gap before the 1980 edition, when we had to come to terms much more with the huge growth in musicology, especially in the USA and on the continent of Europe, and we called there on a much higher proportion of foreign scholars. Of course, it then became necessary to start thinking about the music of the rest of the world, which was admitted almost by grace and favour in earlier editions. The growth factor is something it's almost impossible to control – even Sir George Grove found that. When he originally published it, he started by saying on the title page of the first volume 'in two volumes'; on the second volume it says 'in three', and on the third volume it says 'in four volumes'. Then the next edition was four volumes; Colles's was five; the 1940 edition was six; Eric Blom's was nine, and our 1980 edition was twenty. We are having to work hard to make sure this next one doesn't go up to some total like thirty, which would be too big, I think, for what is required. We were aiming at twenty-four but we think it might be a bit more than that . . . (Stanley Sadie)

History: a thing of the past?

HISTORY, I THINK, really has become impossible, because history implies one thing following another. Now, there was a kind of line that one could follow that started who knows where – say, at the Renaissance – and that came forward to lead to what you will: Cage, Boulez, Shostakovich. But that line, because it kind of split and forked so many times, it's now become a huge tangle. And history is very very difficult to write for the last thirty or forty years. Whether it's also impossible to write a kind of aesthetics of new music, a statement of what music might mean, of what is important now, of who is doing new things with the art and in the art and through the art that haven't been done before and therefore merits consideration – I don't know that that's impossible. (Paul Griffiths)

[WILL THE NEXT EDITION OF *Grove* be produced in electronic instead of printed form?] Not instead of. Probably as well as. Whether it'll actually be CD-rom or whether it'll be some other form of electronic capture, some kind of on-line form, is open to question – we just don't know yet. Conditions are changing month to month and no publisher is going to commit themselves until the last possible moment on the form. But there will definitely be an electronic form somehow. No, it won't replace the book. We have a fairly good idea of how people use *Grove*, what kinds of things they look up, and the fact is that for a very large proportion of queries it's quicker and easier to pick a volume off the shelves and turn to the right page than it is to start playing around with disks or computers and pressing the right things on the keyboard. I think the book still has a quite considerable future. (Stanley Sadie)

I HOPE THERE'LL never be a time when human beings don't get immense pleasure and instruction from a book in the hand, because the machine . . . all right, it's press a button and there it is, but it's a kind of instant reaction, and reading a book you can turn the page back and read again – it's altogether more intimate and you hope it's just the author and you together at that time. That's what one hopes when one writes a book: that it's one chap going to read it and you're trying to tell him and that he'll agree with you, disagree with you, argue with you, and turn the page back – and then go back to the book again. (Michael Kennedy)

Criticism's changing horizons

WE HAVE A DUTY to the public to tell the truth. Everyone knows that not all compositions and not all performers are of equal excellence, though there's usually something to be said in favour of all but the very dullest. So it sometimes seems as though we, who are not good performers (my own piano playing is frightful, and I have a most unpleasant singing voice), are telling the most eminent where they are wrong or, as is more usual, where they are deficient. Our business, however, is not to teach the artist but to instruct the public. Very occasionally one can make a suggestion, perhaps a point of scoring, which a composer will welcome, or a hint about delivery that a singer will appreciate. But it is not necessarily the job of criticism to be constructive. And while in an imperfect world we may often qualify our praise with a 'but', or even say bluntly that something is bad, we have to say what we honestly think. It does occasionally happen that we are in a position to salute a masterpiece or discover a new executant of genius. One cannot salute non-existent masterpieces but when they appear one must have the perception to recognize them and the courage of one's opinions, and proclaim them. (Frank Howes, 1961)

OVERNIGHT MUSICAL JOURNALISM has become steadily less feasible during my thirty-two years on the staff of *The Times*: deadlines become earlier and finishing times later; getting through on long-distance telephones becomes more hazardous and time-consuming; and so more notices are printed a day or so later. We think enviously of our Victorian predecessors, who seem to have had until four in the morning or so to hand in their copy. The latest advance in progress, computer setting with cold metal and the threatened direct input by journalists, will bring the deadline back, they say, to half past nine and overnight journalism will vanish – though football fans, I'm sure, will resist. When I started work at *The Times*, the typewriter was considered newfangled; only one machine was available, paradoxically antique and clapped out, and we all wrote our stories by hand. I taught myself fairly neat, legible handwriting which even ballpoint pens didn't quite eliminate, and I never learned to think on to a typewriter. When direct input of copy is accepted, as sooner or later it must be, everyone will have to learn to type or give up daily journalism. I've chosen the latter course already and since two months ago I've been a freelance writer about music, still contributing occasionally to *The Times*, I'm happy to say, but no longer as music critic. Oh well, it's a job for young people, overnight criticism. (William Mann, 1982)

TECHNOLOGY, WE WERE TOLD, was going to be wonderful for us: you could do these things at the last minute. And all that's happened is you have got to do everything earlier. Technology doesn't seem to be much of a help to the critic at all. Take the Sunday papers – I believe some of my colleagues have to get their article in by Wednesdays because it's in a magazine, which goes to press at a different time. I'm fortunate on the *Sunday Telegraph*: they can take me up to Friday morning, because it goes in the review section (which even so is printed earlier). But I was led to believe earlier on that the new technology would mean that a Sunday-paper writer could even cover a concert on Saturday night – which I believe once upon a time in the old days of hot-metal newspapers, you could in fact do. But the thing that is, I must say, wonderful is having a laptop computer and being able to put your copy into the London computer typed by yourself. The days where, if you were out of Manchester or out of London somewhere, you'd have to find a phone box somewhere out in the wilds and get through and read your criticism by the light of a match almost, somebody the other end had to take it down and you had to spell 'Mozart' and if you used 'adagio' you had to spell 'adagio'. Well now, if the mistakes go in, it's your own fault for typing it wrongly, most times. And it's wonderful abroad, because instead of having to work out what time you phone a notice in so that there's somebody there among the telephonists, you're your own master – you can send it in at the time of day that suits you. For covering a festival at Salzburg or Bayreuth or somewhere like that, from that point of view it has transformed life absolutely for the better. (Michael Kennedy)

How has criticism changed?

TRYING TO LOOK AT IT objectively means looking really at two things: at the critics themselves, and at whether the critics have a chance to say what they think. I think the critics themselves are probably as acute and good, but they have less opportunity to formulate their views for the public. I mean, I wonder if in the 1950s and 1960s there had been a readers' survey conducted, say by *The Times*, whether it would have found that the music criticism to which the paper gave a lot of attention and space was being read, or whether it was simply put forward by editors, by educated editors, who believed this was what *The Times* should be reviewing? I'm not sure that there's a greater public for high music, for music of a kind that is not instantly pleasing but is exciting – the sort of music of which you say, I don't quite understand it but I'm sure there is something there and I'd like to get to know it. I think there's probably less of a public for that kind of music and there's a big public for *The Four Seasons*, and Nige [Nigel Kennedy], which doesn't need a great deal of detailed reviewing – it needs a publicity machine, which has largely taken over from criticism in our press. Until not so very long ago, there was a serious essay once a week in *The Times* on music; it was called 'the Friday article', and it was about some topic that one wanted to read about. Then on Saturday there was the 'World of Music' written by the *Telegraph* critic – who could be Richard Capell, could be Martin Cooper, could be Peter Stadlen, which again taught one something. These were thoughtful essays usually producing some new information and certainly some new thought. All that seems to have disappeared. That was a great strength of the writing – the print as apart from the radio presentation of music. And the two would come together in – I suppose the magazine that of those that disappeared I miss most of all – *The Listener*, which used to have a preliminary essay about some important broadcast of the week, written by a scholar in that subject, which would whet one's appetite for listening, and listening more acutely. In addition to that, there would more often than not be a reprint of some talk that had been given during the week, given a form which would then allow you to study it. Anyone of my age, I think, has a thick file of clippings from *The Listener*, both the weekly articles and the talks that were reprinted. (Andrew Porter)

I'M NOT SURE we're actually that much more diverse. What certainly is the case is that there are many more composers working. I think because the period after the Second World War was so exciting and seemed to open up so many possibilities, it spurred a lot of people who were then children to interest themselves in composition. If you think back in British terms, throughout the first half of the century there were never more than three or four first-rank composers, people whose music was being regularly presented. Now, one would have to say there are – I don't know – maybe a hundred people whose work seems to merit and require being programmed frequently, their new works being considered seriously. That is the huge problem – that there is simply so much material, and anybody is bound to feel themselves highly inadequate in dealing with that. One finds certain areas of interest; one tries to keep up with that, in the knowledge that there's a huge amount that is slipping by. And I think this isn't only the case in music. Anybody in the nineteenth century, any educated person, could have kept abreast with what was happening in scientific developments, say, right across the field. They'd have been aware of Michael Faraday and Darwin and all the rest of it. These days the idea of somebody keeping abreast of what is happening right across the field of scientific endeavour is just completely out of the question. So it's not just in music.

I think we've gone into a new kind of insularity, which is a kind of reaction to the great amount of music being written. If one thinks back to the great Glock days in the 1960s and the Third Programme invitation concerts, there was a feeling that music in Europe and to a certain extent music from America ought to be explored and presented to the public. Now, because there is such a huge quantity of composing talent in Britain the availability therefore of music from the continent of Europe and from America in Britain has gone down. I'm aware of this myself, that the critic's view has become more insular than it was thirty years ago. Maybe it was even more insular another decade or two before that. But I think it is insular now.

That may be one of our problems in musical culture generally but the willingness to say 'this is outstanding and really deserves a wide audience and many performances' in the face of the diversity, I suppose, has become more difficult. Simply so much contemporary music is available now. I remember when I started listening to new music in the 1960s I very rapidly decided that Birtwistle was somebody I was very interested in. Now there was one record that had *Tragoedia* on it and for several years that was all you could get. Nowadays it's very easy to find several records of Birtwistle, composers much less well known, composers much younger – the availability has gone up hugely. The question arises, what trust people can put in critics now and how much they should trust their own judgements. (Paul Griffiths)

I'M AN AWFUL GLOOM MERCHANT about music in this country, not just because of what's going on generally at the moment, but I do think that it is not a high priority to the average member of the public, and if you went out into the street and said to people, 'Are you bothered that there might be no Royal Opera? Are you bothered that there might be no Hallé Orchestra?', in a lot of cases you'd find that they didn't give a damn. As far as the general public is concerned, nobody who writes books or biographies of musicians is ever going to retire to the Bahamas on the proceeds – that is absolutely true. And one wonders why one does it, to a degree. But the great thing in this country is that the people who really love music are absolutely fanatical about it. But then I read the other day that the famous gramophone companies are putting out CDs, 2-CD sets, of 'the classical favourites with all the boring bits cut out', and I thought to myself, have we really been working all these years and got to the stage where people want only the tuney bits, with the boring bits cut out? I find this infinitely, infinitely depressing and that is the thing that worries me most. (Michael Kennedy)

5 Music and Mammon

Music is something that people can get on without. And if it costs
too much – they will!
THOMAS BEECHAM, 1944

IN ANY MODERATELY advanced society there will be a fairly large
number of people who want to be entertained by music, and a relatively small number who have the talent to provide it and have been
prepared to undergo the intensive training necessary to acquire proficiency. In a capitalist society, in short, music is a commodity to be
bought and sold.

It is, by its nature, an expensive commodity. A composer might take
a year or several years to write an opera. When written it will need
several hundred people (singers, orchestral musicians, a conductor and
director, stage and lighting staff, costumiers, front-of-house personnel
etc.) to put it on stage. Some of the artists will have rehearsed for
between four and six weeks and the non-performing staff will of course
be paid a weekly or monthly salary, not a fee per performance. If, say,
300 people are each paid an average (very modest) £500 for each performance, if the composer receives £20,000 per year for two years for
his work, and if the opera is given an initial run of five performances (not
uncommon for a new piece) the expenditure on fees and salaries alone
for each performance will be £154,000. At an opera house seating 2000
and, no less important, *selling* 2000 tickets at each performance, for the
company simply to break even the tickets must cost an average of £77.

This calculation does not, of course, include scenery or costumes, publishers' fees or the theatre's normal running costs – heating, lighting, maintenance, insurance, etc. The economics of an orchestral concert are more modest – no sets or costumes, fewer rehearsals – but because concerts are often given only once the costs of rehearsal cannot be shared between five or more performances, as with an opera. The main costs of a concert, aside from the hire of the hall, rental charges or copyright fees for the music being performed, the printing of programmes, advertising, etc., are the fees or salaries paid to perhaps a hundred or more orchestral musicians, the conductor and one or more soloists. Conductors' and soloists' fees may in some cases be very large – well into five figures sterling for an artist of exceptional reputation and drawing power. Of the musicians capable of demanding such fees several are opera singers. In the case of the imaginary opera cited above, and in the extremely unlikely event of one of the 'Three Tenors' agreeing to appear in it for a fee of, say, £20,000 per performance, the break-even average ticket price would rise from £77 to £87, but the theatre would be assured of full houses and could easily sell its most expensive seats for far more than that.

Although the high fees of a small number of famous conductors and soloists are often put forward as a reason for the majority of concerts needing subsidy nowadays, two less publicized and discussed reasons are that orchestral musicians' salaries, in part because of vigorous action by the Musicians' Union, are now broadly comparable with at least the lower rungs of other professions, and that a high proportion of orchestral concerts nowadays are adequately rehearsed. Many orchestral players remember a time when they were paid little more than semi-skilled craftsmen and had to provide themselves, if they could afford to do so, for sickness and eventual retirement.

The activities of impresarios and artists' agents, cunningly managing 'their' artists' careers for their own profit by charging very high percentages and insisting on high fees, are another reason given for the very high cost of promoting a concert, a recital or an operatic production. At all events this is not a new phenomenon. When, after the modest success of his first opera, Oberto, Verdi was offered a contract to write three more by the then impresario of La Scala, Milan, Bartolommeo Merelli, he was eager to accept: Merelli controlled not only La Scala but Milan's 'second' opera house, the Canobbiana, numerous smaller theatres elsewhere in Italy and the hugely important Kärntnerthortheater in Vienna. He was known as 'the Napoleon of impresarios', just as his contemporary and rival Domenico Barbaja was called 'the Viceroy of Naples'.

When rank-and-file musicians were paid badly it was of course easier to put on a concert, even with a famous conductor or soloist, and make a profit. One or two independent impresarios are still doing so, usually engaging highly competent but young and thus inexpensive conductors and soloists, relying on the professionalism of the orchestra to produce a respectable result with only a single rehearsal, and programming popular works that the musicians will already know extremely well. A really fine conductor, however, aiming for a performance of the highest quality, will normally demand at least three rehearsals; often more where a new work or a very complex one is involved. In such circumstances the concert cannot hope to break even.

In the past, although at certain periods and in certain cities it was sometimes possible to perform concerts or operas and make a profit, orchestras and opera houses often received a form of subsidy. A ruler might guarantee an orchestra or opera company against loss, might even support it generously, to serve his own prestige and that of the state. Opera companies in particular were often supported or even managed by committees of noblemen and wealthy merchants who contributed to the company's costs and received in return a box for the entire season; it was not uncommon for gallery seats also to be provided, so that the subscriber's servants could attend him in the intervals and drive him and his guests home afterwards. In nineteenth-century Italy, when opera was extremely popular with a season at least a few weeks long taking place in every town of substance, it was normal for the theatre's subscribers or lessees to subcontract the opera season to a commercial impresario, who would of course do his best to obtain popular singers and to mount operas that were likely to please, including the new operas which were an invariable part of every season at a major theatre. But the enterprise was inevitably risky, and many impresarios insisted on also being given a gambling licence (Barbaja introduced roulette to Italy), the assured profits from which would insure him against a new opera not drawing an audience or a popular singer cancelling their engagement.

In Europe, especially in Italy and Germany, which for centuries were divided into numerous small states, with rulers normally eager to demonstrate their wealth, culture and status by supporting the arts, concerts and opera had become so much a part of the way of life of the educated classes that they survived the unification of those two countries. In other countries, as absolute monarchy gave way to democracy, the state took over the running and financing of artistic institutions. In Britain, where the court had taken little interest in patronage of the performing arts, apart from such isolated examples as

the brief support given to Handel's earlier opera seasons, opera continued to be supported in the Italian manner (with a skilled impresario
backed by the guarantees of a 'syndicate') until the Second World War,
while most concerts were promoted for profit, with increasing private
subvention for special events: for example the wealthy composer
Balfour Gardiner subsidized concerts of music by his contemporaries,
a concert series more imaginatively planned than most and conducted
by the up-and-coming Malcolm Sargent was supported by Mrs Samuel
Courtauld ('the Courtauld–Sargent Concerts'), and so on.

During the Second World War, the Council for the Encouragement
of Music and the Arts (later renamed the Arts Council of Great
Britain) was established by the government and began subsidizing
music as well as the other arts; since the end of the war government
sponsorship has been crucial to the development of the arts in Britain.
The amount spent has always been low compared with other Western
European countries but in music, for a while, relatively small sums
of money combined with the swiftness and efficiency of British
musicians to ensure not only the survival of existing musical institutions but their expansion and the foundation of new ones. At the end
of the war, for example, Sadler's Wells Opera was already a virtually
full-time organization, and the Covent Garden Opera (now the Royal
Opera) and the Sadler's Wells Ballet (now the Royal Ballet) very soon
combined to form another. In the years since then, major opera
companies have been founded in Wales, Scotland and the North of
England.

At the same time the rise of broadcasting not only made good music
available to anyone with a radio, thus greatly affecting a huge growth
of public interest in music, but also increased the number of musicians
in work. At the height of its activity in this area the BBC, apart from
an exceptionally fine orchestra in London, maintained symphony
orchestras or smaller ensembles playing lighter music in Wales,
Scotland, Northern Ireland, Manchester, the Midlands and the West of
England. Before this, unemployment in the musical profession had
been high, ever since the advent of sound films: the silent cinema had
required at least a pianist, more often a small or even a substantial
orchestra. More recently the number of young people learning to play
instruments has again increased the pool of musicians seeking a limited
number of positions, and many of today's more talented young
musicians can be found doing some orchestral freelance work, at
other times playing chamber music or with groups specializing in
contemporary or early music, perhaps switching with an ease that their
elders find astonishing to a 'period' instrument.

Although government subsidy continued to grow it did not do so commensurately with the growth of the audience for music. There were continual demands for more money to be spent, and continual warnings of the dire consequences of not doing so. At the time at which the series of radio programmes on which this book is based was broadcast, it seemed quite possible (though the risk has at least temporarily been averted) that the Hallé Orchestra would be forced to cease operating. Those who resisted the spending of more money suggested that arts organizations, rather than complaining that Britain spent far less per head on culture than any comparable Western European country, should instead look at the situation in the United States. There, direct government sponsorship via the National Endowment for the Arts is far lower than in Britain, yet the US maintains a very large number of orchestras and opera companies, largely due to private, corporate and business sponsorship. One reason that it can do so is that the US government gives generous tax advantages to businesses and individuals who sponsor the arts, a move that no British government so far has felt able to follow. Another, less easily remediable reason was given by an official of the Metropolitan Opera in New York when asked by the present author why he thought the Royal Opera was so conspicuously less successful than his own organization at raising sponsorship money: 'You have far fewer millionaires than we do.'

Nevertheless, all arts organizations in Britain have had in recent years to take commercial sponsorship seriously, and some have been remarkably successful. Some have been critical of the 'commercialization' involved, though for the most part sponsors have been too sophisticated to insist on concerts, opera productions or commissioned works bearing the name of their product. More serious criticisms have been that commercial sponsors often wish to be associated with a particular arts organization only for a limited period and that they are often reluctant to sponsor any event save those that guarantee maximum publicity, certainly not those that are challenging and unlikely to draw capacity audiences. There have also been complaints that arts administrators now spend far more of their time wooing sponsors than in artistic planning. With the recent promise of large sums of money from the National Lottery (sums initially reserved for capital projects only and thus more likely to help the building of a new concert hall than the running costs of an orchestra that might play in it), arts organizations have often been obliged to take on extra staff to deal with the heavy clerical work that applications for sponsorship and Lottery money entail.

For performers the development of recording has been crucial, not least in economic terms. Without recording, Enrico Caruso would have taken far longer to achieve an international reputation and his consequent ability to demand very high performing fees. With the extraordinary expansion of sales of recordings following the development of the compact disc some artists have not only made their reputations through recordings (prompting allegations in some cases that their careers have been 'manufactured', their live performances not living up to the image presented by their recordings) but have made an ever higher proportion of their income from them. The case of the late Glenn Gould, the Canadian pianist who abandoned public performance entirely, achieving worldwide celebrity and a comfortable income from recording and radio alone, is an isolated but not insignificant one.

At the same time recording companies have changed, and in two directions. Until the era of the long-playing record, and for some while after its arrival, most recording companies were large, and soon became (if they were not already) international in their scope of activity. Most of them accepted, though few would admit it publicly, that their 'classical' recordings were a high-prestige but relatively small part of their output, effectively subsidized in terms of the company's short-term profit by the far higher sales of popular music. Such companies were prepared, for the sake of their reputation and for longer-term profit, to produce expensive recordings that would not cover their costs for many years. Such projects still occur, aided by the fact that recordings can be sold worldwide. But the comparatively recent phenomenon of a 'classical' recording, aided by sophisticated advertising and the projection of the performing artist's 'image', selling as many copies as a single by a pop group has led, perhaps temporarily, to some international companies trying to concentrate on such high-selling material and to a consequent reduction in the number of recordings that cannot be expected to show such large short-term profits.

Over the same period there has been an expansion, worldwide but perhaps most notably and most successfully in Great Britain, of companies who are willing to investigate out-of-the-way repertoire, using artists of high quality but not necessarily international fame. A large part of the expansion of the recorded repertoire, including that of contemporary music, has been the work of these companies, working on narrow but shrewdly managed profit margins but also being ready to take risks on the producers' or proprietors' enthusiasms. Many such recordings, and other musical events, have been aided or sponsored by charitable foundations established either during the lifetimes of successful composers or under the terms of their wills: much work of this kind has been done by the RVW Trust (set up by Ralph Vaughan Williams), the Holst Foundation and the Britten–Pears Foundation.

As far as live music is concerned, since commercial sponsorship is inevitably constrained by commercial decisions, one cannot say that it is the business of sponsors to take similar risks in favour of neglected repertoire or new music, though some enlightened sponsors have done so. State subsidy, however, should be as much concerned with future audiences as with existing ones, as much with the growth of the repertoire as with its maintenance and as much with new music as with old. But when such a very high proportion of public money spent on the arts is inevitably devoted to keeping orchestras, opera houses and festivals ('centres of excellence', as they have been called) in existence, albeit precariously because of the inadequate sums involved, the proportion spent on new art is bound to remain small, perhaps even to diminish still further.

*

Must music lose money?

MUSIC CERTAINLY IS as capitalist an endeavour as anything else, and I don't think that any type of music, whether it's classical or pop, can be estranged from the basic business ethics of the way the whole world works. Certainly in this country there is currently a real problem with the appreciation of whether classical music as an art form should be supported by government, by local authorities and so on, or whether, as has been increasingly happening in the United States, it should be left to fend for itself. And I think this is a real problem that we're facing now. (Simon Foster)

BOTH STATE SUBSIDY and corporate sponsorship have been short-term panaceas. For a while there was a great boom, there was a lot of money rushing in and all was very hunky-dory. But it planted the idea in the minds of artists and their agents that there was gold in them there hills and they could vastly inflate their fees, and once inflated they don't come down again. So now we're faced with declining state subsidy, declining corporate sponsorship and unsustainable, unaffordable fees. Something's got to give. (Norman Lebrecht)

I'M TEMPTED TO SAY no orchestra has ever been a viable concern financially, because of the intrinsic nonsense of the economics. (Cyril Ehrlich)

Selling music

I REALLY HAVE NO DOUBT at all that to call oneself the Chamber Orchestra of Europe – we didn't know it in 1980 – is disastrous, absolutely disastrous. The 'Chamber' is a turn-off for people generally. Worse from a British standpoint has been the word 'Europe' in the title over a period of time – and anyway they muddle us up with everyone else who's got a European-sounding name.

We quite like to play in halls that seat two thousand people – one and a half thousand to two and a half thousand, say an average of two thousand seats. And in the UK context we would be looking at something like an average seat price of £12 a seat, which gives you a maximum on a wholly sold house of about £24,000 of box-office income. Well, obviously you never completely sell a house and we would be budgeting on a considerably lower percentage, but let's say we thought we had a terrific evening, and we were going to sell 80 per cent of the house: you're looking at a box-office income of broadly £20,000. Now, because of the nature of the Chamber Orchestra of Europe and the fact that we have to amortize our travel costs and our rehearsal costs (which are probably four days when the orchestra is operating with no income) over a series of concerts, it's unlikely that we as an orchestra are going to cost much less, including a director or a conductor, than say £40,000 – in other words, double what the potential box-office income is. Now that's almost certainly without a soloist. If you pin on top of that a major international-calibre soloist, you can very easily, or without too much difficulty, be talking – plus expenses and everything else – nearer £50,000 for a single evening's concert, when your income is in the order of £20,000. But let's just stick at £40,000 for a moment. Either someone like me has to come in and meet that gap with sponsorship – and it's almost impossible to raise £20,000 of sponsorship for a concert unless it's a very special one – or alternatively you have to be playing in a city, such as a Berlin or a Ferrara, where they themselves for their own reasons are prepared to come in and subsidize that particular concert, either with city resources or with lottery resources. But, as you can see, before we even sit on a platform, the actual cost just of the Chamber Orchestra of Europe with somebody directing it, conducting it, is probably going to be broadly twice the potential box-office income. (Peter Readman)

Orchestras in peril

BOTH GERMANY AND the United States have seen wholesale closures of orchestras, particularly in Germany where there were far too many, particularly in the north of the country, and they couldn't possibly sustain it. Apart from a couple of BBC orchestras which were closed for tactical reasons, we have yet to see a major symphony orchestra die in the UK for purely financial reasons. And we hear stories about what is happening in Manchester; what happened to my orchestra in the past, the Royal Philharmonic, and yet these orchestras continue. But I don't think any of us in the business really believe that we've got some God-given right that Beecham founded our orchestra and therefore it must go on. (Simon Foster)

ONE DAY AN EMINENT BANKER, meeting me in the street, stopped and said, 'Tell me, T.B., do you owe or are you owed a couple of million? I can't make out which.' I replied 'Both', which in a way was partly true, but left him more mystified than ever. As for the Official Receiver, whose business it was to call in whatever assets a debtor might have anywhere, the income I was receiving under a court scheme set up to administer my father's affairs was difficult if not impossible of collection. As everything else was firmly tied up, there was nothing for the Official Receiver to do but sit down, like the creditors, and wait. As I said at the time, 'For what he is about to Receive, may the Lord make him truly thankful.' (Thomas Beecham, 1944)

What went wrong?

IT WENT WRONG when music lost sight of its economic foundations and started relying too much on the kindness of strangers. If you look at the cost of putting on a recital over the past two generations, in the early 1950s if you engaged the top violinist of the time, Jascha Heifetz, at Carnegie Hall, he would charge you a fee of $3000. When all your costs were told and you had a full house, the house would actually make a profit, and there would be enough to put on recitals by lesser-known violinists and to allow for empty seats. There would be enough surplus both from solo concerts and even from orchestral concerts, without subsidy, to put enough money back into the musical process to enable it to continue. Today the top soloists (Itzhak Perlman, Anne-Sophie Mutter) have fees of $45,000. The hall has to wheel in a sponsor simply to pay the artist's fee and cannot hope to cover its costs in putting on the recital. An orchestral concert in London loses with a full house something like £30,000, for which it receives state subsidy. If the house is not full (and generally it's about half full these days) it loses a great deal more. We've lost sight of the relation between supply and demand and between costs and income, and we've got to rediscover that. It's a simple economic problem: what works, what doesn't work. The rot begins with the mercenary impulse. There are good agents, there are bad agents; there are agents who give their artists good advice and those who give them bad advice. The mercenary impulse which exists both within agents and in artists is essentially what do you put first: the money or the music? I think there are some agents who take too much of the cake and there are some agents who've made too big a business of it. It's very difficult to generalize. There are some small and medium-sized agents who are as idealistic as you and me who would not raise a finger in order to jeopardize musical society and musical performance, and who indeed put a lot of their own money, personally, into sustaining musical performance – one does find such characters. There are an awful lot more who are simply muddling through. And at the top there are these vast multi-national combines that have been formed in order to extort and extract as much money as is possible from the musical process, having realized over the past couple of generations that there are large amounts of money coming in from public sources and corporate sources. These vast agencies have been trying to get their whack of it and that is their priority, and it's a priority with which they have infected many of their artists. (Norman Lebrecht)

IT'S PERFECTLY TRUE that over the last few decades certain artists (and Karajan of course was one of the most famous examples) were able to manipulate the system and earn huge fees. Another example is the visiting tenor who is able to command a very high fee. What's difficult, if you try to argue rationally about all that, is if you ask, 'Well, look, haven't tenors always been paid high fees? Look at what Caruso was able to make.' You see, certainly with agents, while it's true that there's a tendency towards monopoly and therefore for certain international agents to manipulate the system, none the less most monopolies don't survive for long if the pickings are that easy. (Cyril Ehrlich)

Tenors and superstars

'THE THREE TENORS' was an absolute disaster for the whole world of classical music, a total disaster. It emphasized the notion that there were vast sums of money to be made in it. There were – for the Three

Tenors and for their manager. And it also sold a very peculiar and dangerous delusion to people who might have started to become interested in classical music. What the Tenors will say to you is, 'Well, we've brought in a vast audience – this is a great new audience for opera.' Rubbish! After a Three Tenors concert do you see a queue snaking around Floral Street, fighting to get into Covent Garden, or fighting to get into La Scala? Of course not. What they're selling is the illusion that it's not opera if there aren't these three guys singing in it. They're actually damaging the opera industry by their own self-projection. We've seen a huge rise in record sales of Three Tenors records but sales of integral operas, complete operas, featuring any one or two of the Three Tenors, are going through the floor. It's destroying the market for real opera and creating a market for soundbite opera. (Norman Lebrecht)

I THINK WHAT WE'VE SEEN over the last few years is the rise of the superstar artist. Obviously there have been great singers and great opera stars who earned a lot of money in the 1930s and 1940s, but the vast majority of classical music-making is done on a shoestring. It is done with very, very tight budgets; it does not involve these people, and these people are only a very small number. As a matter of statistics, of the number of concerts that take place in London in any one year – in London alone or in the United Kingdom – I would imagine less than 1 per cent would involve people who take fees that are of that type of nature. And I think it's very dangerous to assume that the whole classical music world is dominated by these big stars. (Simon Foster)

IN CERTAIN CASES we've discussed it with promoters and said, 'Look, quite frankly, you're way beyond our budgets.' And what happens in those cases is we don't do the project. And we have had circumstances where we have had to pull out. (Peter Readman)

WHEN I BROUGHT Nigel Kennedy to records – I introduced him with the Elgar Concerto and he made *The Four Seasons* – suddenly a superstar arrived and everyone said, 'This is going to be wonderful. What will happen is that people will rush out after they've bought their Nigel Kennedy record; they'll go out and buy other records of Vivaldi, other records of Elgar.' Well, of course, it's nonsense. Nigel is a great artist but what he did was popularize himself, quite rightly, and his music, and people went out and bought more Nigel Kennedy records. In the meantime the chairmen of big international record companies who had relied on classics being reasonably profitable – bringing in 10 per cent of sales internationally, year in, year out, is a very good comfort zone –

suddenly thought to themselves, 'If Nigel Kennedy can sell a million, 2 million copies of *The Four Seasons*, we must have more Nigel Kennedys.' And the end result was, at a time when the compact disc had been available in the market for so long and most people who were interested in classical music had been able to cover their basic repertoire, the record companies got desperate and started to try to appeal to a broader audience with a very mixed and in fact dangerous message, which is: what you need are soundbites; what you need are records with fancy titles like 'Power', 'Passion', 'Ecstasy' . . . one never knew what was going to come next. And people thought, 'Is this really what classical music is about?' They'd come home and it would be disparate artists on the record, often thrown together as a ragbag, often chosen on some sort of popularity poll. You know: the music was not chosen intellectually; it was which piece of music is more important? Here's the cut-off; that's the album. And I don't think that's doing anybody any good. It certainly isn't bringing people into the concert hall; I don't think it's educating them; I think it is just establishing classical music into the era of Muzak. (Simon Foster)

The musical industrial revolution

WHEN MECHANIZATION TAKES command this enables music to earn serious money. It doesn't happen immediately but the productivity of the musician, the output per unit of the input of the musician, is completely transformed; it's a sort of industrial revolution. So that's the first point: there's the potential there for huge money. The second point is copyright, performing right and so on, which monitors that income and protects it – the Performing Right Society, that sort of thing. The third and most obvious factor is the huge increase in our consumption of music. Today we have music all the time, as background mostly to everything we do. That's a comparatively new thing but it means that we are consuming – buying in some form – music on an unprecedented scale.

The take-off point for the Musicians' Union is 1907 and that was the year of the great music-hall strike. Before cinema came, music-hall was the major form of entertainment. Every music-hall had an orchestra – some very good players came out of that tradition, such as the Barbirollis, for example. But Joe Williams, who was the near-genius who created the Musicians' Union, built up that union and used the 1907 variety or music-hall strike as his golden opportunity, because of course it got publicity. Since the music-halls were on strike famous music-hall artists were on the picket line and the conditions of employment of musicians and actors and so on, for once, were front-page news. Joe cashed in on that, used it for publicity, appeared before the famous arbitration of that strike, and from that time on the Musicians' Union really organized itself. The American Musicians' Union is even more exciting, really, because it got very, very violent: Pedrillo, who was the American equivalent of Joe Williams, used to drive around Chicago in a bullet-proof car.

You have a sort of Malthusian situation in which there is inevitable proliferation, an inevitable glut of musicians trying to make a living. For a performing musician the ideal time to live was in the 1920s and the reason is simply silent cinema, because the silent cinema was of course not silent. It was all over the place and everywhere it required music at the same time and it provided huge employment. The night the talkies arrived, everybody lost their job. Printed music was burned by the tonne and there was a collapse.

Our Performing Right Society was quite a late starter; in fact it started in 1914. Long before that the French had the equivalent and so you had the curious situation, the French composers had their works protected in a way the British didn't, even when French music was being played in London or English theatre music, for example, was being played in Paris. The international agreements on all this under the Berne Convention get under way at about the same time. By 1911 we have in England a decent Copyright Act. The Russians, of course, didn't, so that, for example, when the Chaliapin records were famously earning lots of money before the First World War, they were being pirated everywhere in Russia, and since the Revolution happened soon after that, Russian copyright was a nightmare for most of this century. But in other countries, in Western Europe and in America, in their varying ways they all got this kind of protection. Now the money being handled there is huge, of course, well over a hundred million a year. (Cyril Ehrlich)

Wealthy composers . . .

THERE SHOULD BE a single Art Exchange in the world, to which the Artist would simply send his works – and be given in return as much money as he needs. As it is, on top of everything else one has to be half a merchant; and how badly one goes about it! (Ludwig van Beethoven, 1801)

I HAVE OCCASIONALLY REMARKED that the only entirely creditable incident in English history is the sending of one hundred pounds to Beethoven on his deathbed by the London Philharmonic Society. And it's the only one historians never mention. (George Bernard Shaw, 1932)

THE INTERESTING THING if we contrast Vaughan Williams's relationship with Oxford University Press Music Department and Walton's is that Vaughan Williams knew [Humphrey] Milford, the head of the entire institution, personally and was very much respected by Milford. They never actually had a contract at any point; it was a gentleman's agreement that Oxford University Press would publish anything Vaughan Williams offered, and Vaughan Williams offered them everything he wrote. And that lasted for the rest of his life and has continued ever since. In the case of Walton, the relationship was very much centred on Hubert Foss, who was the first head of the Oxford University Press Music Department. He was exactly the same age as Walton; he was a brilliant young man and he was only in his twenties when he was appointed the first music editor. He took Walton off to all of the International Society for Contemporary Music festivals, he introduced him to Berg, he showed him what was happening in European music, and in a sense we can hear all of these influences coming out in Walton's work during the late 1920s and during the 1930s. The score of the First Symphony and the recording came out within a month of the completion of the fourth movement, which has to be a record really in interwar English music publishing, to have all the material available for the dissemination of a work so quickly.

One of the things that's very difficult of course for a music publisher is having more than one composer or two composers in the house at a time, particularly if they are operating in very similar fields. There's a nice balance to be struck on the publisher's part because they have to have critical mass, which is the concept that they have to have a big enough presence in a certain market to be influential and to be known. But also if you have too many the levels of investment and in a sense the competing demands of composers can become problematic. I think in the case of Benjamin Britten's life with Oxford University Press he was very much aware that Walton had proved his position in the world by the mid-1930s and that there was no question over Vaughan Williams having assumed Elgar's mantle after Elgar's death in 1934 and therefore I think he always felt he was going to be third string. And there was also a sense for the Press in which the level of investment demanded for each of these composers – because all of them were so prolific during the 1930s and, as we've said, the gestation on investment was so slow – that in that particular period the level of losses was huge if they tried to publish all three at once. (Duncan Hinnells)

WE'VE COME TO THE POINT with Britten where we'll have to decide whether we take him up or not. I have a retainer on him, but I gather that Boosey & Hawkes are angling to get him. He's therefore going to take to that firm his *Sinfonietta*, which I'm sure is uncommercial. He now offers me a moderately short work for strings and his Oboe Quartet. Both are long-shot publications, with no target at all beyond prestige for the quartet. It would be a pity to let him go, but it's a costly game and in the case of Britten I'm inclined to think it might be worth while to let Boosey's waste some money on him, so long as we can keep his more remunerative efforts. (Hubert Foss, OUP Music Department, to Humphrey Milford, Secretary to the OUP, 23 April 1934)

. . . and less wealthy ones

WELL, I STARTED LIFE as a schoolteacher and, as any teacher will tell you, you have to do a certain amount of composing, because the school orchestra might not have bassoons or whatever and so you have to kind of start composing. I wanted to do it before then, though, and I actually did write an opera for the school I was teaching at at the time, which was a girls' school in Surrey. And there aren't many operas for girls. *Dido and Aeneas* was the only one I could think of, and I didn't want to do that, so I actually wrote them an opera. And I really got a taste for it, and a taste for quite large forms. So that was that. I left teaching full-time, worked as a viola player and wrote one or two small things. And then it was Richard Hickox who actually asked for a large piece for the Saint Endellion Festival. Which wasn't a commission in that it was paid; in fact, I think I can honestly say I had to pay to do it.

Symphonies of Flocks, Herds and Shoals I can say now quite emphatically was nothing whatsoever to do with the Fens or East Anglia. I have somehow got this reputation as being an East Anglian composer who writes about big flat landscapes with howling east gales. It wasn't anything to do with that, though maybe you can hear that in it. It's certainly an outdoor piece from the title, and I come from Norwich, and I think the BBC Symphony Orchestra liked very much the idea of linking up their sponsor, Land-Rover, with my interests – birds, for example. And so we had a most wonderful day out in Strumpshaw Fen in Norfolk, where I had my picture taken sitting in a Land-Rover – I don't drive, by the way. This was the most exciting bit of it all. It's a wonderful picture and I look very natural as a driver, but I've never learned! Anyway, I think this was one thing they thought would be very nice and sort of tie the whole thing up, and I went bird-watching, and it was very interesting because it's lovely to talk to the Land-Rover people and see the other side of life. They in their turn were fascinated by the workings of a symphony orchestra, and I heard all sorts of exciting projects being set up as I finished the day: 'Well, we must send some of our BBC Symphony Orchestra people out to Land-Rover; Land-Rover must come in and see how we work in our office.' I don't know what became of that project but it's rather nice, I think, the link-up between two completely different organizations.

What I wouldn't countenance – I simply wouldn't be able to do it, actually – is if they were to say (this is just off the top of my head), 'Well, we specialize in antique cars and we'd like something with a 1920s feel to it. Could you write something that sort of suggested that?' I wouldn't be able to do that. I can't. I'm not clever enough, nor would I want to. There are composers that can, but I also feel it would be a sort of compromise, a stylistic compromise for me, so I don't think I would want to do that. (Diana Burrell)

EVERY COMPOSER'S MUSIC reflects, in its subject matter and in its style, the source of the money the composer's living on while writing it. (Virgil Thomson, 1939)

The land without patronage

ONE OF THE ODD THINGS about England is that we've never been any good at patronage at all until roughly about the 1930s. By that I mean the Court was never of any use for the last few centuries. The Court has had no beneficial effect at all. Even in contrast to America, for example, where seriously rich ladies bought, as it were, symphony orchestras, we never had anything like that and therefore real patronage starts here only with the BBC, and later of course with the Arts Council. But the BBC's by far the most important. (Cyril Ehrlich)

Commercial sponsorship – success or failure?

MY OWN PERSONAL EXPERIENCE (which is now quite lengthy, of course, having been involved for seventeen years) is actually that conditions are getting more difficult. Certainly I'm finding the going harder now than I've ever found it. There are many more opportunities for sponsorship in the broader world, in the sports world and other things, and companies can possibly get better value for money elsewhere – at least many companies *think* they can get better value for money, although £20,000 or £15,000 of sponsorship is not a very large sum to some of these very

major multinational companies. Nevertheless the range of opportunities they've got is perhaps broader because more and more enterprises
are seeking sponsorship, and then they've got the whole field, the
medical field, the educational field – there's all sorts of fields in which
they can put their shareholders' money to work. (Peter Readman)

SPONSORSHIP HAS BEEN a very limited stopgap solution. During the
Thatcher–Reagan years it seemed to be the best way of getting society
to pay for music that it could no longer afford. But, as in other areas,
society has discovered different priorities. There is not just a symphony
orchestra or an opera house into which you can put your sponsorship
money these days. You can put it into a museum; you can put it into
an Aids hospital; you can put it into scientific research; you can put it
into a variety of good causes, a multiplicity of good causes, in which
music is just one and it's an ever-diminishing voice. So why should you
put your money into music? And is it bringing you the rewards that
you want for commercial sponsorship? You have to justify this to your
tax inspector and to your board. (Norman Lebrecht)

Grounds for optimism?

IN TERMS OF the sheer dynamic of industry and the whole commercial
world, the compact disc has never changed. It's the same object in the
same rather tacky plastic case and so on. Now at last there is light at
the end of the tunnel. I think the most important thing that will
happen in the record business, which will revive it very quickly, is the
arrival of a new piece of technology called 'digital versatile disc', which
is being used in computer technology. It's a video system and will
replace VHS. Eventually it will be a recordable medium and it will
allow an even better sound quality. Forget all that nonsense, when CDs
first came out, saying it was the finest sound for ever. Absolute nonsense. I think the improvements will be quite dramatic, including for
the first time a success in the so-called quadraphonic area, which was
such a disaster during the 1970s. And those people with disposable
income will be out to buy classical music – that always happens when
there's a new piece of technology. So that's the light at the end of the
tunnel. (Simon Foster)

THE WHOLE CULTURE needs to be changed. I really do think that more
people could appreciate the music of the day – the kind of music that
I call the music of the day, the perhaps more 'difficult' end of contemporary music, not the pop music, the musicals. I just think there needs
to be more of it; there needs to be more risk taken in concert halls. It

becomes ever more difficult for composers as orchestras and festival directors are reluctant to take risks: 'We can't programme contemporary music, we might not get people to it.' And if they do programme contemporary music it's always the very easy-listening sort. And it's fine but, you know, I hate to use this 'dumbing-down' phrase that is on everyone's lips at the moment, but it is a bit like that. And I don't think it need be, because I think it's patronizing to society. (Diana Burrell)

WE'VE GOT TO FIND a way of making it palatable to the audience. We've got to ask ourselves, 'Why are we giving concerts at 7.30 in the evening – for whose convenience? For the musicians, or for the audience? Who are we trying to appeal to at that time? Is it young people that we want to reach? Do young people go out at 7.30 in the evening?' Not the young people I know – they go out at ten o'clock at night. Why aren't we giving concerts later on? Is it the old people we're trying to reach who are afraid to come to the city centres? Why are we putting on concerts at night in city centres where people get mugged? Perhaps we should be putting them out in the suburbs, on Saturday and Sunday mornings. We've got to rethink; we've got to rethink the structure of concerts, the timing of concerts, the location of concerts. And when people have experimented, some of those experiments have been staggeringly successful. (Norman Lebrecht)

IT MAY BE very presumptuous of me to think that perhaps my music does bring a little bit of joy to other people. But of course if it does then they are in the minority. We live in a very star-struck age when it's the big performers that get a lot of money. And, yes, I do find it very sad and I think incomprehensible really that certain opera singers – I don't want to mention any names – could get thousands for just setting foot on the stage and singing an aria. I don't understand why a society feels it want to pay that sort of money. (Diana Burrell)

6 Music and Motown

*My mother was saying . . . 'Why don't you write pop songs
to tide you over?'*
STEVE REICH

LIKE EVERYONE ELSE in the developed world (and much of the
undeveloped or third world) the contemporary composer cannot
avoid popular music. It is everywhere – on radio and television, in
supermarkets, shops, restaurants and bars, in airport and railway con-
courses, blaring from passing cars and neighbouring houses. Many
composers have grown up with its sounds in their heads, even those
who have no interest in it cannot avoid being aware of it, and many
have been forced – willingly or otherwise – to react to it.

Many classically trained musicians will have been taught, or will
have come to believe without being taught, that theirs is a high art and
popular music a low one. But they cannot avoid noticing that popular
music attracts a mass audience, which their own, on the whole, does not.
Contemporary composers especially are bound to realize that at least
some popular musicians address contemporary issues and a present-
day audience as conscientiously as they do, but in terms that the many
rather than the few can understand. Popular music is a vernacular;
contemporary classical music is not.

The divide between classical and popular has never been greater.
Mozart reported, and with pleasure, that all the errand boys of Prague
were whistling the aria 'Non più andrai' from his opera *Le nozze di*

Figaro. Most of the great Viennese composers, Schubert above all, wrote dance music – and Schubert's was for domestic use, not for grand balls at the Imperial Court. Wagner listened, with mixed feelings but without surprise, to his tunes being played by café bands in Venice. Bach incorporated tavern songs into the final section of his *Goldberg Variations*, folk music was widely used by the nineteenth-century nationalist composers and it echoes through many of the trio sections of Haydn's symphonies and through Scarlatti's harpsichord sonatas.

On the one hand the contemporary composer is heir to a great tradition of serious and often complex music that demands intent listening if it is to be fully appreciated. But the same composer is also aware of the immediacy, the instantaneous, visceral appeal, the simple emotional directness of popular music, and aware, too, that many great composers of the past were able to draw on such qualities without compromising their 'seriousness'. In the latter twentieth century this has often seemed hard to do. Some composers have also been aware of, and attracted by, sounds that the worlds of popular and rock music have pioneered, from the saxophone (used by 'classical' composers as early as Bizet, but acquiring its most characteristic voice in jazz) to the electric guitar, many percussion instruments and the synthesizer.

At a time when post-Schoenbergian rigour was in some quarters hardening into an intolerant hegemony, a group of composers (most famously in the US, but in other countries as well) began to explore much simpler melodies and harmonies and repetitive rhythms. Their music was described as 'minimalist', though many of them preferred the term 'systems music'. Some were influenced by studying African or Asian music, others by the apparent *naïveté* of Erik Satie (1866–1925). This tendency or school was ridiculed and attacked by composers and polemicists committed to modernism, but significant numbers of them came to accept elements of it.

Not the least of minimalism's attractions, apart from the fact that it eventually attracted audiences far more numerous than were drawn to most concerts of modern music, was its obvious affinity with popular music. Some of its composers and performers worked in both fields and saw no unbridgeable gulf between them. Americans in particular found it impossible to deny and liberating to accept that many of their greatest composers had worked largely or exclusively in popular idioms. Younger composers in Europe, no longer committed (or never committed) to doctrinaire modernism, found close affinities with various forms of popular (including folk) music and with styles of 'serious' music less complex and more direct than those that had been regarded as the only possible way forward from Schoenberg and his school.

What many of these composers had in common, aside from a wish to address a general rather than a narrow or specialist audience, was a desire for freshness, directness and simplicity of utterance.

The greatest music often demands most of the listener's attention. Popular music, because it serves a different function, often demands less. At a rock concert substantial parts of the audience's attention are devoted to the appearance and apparent personality of the musicians and what that implies, to the staging of the event and the social, political or fashion statement it is making, perhaps to dancing. Inevitably a good deal of such music cannot withstand the sort of concentrated listening that a classical composer expects, and much of it is soon forgotten. But many composers in the latter decades of the twentieth century have recognized that it nevertheless has important qualities that much of the century's 'serious' music has lacked, and that Gershwin, Cole Porter, Duke Ellington, Bob Dylan or the Beatles should no more be omitted from any history of music than Poulenc (who adored Edith Piaf), Ives (who was far more concerned with ragtime, marches, old hymns – 'the things our fathers loved' – than with 'nice music') or Tippett (for whom the blues was central and timeless).

*

Two cultures . . .

THERE WAS RADIO EVERYWHERE . . . A lot of Gershwin, a lot of Jerome Kern, a lot of Cole Porter . . . The most exciting music I heard was . . . gospel music. And the English equivalent . . . Blood Sweat & Tears to James Brown to the Motown music . . . Apparitions, mountain dulcimer . . . Bebop! There could have been Charlie Parker, Miles Davis, John Coltrane, Thelonius Monk . . . Especially in America really almost impossible to grow up exclusively on art music . . . The Beach Boys' 'I Get Around' . . . Haydn to Brahms but very often making a kind of personal view of popular music of the day . . . Pop music was predictable, implausible and I didn't like it – I was a freak! (Laurie Anderson, Michael Daugherty, Judith Weir, Michael Finnissy, Julia Wolfe, David Bedford, Michael Torke and George Benjamin, on their earliest memories of popular music)

MY FIRST EXPERIENCE of listening to music, from the age of three onwards, was popular music and for a few years I remember being very intolerant of classical music. I didn't want to listen to it. It was the age of the Beatles; it was the golden age of pop music. And then I went to a film: *Fantasia*, I'm afraid – it's kitsch but it's the truth – and was overawed by what I heard and what I saw. And literally when I got home I threw my pop 45 r.p.m. discs in the dustbin and for a very long time refused to listen to pop music at all, absolutely refused. The most violent moment of change, I think, in my whole life.

I do believe absolutely adamantly in a classical tradition as has existed in most advanced cultures across the world. This implies a learned music that hasn't automatically made it the highest priority to be popular and in which there's a development of richness in the language, a complexity in the language. It doesn't automatically mean that other types of music are inferior. It's a tradition of constant change and revolution and at certain times across its history the doors are more or less open to music outside it. (George Benjamin)

WHEN I HEAR THE TERM 'classical music', I think of something that is historical. I don't necessarily have a positive or negative reaction to the term but to me it is something historical. It's almost the equivalent of going to a museum. You go to see an artefact and it's very beautiful and it's really rich in meaning and history, and that's what classical music is. Even though somehow in our culture we have put it on a pedestal and made it something very very high art, I think it is great art of a different time and I think it's hard to use the word 'classical' for something written today. (Julia Wolfe)

I'M A CLASSICAL COMPOSER. Broadcast Music Incorporated, a performance rights organization, weights its classical pay-outs with multiples that don't apply to popular music and we're very happy about that! My music is played by musicians who can read music, who are trained in a certain way and, yeah, it absolutely comes out of that tradition. Even philosophically and ambition-wise I feel that I live in that tradition and want to make sure that that tradition doesn't die and that I continue it. If I'm somehow enthused by the energy of popular music it's because it's around us and because I like to listen to it. It's not inconsequential but it almost seems like it shouldn't even need to be talked about. (Michael Torke)

IT WAS MORE THAT I tried to play classical music than listen to a lot of it. I studied the violin. I started when I was about five and then I went to lots of summer music camps. I would listen technically: how do you do that cadenza? It was very competitive, so you were always looking behind you to see who was going to challenge you that Friday to see if they could pull the cadenza better than you could. So some of the romantic pleasure of nineteenth-century classical music was lost on me and became a series of hard-to-play notes. (Laurie Anderson)

A BROADWAY SONG can be sung by anyone of any sex in any key with any instrumental arrangement, and a Schubert song cannot. You don't take a Schubert song, orchestrate it for a lot of saxophones and ask the singer to sort of do riffs around the tune. There is a difference in kind and that difference is crucial and never the twain shall meet. (Ned Rorem)

IF YOU WERE A COMPOSER taking part in the Darmstadt school after the war, the very idea of integrating any music from outside, be it from the Western tradition in the past or non-classical music of contemporary times, would be anathema. It would not only be an aesthetic decision but a moral decision. That led to the greatest schism in Western musical tradition – between the popular and the classical – since the medieval ages. (George Benjamin)

... or more than two?

AT ONE TIME THE CANON was very selective and very limited, essentially white male European music. But now we have so many different kinds of musics and different cultures, and every culture has its significant persons. And so I think that I've just taken a much broader look at things and the way they all look at history as well.

I feel in a really good position because, OK, I can look at what's interesting in all traditions, be it the blues tradition or comic strips, or cinema literature or basketball, whatever. All these different things that are going on in society deal with all sorts of different kinds of classes. I can appreciate what is interesting and offbeat about each one. There's a norm where within each style of anything there's a certain way that's the accepted way to do it. But what always interests me is those people who deviate slightly from that norm. So in country music there are those people; in blues there are those people; in rock there are those people; in ambient music or whatever . . . What impressed me in working with Ligeti was that he liked all kinds of music. Believe it or not, I remember that when the Michael Jackson *Thriller* album came out he found it very fascinating. He was checking out the *Thriller* album! (Michael Daugherty)

PAUL OVERTON TAUGHT Jim Hall harmony. So Hall was, like, one foot in the jazz world and one foot as a composer. First of all Hall introduced me to a lot of things which were just very basically important to me. He also said a number of things to me, one of which was that music from Haydn to a little before Wagner was a common practice and that jazz up to bebop was a common practice, and that we (this was back in the 1950s) had lost this. Caucasians in the Western world post-Wagner had lost an agreement – not an agreement that you get together and shake hands about, but which you just grow up in, and therefore we were in a sense working at a disadvantage because we had to figure out our language. Instead of saying, you know, I speak English so let's get down to writing, we had to figure out our musical language. Am I going to be atonal? Am I going to be twelve-tone? And I think that was a very useful locating device which was very, very helpful. (Steve Reich)

New sounds, new technologies . . .

PART OF WHAT HAS MADE it possible for something like the electric guitar to become a natural being in this world of instruments is that the musical language is evolving and changing, so that the language can now incorporate the sound of electric guitar. The way of playing, the tunes, the fuzzbox, whatever you wind up using, the language is more tied to the original language of the electric guitar: it's allowed to speak in the way that it was born. It's maybe a little less of a speciality item and more of just a natural part of something that eventually found its way into the repertoire in the same way as you might think, 'I really need a cimbalom in my piece.' (Julia Wolfe)

. . . and new performers

YOUNGER PERFORMERS AND CONDUCTORS – people now in their thirties – who grew up on popular music, who've grown up on rock 'n' roll and jazz and film, they really connect to what I'm doing. They're incredible players. They can play their instruments extremely well. At the same time they've also really grown up on pop culture. They really want to put those worlds together. (Michael Daugherty)

WE FELT: WHY SHOULD WE present music in a way that seems so removed from normal life? Most of our fans who weren't musicians never went to normal concert music. Maybe once in a while by accident they wound up at a concert, but most of them, if they were going to talk about art music, they would talk about the Talking Heads. And we felt that, well, there's some other music that's very interesting, other than Talking Heads, and how could those people who go to hear new dance and new film and stuff like that, how can they transfer over and get interested in the kind of music we're doing? So we thought if we changed the atmosphere, and it just seems like 'so show up, however you're dressed, and come see these people who look like you on stage – they're not some kind of spectacular being, they're just up there doing their art', it'll communicate better. (Julia Wolfe)

Minimalism: the background

THIS MUSIC BASICALLY AROSE in the late 1950s and the early 1960s in America. What's going on in America in the late 1950s and early 1960s? Jazz is going on. John Coltrane is going on, with a change of style. Ravi Shankar is giving concerts here. Recordings of African music are coming in. Balinese groups have been here, and Balinese recordings are beginning to come out. There's the Nonesuch Explorer series. So this is not abstract, recherché, trying to be somebody that you're not, some Western colonial trip in musical form. It's reflective (as all good music is reflective) of exactly what time and what place it came out of. (Steve Reich)

How can pop influence classical?

I THINK IT COLOURS harmonic attitudes. There's a certain kind of slidy chromaticism and a certain feeling of unresolved-seventh-type chords, which you get in that sort of music, which I know inform the music I write. They're usually referred to, inaccurately, as jazz chords, those kind of unresolved dissonances that jazz took over from Debussy and Ravel and so on.

I think when I came to consider writing music that was based on those idioms, it was partly because I'd had more recent experience of playing for jazz-dance classes. It seemed that it was a kind of schizophrenia, on the one hand to be regarded as a post-Boulez modernist and on the other hand to be earning a living from improvising jazz. And finally I got around to recollecting childhood in a series of arrangements of Gershwin.

It seemed quite natural to expand Gershwin's chromaticism just a little and to bend the kind of rubato techniques that you use in jazz improvisation and actually to notate more elaborate kinds of rhythm configuration. And I've done about twenty-four or so – more or less reminiscences, memories of a particular kind of music. But the other kind of thing, which I think is very important about this, is the sort of cultural code, the gender stereotypes of popular music versus other kinds of aestheticism. People are looking for an anti-aesthetic stance because aestheticism is still associated, I think, with weakness and effeminacy. Popular music (particularly jazz and rock, of course) has a very butch, macho, masculine kind of image to give music. I think people would rather be thought of as that, particularly if they are men possibly, than they would be thought of as weak, effeminate and sissy creatures, which is what classical music still is in schools. If you teach in schools kids still think that classical music is sissy. (Michael Finnissy)

I THINK THAT BY DEFINITION the language one speaks affects one's music. I strongly do feel that in non-vocal music the language a person is brought up with very definitely is imposed on the music he writes. Beethoven couldn't be anything but German, with all the *achs* and *eins* and *bo-bo-bo-BOM*! Debussy is French . . . *La mer*, which is a non-vocal piece, is French, if only because it has no rhythmic ictus, which the French language doesn't either. As an American I was raised in Chicago. What did we call it then? Not 'pop music'. It was called 'jazz'; all music not classical was jazz, even though it wasn't jazz. The singing of Billie Holiday was far more important to me than the singing of classical singers, because I never heard any. I don't think that I was consciously particularly influenced by it, but by virtue of being an American I think that I was, because my songs are too close for comfort to that world, yet they need a precise singer. I don't like all that vibrato. I don't like to be interpreted. Sing what's on the page, please! (Ned Rorem)

I ALWAYS THOUGHT that the blues was something that belongs to our century. In other words, if you want to put the popular or the vernacular into music now, you can't very easily do it as Mahler did out of the *Ländler* of Vienna; you have somehow to have taken something else; and I thought that the blues had that extraordinary quality of simplicity with complexity. (Michael Tippett, 1985)

THE VOCAL MUSIC that I and lots of my colleagues who would be thought of as serious contemporary music composers are writing today really does attempt to capture the immediacy of what is in pop-music lyrics, folksong and so on. I think it's very often the context in which our music, our serious classical vocal music, is performed that may seem as if it's much more in a frame, much more abstract and formal, but as a composer I have no wish actually to create those circumstances. I greatly envy composers of pop lyrics and musicals, those very good ones who are able just to encapsulate an emotion or thought in everyday words. (Judith Weir)

WHEN THE BEATLES first reared their ugly heads in 1966, I was one of the people who wrote long, learned essays about it all. I'm not so sure

I'd do that now. Cultivated thinking people were allowed to listen to pop music and had to be tied hand and foot to listen to Boulez. Everybody else, all the other smart people, were writing about the Beatles' words, how hip and up-to-date the words were, but words are a dime a dozen. I was talking about the shape of the tune and shape of the harmonies – in other words, the musical values. I think all music, or all song, good and bad, is judged by the tune. (Ned Rorem)

I THINK AS A WRITER I'm probably anxious to reflect at least partially my own time, so I have to think about all other musical reflections of that time. I might not like them but I have to pay attention to what they're doing, and I really don't in serious rock or in serious jazz see that much difference between what people are doing and what I'm doing. I think this polycultural aspect of our society has met all of those things head on in those media too. A crisis, if you like, between modernist formalism and a more relaxed, but then of course less defined, system is something I think jazz composers are interested in too and trying to cope with – where we're going, what we're doing. (Michael Finnissy)

Why not entertain the audience?

ENTERTAINMENT IN AMERICA is actually a very sophisticated art form. I remember in the 1960s watching television shows where a lot of it was improvisation. The structure was there: two people walk on a stage, there is a microphone, you have five minutes. It sounds like a John Cage scenario, right? OK, that is the structure, and to pull it off is a very sophisticated thing.

Some people view the audience as this necessary evil that they have to deal with in some way. The way I use an audience might be a different experience. I used to play in night-clubs. I'm sitting there at the piano doing piano bar. I'm like talking to the audience, and I'm aware of the audience. To me the audience was not an adversary, it was actually someone to play off of. So as I'm writing music I'm thinking of playing off the audience, playing off the experiences, the expectations. I view writing music and the experience of the concert hall actually as an opportunity for communication. If you're a stand-up comedian, if you're a lounge pianist, you have to engage the audience and you have to figure out a way to wake them up. (Michael Daugherty)

IF YOU'RE WRITING a piece of music, whoever it's for, you've still got to go out there and do it, and the minute you're on stage you've got to make yourself feel welcome. Nobody owes us a living: we just go out there and make ourselves as attractive and sexy as we possibly can. If you're teaching composition to people, often the thing is that they get involved in a kind of quasi-academic way of writing, which is very interesting on paper, but if you're performing it, it's as dull as ditchwater. So I say to them, find a gesture that you can go out there and make to the audience. If it's two fingers, OK, so be it, but something so that they know you're there. Otherwise it's 'Is anybody there?' So that is entertainment, that's showbiz. (Michael Finnissy)

THIS IDEA OF MAKING something arresting for the listener and being direct in its expression is a goal of mine. We can always look at popular music as ways in which unabashedly these practitioners found solutions to that. (Michael Torke)

JUST THE FEELING of actually being clapped and cheered instead of slight boos or polite applause (which my pieces might get) made me realize that actually there's more importance to being accessible to an audience – not dumbing-down but being more accessible – than I'd previously thought.

I found that listening to more and more rock music – and of course by that time it became the Pink Floyd and the more progressive bands – didn't affect the way I was writing music at all, because after all I love Delius, I love Elgar, I love Mozart, I love Beethoven. It doesn't come out, I hope, too much in the music – you can write your own music but still love other composers.

I did some arrangements for a show by Bettina Jonic which was called *From Marie Antoinette to the Beatles* and was a selection of revolutionary songs which I'd been asked to arrange for this little tiny group. The manager of a band called Soft Machine was actually the stage manager of this show. At that time Kevin Ayres, one of the Soft Machine members, had decided to go solo, so I was dragooned in for that, and did all the arrangements on Kevin Ayres's first album. Since I knew the tunes and had played keyboards he asked me to join the band. And at that point, of course, because Kevin wasn't the most brilliant guitarist in the world, most of his songs were in E. I discovered that I liked the chord of E major – up till then there were very few diatonic triads in my music (it was mostly fairly dissonant still). Actually playing the music – and of course we supported the Pink Floyd and we supported the Rolling Stones, and I heard all these bands – I realized there was much more value in it than I had previously thought, and I'm sure that some of this rubbed off on my composing style. (David Bedford)

I THOUGHT: WHAT IF YOU really did take some of the structures of pop music – for instance the 1980s concentration on beats two and four – as kind of signposts of organization. You could argue that – oh how boring – we're all so primitive and that's why we like this because it's so simple. On the other hand it's deeply intellectual, that music could be based on that. What does that mean? And then, you know, you draw the analogies that our heart beats regularly and it seems to be the source of life and vigour for us. Then why isn't that true with music? Why are irregular rhythms the only meaningful thing for us composers? And I remember thinking early on: that's interesting, that you can quantify rhythm in the way that serialists quantify pitch. Pitch, I think, is a really complex thing, but rhythm is more primitive. And one of the earliest pieces I wrote that had 'pop influence' was a piece called *Vanada*, where I divided the bar up into sixteen semi-quavers and used every note of the chromatic scale – four were used twice – and developed ways of using a groove rhythm which included two and four plus all these syncopations that were used actually in a very serial way, since I was trying to find a bridge between some of this rigour that I had learned in school and some of the pop influences.

I've written pieces like *Dead Elvis* and *Le Tombeau de Liberace*, integrating concert music, using classical music instruments – strings and trombones and trumpets and percussion and so forth – but the emotional drive of the pieces really comes from my experiences of growing up in America, and I'm very clear about who I am and where I'm coming from.

If I say I took the bass line of Madonna's 'Physical Attraction', then everyone discusses Madonna, or how my music isn't Madonna (which I sure hope it isn't). It's like, 'Oh, he listens to Madonna!' What does that mean? Well, it doesn't mean anything to me.

I'm interested in objects and icons, so that sometimes I do references just as Charles Ives might use 'Dixie' or 'Way Down upon the Swanee River'. In *Dead Elvis* I used 'O sole mio' because actually it's 'Now or Never' by Elvis. And the way that piece came about is that Elvis heard 'O sole mio' when he was stationed in Germany and he said, 'I really like that song – could somebody write some words for that song?' So someone did and that's how the piece came about. But the references are there, I think, partly to place the piece historically. (Michael Torke)

The twain meet, but can they fuse?

RELATIVITY RAG, which is my one obviously jazz- or popular-influenced piece, was an experiment. I had been thinking about computers and the way that they can perform extraordinary graphic transformations by dissecting the tiniest details of an object. So I thought: why not do something like that with musical material in which it would be extremely clear what was going on? So I took a little ragtime, a very very simple one indeed, which I invented for the purpose. Initially, it's dissected and fragmented. Then the harmony begins to get more dissonant, the rhythm ever more unstable, and within two minutes it suddenly bursts out into a completely different world. The reverse process happens at the end: out of a mist of bell-like sounds, gradually reminiscences of the ragtime come back and suddenly you're back into it. (George Benjamin)

I DID AN ALBUM called *Star's End*, which was for orchestra and guitars. It was sort of pop group and orchestra, which sounds as if it could be absolutely horrible. Usually it was done the other way round in the sense that a pop group would decide to use an orchestra and would bung a load of string riffs on to their blues or whatever. I came at it from my end, which is the classical musician's end, and so actually this piece, *Star's End*, is fairly dissonant a lot of the time. (David Bedford)

I BELIEVE IF YOU JUST assemble things left, right and centre and put them together into a hotchpotch, you patronize everything you touch. In any work of art there has to be some deep integrity in the language somewhere. There's a great danger that you lose that when you, in the most extreme post-modern way, just put things together and hope it comes out all right. (George Benjamin)

I LOVED JAZZ and later I loved non-Western music – Balinese and African. But I thought, if you just try to take that material and put it in what you're writing down, you're going to kill that which you love: you're going to kill that jazz, you're going to kill the Balinese music, you're going to kill the African music, and you're going to fail as a composer. You're not going to do either one. What to do? Just forget about it, just absolutely forget about it. It's in so deep you don't have to think about it, it's inside of you, and it'll come out – just do what you're gonna do. (Steve Reich)

The allure of simplicity

I SUPPOSE AS A COMPOSER what I admire about folk music is above all its ability to be often very expressive with very economical means, and the way that somebody will get a huge set of variations or a lovely long melody out of something which is maybe just a tin string stuck on a piece of wood. That seems to me very inspiring and educational for a composer. As classical composers we learn a huge amount of things about variation technique; we study composers like Beethoven who were so great at that sort of thing. But I have to say folk music is where there is that thing of getting a great deal of material out of a small melodic beginning. I think that's the greatest place you can study that kind of technique. (Judith Weir)

THE MOST SIMPLE THING can be so amazing. It has nothing at all to do with how smart you are, how complicated the piece is, how sophisticated it is, whatever. I mean, it's such a magical thing, it's about so much more than that. I guess that's how I would respond to the idea that a certain kind of music is on a higher level. (Julia Wolfe)

DOES INTELLECTUAL SATISFACTION come just from complexity or come from inscrutability? You know, it's really refreshing to begin to think that it has nothing to do with inscrutability at all. And in a way that's what the minimalists were teaching us – among other things. (Michael Torke)

WHEN I LISTEN to a lot of pop music I can't believe how people can listen continuously to some of it – the lack of inventiveness, the lack of variety, the lack of different types of harmony involved. Country & Western, for instance – I just can't imagine why they don't use more chords. I find that very strange. (George Benjamin)

I THINK IF WE WERE LOOKING for a kind of music today that truly tells stories and relays emotion and can really tug at your personal heart strings, it wouldn't be opera or art songs: it would definitely be Country & Western. That seems a really poignant art form at the moment. OK, it's usually presented in a super-kitsch way, but if you actually listen to those lyrics and often the vocal style of the performers, I think that's really a wonderful sincere tragic art form of today. If classical composers could tell stories like that so neatly and yet wrap up so many poignant and complex emotions, I think they would be very pleased. (Judith Weir)

I DON'T THINK that the classical section has a patent on big, complicated ideas. I think a lot of contemporary classical music is incredibly academic and boring – I mean *seriously* boring, especially if it's clever and boring – that for me is like . . . that's the end. I'd really rather listen to anything in the pop section. (Laurie Anderson)

POPULAR MUSIC REFLECTS something in our culture, and always has. We can punish it by saying what it's doing is not very sophisticated, and childish. But we need it. If we are going to be whole we also have to smile and let loose and do all of that kind of stuff, because that's what human beings do. And you can't do that to the *B minor Mass* or *The Art of Fugue*; you really can't let go. And maybe we should say art is that and use that as a definition of what art is. But you can't really ask the question 'Could I do without pop music?' without asking the question 'Could I do without art music?' in the same breath. I couldn't do without either. (Michael Finnissy)

POP MUSIC MAY EAT the classical world in a sense and then fragment so that you have experimentalism on the one side and the Top Forty on the other, which is already the case and may become more so. But it's possible to imagine a world in which the whole classical music world in the broadest sense of that word is a very marginal enterprise – as small or smaller than what we call the early music world today. (Steve Reich)

IN FACT ALL CATEGORIES for me are starting to blur, and it's very hard to define . . . Especially today and certainly in America and certainly in New York, it's hard to say, 'This is art music. This is pop music. This is rock music.' And I certainly can't even think of one music as being the proper music or the main voice of our culture. (Julia Wolfe)

WHY DOES EVERYTHING have to be for everybody? Why can't there be people who devote their lives to listening, to performing, to writing a certain type of music which follows a highly ambitious aesthetic path? I feel there's so much pressure in society today that everybody has to like everything, everything must be popular – you know: if it's not for everybody, it's for nobody. (George Benjamin)

7 Music and Menace

I didn't foresee Hiroshima, but I certainly foresaw Dresden.
MICHAEL TIPPETT, 1973

S OVIET RUSSIA AND ITS 'satellite' states (Hungary, Czechoslovakia, Bulgaria, Romania, Albania, East Germany and Poland); Nazi Germany and its ally Austria (plus, for a time, those countries occupied by Germany); Fascist Italy; Franco's Spain; Salazar's Portugal: during this century many European countries have known totalitarian regimes, and in all of them the influence of totalitarianism on music has been perhaps greater than any school, 'ism' or technological advance. But although Hitler and Stalin, Franco and Mussolini are all termed dictators and their regimes are accurately described as totalitarian, their methods of controlling or suppressing music were quite different, as were the reactions of musicians to them.

After Franco's rise to power, for example, a very high proportion of Spanish musicians left the country, and not only those whose positions were dangerous because of their support for the Republican regime that Franco had suppressed (Manuel de Falla, for example, a devout catholic and temperamentally conservative, left after the shock of the murder of his friend Federico García Lorca, and never returned). In Italy, on the other hand, virtually all prominent musicians stayed, including those of the avant-garde, and many supported Mussolini enthusiastically. The only famous exception was the conductor Arturo Toscanini, who left Italy after a mob tried to break his arms after he had refused to begin his concerts with the Fascist anthem 'Giovinezza'. In Germany the styles of music that the Nazis virulently opposed were clearly apparent from the outset, while the regime in Russia, initially sympathetic to modernism, only later began to condemn it.

Nazi Germany's policy was to promote an art that was distinctly German and Aryan and to suppress that which was 'degenerate' (*entartet*). All Jewish musicans came into this category, as did jazz (the music of an 'inferior' race) and most forms of modernism. As in Spain the exodus of musicians in the years immediately before and after Hitler's rise to power was vast. Most German and Austrian Jews who remained lost their lives in concentration camps. One of these, Terezin or Theresienstadt, run by the Nazis as a 'show camp' intended to demonstrate to international opinion that their intentions towards Jews were benign, was the centre of a remarkable flourishing of musical and other artistic activity. All its inmates were eventually sent to death camps, mostly to Auschwitz.

Of those non-Jewish musicians who stayed in Germany, the most prominent composer was Richard Strauss who, though not a Nazi supporter (he never joined the Party and besides had a much loved part-Jewish daughter-in-law) accepted the position of Chairman of the *Reichsmusikkammer*, the official, regulatory body that organized the musical profession. The conductor Wilhelm Furtwängler also stayed, attempting at least in the earlier stages of the regime to ameliorate its rigidity (he publicly argued against the dismissal of talented Jewish musicians and protested against the ban on the music of Hindemith). Others continued to work as best they could. Many of these, including Strauss and Furtwängler, could not continue their careers after the war until they had been investigated by a 'de-Nazification tribunal'. A few composers went into what has been termed 'internal exile', writing music that they knew could not be performed until the Nazis were defeated or fell from power.

Far fewer musicians left Russia at the time of the 1917 Revolution, though of the most famous Russian composers of the period Stravinsky, Rakhmaninov and Prokofiev were all living abroad at the time; only Prokofiev, after some delay, returned. Dmitry Shostakovich was the first major Russian composer of the Soviet period (he was eleven years old at the time of the Revolution) and his remarkable, precocious talent was at first greeted with pride and enthusiasm. The early Soviet phase of welcoming modernism was not yet quite over, and some of Shostakovich's youthful works reflect this. Soon, however, modernist trends, especially if they seemed to have an affinity with the Western avant-garde, were condemned as 'formalist' and contrary to the principles of 'socialist realism'. Shostakovich's highly successful opera *The Lady Macbeth of the Mtsensk District* was denounced by the official newspaper *Pravda* as 'chaos in place of music', and the opera was immediately suppressed, not to be heard again for many years.

Shostakovich himself, evidently terrified, withdrew his intensely dissonant Fourth Symphony and hastened to write a Fifth, which was described as 'a Soviet artist's creative reply to justified criticism'. Many of his works, from that point on, contain oblique or overt references to his own and other music and to his musical cypher (D, E♭, C, B – DSCH in German musical notation) and ironic or perplexing ambiguities that can often be heard as cryptic or even dissident hidden messages. For much of his life the Union of Soviet Composers (of which Tikhon Khrennikov was First Secretary from 1948 until the break up of the Soviet Union) was all powerful: no composer could work unless he was a member and submitted to its authority.

In Italy Luigi Dallapiccola's *Canti di prigionia* ('Prison Songs') might seem like coded messages to dissident Italians and were certainly so intended, but they were nevertheless performed in Italy, during the early years of the Second World War. Mussolini at least affected to be in sympathy with avant-garde musicians, and Italy was very late and somewhat half-hearted in accepting and enforcing the cultural hard line of her ally Germany.

In Spain, Franco's dictatorship tended to ignore culture rather than either promote or ban it. The Spanish poet Rafael Alberti, who left Spain after the Civil War and did not return until the end of Franco's dictatorship, spent much of his exile writing political verse. On his return, asked by the present author what he would do now, he ruefully replied that he supposed he would have to learn again how to write lyrical poetry. His dilemma was experienced by many artists after the fall of other totalitarian regimes, perhaps most strongly by those who had grown up under them. These composers felt the need to reject all the music that had been associated with the disgraced regime. In Italy this included virtually every living and recent Italian composer save Dallapiccola; in Germany it included a good deal of music from before the Nazi period, that of Wagner above all. The new generation of German and Italian composers needed to write a music that owed nothing to the defiled past. Many of them began to discover the 'degenerate' music that the dictators had suppressed. Thus the influence of the totalitarian regimes extended after their decline, and undoubtedly contributed to the development, in particular, of post-Schoenberg, post-Webern modernism in Germany and Italy after the Second World War and in Russia during the years even before the collapse of the Soviet state.

Portugal, under the long dictatorship of Adolfo Salazar, had a history and an attitude to the arts very similar to those of Franco's Spain. The countries of the Soviet bloc largely followed the Russian line, with local variants, though Poland for a while became a cautious 'shop window' for Western-style musical modernism, some Polish composers (notably Witold Lutosławski) writing music deeply affected by what they were able to discover of musical developments in the West, and many composers from other Eastern European countries attended the famous festivals of contemporary music in Warsaw, though often finding very limited opportunities to use what they had learned when they returned to Budapest, Prague or Dresden. The two most celebrated composers of post-war Greece were both forced into exile. Iannis Xenakis, as an avowed opponent of the Colonels' regime (he was gravely wounded and lost an eye during a street demonstration in Athens), fled the country, was sentenced to death in his absence, and has never returned permanently. Mikis Theodorakis, much of whose music is overtly political, using elements from Greek folk and popular music, was imprisoned by the regime for three years, released only after prolonged international protests, and immediately expelled from Greece; the ban on his music there continued for several years.

Censorship and prejudice are not confined to dictatorships. Even such intensely American composers as Aaron Copland and Roy Harris were accused of Communist sympathies and 'un-American activities' and performances of their music, albeit in both cases relatively briefly, diminished as a consequence. At the outset of the Second World War there were public (though unsuccessful) demands that Benjamin Britten's music should be less often performed, since he was at the time living in America and not contributing to the war effort. The BBC, briefly, instituted a ban on performing music by composers who had registered as conscientious objectors to military service. Britten did so on his return from the US, and was completely exempted on the grounds that the many concerts he was giving with his partner, the tenor Peter Pears, were of benefit to national morale. Michael Tippett was granted only conditional exemption, the condition being that he work in an essential but non-combatant industry (for example, agriculture or mining); he refused, and was sent to prison for three months.

In Nazi Germany the risk of writing protest music was so terrifying and the likelihood of it being performed so slight that there were very few attempts to do so, save by composers opting for 'internal exile' and writing music that they kept hidden. In Spain Cristóbal Halffter and Luis de Pablo, among others, wrote music that defied or mocked the Franco regime. In later years, when asked whether it was less exciting to write without the stimulus of tyranny, de Pablo replied, 'I don't find it exciting to be arrested! I prefer to be bored and get on with writing music.' Shostakovich inspired a whole generation of Russian composers to write music that ignored official decrees. His Thirteenth Symphony, 'Babiy Yar', to poems by Yevgeny Yevtushenko, was his most overtly critical of the Soviet regime; it had a single performance but was not heard again for several years.

*

Spain: too philistine and too poor

SPAIN HAD BEEN a great empire with an immensely rich cultural heritage and of course early Spanish music is vast and endlessly rich. But after the loss, the final loss, of empire, which took about a hundred years over the course of the nineteenth century, Spain was essentially a country going through a major trauma: it was still only gradually coming to terms with the loss of empire. It had an army that was commensurate with a big empire, with a budget that was commensurate with being a very small, backward, third- or fourth-rank country. And that had an impact on the kinds of cultural and specifically musical life. Very few governments could afford to do much in the way of sponsoring the arts. Under the Republic it was slightly better; the President of the Republic, Manuel Azaña, was something of an opera buff. It was rather interesting: on one of the first attempts at a military coup to bring about the Republic, Azaña was actually caught at a performance of *Boris Godunov*. Now the idea of a performance of *Boris Godunov* under Franco is absolutely a surrealistic notion. So part of the problem is that it's a backward country with very little in the way of spare cash floating around in the budget, but it's also a country that after the Civil War is run by a group of generals who essentially believe that all of Spain's ills come from the corruption of decadent Western art – and particularly the art that they associate with France. So the idea of putting money into fostering music is just so alien that it simply doesn't happen. So the two things combine: there's a sort of dogged philistinism combined with real poverty. The consequence is the aridity of musical life under Franco. (Peter Preston)

THE TWENTY YEARS up to the Civil War are in many ways – artistically in general and particularly in the case of music – the most fruitful. Spain's not particularly notable for its music. There's a lot of Spanish influence in other composers – European composers – but there isn't a Spanish school really until Albéniz, Granados and Falla. But that is beginning to grow and beginning to gain confidence in the 1930s: you can now talk about a Spanish music. But it is associated – not necessarily directly – with the atmosphere of the Republic. There's a kind of openness and a cultural excitement in the 1930s. This is not necessarily because the artists were pro-Republican or were in any way overtly political but because they were part of this general atmosphere. That's cut off by an atmosphere of censorship and terror, which Franco quite consciously and quite deliberately practised. It's worth remembering that the number of people who died in the post-war repression is greater than the number of those who died during the course of the Civil War. (Mike Gonzalez)

IF YOU WERE ANY GOOD as a performer you had to get out, because it was impossible to make a living commensurate with your talent if you stayed in Spain. The consequence therefore is that there was nobody to be besmirched by association with the regime because that whole cultural underpinning that we're familiar with both in the Fascist and the Communist dictators simply didn't exist under Franco, because, if you like, his regime was too Philistine and too poor. (Peter Preston)

The exodus from Spain

A HUNDRED AND FIFTY THOUSAND in the year 1939 – a hundred and fifty thousand! You have all our teachers, intellectuals, professors – 80 per cent was out of Spain. In Spain in this forty years was another generation: this is my generation. I was nine years old and all my education was in Spain. I and all my generation grew up without these people, and when these people came again to Spain it was too late. (Cristóbal Halffter)

Italy: *an absence of resistance*

IN ITALY THERE WAS NEVER any massive anti-Fascist movement among musicians. Obviously Toscanini is the shining example of somebody who, although not politically sophisticated, had his ideas and ideals and simply stood by them from the start. There were a few others. There was the young musicologist Massimo Mila, who was gaoled for five years because of his support for Giustizia e Libertà, which was one of the great clandestine anti-Fascist movements. There were a few scattered examples. But the people who actually left in 1938 and didn't come back were Jewish musicians who needed to get out, who realized what was in store for them because they had seen five years of what was going on in Germany. I can't think of any non-Jewish musician, except Toscanini, who did not go back to Italy after 1938. (Harvey Sachs)

WHAT MUSSOLINI HAD TO SAY gave the impression of a change of attitude towards music. Under previous governments, musicians always felt themselves put in the shade, or marginalized. The conservatoires were languishing, for example, and although La Scala had been legally reorganized as an independent subsidized body, the other theatres were run by private impresarios according to a system that went back to the nineteenth or eighteenth centuries. So the arrival of Mussolini with all the new initiatives he adopted seemed to signal a new sensibility. And musicians were captivated by it: there was no opposition; no composers became adversaries of the regime – or, rather, there was only one, and Luigi Dallapiccola distanced himself from the regime only in 1938, when the racial laws were promulgated, because he had a Jewish wife. But until then even Dallapiccola was conquered by the new regime's initiatives, and probably by Mussolini himself. Later Dallapiccola was to write the first Italian works of politically engaged music, works like the *Canti di prigionia*, works written against dictatorship. (Fiamma Nicolodi)

IF, FOR INSTANCE, you had hopes of a successful career as a performer, the thing that you always did, as did all the composers, was to seek a personal audience with Mussolini, and you would see Mussolini at his best when he invited a string quartet round to his house: apparently he would become rapt with attention. There are some wonderful newspaper accounts – listening to Beethoven's Op. 95 Quartet being played to him and sitting there rather in the fashion of D'Annunzio, sniffing at a geranium while listening intently to this overwhelming musical experience. Mussolini, I think, had realized that the most effective way in which you could project the image of the inexorable tough man of steel was for him also to have this interesting sensitive side. The fact that this man could by day govern the fate of Italy and then could relax in the evening playing his violin, listening to a string quartet, or indeed sitting back and suggesting to young composers appropriate themes for their next opera, and so on and so forth – this all made for a certain overall image, which may seem rather camp to us but was in fact very persuasive. (David Osmond-Smith)

IN NAZI GERMANY, it was very clear from the outset, but this was not the case in Italy. After 1938, after the racial laws were enacted in order to bring Italian policy into line with German policy, it is true that music by Jewish composers was no longer performed. On the other hand, in 1942 at the height of the war, Berg's *Wozzeck* was given at the Rome Opera, which would have been unthinkable in Germany at the time. So it was haphazard, hit and miss. (Harvey Sachs)

Germany: an efficient tyranny

THE NAME OF THE GAME was lack of security, to create intimidation in the system. The beginning of the Nazi period in 1933 was clearer in a way because for a number of conductors and *Intendanten* and composers who were Jewish, or were seen to be irredeemably modern, their situation was clear: they had to get out. (John Deathridge)

THERE WASN'T SUCH A THING as a kind of list at this stage. That came later: a list of unacceptable works. In 1933 most people complied or understood what this banning of Jewish music meant, and so Mendelssohn and Mahler, Meyerbeer, Offenbach, all were removed immediately from concert programmes. What's interesting, of course, is that when it comes to the publication of music and the recording of music, in fact it took them many more years to effect a total censorship of composers like Mendelssohn and Offenbach. So, for example, you could buy a disc of Mendelssohn's Violin Concerto in 1936. It was still in the catalogue in Germany. But you wouldn't be able to hear it and probably you wouldn't be allowed to perform it as a student in a music conservatoire. Sadly, most musicians submitted. There were a few protests – and some very brave protests – for example, from a conductor like Furtwängler, who wrote an open letter in a Berlin newspaper arguing that, 'If we are going to reorganize German music, we need to keep people like Klemperer and Walter and the theatre director Max Reinhardt.' Although this letter was published and widely circulated, it was rebuffed quite cleverly by Goebbels the following day. He said, 'Well, I'm also interested in regenerating German music but we basically have to start again with people who are committed to our ideal.' (Erik Levi)

THE BIGGEST STORY happened in 1936, after Toscanini had resigned from the New York Philharmonic, and they had asked Furtwängler to take over the leadership of the orchestra. An imbroglio started in New York: many people protested about this and they said, 'He's a Nazi, he should not be invited', and so on. Furtwängler sent a wire from Egypt saying of course he is not a politician, that he is a musician, but that under the circumstances he would resign from the leadership of the New York Philharmonic. This was something that haunted him to his last days, of course, in the United States. (Friedelind Wagner, 1964)

THERE WAS A PROBLEM, of course, with collaboration between, say, an Aryan composer and a Jewish writer: for example, with Schumann's *Dichterliebe* (poems by Heine) or Mozart's da Ponte operas (da Ponte was a baptized Jew). The way the Nazis got round the Schumann question was to ignore the fact that the words were by Heine; there was no question of banning such a great work as *Dichterliebe*. But in the case of Mozart, a lot of opportunists got their hands on the scores and rearranged da Ponte's words, Germanized them, and so in effect da Ponte's name disappeared from the programme. Eventually one of the things they set up in 1940 was a 'Reich Organization for Music Arrangement', which was a means of rearranging music so that it was politically and racially palatable. This would mean that, for example, if an opera referred to the music or the people of Poland or Czechoslovakia they had to remove the geographical location of the work. In the case of oratorio there was an attempt to recast biblical works as Nordic legends. *Judas Maccabeus* became *Mongolensturm*, and more popular was a rearrangement as 'The Field-Marshal', which was then ironically a portrait of Hitler. So effectively Judas Maccabeus was equated with Hitler. (Erik Levi)

Nazism infects Norway

WE HAD A SERIES of composers who were writing in an international style but with a Norwegian dialect, such as Sinding and Monrad Johanssen. They were accepted as great international figures but unfortunately they saw the rise of Fascism as a way of protecting European culture against bolshevism and against capitalism and they made the fatal mistake of becoming party-political artists. I often think of what would have happened if Elgar had become a follower of Oswald Mosley. That is what happened in Norway, that the great international figures became Fascists and that meant that the entire intellectual tradition was suddenly put in a position where it was discredited. As a result the whole role that had been built up so carefully and over such a short time of the artist as a symbol of national unity was destroyed for ever. (Olav Anton Thommesen, 1990)

Russia: 'socialist realism'

KHRENNIKOV WAS ABLE to balance threats of one kind or another with the largesse of what in the nineteenth century would have been the landowner or the aristocrat offering accommodation, food and all the privileges that a composer might want for themselves or for their family. He could balance that against the dark threats. Earlier on in the Stalinist period – one thinks of the fear surrounding the famous *Pravda* attack in 1936 on Shostakovich or the 1948 Congress – then of course fear was the material dominant everywhere around them. As one composer acquaintance of mine said, 'In those days we did not breathe oxygen, we breathed terror.' He went on to say, 'If you imagine taking terror into your bloodstream, it does very strange things to your mind; you begin to reason in a completely different way.' Although later there were undoubtedly frightening periods – there were anti-Semitic purges; periods when for no reason at all somebody would be arrested and then everybody else would be alarmed – it happened around the invasion of Hungary; it happened around the invasion of Czechoslovakia – on the whole in later years, from Khrushchev onwards, the Composers' Union, partly under Khrennikov's direction, had amassed enough power to offer carrots as well as sticks, and that was very clever. (Gerard McBurney)

ANDROPOV AND BREZHNEV gave a secret order to eliminate me. So I was several times in a position when there were some people provoking around me a kind of mess and I could be easily killed. For example, I had a very fast car, very powerful Mercedes, and they very neatly cut the front left wheel to cause an accident. Then there was a different kind of provocation, you know, KGB – everybody knows what they were doing. So I was in the middle of it and it was very difficult to cope with, I tell you. So eventually it came to complete nervous breakdown after this in these years. And fortunately they all died very quickly in 1984, when I was nearly dying also! (Andrei Gavrilov, 1990)

Un-American activities . . .

Q. ARE YOU NOW or have you ever been a member of the Communist Party of any country?
Mr Chairman, I have heard my colleagues and they considered this question not as proper, but I am a guest in this country and do not want to enter in any legal arguments, so I will answer your question fully, as well I can. I was not a member or am not a member of any Communist Party.
Q. Your answer is then that you have never been a member of the Communist Party?

That is correct.
Q. You were not a member of the Communist Party of Germany?
No, I was not.
Q. From an examination of the works which Mr Brecht has written, particularly in collaboration with Mr Hanns Eisler, he seems to be a person of international importance to the Communist revolutionary movement. In 1930, did you with Hanns Eisler write a play entitled Die Massnahme. *Did you write such a play?*
Yes, yes. This play is the adaptation of an old religious Japanese play, so-called Nō play, and follows quite closely this old story which shows devotion for an ideal until death. (Bertolt Brecht, 1947)

. . . and un-British ones

I DIDN'T FORESEE Hiroshima but I certainly foresaw Dresden. I could never get over this one. I could no more have done anything which would have ended in Hiroshima . . . Believe me, you yourself, you'd better go and see, if you haven't seen, what happens when you incinerate people by radiation. So that as I see it there always has to be a certain number of people who – trying not to think themselves holier than anyone else, because this to me is even more abhorrent – have somehow to stand on some other ground. Let me get it quite clear. When this last war happened and a colleague of mine, Alan Rawsthorne, now dead, who was exactly my own age, went to the war, I'm sure he went with as clear a moral conviction as I went to prison. (Michael Tippett, 1973)

What kinds of music did the dictators want?

Germany

THEY WANTED TO CREATE sort of a neo-Germanic or neo-Neanderthal kind of music-making, of which Carl Orff is one outstanding representative. They would have loved to have more Orffs, and there were quite a number of people actually who imitated that kind of writing, or the very mild style of ex-scholars of Hindemith. Part of the Germanic style seems to be a profusion of fifths and fourths, a real kind of primitiveness. The 'Minister for Musical Composition' would point out what is recommendable to do as a composer and what is not recommendable. Any trace of relationship with Jewish composers already brought you under suspicion, so you had to prove that you were trying to find your own way now that you were liberated from all these terrible Jewish and Communist influences, and had regained purity, and would now serve the Führer for the rest of your days. For instance, they thought that jazz music was Jewish – 'black music', they called it. Jazz was absolutely taboo, and jazz composers and jazz performers were considered like outcasts of mankind, beastly music-making, animalistic. (Hans Werner Henze)

NAZI MUSICOLOGISTS TALKED about a monumental style. They held up as an example of that monumental style the Olympic Hymn by Richard Strauss, which of course is not a Nazi piece. If you read critical commentaries of the time relating to that piece they talk about it being in E♭, this heroic key; it's a nationalist work. In fact, if you listen to the opening you can hear submerged in the musical argument 'Deutschland über Alles'. (Erik Levi)

Spain

I WOULD SAY THAT probably there were three things. Zarzuela – you could always see zarzuela, precisely because Franco was rather keen on it. Then, of course, there was music-hall. Now, there had been rather racy music-hall during the years before the Civil War and particularly during the Republic. After the war it became rather twee. It was the same sort of stuff; it was the same kind of music, but the women wore corsets instead of being naked. The only other area, of course, was music that was rather folkloric – I'm thinking particularly of Rodrigo. In a sense the *Concierto de Aranjuez* became the theme tune of the Franco regime. It did an awful lot in fact in the later period of the regime to help sanitize it. (Peter Preston)

Italy

IT WAS QUITE CONSCIOUSLY FORMULATED as the sort of music that promoted virile values, that was deliberately not pretty, not beautiful, that showed, if you like, the fact that Italy was a race of steel beneath the attractive surface that northern Europe had been so eager to attribute to it. So you'll find in many works from the period of the 1920s and 1930s a tough militaristic tone, both to certain operas – such as, for instance, Mascagni's *Il piccolo Marat*, which is odd in comparison with some of his earlier works because it has this sort of deliberate use of dissonance and a certain sort of insistent militaristic tone to it, which of course is quite appropriate to the subject of the French Revolution.

I think also of people like Petrassi, who was one of the youthful wonders of Italian Fascism; his early works very often make use of an assertive muscular style, lots of brass and lots of deliberately ungracious gestures. I think, for instance, of the finale of the first Concerto for Orchestra which, if I had to pick anything as a typical example of the Fascist sound, I would turn to that. (David Osmond-Smith)

Resisting tyranny

I HAD SOME BOOKS about modern music, about all the great masters of the twentieth century, everything about Schoenberg that one could know then, about Webern, about Stravinsky, and all these things that I had read about and that fascinated me enormously, but that I couldn't hear. They symbolized freedom of thought, individuality, intellectual independence. These Nazis came and put a stop to it. There was a weekly concert the BBC broadcast. It was forbidden to listen to the BBC, of course, but there would be this famous signal, *da da da dum*, and then there would be news and then there would be a concert. And they would play *The Rite of Spring* and Schoenberg's Five Pieces and Berg's *Altenberg-Lieder* and all these things. It was wonderful! But you had to lean your ear to the radio to make sure that nobody would find you listening to a hostile radio station. They would have put you in prison. (Hans Werner Henze)

I HAVE THE LAST SONG of Mikis Theodorakis when he was hiding in Greece before he was arrested. Two days before, he wrote a song. He was hiding in a cellar and all day long he was writing speeches and he wrote music and songs for the Greek people. This is the voice of Theodorakis. I want that the Greek people know that all over the world we work for him, we work for his liberty and for democracy. (Melina Mercouri, 1967)

IF YOU HAVE YOUR PRINCIPLES, then you are doing the right thing. We did so much that after two years they closed the theatre, and then the opera house was closed for the rest of the war. We had to fight the Fascists and the Nazis, of course. For instance, one can mount productions of operas in such a way that the public who comes to the performance feels an antagonism from the stage against the usurper. Or one can build up programmes which are so clear to everybody that it is a provocation. One can do dozens of things. The Czechs did a lot. For instance, they didn't allow us to play *Má Vlast* – you know, the Smetana, 'My Country'. But if you are an ardent human being with these principles, then you always find a way how to fight the evil. (Rafael Kubelik, 1969)

ONE THING WAS very good for us. It was very difficult to explain to the people around Franco that an orchestral piece is a piece against the regime because it was abstract. And then we have more liberty, more freedom to do our music. Some people in the Franco regime think that it's good we have also in Spain avant-garde music. In 1972 in Florence there was a festival, 'Art and Freedom', and I conducted the Spanish National Orchestra, paid for by the Franco regime, and in this pro-gramme there was a piece, *Requiem por la libertad imaginada* – 'Requiem for Imaginary Freedom'. The title was very clear and the music was very clear but Franco's people didn't understand that this was a piece against him and his Spain in this festival in Florence. This is a very strange situation. In Spain, it was forbidden, but in Florence, yes. This is the situation with dictatorship in the south of Europe; it is very different from the north of Europe. (Cristóbal Halffter)

THEY WOULD ASK for our plans a year ahead, written down, and I would write down that I was going to play, for example, the Russian Overture of Debussy, or the 22nd Symphony of Mahler. As they hadn't the foggiest idea what I was talking about, this would be signed and agreed with. So that, in point of fact, when I came to those concerts, I could play whatever I wanted, because it was already permitted. (Gennadi Rozhdestvensky)

IT WAS A FACT OF LIFE that in Soviet culture the Soviet citizen acquired this sixth sense, if you like, whereby when he read any text or he listened to anything, he was automatically geared into listening for some kind of subtext and listening out for some kind of signal. Funnily enough, Shostakovich was one who actually enjoyed using signals and in some of his symphonies, like in the Fifth Symphony, he directly referred to various songs of his – Pushkin songs, for instance – but I think these were very private signals and very few people would have picked them up, simply because they wouldn't have known the music, and in any case you really have to be a fairly knowledgeable musician to be able to analyse and recognize these things. On the other hand, people certainly had their ears out on stalks for signals. (Elizabeth Wilson)

IT SEEMS TO ME that allusion in Shostakovich's music is not sophisti-cated and not intellectual. It's something rather different. It's a very flexible, subtle, mobile playing with a number of levels of possible significance, some of which demand by no means sophistication in the appreciation: they are things that any Russian music-lover would have picked up very quickly. You move from that level, the simplest, lowest possible common denominator of Russian shared assumption, right through specific things like quotations from *Boris Godunov* in the middle of the last movement of the Fifth Symphony, or whatever, to at the peak of the pinnacle quotations that only he himself could have understood. With Shostakovich you're dealing with a man who dealt in allusion as obsessively as other people deal in keys or note rows. Allusion was the stuff of his music, and layer upon layer of allusion is piled into his music. And there is no particular reason to suppose that he ever thought that hard about who was going to understand which particular layer. Allusion was the way he wrote music. Where he had no doubt was that out of this allusion he could create a structure of overwhelming emotional power. (Gerard McBurney)

THERE'S A NICE STORY about one of the Jewish songs, I think it was. Even in my day in Russia, announcers would come out and announce songs like, 'This song is going to be sung by the People's artist Zara Dolukhanova and played on the piano by the People's artist . . .', etc., etc. They would announce the title of the song with great pomposity, and if the song was about the Siberian mines or something like that they would then say, 'This of course happened in Tsarist time.' Of course Shostakovich thought this was extremely funny, and he would be able to say, 'Well, of course, I'm writing about Tsarist time, I'm just writing about how terribly our people suffered, and isn't it a good thing the Revolution came along and swept away everything and gave us paradise on earth!' I think he knew very well how to tackle these things. (Elizabeth Wilson)

I THINK THAT THE PEOPLE who went to the concerts of the Thirteenth Symphony of Shostakovich or whatever, the people who fought to get into the early concerts of Gubaidulina and Schnittke and so on, were all people who would have thought of themselves as part of that peculiar Russian class, that self-appointed class that calls itself and always called itself the intelligentsia. And when they went to hear Shostakovich's Thirteenth Symphony, they thought of themselves as going for the same spiritual and moral experience which they went to the novels of Tolstoy for, which they went to the lyrics of Pushkin for. This was their nourishment in the absence of any other kind of nourishment. (Gerard McBurney)

8 The Language of Music
1: The End of Time

*Now we must speak about the particular rhythm
that is considered part of music.*
ARISTOXENUS, 4th century BC

COMPOSERS at the end of the twentieth century are writing music that not only sounds radically different from that written a hundred years earlier; the language of music and the raw materials from which it is made have themselves changed. Around 1900 few people would have disagreed with the statement that most music involves melody, rhythm, harmony (the sounding together of two or more notes) and counterpoint (the playing of two or more melodies at the same time). All four of these elements have changed substantially during the twentieth century, and composers have added others to them. This chapter and the two that follow examine these changes.

Different musical cultures have tended to exploit one or two of these basic constituents at the expense of others. Indian classical music, for example, eschews counterpoint and all but simple harmony, but incorporates far more melodic subtlety than most Western music: there are twenty-two divisions of the octave, for example, rather than the twelve of Western classical music, and Indian melody is rich in microtonal inflexions. Western classical music has cultivated richness of harmony and counterpoint and subtlety of relationships between keys but (again compared to Indian music) has been content with relatively simple rhythm. Music of the classical and romantic periods is normally divided into very short rhythmic periods (bars), generally of two or three beats or a simple multiple of two or three, and changes of rhythm during a piece are infrequent. Bars having a prime number of beats other than three are uncommon, bars of five beats being rare, of seven rarer still, and of eleven unheard of. Melodies in classical and popular Western music generally proceed in even numbers of bars, very frequently in multiples of four. Rhythmic patterns substantially longer than this, common enough in the fifteenth century (isorhythm, where the rhythm of an entire melody is repeated although its pitches are not), fell out of use with the development of the system of key.

Stravinsky's *The Rite of Spring* made a huge and shocking impact in 1913 with its unprecedented level of violent dissonance, but its rhythmic innovations were no less shocking and quite as influential. On many pages of the score Stravinsky used bars of five, seven, even eleven beats, increasing the rhythmic asymmetry still further by juxtaposing bars of dissimilar length. His rhythmic patterns were not made up of a regular pulse contained within the bar but of asymmetric bars multiplied irregularly. Sir Michael Tippett, influenced by Stravinsky but also by jazz, used the term 'additive rhythm' for a similar phenomenon in his own work.

Stravinsky's revolution led many composers to realize how under-developed rhythm had been in Western art music. Edgard Varèse's *Ionisation*, a score for percussion instruments only, has no melody, harmony or conventional counterpoint, but presents a rich texture of simultaneous rhythms. Charles Ives was fascinated by different types of music, with different speeds and rhythms, happening at the same time. Olivier Messiaen, interested in the way that simultaneous rhythms can react upon one another, was also concerned with longer-term rhythmic divisions, and with the concept of duration. He was influenced in this by his studies of Indian music, which uses metrical structures much longer than the Western bar. Other composers have investigated the subtle and often complex metrical language of the Balinese and Indonesian gamelan, of African drumming, etc.

Arnold Schoenberg's twelve-tone serial technique led some composers, notably Messiaen, Pierre Boulez and Karlheinz Stockhausen, to investigate whether rhythm and duration could be organized as rigorously as pitch was controlled by serialism. These developments and experiments often led to complex irregular rhythms, but the ancient system of musical notation that is universally used in the West (its invention is ascribed to Guido d'Arezzo, who was born *c.* 981) is equipped to deal only with very simple divisions of the bar. For this reason there have been numerous attempts, none of them at all widely adopted, to modify that system or to replace it with some form of graphic notation. The remarkable American composer Conlon Nancarrow, most of whose works were composed directly on to the perforated paper rolls of a player-piano, used the astonishing velocity and precision of which that instrument is capable to write music that is not only unplayable by a human pianist but which would be extremely difficult if not impossible to notate. There is a clear analogy here both with the computer and with electronic music composed on tape. The composer here may use notation as a convenient tool, but both media make available sounds, including complex rhythms and durational patterns, that it would be difficult and perhaps pointless to notate, since much of this music does not involve 'live' performance, and thus no performer needs to read it.

*

Rhythm is everything

MUSIC IS EVERYWHERE – what all the bees do when they hum, the planets when they spin through the universe. All the galaxies make music; the atoms make music. And just a very small range of all this universal music can be heard by human beings. Music is vibrations, rhythms . . . Rhythm is everything. (Karlheinz Stockhausen, 1974)

Stravinsky's revolution

THE FIRST INDICATION of something moving in a new direction was with Stravinsky, and *The Rite of Spring* is really still amazing at this time, because it reversed completely the values of European music generally.

Begin with a whole note and then divide it in two minims and then divide it in four quarters and so on. The metre is regular, so you can make values against this regularity; you can make syncopation and so on, but the metre remains always the same. Stravinsky took exactly the point of view contrary to that. He took the smaller value and he multiplied it irregularly. So you don't have a regular pulse as a division but you have an irregular pulse as multiplication. So it's completely reversed. (Pierre Boulez)

IN CLASSICAL, ROMANTIC MUSIC, rock music also, you have a pulse that is usually medium fast – walking pace, running pace – and the invention in the music divides that pulse, with shorter note values: the melody fits inside the pulse. When you think of any classical melody you'll hear notes that are usually going faster than the background pulse.

However, the pulse Stravinsky used was much faster, so fast that it couldn't be treated in the way that it was before. It's not a great leap of the imagination to think of using these single units not in regular groups of fours or threes, as before, but in irregular groups of five, three, four, two, seven, in which you could not perceive a conventional, steady pulse across the music. (George Benjamin)

IN THE RITE OF SPRING the thing that remains striking to me is the irregularity of the rhythm. It was not an irregularity that was contrived; it was an irregularity that seemed to come out of the particular excitement and the particular liveliness of the music. As I see it, it's a kind of organized rubato, a measured rubato; instead of slowing up bit by bit, it suddenly makes accents a good deal later than you would expect or a good deal sooner than you expect, and that in a sense is like accelerando and ritardando. (Elliott Carter)

THAT WAS A VERY, very important revolution throughout the century: development of rhythm from a very small cell. You start from one and you build outwards. (James Wood)

YOU CAN ADD ENDLESSLY a beat of one–two to a beat of one–two–three and produce a whole series of one–two–one–two–three, one–two–one–two–one–two–three, and so on. (Michael Tippett, 1949)

THE VERY OBVIOUS QUALITY in Stravinsky's music that influenced all of us was the whole freeing up of rhythms. Even if you do something totally different his shadow is somewhere there. (Magnus Lindberg)

CERTAINLY THE RITE OF SPRING turned my head in a whole new direction. I had not heard any music of the twentieth century when I heard that. (Steve Reich)

THAT THE FIRST PERFORMANCE of The Rite of Spring was attended by a scandal must be known to everybody. I was unprepared for the explosion myself. I have never again been that angry. The music was so familiar to me, I loved it and I could not understand why people who had not yet heard it wanted to protest in advance. (Igor Stravinsky, 1972)

Two or more rhythms at once

THE ONLY TERM that makes sense at all is 'polyrhythm', which is what the jazz people do. Over the basic four they are prepared to run threes and twos, roughly going one–two–three, one–two–three, one–two; one–two–three, one–two–three, one–two, which are jazz polyrhythms. (Michael Tippett, 1949)

WE NEVER GET anything together – maybe it comes together but maybe we can fix it so that it never comes together – so there's always a sense of rising tension without a final conclusion. (Elliott Carter)

Charles Ives: 'a sort of floating motion'

THE IMPORTANT THING to remember about Ives: he's very much a one-off, he was just experimenting, he just had fun. That really shows in the music, and some of the music is extraordinarily beautiful, some of it is fun, some of it is completely outrageous. (James Wood)

THE SENSE OF THIS LACK of strong heavy downbeat which Ives also was obviously trying to get – he was trying to get the sense of a great flowing kind of visionary thing which I thought was remarkable. For instance, you have a walking theme in the bass and yet he has managed to construct the melodic line in such a way that it doesn't correspond to the downbeat but runs along separately. And it is something that comes out of jazz, after all; jazz has always had a background of regular beats and against it a kind of improvisation that doesn't fall strictly with the beat at all. I think the 'Concord' Sonata has a side of this sort of floating motion. (Elliott Carter)

LIKE A DUAL PERSPECTIVE – like in cubism – when two things dissociated with each other are going on simultaneously and we observe as listeners the clash between them, the clash in colour, pace and personality, and the point is to enjoy the fact that they don't blend. (George Benjamin)

IMAGINE A SCENE in the theatre with three characters: the first is active, even brutally hits the second. The second character is reactive because his actions are dominated by those of the first. Finally the third character witnesses the conflict and remains inactive. If we translate this idea into the domain of rhythm, we get three rhythmic groups: the first, in which the durations are always increasing – that's the attacker; the second, in which the durations become smaller – that's the victim; and the third, in which the durations never change – that's the unaffected character. (Olivier Messiaen, 1985)

Edgard Varèse: many layers

IONISATION: YES, CLEARLY, there are many layers, many strata, of independently varying and developing, transmuting rhythmic cells, and often these rhythmic cells are apportioned particular colours and sharp-edged or more diffuse sonorities, and these are moving at different speeds. In Varèse the sonic phenomenon is so immediate and primal that we cannot be at a distance from what he's doing. And that is an extremely exciting conjunction of immediate aural experience and formal architecture. (Brian Ferneyhough)

Olivier Messiaen: duration, not metre

RHYTHM IS CONCERNED with time lengths and the perception of them. This is in a way the starting point for the study of rhythm. (Aristoxenus, fourth century BC)

MESSIAEN FIRST INTRODUCED the idea that there was such a thing as duration. He taught duration both as a philosophical concept and as a form of aural training. He sat there banging on the table, leaving a pause while he counted thirteen and then he'd bang on the table again and he'd count fourteen, and he said, 'Which gap was longer and which was shorter?' Of course we hadn't the faintest idea because we didn't know what he was talking about. But gradually we got the idea that he thought that durations of time had character and that one should organize the dimension of duration separately from other things. And from this came a concept called the rhythmic cell, a little rhythm which was then developed independently of pitch and led Boulez to talk about a polyphony of parameters. (Alexander Goehr)

YOU CAN ESTIMATE a ratio of two to one or three to one but if you take, for instance, twenty to one you cannot really estimate anything. It's like coins. If you put a group of twenty-one coins beside one of twenty coins you will not be able to estimate the difference, but if you put one coin and two coins you can. And the perception of the eye is exactly the perception of the ear in this case. So there is a limit to what you can do in comparison between two durations. With Messiaen especially you had durations, no metre. Duration is simply the multiplication of a smaller unit. (Pierre Boulez)

THERE ARE SEGMENTS OF SOUND that you cut up and distribute. The conductor's beat – despite being essential for co-ordination – is designed to be inaudible and everything that everybody does is a syncopation against that unheard beat. All you get are these individual points bouncing off the beat and the listener therefore hears music that floats. (George Benjamin)

Non-Western rhythms

I THINK PEOPLE who study non-Western music can drown. Non-Western music, Indian music, African music, Indonesian music are oceans, representing thousands of years, an entire continent's or subcontinent's music, and you are just one puny little individual. If you decide to submerge yourself in it you can culturally drown in there. It's very difficult to bring that music into your own music without making something that is neither American nor African nor Indian and simply doesn't cut the mustard in either camp. It's to do with a way of thinking. Africans are thinking about patterns that are different lengths, and they superimpose their downbeats. Essentially it doesn't matter to me what that actually sounds like, because I can make any patterns I want out of things that come naturally to me – speech patterns, melodic patterns out of musical instruments. That's the beauty of getting involved in the structure of any music, as opposed to its actual notes. If you copy the *notes* you'll sound like something that exists, but if you copy the *structure* you don't know what you'll sound like and you're sort of curious to find out. (Steve Reich)

IF YOU SAID to a musician in the Congo, 'Well, your drumming is very nice and these are very interesting pieces', and so forth, and 'Listen to this string quartet by Beethoven; all music is just organized sound', I don't think he'd know what you were talking about because he doesn't think music is organized sound. He thinks that music is specific, it serves a particular purpose, it's related to specific occasions, it has a specific tradition and it has specific values. (Alexander Goehr)

TAKE XYLOPHONE PLAYING in Uganda: two people on each side of one xylophone at the same time. What they each play is very simple but the combination of the patterns gives a very complex result. I had the idea of transposing this kind of complexity to the two hands of a single live player. In several of these pieces the inspiration source is the *mbira* from Zimbabwe. I'm deeply interested in African music. It's very very complex. There's no metre and simultaneous symmetrical and asymmetrical grids of pulses. There is this kind of tension between symmetry and asymmetry all the time. (György Ligeti, 1974)

I REMEMBER THE FIRST TIME I heard Balinese music – was it in 1948 or 1950? I don't know – we invited a group of Balinese to perform and I knew people at the theatre and so I was able to stand in the wings. It was very strange because you had this frantic activity but there was a rather elderly man who did not do anything; he was close to a very big gong, you thought he was sleeping, but from time to time, *bang!* If you know the music, you know that indicates the periodicity. It's extraordinary: to see that the frantic activity is simply covering a very long extended period of time. The fact that this periodicity is marked by just one gong means that you have two perceptions of time: a long-duration perception and a very short perception. (Pierre Boulez)

I GOT CLOSE TO THE WORKS of Béla Bartók: changing metres and his adaptations of Eastern European folk music and, most of all, for me, simple canons and less simple canons. I'd heard recordings of African music, and it was exciting – I knew that it swung, but I had no idea how it was made. If you try to write down what you hear you will tend to simplify it, in terms of the way you hear as a Westerner. What A. M. Jones did was to build a machine – basically moving graph paper with little metallic pencils, and figured by two copper plates. He had a master drummer from Ghana come to the University of London. There's sort of a time-keeper in Ghanaian music and he basically plays a pattern. So then on a moving sheet of graph paper he had the sound written down in graphic notation. Out of this came a notation that he never would have arrived at if he had simply transcribed what he heard because what he saw was that these things were staggered; they were not lined up. I even have a notebook back in New York with graph paper – which of course a lot of composers used at the time – which I use basically as a rhythmic device. Pieces like *Clapping Music* and *Drumming* were conceived of as rhythmic structures. (Steve Reich)

Systematizing rhythm and duration

THE SAME SPOKEN PHRASE or sentence with different arrangements of its parts takes on as many differences as there are differences in the nature of rhythm. (Aristoxenus, fourth century BC)

SERIALISM WOULDN'T HAVE EXISTED without Stravinsky making rhythm important, back in the early part of this century. That brought us to the point in the late 1940s or early 1950s where parameters were considered, if not of equal importance, of closer importance than was the case back in the past. (Magnus Lindberg)

WHEN WE SAW HOW Schoenberg organized his world, of course we saw that he was in a certain sense inconsequential because he took very drastic measures with pitch, but with nothing else – everything else was still very traditional, in a way. We took his type of organization but expanded that to all the characteristics of the sound, all the parameters of the sound. Pitch of course first, and then duration especially: not rhythms but duration – I insist on that. After a while we saw that kind of organization pushed to this extent was producing chaos. The excess of organization goes to chaos directly, and that of course could not really satisfy me, at least, or us generally in my generation, so we began to think a little further. (Pierre Boulez)

THERE'S A PIECE I'm in the middle of writing for the Millennium, *Fall and Resurrection*. At the beginning of that piece I was confronted with the necessity to express utter chaos, before God as it were loved the world into being, so here I took the way of someone like Brian Ferneyhough, for instance. I decided the only way I could do this was to create about a hundred and fifty different matrices taken from a Greek chant. It was a nightmare for me to write that music and actually physically to write out on a page – because we're talking about different tempi with probably sixty-four staves – it took me about two months to write out each page of that, literally write it out once I'd worked it out. (John Tavener)

Towards chaos?

TIME DOES NOT divide itself. It needs an agent to divide it. (Aristoxenus, fourth century BC)

THERE ARE TWO really very different categories in the organization of durations in music and of rhythms. You have an arithmetic ratio (two to three, three to four, and so on) and you also have division into five, four, three, which makes things confused. And the speed is different. The speed is there to contradict or, on the contrary, to emphasize the regularity, because if you have an accelerando your regular pattern is in fact irregular. (Pierre Boulez)

THE FIRST PIECE OF THIS KIND – a piece for a hundred metronomes – I wrote in 1962. Oh, a very bad scandal! If there is only one metronome and it's very fast, it's not interesting, it's *da da da da da da da*; but if there are many metronomes, their combination, when all the

metronomes are in movement, is quite continuous. The piece was prepared so that some of the metronomes will stop earlier and some will
continue. So, as more and more metronomes stop, the whole texture
of pauses becomes more and more clear. (György Ligeti, 1974)

MANY COMPOSERS HAVE BEEN TROUBLED by this common, audible,
dependable regular pulse. That was at its extreme in the 1950s: the
hyper-hyper-active, hyper-irregularity of the rhythms and the very
staccato, jagged nature of the outlines of the music, verging on neurosis
at some points. I suppose that was asking for a reaction the other way:
minimalism. (George Benjamin)

Flying, and 'hyper-rhythm'

MY MUSIC IS CONSIDERED to be very complex, and was considered
for many years to be impossible to play. Rhythm, metre, density are all
different aspects of the disposition of events in time. If you have a set
of measures, let's say 5/8, 3/8, 4/8, I may in the 5/8 measure take subdivisions of 5, 3 and 4. That set of proportions then anticipates the
sequence of measure lengths (5, 3, 4) on the larger scale. Inside that 5,
3 and 4 it's possible to embed 5, 3 and 4, so that I have three levels of
5, 3 and 4. Even the addition of rests, for instance: if in that 5, 3 and
4, I then look at the impulse sequence 5, 3 and 4, I say, 'OK, I'm going
to leave out every fifth note', or I say, 'Take five notes, leave out the
next three notes, play four notes, leave out the next five notes', I am
creating a hyper-rhythm. I do think that the shapes, and shapes of
shapes, and shapes of shapes of shapes, do create a sort of resonance
in the spirit that contributes greatly to the sense of identity, the sense
of thusness, of a particular composition. (Brian Ferneyhough)

COMPOSERS ARE NOW DEMONSTRATING a form of chaos. An example
would be a work like Ligeti's *Melodien*: in certain complex places there
is an absolute plethora of different little pulses ticking away, none of
them related to any other except in the way they're organized. An
extreme example would be Elliott Carter where in his marvellous
Concerto for Orchestra you have on certain pages in the score
something that is slowing down, something that is speeding up, and
something that seems steady in tempo, all going simultaneously.
(George Benjamin)

WE HAD A HORSE AND CARRIAGE and a great deal of the older music
was just the clump, clump, clump of horses. And then we added the
automobile and the aeroplane, and that's what I'm getting into. It sort

of flies along and that's what I'd like to suggest. Charles Rosen said some very interesting things about my music that I never thought of, and one of them was that my music was remarkably original in its concept of time. I don't think listeners think about it this way. What it does is to give a sense of constant forward flow in a piece of music. The way things flow is not something found in other music at all. One of the fundamental thoughts that I found is the notion of the upbeat leading to the downbeat. A great deal of contemporary music in my opinion falls flat because it doesn't have any sense of the upbeat, and that's tiresome. (Elliott Carter)

Dividing time

THERE SEEMS TO BE A LIMIT when the time lengths into which fractions of a movement are to be fitted are not reduced any further. (Aristoxenus, fourth century BC)

YOU HAVE A TIME that is suspended, that has no pulse at all; you write simply, 'Wait for the resonance to disappear, and then play the next chord.' So that's a time absolutely without any pulse. I wanted to do a piece with resonant instruments. I thought first of the group of instruments, with very different types of resonance, from the piano, which is the longest one, to the mandolin, which is the tiniest one. I don't want to write rhythmically for these instruments, because I skip the main quality of that instrument, which is the duration of the resonance. (Pierre Boulez)

ANYONE WHO'S SPENT ANY TIME with Cage benefits by not being forced into particular ways of writing music. What he does is enable you to think for yourself and to develop your own approach. So there's no, if you like, Cage style or post-Cage style of composition; there is simply an approach. Cage in a way is rather like a sort of philosophical position, where he reduces music to a condition of zero, with a so-called silent piece, 4'33". If you accept that (and I do) then after that you can go in any direction you want, provided you in a sense, as Cage would say, take nothing for the basis. So you don't build on the past, you start from zero, and that is the fundamental difference between Cage and, say, the European avant-garde. (Gavin Bryars)

Notating complexity

MUSIC ISN'T SOMETHING you think of in your mind and then just write down on paper. The relationship between the paper and the sound, the paper and the invention, is much more complex than that. However enormously radical the changes in composition have been in the twentieth century, the way it's notated has changed surprisingly little. The idea of having five lines and bars and tempos and sharps and flats and semiquavers, demisemiquavers and things – you know, they're still as valuable to us as they have been for centuries. (George Benjamin)

I THINK COMPOSERS have had to resort to all sorts of tricks in order to make sense notationally of their musical ideas, especially if one is thinking in terms of maybe not standard tuning – forty-eight notes to the octave or whatever. If you want to do things where you want to get rid of the idea of continuous rhythm, you want to freeze things, or you want to introduce some kind of aleatoric element or some improvisation element, then you have to think, notationally, away from the conventions of the old stave notation.

Some of Cage's scores are incredibly beautiful pieces of graphics. Cornelius Cardew was a fantastic graphic designer and *Treatise* is a wonderful piece of graphic design, as well as being a really fantastic piece of music. Generally when composers do graphic scores, they have to give some clue to the performers what these notations mean, so you get a kind of table of interpretation at the beginning. (Gavin Bryars)

IN DARMSTADT EVERYBODY was thinking about notation. One composer, for instance, put only sharps and nothing else, and another one composer flats and nothing else. Another composer put all the dynamics with bigger notes or smaller notes and so on. Everybody had an explanation, and you had to read maybe four pages of explanation before reading a bar. And then in the next piece it was exactly the contrary. So I remember once, there was one point in Darmstadt – it was a symposium on notation – and nobody could agree with anyone else. (Pierre Boulez)

THE MAIN THING IS to find the optimum notation, so that your ideas can actually be communicated. And if the best way is through inventing some ideal notation, then that's what you should do. Music went through a lot of that in a sense to open up the question of how you can approach musical performance. I now use conventional notation again. (Gavin Bryars)

THERE ARE PEOPLE, Stockhausen included, who want to make a kind of notation that includes everything in the same sign – staccato, dynamic, pitch and so on and so forth. But if you see a condensed sign like that you have to analyse it and it takes time. When you have, on the contrary, different markings – for instance, a minim and a dot and a *piano* and a crescendo – then you make the synthesis, and making synthesis is much quicker than analysis. In the analysis you have to extract; in synthesis you reduce. The more I go, I go in this direction. You organize and then you make a tablature, very easy, and then you hear the result. And if you want to check the result, you check the result, note by note. (Pierre Boulez)

Conlon Nancarrow: unplayable by human hands

I DISCOVERED THE EXISTENCE of Nancarrow by chance in 1980. I never heard about him. Elliott Carter knew him, and John Cage knew him. This kind of rhythmical folly I never could imagine – it's not possible to be performed by a human being – but the mechanical piano, the player-piano can do it. (György Ligeti, 1997)

ONE VOICE COMES IN quite slowly, then the top voice comes in all over the place: very very fast. And gradually over the composition the very fast voice slows down and the very slow voice, or the relatively slow voice, speeds up. He liked fugal, contrapuntal structures very much and he started out doing tempo relationships where you could have one voice coming in at a certain speed, another one coming in 50 per cent faster, another one another 50 per cent and so on, all building together. First, he would mark out the rolls with the position of notes that he wanted – if one calls that rhythm – then he would remove the roll from the perforating machine. He would copy that across to manuscript paper, blank manuscript paper, and at that point he would put the notes in. So he's very definitely thinking in terms of the positioning of the notes rather than their pitch. (Rex Lawson)

MANY OF THE WORKS you cannot listen to without smiling – they're so exciting visually. Sometimes you suddenly become aware of a process, of a canon; you can suddenly hear the thing as it happens on the pianola. But that's not then an analytical experience; it's always a very exciting experience, actually noticing the canons – as though you've suddenly understood why a mysterious small animal moves in the way it does and you suddenly realize what it's doing. (Thomas Adès)

Electronics and the computer

WHEN YOU WRITE an electronic piece you are like a painter, in that the situation's immediate: you put the pigment on to the canvas and there is no interpretation. Whereas, if you are writing a piece for an orchestra, you put hieroglyphics down on a piece of paper, and you might hear it in your head to a certain extent, and then it has to be performed. (Harrison Birtwistle, 1974)

THAT BROUGHT ME to the microcomputer world back in the early 1980s, when I started to develop software that allowed me to stretch and compress rhythms, to make interpolations, to make gradual changes of characters in a very precise way. (Magnus Lindberg)

WITH SAMPLING AND THE SYNTHESIZER you can have really very extraordinary scales because you can organize it very easily – much easier than trying to notate it. (Pierre Boulez)

THE COMPUTER WITH THE USE of Midi and with sampler instruments became a tool for orchestration and to enable you to hear what you'd done in a mock-up version as you're doing it. That's very, very helpful. Beyond just being a compositional aid in a mechanical sense, being around any device or musical instrument will tend to affect the music that you do with it, obviously. *Different Trains* would have been inconceivable without it and without the sampler keyboard, which was really another form of computer. I became aware of the sampler keyboard about 1986, 1987. I had no interest in synthesizers. I'm not interested in electronic waveform imitating a violin. Buy a violin! But a sampler is a totally different kind of a device. I can get these bird sounds, or your voice or my voice, to come in on the end of the third beat of the fifteenth bar by simply playing it or by programming it in. (Steve Reich)

I WAS ALWAYS VERY KEEN on developing the kind of computer techniques that could free the performer from following something stored, on a tape for instance. For instance, when I was beginning with IRCAM in the early 1970s, I could not foresee at all the development of the computer. At the beginning you had a big computer – in 1976 even, twice the size of this room – and time-sharing, so people were waiting. They were typing and then waiting for the answer, which is unthinkable now: everybody has a screen in front of his face. (Pierre Boulez)

SPEECH WILL DIVIDE the time by its own parts, namely letters, syllables and words. (Aristoxenus, fourth century BC)

I AM SOMEBODY who's interested in the rhythm of speech and I like to translate it into musical terms, as opposed to people who like to play around with the syllables – I'm not very fond of melisma in song. Listening to a conversation always has musical quality to me and has to do with inflexion and emphasis. It's all music to me; I like to translate that. (Stephen Sondheim)

THERE'S TWO THINGS that music can do: it can start and it can stop. (Harrison Birtwistle)

9 The Language of Music
2: Tabula Rasa

There is no theory. You merely have to listen. Pleasure is the law.
CLAUDE DEBUSSY, 1883

ONE OF THE REASONS that some twentieth-century music is perceived as difficult is that its harmonic language bears little or no perceptible relationship to that of preceding centuries. Most traditional Western music, classical and popular, depends for its sense of structure and movement on a tension between dissimilar keys, often expressed in contrast between dissimilar harmonies. Composers have been breaking the 'rules' of harmony since Beethoven reintroduced the main theme of the first movement of the 'Eroica' Symphony while the accompaniment was in the 'wrong' key, or since Mozart's 'Dissonance' Quartet or earlier, and they broke these rules in search of greater expressiveness. But however often the rules were broken, they were broken against a background of a harmonic system that was not only generally accepted but rooted in the laws of physics and the nature of the human ear.

A note is perceived as having a particular pitch because a string, a column of air or a vocal cord vibrates at a particular frequency, which the ear receives and transmits to the brain. The reason that two notes an octave apart seem to have such a close affinity, and to sound especially euphonious when sounded together, is that the ratio of the

125

upper note's vibrations to those of the lower is precisely 2:1. All other intervals between notes that are accepted by the ear as 'harmonious' have similarly simple mathematical relationships which the inner ear is finely equipped to perceive. Those notes that have such simple relationships to one another are known as the 'harmonic series'. This principle was known and understood by the ancient Greeks, and was first described by Pythagoras in the sixth century BC.

The search for greater expressiveness during the nineteenth century, which reached its high point in the music of Wagner and some of his contemporaries and successors, led to the breaking of more and more of the 'rules' of harmony, to such an extent that tonality, the sense of key, was weakened. This was seen as a particular hazard in music relating, as Wagner's did, to the great Austro-German tradition. Schoenberg's radical abandoning of all sense of key (atonality) and his subsequent invention of a system (twelve-tone serialism) to provide an alternative to tonality, were attempts both to solve the problem and to follow in the direction that Wagner's discoveries pointed. He was more concerned to preserve a tradition, however radically transformed, than to break with it: one of his biographers has called him 'the conservative revolutionary'.

To many his music was perplexing, even incomprehensible, but the rigorous logic of his system attracted composers. For a while, in the years after the Second World War, there were many composers, theorists and critics who held that Schoenberg and his followers had indicated the only possible route by which music could move forward. As with Marxism, the adherents of serialism described it as 'historically necessary'. However, other composers – for the most part not those who owed any special adherence to the Austro-German tradition – had enriched their melodic and harmonic languages by studying the ancient modes: scales that are neither major nor minor, that were in use before the development of the tonal system, and which are also found in Eastern and Western folk music.

Gabriel Fauré's musical style, for example, owes a great deal to his training in modal harmony, a training devised to enable church musicians to provide accompaniments to the modal melodies of Gregorian chant that would not distort them, as harmonization according to rules laid down for non-modal melodies would have done. Claude Debussy, who had been deeply impressed by the Javanese and Vietnamese music he heard at the World Exhibition in Paris in 1889, was also aware of the modes and expressed his impatience with the tonal system: 'Music is neither major nor minor.' Béla Bartók, meticulously collecting and studying East European folk music, was excited by the quality of the melodies he found, but no less so by realizing that some of them used the whole-tone scale, a mode 'neither major nor minor' much employed by Debussy. As a young man Debussy had made two extensive visits to Russia, where the use of modes or scales other than the major and minor was widespread; one of these, the so-called 'octatonic scale', much exploited by Rimsky-Korsakov, was to be an important influence on Rimsky's pupil Igor Stravinsky. The attraction of all these 'alternative' scales was that they gave composers an enriched harmonic and melodic language without implicitly denying the sense of key, as Schoenberg had done. In many of the works of these composers melodies are heard that are, for example, seemingly 'in C' but are in neither C major nor C minor. In a modal scale starting on C some of the notes that in tonal music would confirm its key, and establish whether it was C minor or C major, are missing. Thus some chords that in tonal music are important for giving a sense of direction or movement are absent from modal music.

Olivier Messiaen, who enthusiastically studied Schoenberg's system and analysed atonal and serial works in his famous classes at the Paris Conservatoire, nevertheless also investigated the modes even more closely than Fauré had done. He was, however, more interested as a source for his own compositions in the modes encountered in non-Western music, and he invented for his own use seven 'modes of limited transposition'. (The 'modes of unlimited transposition' are the major and minor scales.)

At the end of the twentieth century there are still composers who find it important and valuable to follow in the direction pointed by Schoenberg. Even some who have been unconvinced by his theories have found the rigour and economy of his method a useful and productive discipline. Stravinsky, who for many years was seen as Schoenberg's antithesis, at the end of his life (and after Schoenberg's death) surprised and disconcerted many of his admirers by wholeheartedly adopting serialism in such late masterpieces as the *Canticum sacrum* and the *Requiem Canticles*. But it has often been remarked that in his exhaustive development of short melodic cells Stravinsky had been writing 'quasi-serially' for much of his life, during which he had built up a personal harmonic language which continues to be audible in his late serial works.

As a reaction to the post-Schoenbergian modernism of the 1950s and 1960s, which in some quarters had hardened into a rigid orthodoxy, a group of composers (mainly but not exclusively in the United States) began, in some cases under the influence of non-Western music, to investigate a music of much greater simplicity. Soon described as 'minimalism', this music is characterized by regular rhythm, simple melody (often changing by gradual permutation of notes within a repetitive pattern) and very simple, sometimes modal harmony. Other composers have rejected orthodox modernism without accepting minimalist techniques, turning instead to Debussy, to Bartók, to Messiaen or to other composers as an alternative to the Austro-German tradition. Others, like John Cage and for a while the Englishman Cornelius Cardew, revelled in a music with few rules or none, music that was metaphorically and literally democratic, in which the random was the rule. The result, at the turn of the century, is a plethora of styles amid which it is hard to recognize any one as central. Most of them, however, have one thing in common: a recognition of the expressive power and structurally functional importance of harmony.

Schoenberg emancipates dissonance . . .

SCHOENBERG'S FIVE ORCHESTRAL PIECES, Op. 16, made a profound impression on me; it's an extraordinary piece. I've since had the chance to perform it a number of times over the years, and it's stayed profoundly impressive. I think it simply demonstrated – without the twelve-tone system yet having been developed – that it was possible to write a very substantial, large piece, with extended movements, without recourse to tonality. (Charles Wuorinen)

MY FATHER [WALTER GOEHR] used to say that Schoenberg had told him that he originally wanted to write eight [Orchestral Pieces], but that he was frightened by what he had done, that it was so radical at that time that he actually lost his nerve. It would explain why the fifth piece peters out in a strange way. It doesn't come to any sort of meaningful conclusion.

Each of the Five Pieces contains an attempt to give expression to an idea about space and time. A painter friend of mine pointed out that in Cézanne, if you look at the pictures of the Mont Ste Victoire which he did at the end of his life – there are many of them – you find that what he is painting in the sky, where there used to be just a white cloud and some blue sky, is now as dense and as complex as what he is painting in the landscape, and that this is in some way an important statement about pictorial space. Schoenberg is filling space – space in the sense that an orchestra has a top note with a piccolo, and a bottom note, double-bass or tuba – in a way fundamentally different and more radical than any composer of the nineteenth century. It's a piece where the concept of dissonance is abolished, and consequently everything can be combined with everything, and everything *is* combined with everything, so that the space is filled. (Alexander Goehr)

. . . but creates a further problem

IF THE RULES OF HARMONY and counterpoint are broken down and dissonance is emancipated, as Schoenberg argued, and you don't have common simple chords in the background, what is a passing note? What isn't? You can't tell. What's a dissonant note? You can't tell either. The reason for having all twelve notes going is so that no pitch can appear more important than any other: they're all equally important.

In some of the best Webern, like the Symphony, you get a form of weightlessness, you get no polarity between the pitches. Everything is of equal importance: it's like listening to a most perfect crystal. But there are great problems in that technique. One is that if you use all twelve pitches all the time, there's no air in the texture. You also get no sense of harmonic rhythm, because statistically everything's moving at the same pace. (George Benjamin)

SERIALISM IS A WONDERFUL THING because it really sorts the men from the boys: it's such a kind of dry and unhelpful form of writing. On paper, when you describe it, it has no attractions at all. (Thomas Adès)

I THINK PEOPLE do find it very difficult to listen to serial music, especially Schoenberg. Even today, seventy-five years after Schoenberg's serial music, people are still finding it very, very difficult, in spite of the fact that it's not new, and lots of other much more shocking things have happened since. I don't believe that the twelve-tone system will prove ultimately to be the most important revolution in this century's music. (James Wood)

IT IS NOT BECAUSE people are stupid, it's because the language is such that it's something that you only rarely want to hear. It violates so many of the conventions (which is basically what they are, perhaps based on some physical reality of the harmonic system) that it becomes a very rarefied and rare item on most people's listening agenda.

There were unfortunately many composers who followed Schoenberg. I say 'unfortunately' not because Schoenberg wasn't a good composer but because I think the idea, as Boulez says, that this was the historically necessary thing to do is a mistake. Nothing's historically necessary. (Steve Reich)

Debussy: pleasure before theory

CLAUDE DEBUSSY: I do not believe in the supremacy of the C major scale. Music is neither major nor minor. Major and minor thirds should be combined, thereby making modulation more flexible. The mode is that which one happens to choose at a particular moment. It is inconstant. (*Plays series of chords.*)

ERNEST GUIRAUD (his composition teacher): What is that?

DEBUSSY: Incomplete chords, floating. You must blur the sound. One can travel where one wishes and leave by any door.

GUIRAUD: But when I play this (*plays chord of Ab, C, D, F♯*) it has to resolve.

DEBUSSY: I don't see that it should. Why?

GUIRAUD: Well, do you find this lovely? (*Plays series of parallel triads.*)

DEBUSSY: Yes, yes, yes!

GUIRAUD: I'm not saying that what you do isn't beautiful, but it's theoretically absurd.

DEBUSSY: There is no theory. You merely have to listen. Pleasure is the law. (Conversation overheard by Maurice Emmanuel, 1883, published by him, 1926)

Chords in their own right

DEBUSSY'S IDEA WAS a chord being able to have a certain sonority, a certain flavour which can exist in its own right. (James Wood)

KANDINSKY'S WIFE SAYS in a book she wrote about him that he far preferred tubes of paint to the subject matter that he was painting. What really thrilled him was a tube with vermilion in it. Harmony has essential content. It's, as it were, tactile. (Alexander Goehr)

WHY NOT GO a bit further? Why not stretch, like Mahler: immense chords for angst and pathos? Other more subtle uses of complex chords can be found in Debussy and Ravel, where, just for the pleasure of sensation, they began to investigate harmonies of sometimes six or seven notes, and which got further and further away from the nice, clear three- and four-note chords that had defined harmony for centuries. In *Daphnis et Chloë*, for instance, one of the most atmospheric passages starts with a nine-note chord. (George Benjamin)

I'M TERRIBLY INFLUENCED by Ravel, period. I even stole the first chord of the *Valses nobles et sentimentales* for 'Liaisons' – Ravel should get royalties! I've no hesitation about either stealing or admitting what I steal, because if you steal eventually you digest it; it becomes your own. All those sevenths and ninths are what it's about. (Stephen Sondheim)

I THINK THAT STRAVINSKY thought of some of his *Rite of Spring*-type chords as being almost noise. I remember an anecdote about him changing the last chord of *The Rite of Spring* because, he said, 'Before it was a noise; now it's a sound.' He started to listen to this thing that he created, which at first was a very angry sort of crash; he changed a few notes, and it made all the difference to him. (James Wood)

Stravinsky's harmonic language

THROUGHOUT MY ENTIRE MUSICAL LIFE, from the time I was fifteen, I never ceased to admire the works of Stravinsky. I think he's an absolutely fabulous composer. It doesn't matter what style. The thing that was important was that there was this mark on all his works: this is very strongly Stravinsky's music, whether it was *The Firebird* or *The Rake's Progress* or the *Requiem Canticles*, whatever; I think that's extraordinary. (Elliott Carter)

THERE ARE PEOPLE who experiment with different kinds of harmonic style, like Stravinsky. I think part of it, sometimes, is orchestration, but essentially I think you can tell who's written what, even in piano reductions. Harmony is what characterizes music. That's how you can tell Brahms from Rakhmaninov. It's also how you can tell Rodgers from Kern. It's the fingerprint, and all the first-rate composers have eventually developed a style that is harmonically individual. Everybody said, 'Oh, Gershwin: you can always tell him rhythmically.' No, you can't. You can tell him *harmonically*. That's how you can tell him. (Stephen Sondheim)

The basis of harmony

YOU CANNOT DENY the importance of the harmonic series. Classical harmony is based on the first few partials of the harmonic series. The reason for that is because those partials have a very satisfying concordant feel to them. When you hear a triad you feel relaxed. (James Wood)

THE RUSSIAN CHURCH SAYS that the triad is allowed because it represents the Trinity. It's natural if it's stemming from the harmony of the spheres. (John Tavener)

WHEN YOU HEAR a seventh you feel a little bit more tense. All these intervals have a very, very potent feel to them. The further you get away from the harmonic series, the further you get away from the soul. For example, a piece like Stockhausen's *Stimmung*, which is one chord for an hour and a half: who would have thought that one could seriously sit down and listen to that? (James Wood)

THAT NINTH CHORD in Stockhausen's *Stimmung*: of course it is like the harmonics in a good ninth chord, like Debussy himself. But I think you cannot base a work on a simple chord. I don't like this simplification of the vocabulary because I find it too restrictive. You know, if you make a chord of E major, even if you add phase-changing and everything, it remains a chord of E major! (Pierre Boulez)

Minimalist harmony . . .

THE CHORD IN *FOUR ORGANS* is a dominant eleventh chord. You've got the tonic, the A, as the top voice, and the dominant, the E, is in the bass. The way I would describe that chord, I would say, 'Stand up and lean forward and just stay that way.' It's always being pushed to go to A, and the A is sort of saying to me, 'Well, look, you know, we're there, now.' 'I don't care, I want to go there.' So there is this dynamic stasis: there's energy and yet there's stasis at the same time. That makes it possible to write what I think is a viable piece that's about twenty minutes long, based on that harmony, which you find in Debussy: you find that eleventh chord voiced with the tonic on top. And in *Music for Eighteen Musicians* I wrote eleven chords, and each of those chords appears in the middle register. First I wrote the right hand or the treble clef with the middle-register material, and only later did I write in the bass, but the bass is not always the same. So the functional part of the harmony resides in the middle register, which means that the bass becomes colouristic. Now we're talking *L'après-midi d'un faune*! (Steve Reich)

THE CHORDS THAT ARE PLAYED are actually the same four chords repeated all the way through. At any moment of the piece you'll be hearing one of those four chords, and in that sequence. What happens is that the piece expands rhythmically: over each chord more rhythms get played each time, so you may be hearing the same four chords, but you'll be hearing them in a longer and longer phrasing. (Philip Glass)

... for and against

THE ONE THING I can't stand is that genre of composers – and let no names be named – who at some point in their career got very snotty and said, 'In those days my teachers forced me to write serial music in order to get my pieces played. I had to write this nasty-sounding, gritty stuff. Now, finally, I write what I wanted to write all along.' Well, what pathetic people those are! If you couldn't tell your teacher to go and take a hike ... well, I don't know, there's not much of an artist or rebel in you. (Brian Ferneyhough)

WHEN I WENT TO MUSIC SCHOOL – I was at Juilliard, and at Mills College – there was one way to write, and if you didn't write twelve-tone serial music you were just a joke. You just weren't to be taken seriously. So the only way to deal with that, for me, was to leave that world. (Steve Reich)

THE INTERESTING THING in the last fifteen or twenty years is the enormous popularity that we've seen for music by the Góreckis, the Taveners, the Arvo Pärts, and I think this has come about as a kind of sigh of relief. It shows that there is a kind of desperate frustration among people who want to listen to music and want to hear new music, and they have aspirations of their own about what new music is, and they hear consonance, they hear some harmonic sense out of the kind of darkness of post-serial music. (James Wood)

WHEN TERRY RILEY and LaMonte Young and Philip Glass and I started to do what we did, we had the benefit of being in America. Music does come out of a time, it does come out of a place, and what's called minimalism really did come out of America. Now it has cropped up also, very remarkably, in Eastern Europe. (Steve Reich)

IF THAT WORD had been used in the days of the Fathers, in the fifth and sixth centuries in Egypt, I think the word 'minimalist' then would have been exceptionally flattering. (John Tavener)

MINIMALISM IS A TERM, like Impressionism or Expressionism, that was taken from painting and applied to composers. I think it may be descriptive of pieces like *Clapping Music* and maybe even up to *Drumming*, but starting to get to *Music for Eighteen Musicians* and beyond, I don't think that's the word that people would have chosen. But at that point the die had been cast. If I were to copy out a Mahler score and change a few notes, they'd say, 'Aha! A new kind of minimalism!' I suppose if you dug up Debussy and asked him how he liked the term Impressionism, he'd say 'Goodbye and good luck.' (Steve Reich)

I HAVE HEARD RECENTLY a work by Arvo Pärt, and I find that it's really a waste of my time to listen to it, because if after two seconds – or maybe twenty seconds, let's say, to be generous – I have understood that the piece begins in the low register and it will be ending ten minutes later in the top register, I don't need to listen to the piece because I can foresee it. (Pierre Boulez)

LOOKING AT WHERE WE ARE NOW, in the 1990s, and the kind of music that's being written, it is very clear that many, many composers, particularly in this country, have gone back to a kind of tonality. Not a new tonality, but really rather an old tonality.

You can hear this resonance, this harmonic resonance, coming through – I happen to love Arvo Pärt's music. There's not a living European composer I would rather listen to than Arvo Pärt. (James Wood)

THIS IS AN ACTUAL CASE: key signature of D major and it seems to be a slow two-part invention basically on the structure of D major. What aspect of D major-ness, or of tonality or of the historical emplacement of this re-evocation of the desuetous rules of D major-ness are you attempting to evoke? I think it's important to make clear to a young composer that D major also has sharks' teeth hidden behind the nice gentle smile. (Brian Ferneyhough)

Messiaen invents new scales

FOR ME THE LINKS between sound and colour are intellectual ones. A complex of sounds, a chord, corresponds to a particular ensemble of colours, and this ensemble of colours accompanies the chord at every octave, getting lighter as you go up towards the treble, and darker as you go down towards the bass. The colours are the same, just lighter or darker. This happens only if you transpose the chord by octaves. If you move it by a semitone or a tone, or a third or a fourth, the ensemble of colours changes. (Olivier Messiaen, 1985)

MESSIAEN WAS BUILDING new scales to replace the old scales, but the new scales were able to have harmonic tension, they could move from one place to another, to the point where he could actually control the colour of the chord. If you follow that path, the idea of keeping natural harmonics as a very central part of the harmonic world, you have then to look at the so-called 'spectral school' of composers such as Tristan Murail and Gérard Grisey, who started to look a little bit further up the harmonic spectrum than classical harmony had ever done, and you start to get some absolutely beautiful harmonics which don't coincide at all with the chromatic scale, and you start getting into microtonality. A lot of people think microtones sound very weird, but actually they don't always sound very weird.

There's this marvellous story about Ives and the church bell next door. There was a thunderstorm, it was quite late in the evening, and the church bell was ringing, and he was absolutely determined to try to capture the sound of this church bell, and he played it over and over again on the piano, and he couldn't get it. He was rushing in and out of the house, coming in completely drenched, and he was up all the night trying to find this chord on the piano, and of course what he was hearing was a non-linear spectrum, and that is the reason: because the partials have nothing to do with the harmonic series. (James Wood)

Sound and noise

IN EDGARD VARÈSE'S OCTANDRE the instruments are not balanced in the same way that a Stravinskian chord is well balanced, for instance, but each chord is somehow balanced in spite of itself, and the balance, the weighting of the different instruments in the different registers, is very convincing. (Brian Ferneyhough)

ONCE YOU GET INTO THE WORLD where a harmony, a combination of pitches, produces a certain colour, that is where Varèse is important. He showed the world the importance of the *objet sonore*, a sound that is totally unique. People thought it was noise. What is the difference between noise and sound? When you play an oil drum, it sounds like a noise, maybe. When you start to look at it, and extract the harmonics, it's extremely beautiful and it's certainly not noise. (James Wood)

Getting away from harmony

I REMEMBER GOING TO SEE Michael Tippett, and he said, 'Well, how are you getting on? What are you up to?' And I said, 'I'm very worried about harmony.' He said, 'Why?' And I said, 'It seems to me that what I write is arbitrary, because there's no sort of underlying harmony. It seems all right while I'm writing it, but very often I can't remember it.' He said, 'It's strange you should say that, because if I were to describe the whole enterprise of my compositional life, it's trying to see how one could write coherent expressive music without harmony: how to get away from harmony.' (Alexander Goehr)

To WRITE MUSIC you need negative areas, you need forbidden territory, you need borders, you need things that at any moment you mustn't and you can't do. Without those, you can't compose. (George Benjamin)

IF ONE WANTS TO THINK of a musical avoidance in which one makes up a real or virtual list of forbidden sonorities, forbidden gestures, I think one is limiting, unduly and unnecessarily, that very expansion which we've enjoyed in our period. (Charles Wuorinen)

Freedom and 'foolishness'

I DON'T WISH TO BE THOUGHT to be as foolish as I sound. And I frequently, very consciously, put into my life experience things where conclusions that I've reached in the field of music cannot possibly be held, for instance my interest in mycology and my gathering and eating of wild mushrooms. Now if I were as free and easy with the mushrooms as I am with sound, I might not be here this afternoon to talk with you. Indeed not. (John Cage, 1967)

JOHN CAGE, I THINK, is a very minor figure, who simply hit upon a very clever way of self-promotion at a certain critical moment. All the philosophy and the half-digested orientalism and the mushrooms and the happenings and all of this other stuff is just so tedious. Assessing a phenomenon like Cage is to try to imagine the consequence, the legacy that follows. What, when you have shattered every single convention of concert life, do you put afterward? Interestingly enough, of course, the answer is nothing, and I don't see any legacy, aside from the wistful reminiscences by certain figures who are affected by John Cage. You know, these wonderful remarks: 'John taught us to hear', which is one of the most vacuous statements I've ever heard in my life. Aside from that, there seems to be very little impact from all of that activity which was so widely publicized and heralded, and which offered a rich field of opportunity for so many deeply untalented people. (Charles Wuorinen)

THE ESSENCE OF SCRATCH MUSIC is that people are asked to write accompaniments. So each person writes and plays these accompaniments; everybody plays their accompaniments together. So, in fact, this whole body of sound – a lot of people playing Scratch Music – could be used as a background for somebody playing a solo . . . [Explosive noise. INTERVIEWER: What on earth was that?] Well, accidents will happen. That must have been somebody who was playing Scratch Music on a balloon and suddenly decided to play Scratch Music so hard that the balloon burst – a solo performance that came about unintentionally. (Cornelius Cardew, 1972)

IF, FOR INSTANCE, A STUDENT becomes obsessed with work with jam-jars or waste-paper baskets or mucking about with the inside of pianos, the teacher should at first welcome this (if it's an improvement on what the student's done before) and then first gently and then more forcefully point out that the world of music is wider than that represented by jam-jars. If, on the other hand, the student obstinately, after three or four years, still produces Brahms intermezzi, or pastiches of them, he should point out, with equally increasing force, that a lot of water has flowed under the bridge since then. Of the two students, I think that the jam-jars one would be potentially the more hopeful, because he is reaching out. (Hugh Wood, 1967)

Anything goes?

IF SOMEBODY SAYS they can play the piano, and then bangs with their elbows, one is entitled, fairly, to say, 'I'm terribly sorry but you can't play the piano.' But when somebody comes and says, 'I am a composer', and they bang with their elbows, it's a question whether you can say, 'I'm terribly sorry, you're not a composer.' Even if you can say it, you tend to bite your tongue and keep it to yourself, either because you may be driven out as a hopeless renegade reactionary, or as a totally intolerant person. (Alexander Goehr)

The pluralist century

WHOEVER COULD POSSIBLY, with a straight face, maintain now that only by imitating Tchaikovsky is one finally one's innermost self? Never before in the history of the world have so many different sorts of music been equi-distant or equi-valent, and I would be very rash to suggest that any particular sort of musical style or practice would be more relevant and would be seen in fifty years' time as standing for all other sorts of musical practice in the late twentieth century. Maybe that's what it will be: the period of plurality, but maybe it will be so obvious and so natural to those living in fifty years' time that everything is fractured plurality that it won't occur to them to call the second half of the twentieth century anything of the sort.

The problem is that today there are so many different ways of writing music – which I have to accept as being in some way uniquely valid to the people doing it. At the same time, clearly, some of the

products are not equal to the ideals the composers are trying to transmit, and that will never change, that will go on getting more and more
pluralist. Fifty years ago, if somebody had asked you, 'What do you
do?', and you'd replied, 'I'm a composer', they would have known
more or less what your music might sound like if you were a 'serious'
composer. Nowadays if somebody asks what you are, and you say
you're a composer, they'd say, 'What does it sound like?' It could
sound like anything. Perhaps there you have it: the label for the century
is 'the pluralist century'. (Brian Ferneyhough)

WE ARE PAYING ATTENTION to the notion that pluralism is the natural
condition for a so-called democratic society, and that pluralism means,
in music, that different kinds of music can co-exist, and different publics
can co-exist. However, this is perhaps rather an optimistic view of the
situation, because it leaves out the distortions wrought by commercialism upon any sort of idealistic notion of democracy and the
pluralism that is its cultural equivalent. In that sense I'm much more
optimistic for Philip Glass than I am for myself. (Alexander Goehr)

What is harmony?

DO WE ALL KNOW what we mean by harmony? We could have that
discussion: what do we mean by harmony? There are things that I very
carefully control, and what I control are the intervals. (Harrison
Birtwistle, 1998)

I PERSONALLY DON'T REALLY FEEL there is a very large distinction
between the vertical and the horizontal. (Brian Ferneyhough)

IF YOU SING A MELODY in an enormously reverberant acoustic it will
produce a harmony. (John Tavener)

SCHOENBERG IS REPUTED to have died saying the word 'Harmony'.
(Alexander Goehr)

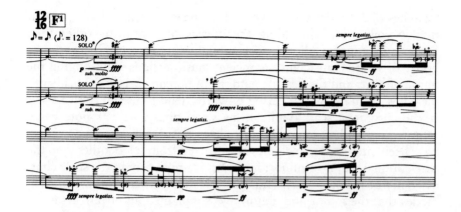

10 The Language of Music
3: New Adventures

I think there's been a need perpetually for melody.
GEORGE BENJAMIN

ALMOST THE COMMONEST accusation against much twentieth-century music is that it is tuneless. It is true that some composers have been so absorbed in areas of musical language that had been all but unexplored until this century that in some of their works melody is of less than primary importance. Some modernist works of the 1950s and 1960s are perceptible as rapid sequences of brief events, in which it is hard to pick out anything as sustained as a melody. Other works concerned themselves with patterns of points or clusters or with gradations of texture, with pure rhythm or with sounds from the natural and man-made worlds that until then had been regarded merely as noise. In fact melody has remained central to the vast majority of music written in this as in previous centuries. Twentieth-century melodies rise and fall in pitch, they pause and continue in their phrase structure, they build and release tension as melodies always have. But in this century the rises and falls have often been over greater extremes of pitch than ever before, the phrase patterns and rhythms have often been more irregular, the tensions and releases more extreme and less predictable.

Not all twentieth-century composers have been concerned to write melodies of an entirely new type. Many have sought melodic inspiration in folk music, including the musics of continents other than Europe, in popular idioms once thought foreign to or beneath the notice of serious musicians, in ancient music such as plainsong, in the music of birds and the flexible patterns of human speech. Schoenberg's melodies, from his atonal period onwards, tend to use all twelve notes of the chromatic scale (with, in his serial phase, no one note being repeated until all eleven others have been heard), but other composers have been interested in melodies constructed from scales other than the conventional major or minor: from the five-note pentatonic scale characteristic of much Eastern and Western folk music, from the ancient modes that the minor and major keys supplanted and from 'artificial' modes constructed on similar principles. Some of these modes, like the octatonic scale much used by Stravinsky, have the advantage of sounding unlike major or minor, thus seeming 'new', but without denying a sense of key.

In the past, musical form depended very largely on readily perceptible repetition or variation. In a piece in which there is little or no obvious repetition the principal thematic ideas may be hard to grasp, but a firm and readily comprehended structure – perhaps involving the clearly perceptible repetition or variation of elements other than melody – may be of great help. In music based on serial principles, where a pattern of notes may appear in its original form, in inversion (played upside-down), retrograde (played backwards) and retrograde inversion, and where in certain cases the distances between notes may be expanded or contracted, the difficulty arises of how far the average human ear can perceive such relationships.

In the past, likewise, melodies were so often constructed in regular patterns of four, six or eight phrases, usually in a regular rhythm and proceeding from a key note, away from it and back again in a variety of well-established ways, that a strong opening idea would often suggest its own continuation and conclusion. This is more difficult when so many types of melodic language are available to the composer, and when all aspects of melody may be unpredictable. Yet of the imperatives that compel composers to write music that sounds new and responds to changed times, circumstances and environments, none is more pressing than the need to write melodies that seem new. Even those composers who have drawn most fruitfully on the past have done so in order to find a language that, though rooted in history, sounds new.

Defining melody

A LINE THAT BEGINS to breathe at the start of the piece and stops breathing at the end of it: it's a very organic thing. (Thomas Adès)

IF MUSIC CAN'T BE SUNG, it is no longer music. (John Tavener)

MELODY IS A WORD with certain connotations. It's not enough for me to say, 'I've written a melody.' Someone has to be able to recognize it as such.

What do people mean if they say, 'That's a nice tune'? If I say, 'I think that *Gruppen* by Stockhausen has some absolutely lovely tunes in it, I whistle them every night', people would look at me sceptically. In simpler days amateurs used to come to one and say, 'I've thought of a lovely tune; could you help me write it down?' (Alexander Goehr)

I THINK THERE'S BEEN A NEED perpetually for melody, and when composers haven't written melody they've intentionally repressed the melodic instinct.

Melody is not tune; melody is the contour of an instrument along time, along a line. There are some composers for whom their natural lyricism has flowered as spontaneously as in any other century: look at the music of Tippett, say, or in many cases Messiaen. (George Benjamin)

IT CERTAINLY IS the most complex parameter in music because to write a melody involves all parameters. At the same time it's the most difficult to deal with. As Messiaen said, 'It's the most refined quality in music, to be able to write melodies.' (Magnus Lindberg)

I THINK EVERYBODY can pick out the beginning of a melody on an instrument. If you have a child, when it's finished actually clouting the instrument, it will pick out the beginning of quite acceptable melodies. (Alexander Goehr)

A too restricted definition?

GENERALLY, WHAT PEOPLE CONSIDER as melody has to do with a kind of Italian tradition, of a very small part of Italian opera especially. Melody is not the only thing; it is very important, but to put the emphasis just on melody is not valid. When I read sometimes that melody is 'the most important element', the 'more intuitive gift', etc., etc., that's just baloney! [INTERVIEWER: But Messiaen said that, didn't he?] I know. I did not want to quote him, that's all. (Pierre Boulez)

ALL THESE COMPOSERS felt that this older music was no longer able to express the experience and life that they felt around them, that they were living. It was something that was part of the old time when there were crystal chandeliers and emperors and empresses and wonderful waltzes and beautiful costumes. Suddenly the twentieth century came in and an enormous number of new things began to happen in every field. Music was reacting that way as every other field did. The theory of relativity is a good deal less comfortable than Newtonian physics. (Elliott Carter)

Melodies with ancient roots

I WOULD IMAGINE in fact there were percussion instruments first, and then we have the voice, obviously, and these are the first musical expressions of mankind, and we share it with some other animals, only we do it differently. (Steve Reich)

QUITE RECENTLY IN RUSSIA, listening in a church there, I heard this melody which is part of a liturgy, and there it is at the beginning of *The Rite of Spring*. I don't believe for a minute that Stravinsky deliberately used it. I think folk music and church music are connected anyway. (John Tavener)

PLAINSONG HAS A SENSE of constant flow that remains within the particular style and the particular character that is established by the melody and it remains there and flows on, constantly developing new ideas out of this fundamental material. (Elliott Carter)

SINGING, UNACCOMPANIED SINGING, monody, is often amorphous. Above all, in plainchant, one of the most important sources of Western music, perhaps the most important, there's no regular pulse, and the rhythms from note to note are liquid. (George Benjamin)

MELODY CANNOT EXIST without rhythm, obviously. You can't have a melody without having some rhythmic shape to it, even if it's a liquid, flexible one like in Gregorian chant, which still has some movement in time. (Steve Reich)

THEN ALONG COMES a composer like Stravinsky, and he takes hold of this man-fabricated technique, as it were, and he can make something fantastically fresh and even traditional, with a capital T. In pieces like the *Canticum Sacrum*, in the *Surge, Aquilo* section for tenor and double-bass harmonics, harp and flute, there's a bit: if you just sang that to me I wouldn't be able to tell you that was Stravinsky. It could be a Byzantine chant. In a piece like *Abraham and Isaac*, there's something incredibly ancient about the vocal line, even though it's very difficult to sing. It's serial, but it sounds to me very like ancient Hebrew chant. But I don't believe Stravinsky made academic studies or even perhaps knew much of this music. (John Tavener)

. . . and exotic ones

'STRAVINSKY HAS NO SENSE OF MELODY, he just repeats four notes': that's true. But that's a different way of conceiving melody. For instance, in folk melodies, especially in the East, you have only four or five notes, mostly five, and these melodies are condensed and expanded. (Pierre Boulez)

I WAS BOWLED OVER BY – in love with – the voice of Sarah Vaughan, especially by some of her recordings of songs like 'Lover Man', above all, in a recording made at Tivoli. She made many recordings of it, but there's always an element of improvisation in jazz. Her voice had this extraordinary range and she had such an instinct for rhythmic freedom as well. She always chose her partners very well (a pianist and a double-bassist, for example), but on that day they were so inspired that in this interpretation the song equals the greatest passages of all music. (Henri Dutilleux)

IT'S PART OF A very, very rich Romanian musical culture, in a very small area in the northern Carpathians. They are called *Hora Lunga*. *Lunga* is like 'long', and it is always on descending patterns, and always certain repeating rhythmic melodic patterns, mostly in pure intonation. I applied this in my Viola Sonata, in the first movement called *Hora Lunga*. It's not folklore, but the idea. (György Ligeti)

A more flexible melody

WHY NOT, AS OPPOSED TO creating a strictly symmetrical poem, go for slightly irregular lengths of lines like you might find in Brahms, of five bars instead of four? Why not make it more developmental as it goes along, more like prose than poetry? Then there's also amorphous rhythm: a lot of music started from amorphous rhythm. The rhythm of our speech is amorphous: you can't find a pulse by which people speak. (George Benjamin)

SPEECH MELODIES ARE AN EXPRESSION of the whole state of the organism and all phases of spiritual activity which flow from it. They show us the fool and the wise one, morning and evening, light and darkness, scorching heat and frost, loneliness and company. The art of a dramatic composition is to make speech melodies which like magic convey the vitality of human beings. (Leoš Janáček)

Organic melody

I PUT THINGS TOGETHER very much like a body is put together. (I don't know: are we built up from the feet up or from the top down? I don't know!) But I think that a lot of young composers and a lot of professional musicians have a fantasy about how things are made in general. They have some kind of idea that things *became*, like an embryo, like a natural growth, so to speak, and the form and everything is handed down. (Morton Feldman, 1984)

Following or finding the tune

MY FATHER [WALTER GOEHR] used to tell a story that he was sitting in the Schoenberg composition class when Furtwängler phoned up the morning after the first performance of the Op. 31 *Orchestral Variations*, and Schoenberg apparently said, 'Mr Furtwängler, you are an experienced enough musician to know that the melody is not always in the first violins.' (Alexander Goehr)

IT WAS AGAINST ALL the sense of creativity to look at twelve tones all the time. You know, with these twelve tones you cannot write a melodic line which is very rich, because it will always go note to note to note to note to note. (Pierre Boulez)

THERE WERE SOME PERIODS in this century when melody was not only weak; it was, I could almost say, banned. In the post-Second World War atmosphere and in the Cold War period much talk was along the lines of: 'The past is evil'; 'This is Year Zero.' What's the obvious thing that defines all music of the past? Melody. So let's get rid of melody. Even to the point at which in a certain instrumental part within a texture you couldn't have two notes directly following each other. (George Benjamin)

I WAS JUST READING a letter Schoenberg wrote to Rufer, in which he said, 'Well, even if they don't understand the music no one talks about my beautiful form.' (Morton Feldman, 1984)

'MANTRA' IS THE NAME for a sound formula which I have used throughout the composition. This sound formula has four limbs. Now in the piece the first limb is combined with the mirror form of the second. But they are not only used in the original forms, but in many different transformations and expansions where the intervals are stretched over more space, melodically. (Karlheinz Stockhausen, 1971)

Melody and form

THERE ARE THINGS which are very simple but very effective. You use, for instance, a line for an instrument. Then you use just a transposed line, even exactly the same one, but you make a different rhythm, and then it's as though the lines are coinciding and not coinciding. Or you have a line which is very simple rhythmically, and you make the same line but with a lot of ornamentation, and then you have a kind of acoustical phenomenon like writing on wet paper, and the ink goes in all directions. It's very simple. (Pierre Boulez)

WE'VE BECOME USED TO TERMS such as 'tune' and above all 'theme' and 'motive'. In the past, the form of a piece of music would be their statement and then their development, combination, contrast. The perception of the form would be the recognition of these themes and of their manipulation across the structure of a piece. (George Benjamin)

SOME PIECES OF MINE, *Explosante-fixe* for instance, are built like a mosaic. So you have elements that are blue, elements that are red, elements that are green. The blue ones have one type of instrumental combination and are in a specific register. The red ones are at a very specific speed, with another instrumental colour and so on and so forth. And you have sections that are developed independently. And then I put them, not by chance of course, but to make contrasts and so on, and people can recognize the blue elements, the red elements, the green elements, but they will never know when they come, so you have an element of security because they recognize, but at the same time they are surprised because they don't know *when* they will recognize. Memory works retrospectively. When they say, 'Oh, I have heard that already', it's not exactly the same, but they remember. (Pierre Boulez)

Beginning, continuing and ending

IN MUSIC IT'S ESSENTIALLY one concept in Western civilization: beginning, middle and end. I got very into the best aspects of composers, and their handling of the problem of beginning, middle and end. I actually tabulated who was good for beginnings, who was good for ends. Varèse's beginnings are sensational. Nobody has a good middle, really. Stravinsky's endings are sensational. I think out of bore-dom. He wants to get out of it or something. (Morton Feldman, 1984)

WHERE THE PROBLEM COMES is in the continuation. The problem is how to complete a melody. I can begin you a dozen between now and one o'clock, no problem at all. The problem of ending a melody, or continuing, if you like, is to make it feel that it has made a journey in terms of itself. It's rather like continuing a sentence. You say some words and then you can say some other words, and you might ulti-mately come to something that sounds like a full stop, but it won't be a sentence unless the sentiments contained in the subject are realized in the predicate: it simply won't be a sentence. (Alexander Goehr)

I'LL TELL YOU HOW I worked as a kid. I was starting one of my piano pieces in the early 1950s, and everything was just too marvellous: you open up, you get that chord, you get that little two-note or three-note thing that can make a piece, but I wanted immediacy. You know, for teenagers in New York at that time, Kafka was very important, he was a big influence. I wanted an opening that was: 'Someone must have been telling lies about Joseph K.' I wanted that immediate opening, and there was always a set-up, a preparation. What I did was write six bars, seven bars, and then I found myself there: there was the begin-ning of the piece. In recent years, I've started with the codas of certain pieces, and I liked it very much. (Morton Feldman, 1984)

I WAS ALWAYS CONCERNED about the endings of my pieces, and I went through a phase of writing the endings first so that I would have them ready, and I could usually work up to the hour or so before the thing had to be sent to the copyist. I mean quite literally put the piece of paper on the end. (John Drinkwater)

YOU END WHEN you run out of time. To get away from the cliché of fade out or crash. (Julian Anderson)

YOU HAVE TO END EFFECTIVELY; you're as good as your ending. Most people, they don't remember too far behind the ending. (Morton Feldman, 1984)

Improvisation and freedom

WE ARE AT THE DAWN of a new era. For the first time an orchestra in the Western tradition is playing without a conductor, and it's playing a music that has not been determined in detail by another man.

Set sail for the sun. Play a sound for a long time, until you hear its individual vibrations. Listen to the sounds of the others, and slowly move your sound until you reach complete harmony and the whole sound becomes gold. (Karlheinz Stockhausen, 1971)

THIS WAS THE BIG MISTAKE with the improvisation groups that were the rage in 1968. You could see ahead of time what they would do, because, you know, it was very simplistic. I remember I tried a test with a man I know. I said 'I can tell you what will happen', and I was never wrong for the whole evening. That was the only interest of the evening!

Of course there was some excitement and so everybody just made more activity, more activity, louder, louder, louder. Then they were tired, so for two minutes you had calm, calm, calm, calm, calm. And then somebody was waking up so they began again, and then they were tired, sooner this time, and so the rest was longer. You cannot call that improvisation. That's absolutely the contrary of improvisation because you know very well that it will be up, down, up, down, up, down. (Pierre Boulez)

Setting words

BASICALLY MY EXPERIENCE with the human voice has been very different than traditionally was the case. The very first pieces of mine that came to public attention were taped pieces, recordings of people speaking, not singing. I actually did drive a cab, and recorded people in it, made a tape piece out of it which I bulk-erased, then I did the piece *It's Gonna Rain*, which really began the whole direction in which I've gone. It was recorded by a black Pentecostal preacher in Union Square, downtown San Francisco, in 1964; the piece was made in 1965.

You don't think of that as music, but after you hear the repetitions of the loop, that *da-da-dee* becomes as important as 'It's gonna rain'. It isn't that 'It's gonna rain' disappears; it stays there, and as a matter of fact the emotional tone of the piece is a very good setting of the words. I think the second half is such a good setting of the words that I was afraid to play it in public for a while. I thought it was just too grim.

Having done the tape pieces, lo and behold, in 1980 I got this idea: if I write a melody and set some words to it. Berio said to me he liked such and such a piece, and he said, 'It's syllabic', meaning that he was just fed up with melismas, you know? 'I just want to hear it the way it's said; can you deal with that reality?' (Steve Reich)

The melody of the future

I DON'T LIKE PEOPLE who abdicate, and say, 'Oh, there is no more to look for, there is no experiment to be done, everything has been done, and now we must put ourselves in a kind of historical perspective.' You have to go further, but go further where? That's very difficult to know. You can organize the next step for yourself, but that's all. (Pierre Boulez)

EVERY TIME I GET A LETTER from any young writer I always say, 'Get formal training. Find out what a leading note is, and why it's a leading note. Then you don't have to use it as a leading note, but you cannot abandon tools till you know what they're for.' (Stephen Sondheim)

NOW WE'RE NEARER THE END of this particular century rather than in the middle, I've found that it isn't possible to devise one way of writing new music which is pertinent and to the point. It's an absurd 1950s concept represented at that time most characteristically by Boulez; it really is a god that failed. I call it that because it's the title of a collection of essays, edited by Arthur Koestler, about Stalinism by ex-Stalinists. (Alexander Goehr)

IF YOU HAD ASKED ME fifty years ago where music would be in 1998 I would have told you maybe a nonsense: 'Everything will be organized, serialized and so on' – and it wasn't the case. At least experience makes you modest. (Pierre Boulez)

THE REASON I FIND I'm not peculiarly interested in what's going on in music is because I don't know where music's going any more at all. (Richard Rodney Bennett)

IN TERMS OF NEW MUSIC, perhaps there won't be any. It's very difficult to say what is going to happen in fifty years' time. I do think that if one looks at the history, the very unhopeful history of the twentieth century, I cannot help but believe, against my will and against my better judgement, that art is one of those very few phenomena which allow us to recondition ourselves, to recalibrate our spirits, such that we're not entirely deadened from day to day by this very mass of often superfluous and manipulatory information in what seems to me can be only a highly manipulatory and administered twenty-first century. (Brian Ferneyhough)

11 Music and the Movies

Imagine what the music world would have been without *film!*
LEONARD SLATKIN

UNTIL THE ARRIVAL of television, film was the most popular form of entertainment throughout the developed world. At the height of the medium's popularity there was scarcely a town of any size in Europe, America or Australasia without a cinema, and they soon spread to many parts of Asia and Africa as well. Although many countries developed their own film industries, cinema was from the beginning an international art. And from the beginning even silent films had music, provided often by a pianist (who was expected to improvise, perhaps using established 'classics' as a basis), not infrequently by at least a small orchestra or ensemble. The cinema soon developed its own specialist composers, but many composers from the concert hall were also drawn to it. For very many thousands of people the cinema was the place where they first heard 'serious' music. Because of the medium's vast audience, the music of, for example, Max Steiner (who wrote the scores for *Gone With the Wind*, *Casablanca*, *Now Voyager*, *The Big Sleep* and dozens of other popular films) is almost certainly more familiar to more people than the symphonies of Beethoven, and of those concert-hall composers who also wrote for the cinema many more people will have heard Sir William Walton's music for *Henry V*, *Hamlet* and *Richard III* than his works for the concert platform, the recital room or the opera house.

149

Some critics and composers have disparaged film music: Stravinsky did so (though only after repeated, unsuccessful attempts to obtain work from the Hollywood studios himself). Being a mass medium film needs to cultivate popularity, and many of the most popular films have been undemanding. Music is also, inevitably, a subsidiary art in film in a sense in which it never is in such other collaborative media as opera and ballet.

Nevertheless many composers, in collaboration with directors who have fully understood the power of harnessing visual and musical imagery together, have written scores of such high musical quality that the film would seem incomplete without them. Some are so well integrated with the visual images that the reverse is also true: Benjamin Britten's scores for the documentaries *Night Mail* and *Coalface* are little known, despite their distinction, because of this: they make their full impact only in a cinema, not in a concert hall or on record. Other scores, such as Prokofiev's for Feinzimmer's *Lieutenant Kijé*, Jacques Ibert's *Divertissement* (drawn from his music for René Clair's *Un Chapeau de Paille d'Italie*) or Virgil Thomson's for Pare Lorentz's *The Plow that Broke the Plains*, have achieved a concert-hall existence independent of the cinema. Film specialists would argue that the best film scores cannot be separated from the visual and verbal images for which they were written, and many scores by major composers are unknown to their admirers because the films for which they wrote have been forgotten or in some cases have not survived. Vaughan Williams 'recycled' much of the music that he wrote for Charles Frend's *Scott of the Antarctic* in his *Sinfonia Antartica*; the film itself is seldom seen. His scores for Michael Powell's *The 49th Parallel*, J. B. Holmes's *Coastal Command* or Jeffrey Dell's *Flemish Farm* remained unknown for many years, until concert suites from them were recorded.

The work of such skilled specialist composers as Max Steiner, Erich Wolfgang Korngold, Miklós Rózsa and (from a more recent generation) John Williams has been greatly valued by directors who have realized how much music can contribute to the impact and the emotional mood of a film. Examples of films that were modified to suit the music written for them are rare (one scene from Alexander Korda's *Things to Come*, directed by William Cameron Menzies, was shot to pre-composed music by Arthur Bliss, following a suggestion by the author of the film's screenplay, H. G. Wells), but the popular success even of a finely acted and expertly directed film has often been sealed by the music. As many people remember the theme music to *Gone With the Wind* as remember its most crucial lines.

The craft of composing for films is demanding. Except in very special cases the film will be shot before the composer sees it, and editing may not yet be complete. He will then have to write, very swiftly, music timed to the second and in accordance with the director's instructions. Some composers have regarded this as hack work, others as a valuable (and reasonably well-paid) discipline, some as a musical form that in ideal circumstances is in no way inferior to any other. Some indication of the appeal of the best or most evocative film music is given by the fact that concerts devoted to it have become popular, as have recordings of it, using either the original soundtrack or a new version in sound often superior to that of the original.

Works from the concert and operatic repertoire have quite often been used in films, in many cases introducing the music in question to a much larger audience than would otherwise have heard it. There has been a decline in the use of specially composed music in recent years, with many films relying instead on compilations of popular songs or dance numbers, while some more serious films have used no music at all save that which would be naturally present at the location. It is significant, though, that in a medium in which nostalgia plays a not unimportant part high-budget films are still more likely than not to have a specially composed score, normally for full orchestra, often with a 'theme tune' first heard over the opening credits and often more or less overtly referring to the romantic or melodramatic style of such composers as Steiner, Korngold or Rózsa.

The discipline

I WENT ONCE to a lecture where there was a very famous German philosopher and historian, Emil Ludwig. He said, 'Film music cannot be good because they say it has to be four minutes and twenty-two seconds. Now, how can you tell an artist to write for four minutes twenty-two seconds when his inspiration would take him to six minutes?' My answer is when Michelangelo came to do the ceiling of the Sistine Chapel he could have said to the Pope, Julius II, 'I would like to have two metres more.' And what is space for art is time for music. When you have to act for four minutes twenty-two seconds, you can arrange it. (Miklós Rózsa, 1984)

THE THING ABOUT WRITING film music is that you write it and you hear it immediately, or the next day. I think film music is a very essential part of any composer's technique: to be able to do something very quickly. And it's hit or miss, really; either good or bad, it's very good for you. (William Walton, 1972)

Art or journalism?

FILM MUSIC IS SIGNIFICANT, in many ways, of course, but not as music, which is why the proposition that better composers could produce better film music is not necessarily true: the standards of the category defeat higher standards. Still, I must express my respect for the craftsmanship of the many good musicians employed by the films, especially the arrangers, who are responsible for more than the word 'arranger' would seem to imply; in fact, it is said that in Hollywood Haydn would have been credited as the composer of the *Variations on a Theme by Haydn*, and Brahms as their 'arranger'. (Igor Stravinsky, 1959)

I THINK THE PREJUDICES about film music are really old hat – I can't believe that any serious critic can denigrate Shostakovich's film scores or Aaron Copland's. He's America's greatest composer; his two film scores for *The Red Pony* and *The Heiress* are absolute masterpieces; they could be ballet music. What's wrong with film? (Ken Russell)

I'VE DONE ABOUT SIX or seven films in all. I don't see why it isn't just as serious as the writing of stage music or the writing even of an operatic score. I don't see that the fact that so much run-of-the-mill film music has been written by run-of-the-mill professional composers who do nothing but film music should prejudice one's mind about the whole subject to such an extent that you'd be suspicious of any music written for any film. (Aaron Copland, 1971)

I THINK OF DOING film music as journalism. I happen to love it because I'm a great movie person. But it's journalism: one is using a very small part of one's creative ability, and it has to be done very fast. And it's a collaboration. I think composers find it difficult to accept that a lot of the time in film music they are just the servant of the film, and if you go in thinking you are going to write important music which everybody's going to listen to and admire, you're wrong. (Richard Rodney Bennett, 1974)

FILM AND TELEVISION MUSIC belongs in the market place. When you write for film, you are serving the product. Music is one element of a script, a script that will consist of spoken dialogue, sound effects, props, costumes, a style, camerawork, etc. Music is one of those ingredients. It does not exist on its own. (Carl Davis)

IT'S ALWAYS DIFFICULT to pit one musical form and genre against another, so to some degree the comparisons are not fair. It would be similar if you said, 'Who had a greater impact on the vocal art: Frank Sinatra or Dietrich Fischer-Dieskau?' Each impacted their own forms and their own audiences in their very separate and unique ways, and each was a great artist. If we took an example of Beethoven and compared him with Max Steiner, one could say that arguably each was a master in his own field; and to try to say that Beethoven might have been a lousy film composer, whereas Max Steiner might have written a lousy symphony, is just too speculative. I find criticism of that nature tends to want to lump all music into one pot, and you simply can't do it. Yes, it's all music, but there are so many different kinds of musics. And that's what's wonderful about the public these days: despite the fact that commercial interests such as motion pictures and recordings do dominate our society, they have allowed us to broaden our tastes. Imagine what the music world would have been *without* film, and one could see this century as having dissolved even further into some lower form of art! (Leonard Slatkin)

FILM MUSIC CAN BE real music. It depends how good it is and how well written. It is a very specific job. It is a craft: you have to learn how to make your creation, make your composition live inside very given circumstances. I think a sustained discussion of whether a composer who writes for film is a real composer or not is a spurious debate because it's a question of how much you invest in it, how gifted you are. Can you write good music for it? From my point of view a composer who writes only for film is someone who leads a limited musical life. (Carl Davis)

IT MIGHT BE INSTRUCTIVE to remember that one of the very first pieces of music for films was actually written by the French composer Camille Saint-Saëns [*L'Assassinat du Duc de Guise*, 1907], so there is certainly a tradition in history of great composers from one medium writing for another. I think that as the technology of films developed, more and more composers felt compelled at least to try a little bit to feel what it would be like. And certainly by the time we got to the 1930s and 1940s it was becoming apparent that film was going to be the operative medium of dramatic work, rather than the operatic or balletic stage, and indeed that has probably been borne out – in fact I believe it was John Williams who said that, for him, film was the opera of the second half of this century. (Leonard Slatkin)

A necessarily conservative art?

EDMUND MEISEL'S SCORE [for Eisenstein's *Battleship Potemkin*] is very interesting because it was a very contemporary score: it is very dissonant and difficult to listen to, which in the case of that film is actually very good – it really is quite gripping. Like Meisel with Eisenstein, Arthur Honegger had a very strong relationship with Abel Gance and worked on two films for him. The first was a film called *La Roue* (*The Wheel*), and then he followed that with writing and organizing music for *Napoleon*. Legend has it that he redeveloped the music he wrote for *The Wheel* to form a concert piece called *Pacific 231*, a very graphic depiction in the orchestra of a train starting up and gaining momentum and then coming to a halt. (Carl Davis)

DOUBLE INDEMNITY IS A VERY STRONG FILM, a very good film, still a classic, and Billy Wilder didn't like my music at all. He said, 'This is full of dissonances. This is not music for films; this is for Carnegie Hall.' This is the biggest swear word he could say. And I said, 'I take it as a compliment.' 'But I don't mean it,' he said. 'In one part you have an F♮ in the violins, and there is an F♯ in the violas. That's a dissonance. We hate dissonances.' I said, 'I don't. This is a dissonant film about dissonant people and the score will have dissonances.' (Miklós Rózsa, 1984)

WELL, SCHOENBERG WENT to Hollywood, and thought he'd try his hand at being a film composer, but he wouldn't compromise his aggressive, serial style, so he was a complete failure there. It wasn't until slightly later that serialism and atonality was accepted by Hollywood. Ironically it was in a Tom and Jerry cartoon called *The Cat Who Hated People*: that was the first time that serial music hit the cinema screen, in a score by Scott Bradley, who devoted his life to Tom and Jerry. Then it was used, later on in the 1950s, by Leonard Rosenman in a film called *The Cobweb*, set in a hospital and all about disordered brains. But I suppose the most famous use of it was in a horror film made in England by Hammer Films, when Benjamin Frankel scored the 1961 *The Curse of the Werewolf* with Oliver Reed. That was an interesting use of a serial film score, because it was a bit like how Alban Berg used his note-rows. What Frankel did was to take a note-row that has tonal implications – softening the blow – so he was able to have a serial style, which fitted in with the horror of the picture, and it was also usable for the more romantic parts. And he mixed it with tonal music as well. So serialism, which Schoenberg tried to bring into the cinema, eventually made it, and it was in horror films in England,

and in a comedy film in America, that it first made its big impact. (David Huckvale)

IT's FUN IN FILMS to be able to use orchestras which you wouldn't actually use in the concert hall because they'd be impractical. There was a film I did called *Billion Dollar Brain*, in the late 1960s, and in that I used an orchestra of three pianos, eleven brass, four percussion and ondes martenot (a beautiful electronic instrument which I've used a lot), just to get a very hard, almost an inhuman sound which was in keeping with the film. And of course in the concert hall you couldn't usefully write for three pianos and eleven brass, because it wouldn't get played. But it was nice in the context of the film.

I started writing movies in the mid-1950s and it was a time when I think the old traditions of film music – the symphonic 1930s/1940s style – were starting to fade, and styles of film-making and acting were changing, and similarly styles of music were changing. And I remember between when I was about sixteen and eighteen I heard some very important film scores – for example, *A Streetcar Named Desire* by Alex North, *On the Waterfront* by Leonard Bernstein, and particularly *East of Eden* by Leonard Rosenman, and they were all scores where there was some awareness shown in the music of what was going on in contemporary music. Not bang-up-to-the-minute avant-garde music, but it sounded as though the composers had heard Bartók and Berg and Stravinsky, as opposed to just Rakhmaninov and Tchaikovsky and Debussy, which was the tradition in film music earlier. (Richard Rodney Bennett, 1986)

The silent-film pianist

IN ONE INSTANCE a great composer started off as a silent-film pianist, and that's Shostakovich, who worked in a cinema during his teens. But he was actually fired for laughing. He was playing for a comedy (I believe it was a Buster Keaton comedy) and evidently was laughing so much that he couldn't play any more and the management just wouldn't accept that and kicked him out. (Neil Brand)

'HERE's A CHORD you can't do without,' he said, 'if you're a picture-palace piano-player. You use it for fights, burst dams, thunderstorms, the voice of the Lord God, a wife telling her old man to bugger off out of the house and not come back never no more.' And he showed me: G, E♭, G♭, A♭. 'Always the same like dangerous sound,' he said, 'as if something terrible's going to happen: soft for "going to happen", loud for "happening". And you can play whole strings of these chords, each one based on a different white or black note at the bottom. And you can arpeggio them to make them like very mysterious. Here's just one more chord,' he said, 'very, very mysterious. I see the buggers are starting to come in, so I'll have to show you quick. It's this one: C, E, G♯. Make it on any note. Good for ghost music, *Frankenstein*, that sort of thing.' (Anthony Burgess, from *The Piano Player*, 1987)

GIUSEPPE BECCE'S CATALOGUE, *Kinobibliothek*, made in Berlin in 1919, became extremely well used throughout Germany, and there were others throughout the world, which were available to piano players and gave them indications of the kind of music they could actually use. This assumed that they couldn't improvise, so they had to have the sheet music in front of them. For instance, they have 'Dramatic Expression, Main Concept' – in other words this is assuming you have a main theme going right the way through the whole film. They give you '1: Climax, Catastrophe' and then after that, in brackets, subdivisions, so there are subdivisions of catastrophe (whether it's a better or worse catastrophe, so it would seem!) – 'Highly Dramatic, *Agitato*', 'Solemn Atmosphere', 'Mysteriousness of Nature'. Now these are three different pieces all coming under the heading of 'Climax'. (Neil Brand)

I SUPPOSE IN THOSE DAYS the themes from opera, ballet, concert hall, were very strong indeed. There are many, many letters, when you look back on the old magazines like the *Picturegoer* and *Cinema Weekly*, *Picturegoer Weekly*, *Picture Show*, over and over again in the 1920s you get letters from people saying, 'We have a lovely pianist and he's played so many interesting things I've never heard of before, and the other night he played a thing from something called *Aida*, and he played it against a scene from an old Cecil B. de Mille silent movie, I think it was *Ten Commandments* or something.' Over and over again you get these letters with people responding to it. (John Huntley)

THEY WEREN'T PRODUCING film music, as we would think of it. They were producing normally a series of tunes which would be quite well known, probably, but audiences didn't expect a seamless and original piece of music for every film they saw. They expected, I think, to be pleasured by music in a kind of palm-court-orchestra way. It was enough to have a link with what was happening on screen but it didn't have to support it or be part of an organic process, which we would now expect from modern film music. Of course I'm thinking about American audiences now – American audiences wouldn't go to the opera before the mid-1920s and they wouldn't have had a radio. And so to hear music of this standard they would have gone to their cinema. But they wouldn't have gone for the music; they would have gone for the film. (Neil Brand)

The silent-film orchestra

FOR YEARS AND YEARS I don't think any of us really understood the impact of silent films. We saw awful 16 mm. copies of *The Cabinet of Dr Caligari* and *Birth of a Nation* in our film societies. Then one day we saw *Napoleon*, a film that went on for eight hours, with Carl Davis and a fifty-piece orchestra and it was utter magic. You suddenly realized that when you had got a really good orchestra in the pit and a big West End cinema and a silent film on the screen – and very often you had a kind of overture, a prelude and all the rest of it – there must have been an enormous amount of music communication going on. (John Huntley)

I ACTUALLY HAD NO IDEA how I would approach creating a score that would have so much music. It was really like writing a Wagner opera quickly. What I did – which was something that the composers of the time did themselves, because they also had very little time – was to provide a mixture of existing music with things that one couldn't find and so I created. I decided I would make the music I found or chose to be reflective of Napoleon's own story and Napoleon's own time, using the composers who were contemporary with Napoleon: Haydn, Mozart, Beethoven. (Carl Davis)

The Hollywood style

BECAUSE THE LEVEL OF THE PLAYERS in the Hollywood orchestras was so stupendous – each orchestra, literally, could hold its own with any concert orchestra in the United States at the time – I believe that's what accounted for the sound: the composers tried to take advantage of these extraordinary musicians. Plus which, many of the composers of the time had come from both Central and other European back-grounds, so their tradition and training would have been in roughly the Elgar–Richard Strauss mould. They knew the sound of the lush orchestra and brought it to their film scores. (Leonard Slatkin)

THERE WAS A KIND of well-known film-music style: it was applied almost without regard to the subject matter. It didn't matter whether the plot happened in the fourteenth century or the twentieth century; it got more or less the same kind of musical treatment – a large fat sound, very lush usually, fully orchestrated and known as 'Hollywood film music'. And having been given this simple story [The Red Pony] that took place in the Far West, I naturally tried to reflect the scenes that one saw on the screen with music that somehow was related to those scenes and only those scenes, and couldn't have been applied to a Russian story or a French story – which was thought of in those days as being rather revolutionary. (Aaron Copland, 1971)

I'M NOT EVEN CERTAIN that I'd call them particularly great scores in relationship to what they were trying to accomplish in the films. In some cases the films weren't particularly good. John Steinbeck himself thought that the film version of The Red Pony was just not very good at all, but the score in many ways has outlived the film. That's probably not a good thing. The ideal film score is one where the music is just part of the overall texture. (Leonard Slatkin)

Erich Wolfgang Korngold

ERICH WOLFGANG KORNGOLD was the first composer to write for films who received fan mail. King's Row, I understand, according to the studio files, resulted in him getting many, many thousands of letters from people asking for a recording of the score. They were unable to supply a recording so what was produced was a one-page written-out musical realization of the main theme which he autographed and then sent off.

A score like King's Row becomes almost like a cinematic Ein Heldenleben, and the music is of such quality that it stands up every single time as a piece of absolute music, without the pictures and often the cardboard events on screen which it was meant to support. He never compromised: if you look at a score like King's Row or The Seahawk, there is so much going on in the orchestra, so many counter-melodies and embellishments that could never be heard on the mon-aural soundtrack with everything else that was going on, like dialogue, sound effects and so on. One wonders, now, why did he do it? I think the answer has to be that one day he hoped that this music would be rescued and performed as concert music.

William Walton, writing for Laurence Olivier's Shakespeare trilogy, is a totally different kettle of fish to Korngold writing for a film like The Seahawk, which is popular, escapist entertainment, wonderful though it is. I would really be hard pressed to look at any of the films Korngold composed for and say they are in the pantheon of great cinematic masterpieces. They are very fine films, some of them. Robin

Hood is probably the best version that's ever been made of that story, but it's a children's adventure story and it's enormously successful popular entertainment. Whereas Walton was writing for *Henry V*, Arnold Bax was writing for David Lean's *Oliver Twist*, Ralph Vaughan Williams was writing for *Scott of the Antarctic*. These are somehow more sophisticated art-house films which are appropriate for these composers to be involved with.

Korngold's use of film themes in his concert works was not immediately apparent to an audience going to hear, say, the Violin Concerto. The original programme booklet for the première of the Violin Concerto makes no mention of the films from which these themes came, nor for that matter do the critics of that time say, 'Oh well, we heard that theme in *Juarez*', or 'We heard that theme in *Another Dawn*', because those films were not in circulation any more. They hadn't been seen for some years – in fact over ten years. I think the main criticism of a piece like the Violin Concerto was that it sounded very much like Korngold! And Korngold of course had become the yardstick of musical style in films. It was only in the 1970s and 1980s when far more knowledgeable people detected or recognized where these themes came from that suddenly critics were able to say that it was a 'film concerto'. In actual fact Korngold's Violin Concerto was composed in draft before these films were ever thought of. (Brendan Carroll)

Concert-hall composers in the film studio

IT WAS IMPOSSIBLE in the early days of sound to record music separately: it had to be done live on the sound stage. Once they had finally sorted out the problem of multiple tracking in the 1930s, there was the immediate appeal of being able to put music to films, the whole new challenge of being able to write music that was absolute music for the screen, rather as composers in the nineteenth century would have written incidental music for the stage. (Brendan Carroll)

LOUIS LEVY DID THE HONEGGER SCORE for *Pygmalion*. And I might add that Louis Levy was quite a rough 'erb in his own way; he wasn't a very posh gentleman. I always remember recording sessions with Honegger doing the score for *Major Barbara* and he was very particular. He wanted everything absolutely right about the score and he kept rehearsing and going back with the orchestra. And in the end poor Louis Levy couldn't take this any more. He came up on the loudspeaker saying, ''Onegger, tell 'em to play it faster or play it slower, but for God's sake get on with it!'

It was Louis Levy who got them to make the film of Paganini's life, *The Magic Bow*, with Stewart Grainger in the part of Paganini – not a total success, but what a way to introduce people to the music of Paganini! And quite a number of the films like that, made at Gaumont–British, were the result of Louis Levy saying, 'Hey, why don't we not only use the music of Paganini; why don't we make a story about his life one day?' – which is precisely what they did. (John Huntley)

ALEXANDER KORDA, IN HIS HEYDAY or even when he started, would employ only the greatest painters, the greatest make-up people, the greatest everything he wanted. They all had to be absolutely top people in their jobs. And so I said to him, 'Well, you're hiring all these wonderful artists; in the music side we must be able to have the finest composers.' But he said, 'Well, X' – my predecessor as his music director – '*he* wrote the music as well as conducted it.' And I said, 'Yes, and you've just fired him, haven't you?' So I said, 'I will take on the job as music director only if you will give me the greatest composers.' (Muir Mathieson, 1971)

I THINK IN WRITING for the films I was tempted first by the excitement of the new medium. I'd written music for the opera stage, for ballet, concert hall, recorders, chamber music, soloists, brass bands – the only medium I hadn't tried was the film and that was a great incentive to me, to see what the problems were. And the second thing about writing music for the film is that I find it a very good discipline for a composer. To begin with, he has to use the blue pencil, which he might do with a great deal of advantage sometimes in the concert hall. You have a timed sequence lasting three and a half minutes; you write music which you think fits the scene like a glove; a cutter comes in and cuts it down to forty-five seconds. You have got to get in those forty-five seconds exactly the same punch as you did in the three and a half minutes, and that is a discipline. (Arthur Bliss, 1964)

VAUGHAN WILLIAMS APPROACHED *me*, actually, through my piano professor at college. He wanted to write a Cowboy-and-Indian sort of film score, but as I pointed out we didn't make Cowboys-and-Indians in this country. So he settled for *The 49th Parallel*, which was at least set in the Americas. (Muir Mathieson, 1971)

MUIR HAD BEEN TRYING to talk to Vaughan Williams about this for a long while but not really getting anywhere, and he went down to Dorking, Vaughan Williams's home, and he found the chap in a rather sort of sad position. He felt that composers were not making much of a contribution to the war effort. He himself at that time was going round with a little wooden handcart collecting scrap iron from his neighbours for the War Office to build Spitfires. Muir said, 'I think we can do something better than that. Come and have a look at this film and do the music for it.' Vaughan Williams, I suppose, looking back on it, was most impressive, really. He accepted the whole thing as a challenge. He was nearly seventy, but he seemed like somebody aged twenty. He came to the studios. He just wanted to know what it was all about, wanted to learn, wanted to know how to do it. (John Huntley)

[VAUGHAN WILLIAMS] SAID THAT FILMS had a possibility of a dramatic cohesion of all the arts that even Wagner had never dreamed of. His famous line was: 'If you write music for films you must be prepared to have your head cut off, your tail cut off, even your entrails taken out, and you still must make musical sense.' (Muir Mathieson, 1971)

VAUGHAN WILLIAMS GRADUALLY EVOLVED a particular approach to the movies. He liked to have the script right from the beginning, and he liked to write the outline of the sketches of the music before the filming in some cases had even begun. Now the other chaps, the professionals particularly, nearly always wrote when the film was finished and they timed it and they measured their music against the finished film. Vaughan Williams would pick up a theme; in, say, *Scott of the Antarctic* he evolved this rather marvellous sound of an echoing voice to represent the iciness and the barrenness and the emptiness of the Antarctic. He wrote quite a substantial piece for this, and when he brought it to the studio everybody was horrified, and said, 'This is far too long – can't possibly do that – this is the opening bit of the film. And these scenes of the Antarctic are boring anyway, you know; those endless shots of ice floes and all the rest of it.' Then they tried it with Vaughan Williams's music, and it worked like a dream. And the result of that was that Charles Frend, the director of the film, said, 'Get every out-take you can find of the Antarctic and open it up, and lengthen it, to fit the music.' That was very unusual. In that case the actual film-makers were so impressed by what Vaughan Williams had done that they re-edited and cut the film to fit his score. (John Huntley)

The 'Warsaw' and other concertos

WHAT WE REALLY NEEDED [for the 1941 film *Dangerous Moonlight*] was a miniature concerto of exactly seven minutes which included an introduction, a first tune and a second tune (or a first subject and a second subject), the feeling of cadenzas and a very, very exciting ending, so that the whole thing [by Richard Addinsell] was a potted concerto in a way. But I think it was an absolutely magnificently conceived potted concerto. (Muir Mathieson, 1971)

IT IS IN A SENSE of course a pastiche of Rakhmaninov, but also there are elements in it of the Grieg Piano Concerto, for that matter. Do you know, it never even had a name when it came to the studio? When I first heard it, I knew the 'Warsaw' Concerto only as '3M4' – that's reel 3, music, section 4. It had no other name at all except that. Louis Kentner, who came to play the piece, said, 'Under no circumstances does my name appear on the screen or any subsequent use of the music at all. But I'll do it for you because the money's good.' The film went on at the old Odeon, Marble Arch, and what happened was that people came out of the cinema and went up to the cinema manager and said, 'What's that extraordinary, wonderful piece of music in it?' The manager hadn't actually seen the film then, so he nipped into the cinema and said, 'Oh, it's all about Warsaw. Tell 'em it's the "Warsaw" Concerto.' And that's how it got its name. Columbia Records wanted very much to issue it because it was obviously going to be very popular indeed, so they rushed down to the studios and we pulled off the shelf 3M4. Now by accident we pulled off the shelf an NG take, a 'no-good' take in other words, which had a 'wow' in it; we didn't even notice at the time. Columbia rushed away; they translated the soundtrack (of course of the music only, without the dialogue and the speech and sound effects) and they put it out as a twelve-inch Columbia record. If you listen to it very carefully, it's a rather poor piece of recording, and the fact that it's got a slight 'wow' in it if anything adds to the romantic feel of the whole thing. It just went romping home. In the end no NAAFI pianist in any camp in the British Army or Air Force or for that matter any part of the services during the Second World War could sit down at piano without being asked for the 'Warsaw' Concerto. In a sense, I suppose, it worked quite well, because they weren't the sort of people who in a million years would have listened to a Rakhmaninov or a Grieg piano concerto, but now they were hearing something a bit like it and – who knows? – when they actually heard a Rakhmaninov or a Grieg piano concerto, perhaps it meant a bit more to them. (John Huntley)

I THINK THE FIRST FILM that turned vast audiences on to classical music, myself included, was *Brief Encounter*, which had Sergey Rakhmaninov's Second Piano Concerto as its theme. That spawned a whole host of mini piano concertos that jumped on the bandwagon, as it were: *Dream of Olwen*, Cornish Rhapsody, *The Night Has Eyes*, and the 'Warsaw' Concerto. They were all mini concertos, and I think that they did expose people to the orchestra and the sort of themes and rhythms and the bravura use of the piano, the almost Lisztian use of the piano, and it did turn a great number of people on to classical music, without doubt. (Ken Russell)

THAT HAS ALWAYS BEEN my argument against using music that's known, because if you suddenly bring in one of the standard classics at a highly emotional moment, somebody is bound to say, 'What's that music? I know that', and the moment of tension has gone. That's why I've always maintained that it's much, much better to have a score specially written for a film. There are occasions, of course, when you can use [a standard classic], so long as you establish that that is what the work is. (Muir Mathieson, 1971)

WHAT ABOUT ALL THOSE FILMS where other pieces of music were used? Kubrick's *2001* did have an original score but they ran out of money and they couldn't use the music. That was how they came to borrow Strauss and the works of Ligeti. All these things add more fuel for people who are critics, of course, saying, 'Well, if you can make a film without an original score: horrible, the whole form's being ruined!' On the other hand it shows the incredible diversity and the broad range that a film can inspire from the people who have to create the music. I find it perhaps the most open and honest category for the composer and creator. (Leonard Slatkin)

'Film composer': a stigma?

MANY COMPOSERS WENT into film music and virtually destroyed their concert-hall career in doing it. William Alwyn certainly did that; Benjamin Frankel did that. It's only recently that the concert works of Alwyn and Frankel have even begun to get any kind of recognition. But, you see, in their day, 'Oh, he's a film composer. Oh, we don't want him in the programme. He writes for the movies, you know, writes for the flicks' – this was very much an attitude. So some of the composers had to make a very conscious decision: make the money out of the movies; write what you like for the concert hall, but don't expect anybody to listen to it, because once you're stamped as a movie composer the concert-hall world will not want to know you. (John Huntley)

WHEN I FIRST STARTED researching Korngold the very term 'film composer' was the greatest insult one could level. I think as time has gone on it's slowly but surely become apparent – even to the most staid music critic – that writing music that is valuable for the screen does have a place in this century's musical tradition. Film music is tainted, I suspect, because of where it is created. Film music is created in a place called Hollywood, which is always regarded, even now, as some kind of downmarket feeder of people's dreams. Films that came out of Hollywood were never as highly regarded as those that came from Europe. If Korngold, for example, had written music for the German cinema, which he nearly did, he would be regarded as one of the great pioneers who had worked with the great directors, because German cinema was art cinema, whereas Hollywood was fuelling popular taste and popular culture and never really tried that hard to raise itself above that. The films that were made in the 1930s and 1940s were fairly simplistic; they were not great literary masterpieces. Technically they were fantastic, but they're never going to be intellectually challenging. (Brendan Carroll)

Titanic *and after*

DURING THE TIME of the contract studios in Hollywood, each composer turned out maybe two films a year. In the case, say, of Miklós Rózsa, when he was writing *El Cid* he had six months to research the music and prepare the score appropriately. These days it's very much more a commercial venture, in the sense of how much product can be put out. Composers in many cases don't have to write quite so much music as they did, because they're having the assistance of pop singles to add to it, using other sources. All you have to do is watch pretty much any film and see the end credits and the interminable list of songs that comes on. To me that doesn't smack so much of originality as . . . well, it's less music for the composer to write. It'll be interesting to see, as the next century develops, how these composers impact and affect our listening habits. I still believe that memorable film scores tend to be ones that harken back to the traditions of the 1930s and 1940s. So when we look at a film like *Titanic* – and whether we like the film or whether we like the film score is completely incidental in this case – what we see here is that this was the most successful of all the film scores of its year, certainly, and it's very much in the tradition of the great film scores of earlier years. And if you look back at the film scores that seem to achieve the most success, you'll find that element is running almost throughout.

When we see programmes devoted to music from films, or with suites or extractions of film music in a concert programme, some people raise red flags. They don't like it; they think it's a bastardization of the sacred nature of the concert hall. Maybe it's our fault, maybe we've made the concert hall some bastion of culture that needs to expand a bit. It's all music, and I think to deny film a place in the concert hall would be the same as denying excerpts from opera or ballet – things that appeal immediately and were inspired for and created for other mediums. So film music certainly has a very distinguished place in the concert hall. I find that in many cases if you place it alongside existing concert works, that these scores, when they are of high quality, stand up well and don't even invite comparison. They are simply wonderful pieces of music that need to be listened to. And maybe the great beauty about a film score for an audience member in a concert setting is they have two choices: they can reflect on the film, if they've seen it, and recall the wonderful visual moments that the director and artists have presented, or they can do the more intriguing thing – that's create their very own film. (Leonard Slatkin)

A VERY STARK OR very powerful image is the same to anyone, all over the world. It's a universal language. Whereas music isn't universal at all, I think. But giving people pictures helps. I know that for a fact because of the Elgar film I did, which was seen by millions and shown many times, and people have come up to me and said, 'Oh, you're the man who made the film of the boy on the white horse.' And that was an image they could grasp hold of. You know, I think if they didn't have that image people wouldn't have latched on to it, but once on to it they had that in their mind and then every time they hear the music they get to know it more and more. And that's the thing about classical music, you know – repetition brings more understanding and more love for the music. (Ken Russell)

12 Music and the Marvellous

*The music is fantastically rich . . . At last I'm beginning to catch on
to the technique, but it's about as complicated as Schoenberg.*
BENJAMIN BRITTEN, BALI, 1956

WORKS OF ART AND CRAFT can readily be exported, but for music to pass frontiers it must either be written down or printed, or musicians themselves must travel long distances, taking their music to far-off lands or studying the mostly unnotated music of other civilizations. Thus Europe was familiar with Chinese porcelain and silk, Indian metalwork and Japanese lacquer long before it knew anything of the music of those countries. Sir Francis Drake and his companions heard Javanese 'country music' in the sixteenth century but it is impossible from their brief description of it to know what it sounded like or whether it in any way resembled the gamelan music of present-day Java. Exotic settings were often chosen for operas and masques from the seventeenth century onwards, but the 'Chinese Man' and 'Chinese Woman' who dance in Purcell's *The Fairy Queen* do so to characteristically Purcellian music. The four acts of Rameau's *Les Indes galantes* are set respectively in Turkey, Peru, Persia and North America, but no attempt is made to distinguish them musically.

The military music of Turkey was known in seventeenth- and eighteenth-century Europe because the expanding Ottoman Empire had mounted repeated forays westwards, at one point laying siege to Vienna. The advance was repelled but left behind it, along with a taste for coffee, the memory of 'Janissary music', which was imitated by composers by using cymbals, triangle, bass drum and piccolo. An assemblage of bells hanging from a crescent mounted on a staff remained for many years an instrument in military bands, known as a 'Turkish crescent' or 'Jingling Johnny'. It is perhaps indicative of Western ignorance of Eastern music that it is known in French as the *pavillon Chinois*.

Although Britain, France and other European powers had colonial territories in Africa and Asia, and although missionaries and others published occasional scholarly accounts of Asian music as early as the eighteenth century, opportunities for Westerners to hear non-Western music remained very rare until the invention of recording and the development of rapid international transport. Even in the nineteenth century, when opera, ballet and song began to reflect a growing interest in the exotic among painters and writers, musicians were as a rule content to evoke the Orient with the most generalized means. Léo Delibes's popular opera *Lakmé* is set in India, but contains no trace of genuine Indian music. The exoticism of Camille Saint-Saëns's *Samson et Dalila* is due largely to the use of sinuous melodies featuring an interval (the augmented second) that finds no place in the major or minor scales; Verdi used the same device to evoke ancient Egypt in *Aida*. Non-Western music was widely thought of as 'primitive', and was little studied in Europe until the twentieth century. It is paradoxical but perhaps significant that one of the first scholars to make a detailed study of Eastern scales, Alexander Ellis, was drawn to the subject not out of attraction to non-Western music (he was tone-deaf) but as an extension of his professional interest in phonetics and mathematics.

The development of transport enabled Western musicians to travel more widely (Saint-Saëns became aware that non-European peoples had scales other than those used in the West on his frequent holidays in Algeria and Egypt) and Eastern musicians to visit the West. At the Exposition Universelle, held in Paris in 1889 to celebrate the centenary of the French Revolution, foreign nations were invited to exhibit their wares and cultures. Among the pavilions clustered on the Champs de Mars around the Eiffel Tower, which had been built as the exhibition's centrepiece, were a Javanese *kampong* or village, featuring a company of dancers and a gamelan orchestra consisting of gongs, bells, drums and metallophones, with only a single stringed instrument. Near by was a booth housing a travelling theatre company from Indo-China in which semi-improvised plays were performed to the accompaniment of instruments equally strange to European eyes and ears. Both orchestras were tuned to scales unfamiliar to a classically trained Westerner; both produced music that seemed to have quite different objectives to the music of the West. Among the visitors to these two pavilions were many composers – Erik Satie, Emmanuel Chabrier, Nikolay Rimsky-Korsakov – including the fourteen-year-old Maurice Ravel and, obsessively returning day after day, his senior by thirteen years, Claude Debussy.

Even those, like Gustav Mahler, who did not visit such exhibitions or travel to far-off countries themselves could become aware of non-European music through the new medium of recording. Travellers brought back firstly phonograph cylinders, then gramophone discs, and later tape-recordings of music from all over the world. Folk-music collectors used these new media, which facilitated the close study and notation of the melodies that they collected. This wide variety of means by which Western musicians became aware of non-Western music is paralleled by the variety of ways in which they made use of that awareness. At the turn of the century and in the wake of Wagner many composers felt that the musical culture of Europe needed renewal. For Debussy, already dissatisfied and frustrated by the rule-bound rigidity of his conventional musical education, Asian music demon-strated that other paths were possible and confirmed him in his continuing search for them. For Ravel, the music of the East was more of a captivating magic garden. Later, Olivier Messiaen, learning about Indian rhythms from textbooks – he was especially fascinated by palindromic rhythms – and about the gamelan from direct experience, used both as elements in a musical language that was also enriched by detailed study of other non-Western musics, birdsong and the modes used in plainchant.

None of these composers merely imitated non-Western music; they found in it resources and techniques that answered to their needs, and absorbed those elements into their own language. Benjamin Britten was introduced to Balinese music indirectly, by meeting the Canadian composer Colin McPhee who had lived for some while in Bali and had transcribed some pieces of gamelan music for two pianos. Britten seems to have been initially unimpressed, but he played through the transcriptions with McPhee and they made commercial recordings of some of them. Aspects of gamelan technique soon began to be heard in Britten's own music, and his first direct experience of it, on a tour of the Far East in 1956, had a profound impact on the style of his later music. Not long after his visit to Bali he experienced the Nō plays and the court music (*Gagaku*) of Japan, and these too affected not only his musical style but prompted him to create a new form of ritualized music theatre in his church parables, the first of which is directly based on the plot of a Nō play.

As has already been mentioned in chapter 8, Western music until the twentieth century tended to underdevelop rhythmic complexity because of its concentration on tonal, harmonic and contrapuntal richness. For the same reason percussion instruments were relatively neglected: the classical orchestra used only two or three timpani, with occasional resort as the nineteenth century proceeded to bass drum, side drum, cymbals and triangle. A greater knowledge of non-European music has assisted the development of rhythm and has contributed greatly to the far more important role given by modern composers to the percussion section of the orchestra. The influence of the gamelan is perceptible in Ravel's music for conventional Western instruments; it became clearly audible when, for the first time in Western concert music, Messiaen used a vibraphone (rather close in sound to the Balinese *jegogan*) in his *Trois petites liturgies de la Présence Divine* in 1945; it was directly imitated in 1957 when Britten, in his ballet *The Prince of the Pagodas*, used authentic Balinese melodies played by a 'gamelan' ensemble within the orchestra made up of vibraphone, xylophone, celesta, two pianos and gongs. In a similar way but to quite different effect Pierre Boulez in *Le marteau sans maître* (1955) used a small ensemble of Western instruments chosen for their kinships with instruments from a variety of non-European cultures, the guitar 'representing' the Japanese *koto*, the vibraphone the Balinese *gender* and the xylophone the West African *bala*. His aim was 'to enrich the European sound vocabulary by means of non-European listening habits'. György Ligeti, fascinatedly discovering that the African *mbira* or 'thumb-piano' (a resonating box fitted with tuned steel tongues) has its lowest note at the centre with the others radiating from it, tried to imagine a piano tuned in that way.

Just as composers at the beginning of the twentieth century sought new directions, and some found them through discovering the alternative paths pointed by a study of Eastern music, so many composers in the latter half of the century have rejected what they see as doctrinaire modernism. Some of them, too, have found inspiration in non-Western musics, whether experiencing it directly or finding in it a confirmation of what they were already trying to do. But by the latter years of the twentieth century, with symphony orchestras playing the Western repertoire flourishing in Japan, Korea and elsewhere and with Asian countries producing some of the world's best-known exponents of that repertoire, a composer such as the Japanese Toru Takemitsu found himself inhabiting both worlds. Trained in the European tradition in a country that had gone a long way towards accepting that tradition as its own, he rediscovered Japanese musical culture in a number of works that combine Japanese and Western instruments. Later still he abandoned these attempts at 'blending', as he called it, but continued to welcome influences from many disparate sources and cultures.

At the beginning of the century (1901–5) the scholarly and influential *Oxford History of Music* concerned itself solely with Western music since 1300. Its second edition (1929–38) added a supplementary volume surveying the Middle Ages and antiquity. Not until the book was completely rewritten, as the *New Oxford History of Music* (1957), was any attention paid to Eastern music, though even then the word 'Africa' did not appear even in the index. By the end of the century there is a general realization that Western classical music is only one of a rich and wide variety of musical traditions, and it seems likely that that realization will continue to affect composers and audiences profoundly. The world has become a smaller place, but there is a strong possibility of it becoming culturally richer as a consequence.

*

'Very strange . . .yet pleasant and delightful'

ON THE MORNING of the 9th of March 1580 we espied land; and bearing farther north, and nearer shore, we came to the island Java.

The 13th of March, our general himself, with many of his gentlemen and others, went to shore and presented the king (of whom he was joyfully and lovingly received) with his music.

On 21st March, the king coming aboard us, in requital of our music which was made to him, presented our general with his country music, which though it were of a very strange kind, yet the sound was pleasant and delightful. (Logbook of the *Golden Hind*)

But the twain do not meet

THE ONLY WAY THE EAST had infiltrated, it seems to me, prior to the nineteenth century, was in the use of Turkish music, a sort of exoticism which you would find in the opera house, as in Mozart's *The Abduction from the Seraglio* and to a certain extent *The Magic Flute*. You find changes in mode, a specific sort of tempo, changes in orchestration, use of the piccolo and percussion . . . (George Benjamin)

YOU COULD SEE IT most easily in literature and painting, where, for example, the rendering of scenes from what is supposed to be the

Orient really follows a set of quite predictable patterns. They become stereotypes – the palm trees, the robed figures – who seem exotic, sometimes violent, obviously distant. And visual representations like the paintings, for example, of Delacroix: a lot of dash and cruelty and colour and tremendous emphasis on the Oriental female, who's almost always a slave or a concubine or a dancer or something of that sort. This Orient is really an object of European consumption: it's something to be looked at; it's supposed to be exotic; it's something that you don't really enter and feel the life of it. (Edward Said)

IT REALLY BEGINS to take off halfway through the nineteenth century in France. There's a very strong tradition of Orientalist stage works, with composers such as Bizet (*The Pearl Fishers*, of course), and even Saint-Saëns, the arch conservative, dabbled with Arab scales and all sorts of exotic things, and in the late 1870s was getting rather alarmed that there would be so much coming in from the Far East that tonality would disintegrate altogether, and Delibes's *Lakmé*, which Debussy dismissed as sham Oriental bric-à-brac. (Mervyn Cooke)

IN *AIDA* VERDI TRIES to give a sense of verisimilitude with regard to the Orient; there the Orient is not associated so much with the male characters as with the female characters. Take, for example, in the second scene of the first act, the chorus of the priestesses of Ptha, with the harp and the cymbals. He saw pictures, partly due to the Egyptologist Mariette, of what people in the Orient played: certain kinds of flutes, certain kinds of harps, a particular sound. (Edward Said)

Ellis's step forward

THE BIG LESSON of Alexander Ellis is his discovery that other cultures have different scales which do not conform to our notions of what a scale should be, and certainly not to what we might consider the natural laws of sound and tonal organization. Saying that they are accepted, and that they work, rather than saying that they must all be inferior or wrong in some way, is actually an enormous step forward. That really got the whole thing going, and when composers then started taking that attitude, it did change everything. (Neil Sorrell)

Debussy discovers Asia . . .

TO SOMEONE WHO'S BEEN trained in harmony and counterpoint and is used to playing the piano, these weird Javanese instruments would have sounded completely out of tune. The music is so anti-directional;

it just revolves. The bass line of the low notes is vague and weird; it doesn't seem to have any function. It *doesn't* have a function in the traditional sense. The rhythm of the music – and not only the sonority but the philosophy behind it – is so foreign that it took somebody with a very special sensibility to understand it. (George Benjamin)

REMEMBER THE MUSIC of Java which contained every shade of expression, even those one can no longer give a name to. There, tonic and dominant were no more than empty ghosts for the use of stupid little children. (Claude Debussy)

DEBUSSY IS LESS INTERESTED in goal direction than many a Western composer. He's less interested in friction and dialectic than many a Western – particularly German – composer. In other words his music rotates, and it's fascinated by the quality of sound itself and of comparison between materials rather than forward motion and narrative and conflict between materials. That is the influence of the East: savouring things for what they are rather than for what they do. (George Benjamin)

. . . but if he had not?

FIRST WE WOULD HAVE LOST purely evocative pieces like *Pagodes*, the gamelan-ish things in the String Quartet, in *La Mer* – especially the first movement – where he orchestrates in layers, overlapping pentatonic material, at different speeds, with different tessituras – that's clearly a gamelan kind of texture. For Debussy the gamelan is a precipitate. It found a natural affinity in him. A tremendous influential thrill like this at a seminal point in a composer's life is a short cut that can save him years and years of what Boulez would call research. (Robin Holloway)

Ravel adopts a genre

LAIDERONNETTE, EMPRESS OF THE PAGODAS – the title, the concept, produce a lovely little dinky gamelan piece of the greatest refinement: there's nothing seminal or radical about that. There are no tonics and dominants dissolving away like ghosts. It's already a cultural thing for him to be doing, well understood, well established. He's writing in a genre – the gamelan genre – and doing one of its most attractive numbers ever. (Robin Holloway)

Chinese music in Vienna

AT THE TIME when he was thinking about *Das Lied von der Erde* Mahler actually heard some phonograph cylinders of authentic Chinese music. We don't know what was on them, but there was a lot of interest in Vienna at the time in the Orient, and there were all kinds of early examples of a figure who's very much part of our own musical culture, the ethnomusicologist. Mahler certainly knew Guido Adler, for example, who was very close to the people who were looking into that area of music, and who published papers in learned journals about it. So he would have known about some of the techniques employed in South-East Asian music, above all the idea of heterophony. Heterophony may sound rather forbidding, but in fact it's a quite simple basic idea. One could express it as a question: 'How much can you get out of a unison line?' And a prominent feature of South-East Asian music is indeed this capacity to take a single melody as a unison and then by simultaneously combining it, very often at the octave above or the octave below, with different rhythmic versions of the same tune, you get the most wonderful kind of heterophonic counterpoint. There are many, many examples of that in *Das Lied von der Erde*. (Donald Mitchell)

Messiaen the collector

WHEN MESSIAEN MET the rhythms of India for the first time, he did not really know the music of India. He had read about it in books, but don't forget that at this time there was no possibility of listening to it: there were no recordings, or very few, just in the collections of museums. (Pierre Boulez)

HE DISCOVERED THESE INDIAN RHYTHMS in a very obscure encyclopaedia. They're extremely old – thirteenth or fourteenth century – and I don't know if he was aware of this, but it's highly dubious that they were ever used for real music. I think they were more a philosophical and purely esoteric invention. What he found in these rhythms, apart from their extraordinary names, was suggestive shapes: accelerations or the opposite, slowing down, circular motion, symmetries, very large values in the middle of which you'd find very short values. Intellectually these ideas appealed to him. As a composer he was a collector: he assembled things, and this was another thing to use. So when in later works, in the 1930s or above all the 1940s and 1950s, when he wants to provide a tapestry of clicking rhythms in the percussion department as a background and a support to collages of birdsong, instead of just sitting down and writing them from nothing he makes a collage based on his favourite Indian rhythms, and they provide him with a way of producing non-pulsed and interesting streams of simple durations.

Palindromic rhythms are thought-provoking. When you hear, especially in the middle of a texture, a rhythm that is the same backwards and forwards, you don't usually think, 'Ah! There's a rhythm that can be played backwards and forwards'. Our perception of time doesn't work like that. I think it's on a more philosophical level that they're important, and it's this: that in Western music, until this century and for an awful lot of centuries, we've been used to goal direction in music. In terms of harmony, everything's pulled towards a cadence, small cadences *en route* every eight or sixteen bars, big cadences at the ends of sections, one huge cadence at the end of a movement and one gigantic cadence at the very end of the work. Equally in rhythms we're used to cadences. Those big cadences, harmonically, happen on the beat, and they usually happen after a symmetrical number of beats. In terms of every element of composition – the melodies, the orchestration even, the tempos – we're used to starting some place, going somewhere else and coming back. Here's someone who's saying that there isn't a goal, that the destination of this rhythm is to revolve around a still, central point, because leading up to that central point is exactly the same backwards as leading away from it. It's completely symmetrical. So that defines the philosophy of composition in which you're not heading towards something but you're revolving around something. (George Benjamin)

I THINK THAT THE INFLUENCE was right and at the same time was wrong, but I find the wrong influences the best, always, because you're absorbing, assimilating the music you want to assimilate, and you transform it completely. The influence of Asia on Messiaen is an influence he absorbed completely, and which has very little to do with the original music. The more you know the original music, the more you see how different the music of Messiaen is from the music of the Far East. (Pierre Boulez)

Boulez invents a country

THERE WAS THE DISSATISFACTION if not the distaste at the whole idea of the West at the end of the Second World War, the feeling of a need to start completely again, discarding if possible the whole of the European tradition. That meant the history but also the thought of

Western music, and there were various models for that, the purest constructivism being one of them (through serialism), but another was to
go and raid all the other music that had not really been considered, at
least until the twentieth century, as being music – the musics of the Far
East and Africa and elsewhere. Simple curiosity – particularly in the
age of air travel, recording and broadcasting – is also a very important
factor, as is the end of colonialism, when countries which had been
subservient to the West restated their nationhood and autonomy. All
these influences made a big impact on composers sensitive to them,
from the end of the Second War onwards, and it's difficult to find an
important composer since the war who hasn't in some way been
changed or influenced by non-Western music.

One of the best ways to listen to some of Boulez's works, like *Le
marteau sans maître*, is to imagine that he's invented a country in the
middle of nowhere which has its own rules of language – and very
strict ones, as Eastern musics often do – but he's invented them, based
often on the model of Eastern musics. There are rules of rhythm, there
are rules of timbre, and in a sense the piece is a sort of display of a
musical culture he's invented purely from his imagination, though
alluding often to non-Western music. (George Benjamin)

Britten in Pagoda-land . . .

EVEN WHEN WORKING on *Peter Grimes*, something was already
flowering from that contact with the ceremonial Balinese music that
he'd played in New York. Even in the famous *Grimes* interlude *Sunday
Morning* the technique certainly has its recognizable and demonstrable
technical roots in what he'd learned from playing that Balinese
ceremonial music with Colin McPhee on Long Island in the early years
of the war. (Donald Mitchell)

BRITTEN HAD BEEN HAVING great difficulties with the ballet *The
Prince of the Pagodas*, and had got stuck at the beginning of Act II.
Very uncharacteristically for him, he'd cancelled numerous deadlines.
He was normally extremely efficient, and I think the fact that he wasn't
living up to these deadlines with this important piece weighed very
heavily on him as he travelled through Europe and India and into the
Far East on this concert tour. He got to Bali and he spent two weeks
there, which was really a holiday from this very punishing recital tour,
and the ballet was clearly very much on his mind. It seems that almost
immediately, as he began to explore the island's musical culture, he
realized that here was the solution to his compositional block. So when

he came home he set about reconstructing the gamelan music he'd heard from various sources, tape-recordings he'd made, commercial gramophone recordings, sketches he made on Bali as well – there are about four pages of manuscript he filled out with musical notations – and then from that point onwards it became really a very central feature of his style. (Mervyn Cooke)

THE PRINCE OF THE PAGODAS really registers for the first time on a public scale the Balinese input that had been there ever since the early 1940s. It is an absolutely crucial work, and in terms of the general twentieth-century picture it's one of the works by a major composer that really does show how important the Oriental dimension had become. Britten is one of the great exponents of this extraordinary manifestation of the East fertilizing the West in a major way. (Donald Mitchell)

. . . and in Japan

WHEN HE FOUND HIMSELF in Tokyo, he went to the Nō theatre, and although the tour group initially found that Nō was rather humorous to them, because they didn't understand a word of the text, and there was this rather curious vocal chanting, and terribly slow action, Britten very quickly caught on to the intensity of the dramatic experience, and that's the most important thing about Nō as far as he was concerned. He later described it as one of the greatest theatrical experiences of his entire life. The particular Nō play he saw, *Sumidagawa*, had a plot that was so much in line with Britten's own preoccupations that it could almost have been written for him. It was all about the abduction of an innocent child, and the deranged mother in search of that child: innocence and experience, the classic Britten preoccupation. Over the course of the next eight years, he reworked that Nō play into the church parable *Curlew River*, and built in aspects of other types of Japanese music: the court orchestral music, *Gagaku*, and also traditional Japanese songs with *shamisen* accompaniment. (Mervyn Cooke)

AGAIN, YOU'VE GOT TO SAY that there was a predisposition from the start. Britten's tendency to heterophony, to harmonizing by drones, to reducing the power of the bass – these things were latent. They made *Curlew River* possible and culminated in *Death in Venice*. It was an influx of the Orient to wider and stranger places than were ever allowed even by Debussy. (Robin Holloway)

Rhythm and percussion

RHYTHM WAS NEGLECTED, particularly in the nineteenth and eighteenth centuries, and as a result Western composers have found a way of renewing the language by looking at rhythm, and one of the best ways of displaying rhythms is through percussion. (George Benjamin)

WHAT THE GAMELAN DID was that it first of all opened up people's minds to the idea of an orchestra entirely of percussion. Virtually all the instruments are what we would call percussion; the strings and wind are fewer in number. To borrow a phrase of Debussy's, he talked about 'the charm of their percussion': the idea that percussion is now used in a subtle, delicate way, and it isn't the bang-crash-wallop 'kitchen department' any more. (Neil Sorrell)

Steve Reich gives it all a good shake

AT THAT TIME IN AMERICA, in the pop music world of Motown, there was a guy by the name of Junior Walker, and he did a tune called 'Shotgunned', and the bass line was repeated through the whole piece: there was no B section, there was no release, there was no bridge. We were also hearing Indian musicians for the first time in concert; we were hearing a lot of recordings of African and Indonesian music. What you could hear in this was music that didn't modulate, music that didn't change key, but which substituted rhythmic complexity in place of the harmonic complexity of Western music. Another big influence was John Coltrane. He was a jazz musician who at that time – 1962, 1963 – was playing an enormous amount of music on one or two chords: his 'Africa Brass' is on F for half an hour. So the idea of harmonic stasis was in the air, it was something that was coming from the rock 'n' roll world, from the jazz world, and from the world of non-Western music. And if you also had, as I did, a love of renaissance and medieval music and the structures thereof, if you mix that well, give it a good shake with the idea of little tape loops that repeat, then I think you can begin to see, with someone who was trained as a drummer as I was, how this might have taken. Certainly I should also give thanks to Terry Riley and his piece *In C*, which began this, and before that there was LaMonte Young who by holding long continuous tones had a marked effect on Terry, and then Terry had an effect on me, and then I had an effect on Philip Glass. So, there's your minimalism.

Going to Africa was getting a huge pat on the back, so to speak. There are civilizations, of which West Africa is one, that have spent thousands of years developing rhythmic counterpoint. The sound can be more complex than electronically generated sound. Repeating patterns combined so that their downbeats do not coincide have a long and honourable history. There's no new technical information in *Drumming* that you won't find in *Piano Phase* or *Violin Phase*, but the encouragement to go ahead and to put it on Western drums, Western bells and Western marimbas came from being in Ghana. It was a big green light. (Steve Reich)

Ligeti rediscovers the piano

ON THE PIANO there is no possibility of the two hands playing the same pitches as they can on the *mbira*, because the piano was constructed having the bass on the left and the treble on the right. I have no symmetrical possibility, but I want to combine two patterns, and I came to see how I can play with two hands at the same place, doing with one hand the white keys and with the other the black. The idea is simply a topographical idea of the piano. It's not a musical idea. (György Ligeti)

Takemitsu walks in a garden

SUPERFICIALLY, WHEN YOU LISTEN to Takemitsu's works, the similarity in harmonic language to composers such as Berg, Debussy and Messiaen is sometimes so close that you can lose sight of the fact that he does have a very original way of making the music breathe, and of walking through the form – 'walking' being the term, because he would see his forms as being metaphors for the beautiful Japanese gardens that he loved. (George Benjamin)

TAKEMITSU ALSO USED Japanese gardens in a very practical kind of way in composing his music. He told me that if he got a commission for a piece that had to be, say, twenty-two minutes, he might go to a particular garden and start at one point at a sort of key rock, and walk around it for twenty-two minutes, and experience the shifting points of view towards that particular rock to see how it changed with light, to see how the shadows of trees or grasses would change as he moved around it. So in a sense he was using the experience of walking through a garden as part of the planning for the composition of music. To him it was a very practical kind of resource. (Peter Grilli)

I MUST SAY THAT I AM influenced by every composer nowadays, from John Cage to Stockhausen – many, many. Also by traditional Japanese music, Indonesian, Javanese music. I don't care: I like music! (Toru Takemitsu)

The twain meet

THE TWENTIETH CENTURY has been the century in which there has been this increasing interest and contact with the Orient – with the other half of the globe. The West has become much closer to the East. (Donald Mitchell)

THERE'S SOMETHING ALMOST PACIFIC about music, in a way. It gives one the possibility of perhaps reducing these horrible conflicts that come up from these ideological constructs called the Orient or the Occident. (Edward Said)

IT'S VERY GOOD TO KNOW a lot of cultures and a lot of languages, because you have the relativity; you regard your own language as one of many possibilities. (György Ligeti)

NOW THAT THESE ETHNIC SOUNDS are so easily available, maybe the kind of thrill of discovery that you could get from something absolutely rare that was still possible to Britten in the 1950s might no longer be. 'Ethno' is PC; to build a body of music out of imitating the Western canon is not; so the going thing is to raid the wide world, especially if it's not Western. This is the topsy-turvy upside-downness of our times. (Robin Holloway)

A LOT OF THIS MUSIC is full of Eastern promise, but rather a lot of the promises are not kept. (Neil Sorrell)

THERE'S A WAY OF DIGESTING the influence of non-Western musics that doesn't try to mimic them. You don't imitate the surface of what you're interested in, trying to do a gamelan with lots of vibraphones or glockenspiels and gongs, but you look deeper into the essence of this other music and you abstract from it. You're not, I think, doing a dis-service to the music then, and you're enriching your own palette by seeing how other human beings from a different culture have organized their music, and how you can. The world of our central classical music, going from about the late seventeenth century to about 1910 is an incredibly rich and extraordinary way of organizing and conceiving music, but not the only one. (George Benjamin)

13 Mastering Music

Nobody is too great to write for children.
ZOLTÁN KODÁLY, 1929

FOR MUCH OF THIS CENTURY, music teaching in most British state schools involved singing hymns and folk songs by rote, with perhaps an occasional period of 'musical appreciation' involving a teacher playing records of established classics and talking a little about them. Such teachers were rarely professional musicians and few had any training in musical education. Instrumental teaching, where the school offered it at all, took place after school hours and in most cases the instrument in question had to be provided by the child's parents. The pioneering work of the composer Gustav Holst, who from 1905 taught his pupils at St Paul's Girls' School in West London to sing, play instruments and compose simple pieces, was not much imitated elsewhere.

The spread of broadcasting enabled many children as well as adults to hear music to which they would otherwise have had no access. In 1923 the German-born industrialist Robert Mayer founded a series of concerts for children in London, retiring from business shortly thereafter to devote himself entirely to expanding the scheme. By the outbreak of the Second World War he was promoting concerts in twenty-five British towns and cities. In 1954, with little support from the musical profession, he set up Youth and Music (based on the *Jeunesses musicales* movement, established in Belgium during the

1940s and widely imitated elsewhere in Europe), one of whose main objectives was to attract older children to concerts by offering them tickets at reduced prices. Although Mayer continued his work until after his hundredth birthday it was eventually overtaken by new attitudes to musical education, and the Robert Mayer Concerts were recently discontinued.

Those new attitudes, away from passive 'appreciation' and towards practical music-making, began to be felt during the 1960s, and were given greater impetus by the publication in 1970 of the extremely influential book, *Sound and Silence* by John Paynter and Peter Aston. This prompted a realization, further fostered by knowledge of the educational work done in Hungary by the composer Zoltán Kodály, that children could and should be taught to make music, not merely to listen to it. This led, firstly, to the establishment of a network of what were termed 'peripatetic' instrumental teachers: skilled instrumentalists who would travel from school to school within a local education authority area, coaching children at each of them. Some used methods modelled on those pioneered by the Japanese Shin'ichi Suzuki, who taught very young children to play the violin in large classes (his first experimental class numbered forty children) instead of the 'one-to-one' approach that had until then been considered essential and which inevitably restricted the number of children receiving instrumental tuition.

The number of children learning an instrument, and being regularly tested for proficiency and progress by examiners appointed by the Associated Board of the Royal Schools of Music, grew enormously. School orchestras became widespread, often with the best players from each being selected for more advanced training and for membership of a county youth orchestra. The summit of this pyramid was the National Youth Orchestra, founded by Ruth Railton as early as 1946, many of whose members subsequently joined professional orchestras. All this activity centred on the performance of Western 'classical' music, but two other developments expanded the scope of music teaching still further. One was a growing belief that children should be taught to compose as well as to perform. The other was a feeling that concentrating on classical music bred an élitist attitude to other forms.

Using elements of 'pop' music in the classroom was seen by some teachers as a useful way of drawing children gradually towards a more serious repertoire, by others as a culture to which most children responded more directly than to music from the classical tradition, and which had its own value and validity. In many schools, those in cities especially, a substantial minority or even majority of the pupils came from cultures other than the Western European. In 1985 the national curriculum for the General Certificate of Secondary Education (GCSE) recognized these factors by stipulating that musical education in all state schools should involve composition as well as performance and that the styles of music taught should include popular forms and non-Western music. 'Composition' included improvisation, which is central to jazz and to many non-Western musics.

This remarkable growth in the quantity and range of music teaching in schools was much admired abroad, and the British approach was widely emulated, but in Britain itself it was seen to be expensive, and music tended to be one of the first areas to suffer when attempts were made to reduce expenditure on education or to concentrate educational resources on what were perceived to be the more essential disciplines of literacy and numeracy. A reduction in the number of peripatetic teachers employed coincided, ironically, with research evidence that children who are trained in practical music-making tend to do better academically than those who receive no musical education.

During the same period attention was also paid to the fact that in Britain, as in many other countries, two forms of advanced musical education are available: the conservatoires or music colleges concentrating on the training of performing musicians (although in fact a high proportion of their graduates become music teachers) and the music departments of universities providing more academic courses (although many music graduates have become performers, their talents first attracting attention at concerts promoted by students). In recent years there has been a growing tendency for performers to attend universities as well as music colleges, for universities to encourage performance and for conservatoires to pay more attention to such disciplines – formerly perceived as 'academic' but in fact essential for performers – as music history and research into sources. Many music colleges, instead of the certificates of competence that were formerly bestowed on graduating students, now award degrees in music; similarly numerous universities now offer degrees in musical performance.

Widespread anxiety is currently felt by music teachers and others about the future of musical education in Britain. Although the broadening of the range of music taught in schools is generally welcomed, as is the increased concentration on composition and improvisation, the time available to encompass this variety has not expanded. Much musical education still takes place in the children's (and the teachers') spare time, during lunch breaks and after school, putting considerable strain on the endurance and the dedication of all concerned. Attempts to halt the increase in spending on education have led to a reduction in the number of peripatetic instrumental teachers employed in schools, a tendency that was further exacerbated by statements from government ministers calling for a greater concentration in primary schools on reading, writing and mathematics. It has been claimed that large numbers of children now have no access to instrumental training, and that the effects of this are already perceptible in lower standards in some youth orchestras. Despite a recent government announcement that extra funds are to be made available for musical education these anxieties have still not been allayed.

*

Why musical education?

1 TO PROVIDE A PLEASING RECREATION and amusement for the singer and his friends.
2 To cultivate the aesthetic faculty.
3 To afford training in morals and patriotism through the words of the song learned.
4 To train in distinctness of articulation.
5 To provide healthy pulmonary exercise.
6 To aid in schools' discipline, because in the singing lesson all are taught the necessity of submitting to the direction of the conductor.
(*School Management*, 1900)

Ears like needles!

GOOD AFTERNOON, SCHOOLS! I think we'll begin our lesson this afternoon by singing a scale or two, just to practise your voices to try and get them even and clear, and at the same time we shall be reminding ourselves of the sound of the major scale which we've been learning about this term. Miss Godley is here with me in the studio, and she's going to pattern these scales for you, and I'm going to ask you to sing the whole scale after her. I'll tell you when to begin, so wait for the word, and each time that Miss Godley sings, please listen as keenly as you can, ears like needles! (BBC Schools broadcast, 1937)

Before the change

WE HAVE THE FOLKSONG ENTHUSIAST who can see no good in sight-singing or part music; the pianoforte-trained person who will try to put the clock back a long way on some matter of mere notation; the enthusiast for the 'appreciation' of music who thinks that all definite ear-training should go by the board, and that children should be given instead some washy sort of general impression of masterpieces – we might as well try to teach the appreciation of English poetry before teaching English – and lastly we still have the Methuselah amongst us who thinks that music in schools should consist only of song-singing, and that the number of songs is limited – either by Magna Carta or by the Education Act of 1870 – to five in one year. (John Borland, 1927)

AT THE MOMENT I ENTERED the music teaching profession in 1971 I was the first full-time music teacher in that grammar school. That was a pattern that was not uncommon across the country: full-time music teachers in secondary schools and grammar schools really only date back to that period. Until then there would have been somebody on the staff who was good at music – somebody perhaps who played the piano, or could do the choir. At a neighbouring school a local church warden who was also something of an organist was brought in for a couple of days a week to teach music. A third school had nobody. Characteristically the girls' grammar school did have a full-time music teacher. That tells you something about gender and music education. (Roger Durston)

Music appreciation

APPRECIATION OF MUSIC: unfortunately this subject has suffered much from a misapprehension of the meaning of the term 'appreciation'. At first many teachers understood the word in its secondary and colloquial sense. They therefore set out to teach children to 'like' music, forgetful of the fact that children already do like music. (*Recent Developments in School Music*, 1933)

MUSIC APPRECIATION WAS SEEN TO SAY, 'Well, there are these great musical artefacts. Clearly children ought to know about the Armada and the Battle of Trafalgar, so they ought also to know about Beethoven's Fifth Symphony, Haydn's *Nelson Mass* and probably Tchaikovsky's *1812 Overture*.' The idea was that even if they didn't like them while they were at school, perhaps in later life they would come to them and learn to love them. (Roger Durston)

IT USUALLY MEANT THAT they were bored and fed up, and thought, 'Let's get on to the next thing where we can do something ourselves.' They didn't actually want to be told that Beethoven was wonderful; they wanted to discover that the tunes of Beethoven were fun to do, even if they played them indifferently on the recorder. That's much more vital. Music is about actually doing things, not just about receiving. (John Manduell)

Zoltán Kodály: doing, not just receiving

ACTIVITY IS THE CHIEF THING, therefore the so-called music appreciation with gramophone records is only of secondary importance for us, because it's too passive and if children are not prepared for it sufficiently it has no use at all. And then it is only good if they can hear the work also in a living performance. (Zoltán Kodály, 1964)

[KODÁLY'S MELODIES FOR CHILDREN] are of an originality, a simplicity yet richness which is quite startling. We can all learn from these: from their beauty of sound, their freshness. One is reminded of his famous words: 'Nobody is too great to write for children. In fact, he should try to become great enough for it.' Not only did he leave these countless miniature masterpieces for children, but he worked for and replanned their musical education: new methods of sight-reading, vocal training, new curricula. One result of his educational efforts is that, at this moment, over 80 per cent of the state schools in Hungary – and I do not mean the musical schools – have a one-hour general music period every day. (Benjamin Britten, 1967)

KODÁLY'S WORK HAS BEEN very, very important, but sadly it is not used systematically in schools now. I think it would be absolutely wonderful if we could have every primary school with a Kodály specialist in it, and they could teach the children to sight-sing. (Lucy Green)

Gustav Holst: learning by doing

OF COURSE [HOLST'S] SORT OF TEACHING wasn't just harmony lessons, it was always composing. At Morley College he had adult beginners (and they really were beginners!). He taught them to make up rounds, and then they spent the lessons singing them. He did that with his schoolgirl pupils too, and we very soon learned – because it was a positive nuisance not to – something about harmony from the inside. Some of the rounds we wrote came off, and others didn't, and so we learned from trial and error, which was his way of teaching: learn by doing. We learned that you had to have a give and take, a to and fro between tonic and dominant, to make it work, and learning that from the inside instead of from a textbook was wonderful, and part of his great work as a teacher. (Imogen Holst, 1970)

The Russian way

A VERY SERIOUS NETWORK of music education was established in the Soviet Union. There were some political reasons for that, because the Soviet Union made a lot of propaganda, and in order to show that Communism is the best system, they wanted to show that they are best in everything. I think they succeeded because that made a very good face for them, and it was good for music, of course, at the same time. What was important as well was that children (their parents when the children were small, but then later the children themselves) were so dedicated to that. (Irina Zaritskaya)

The National Youth Orchestra

IMMEDIATELY AFTER THE WAR I realized that there was wonderful talent among the young in the British Isles, which was very often wasting for lack of development, and to me for any talent, any gift in a child, to be going to seed just because it isn't developed is a terrible thing. So I went to all the famous people and Ministers of Education and high-up and powerful musicians, and said, 'Couldn't we have a school in which some of us who were very keen about this would be only too willing to help?' They said that it was a very fine idea, but of course it couldn't possibly be done, because there were no premises and no money and anyway there wasn't very much talent, and the great musicians would never teach the young. Finally, after trying to persuade many people to do it, I decided that I would just start myself, because I knew the talent was there, and I knew that all my friends among the great musicians would help and be interested in this. (Ruth Railton, 1964)

Concerts for children

WE BOMBARDED ALL OUR FRIENDS to bring along their children, and there they were: there was Victor Gollancz; there was Bernard Waley-Cohen. They all came along with their children, and from there my social conscience pricked me: what about the poor? So we said, 'All right, why *not* the poor?' Nobody's poorer than the people who live in the East End of London, so we went to the People's Palace, along Mile End Road. Now this you must imagine: they had never heard or seen an orchestra before, they never knew music of any kind, and yet we played a movement of a Bach concerto and you could hear a pin drop. That gave us enormous courage. (Robert Mayer, 1979)

I WAS A FLUTE PLAYER in the LPO, and in the orchestra we all universally detested what was done in the name of schools' concerts. We used to sit there; we played whatever ambitious would-be conductors wished to conduct; they gave introductions about the history of the composer, and we played to what we could clearly see were bored audiences. (Richard McNicol)

John Paynter: inviting children into music

IN THE LAST TWENTY-FIVE or thirty years there's been a huge number of developments in music education. It was in the mid-1970s that John Paynter and Peter Aston wrote their wonderful book, *Sound and Silence*, and there were a lot of other people at the time – Brian Dennis, George Self, Murray Schaefer – doing the kind of work in which children were encouraged to experiment with the materials of music in classrooms rather as they experimented with the materials of art. (Lucy Green)

WHEN I WAS YOUNG, music was taught to you. You were taught facts about music; you were taught to analyse music – basically you were instructed. Now the way of teaching that was piloted by John Paynter in *Sound and Silence* – and for me was the ultimate inspiration – was the idea that everybody can deal with musical material and build it into things just as they do with clay or whatever. That's the fundamental change: that we now invite people into the music. (Richard McNicol)

WHAT [JOHN PAYNTER] WAS DOING was regarded as being quite different, quite challenging, but he was able to demonstrate that his ideas were musically grounded, and it was the strength of that musical knowledge and understanding that provided a base on which people built. (Janet Ritterman)

AS A STUDENT I had come into contact with a very wonderful lady named Gladys Partick, and she imbued me with a feeling that music was part of everybody's natural way of thinking. She had a number of little phrases, one of which stuck very much in my mind. She would say, 'The sound first and then the sign.' In other words we need to come to terms with the way the thing sounds, and then we can call it something.

I became a school teacher, and you have to remember that my main enthusiasm was to be a composer, not a performer. I thought, 'How do I deal with this business of being a school teacher?' First of all, whatever I did must apply to every child I teach: you can't have music teachers who are addressing only like-minded people. It seemed a very obvious step then to say, 'I'm a composer, that's what I do musically. This seems to me to be where music begins.' (John Paynter)

ONE OF THE PROBLEMS of the *Sound and Silence* creative movement is progression. As teachers found very quickly, you can do this sort of thing with children up to a point, but how do you get them to do it better next time? In the 1970s Keith Swanwick began to argue that children should not only compose in the classroom, but that they should perform and listen in a way which was integrated: listening to your own music, listening to your classmates' music, and listening to 'real' music. (Lucy Green)

Teaching other musics

THIRTY YEARS AGO, twenty-five even, the curriculum was virtually entirely classical Western music. Gradually popular music began to enter the curriculum, but it remained as a rather inferior second cousin which was used by teachers as a way of building up a pleasant relationship with the children before you got on to the 'real stuff'. Then, in 1985, when the GCSE exam was first introduced into schools, that syllabus turned things right on their heads, because it laid equal emphasis on composing, performing and listening, and because it stipulated that the music used in the classroom should include popular music and music from around the world. (Lucy Green)

IN THE LAST TWENTY or twenty-five years very astonishing things happened. Teachers discovered that with new music, with rock and pop music, they come near to the pupils, they interest the pupils, and from this point they have a better chance to explain Beethoven. In my school it's funny to see that the same pupils who are very enthusiastic about playing Beethoven or Mozart just go to the rock band in the other room and play rock music there. (Josef Frommelt)

IN 1982, WHEN I ASKED TEACHERS to grade the importance of the different musical styles, classical music was way up the top, followed by popular music, then twentieth-century classical music, and folk music at the bottom. Today, in the rough analysis I've just done, folk music and twentieth-century classical music remain at the bottom. Popular music has superseded classical music and is way above it in teachers' estimates of its importance, its educational viability, its enjoyment factor and its value. Next to classical music is world music, which seems to be taking equal or even greater importance. That is something that was completely absent from the curriculum sixteen years ago. (Lucy Green)

A POP GROUP WILL EXCITE; a string quartet will enrich. Or is it the other way round? It's according to your perception. (John Manduell)

PERIPATETIC MUSIC TEACHING lost some ground because it seemed to be associated with only one form of music-making. There was a feeling that unless children were involved in great works of art, they weren't really engaged in worthwhile activity. If they were involved in what appeared to be ephemeral fancies, like pop music, somehow this was not a worthwhile study at school. Now once people understood that we're actually dealing with the musical components rather than the artefact, then popular music, jazz, rock and all sorts of other improvised forms came much more to the fore. I think there's a general understanding among music teachers that they cover a wide range of styles and genres, and if you go to schools proms now, seven out of the ten items are likely to be crossover-, fusion-, jazz-, rock- or world-music-based. (Roger Durston)

THE MISTAKE AT THE MOMENT seems to me that there is an orthodoxy about this, that teachers are being put in the position of having to accept – quite irrationally, from my own experience – that all young people will automatically respond to popular music, and that, therefore, is where you begin. I've always believed you begin with music, particularly with what the children themselves would do.

The first thing I would do when I went into a classroom was to say, 'Put yourselves into groups of five and make me a piece of music.' They would say, 'How long's it going to last?' I'd reply, 'As long as you want it to – not too long, or we'll be here all night, but you decide. That's important. What do you want? It's not for me to tell you what I want. You know what music is. If you've got to your age and you don't know what music is, then something's wrong.' Now, some of them will come up with things that sound like the latest pop music – there's no reason why they shouldn't. Others will come up with things that don't sound like any other music you've ever heard. Teachers ought to be able to teach from the basis of what they themselves believe. (John Paynter)

British musical education exported

SCANDINAVIAN COUNTRIES ARE VERY QUICKLY implementing our sort of curriculum. Norway is introducing its own; Sweden is. Japan has looked very, very closely at our curriculum, because of course Japan is saying, 'Look, we've got too much directed teaching. We need people who can express themselves, who can develop musical and other concepts.' So, curiously, under the last government, while we were entrenching, they were all saying, 'We must adopt the English model.' The English model is very, very well known throughout the world. (Richard McNicol)

BRITISH MUSICAL EDUCATION in the 1970s and 1980s became an exportable commodity, and I myself and many other people like me were being continually invited, not just to go and talk about it but to run workshops for teachers, to help to train teachers in these techniques. To some extent that is still true. In many of the countries that I have worked in, there isn't any musical education in schools; all the musical education is organized privately, in the Scandinavian countries very often through the little local music schools, which is something we don't have in this country. But they have consistently wanted to learn from us about the place of creativity in the musical curriculum. (John Paynter)

IN SWITZERLAND FIVE YEARS AGO we carried through a very interesting and important pilot project. Waldemar Webel, the leader of this project, compared sixty classes with increased music tuition of seven hours per week with sixty classes without music. The time for these seven lessons was taken away from mathematics, from languages, from sciences and so on. The result was that the pupils with more music education had the same or better results in the science subjects, and they also developed more social competence, more fantasy, more creativity. (Josef Frommelt)

Instrumental teaching proliferates ...

I THINK WE HAD a couple of thousand candidates for Associated Board examinations in our first couple of years. Right now we examine in eighty countries, and last year it was over six hundred thousand. That's an awful lot of candidates. At the beginning we had piano, the four strings, wind and brass, but we've added percussion and guitar. The piano still accounts for 77 per cent. It's very high. Between violin and clarinet or flute, it swings. Sometimes the violin's taken over. Strings become important for a couple of years, and the wind goes down, and then suddenly we find the entries sweep up on flute and clarinet. Recorders we started, and of course that's very popular because of schools. (Jean Harvey)

THE MORE INSTRUMENTS we brought into the classroom, the less singing we did, and one of the depressing things about the present time is that singing is not perhaps as widely seen to be good as it used to be years ago. We've placed so much emphasis on instruments that there's been an enormous proliferation of youth orchestras, and all of them are wanting to tour the world. I have mixed feelings about this, because if I had to put my finger on what was the single most important development in musical education in this century, I would have said peripatetic instrumental teaching. (John Paynter)

... and declines

BRITISH PATERNALISTIC CHIEF EDUCATION OFFICERS, often Oxbridge-educated people, would, from the resources that they had available, offer to their music adviser a few more teachers each year. In the music adviser's mind had been a symphony orchestra for young people, and therefore they would appoint instrumental teachers in the proportion that was required to produce an orchestra, and that went on until 1974. The oil crises, the realization that no longer could we live off overseas earnings, meant that we had to cut back and trim our education system, to the point that a music adviser could no longer go to the chief education officer in February and say, 'Do you think you could let me have a couple more teachers?' and he would say rather grandly, 'Of course, Bill, have another couple.' That came to an end.

In that the peripatetic instrumental teaching service brought live music-making to children, it was the single most important thing. In that it failed to bring it to all children, it was an extremely damaging thing, because it created a sense that practical musical activity was something for an élite, who had to be selected in some sort of way. (Roger Durston)

Learning music is not easy

AS AN INFANT OF SIX OR SEVEN, my innocent life was blighted, yes positively blighted, by the simplest little piece of music Beethoven ever wrote, namely the Sonatina in G. There were certain bits in it which my infantile fingers couldn't cope with, and every time these bits were reached, down came a sharp rap on my knuckles with a round, black and quite hefty ruler, wielded by the worthy governess who was then in charge of my studies. Did the said difficulties vanish in consequence of the ruler treatment? No, they didn't, but my terror and incompetence increased. So between the ages of six and ten I learned to associate the name of Beethoven and his music with punishment and physical suffering. (John Ireland, 1945)

THE FIRST TIME I PLAYED in public, as a little child at the Watford School of Music, I had to play at a pupils' concert. A few little girls and little boys with their mothers were there, that's all, an audience of about twenty people, and the head of the school called out, 'Now Master Gerald Moore will play a sonatina by Gurlitt.' Well, Master Gerald Moore *did* play a sonatina by Gurlitt. I burst into tears, but my mother seized me by the scruff of the neck and the seat of the trousers and marched me up on the platform, and I played through my tears. (Gerald Moore, 1969)

WHEN I PLAYED THE PIANO it was for me as natural as to sleep or to eat. Then they were all over me, you know, they covered me with chocolates, kissed me all over and so on, and that angered me. I thought I was let down, you understand? The things which I wanted to be praised for I missed. (Artur Rubinstein)

YOU MUST BE LISTENING to your playing. Don't forget to listen, to have this possibility of being at the same time the player and the listener who is seated in the audience. Otherwise, if you are too absorbed in your own playing you won't hear yourself very well. And then if you listen to yourself as a critic would do in the hall, you will hear yourself without so much sympathy, and that's good. Don't hear yourself with much sympathy. (Paul Tortelier, 1961)

I LOVE TO TEACH. I love to be with the students. I feel it's a very great privilege, and I think that I help them to withstand stages of development which are arduous, which are severe, which are difficult. I encourage. In a way I impose a certain law, a certain habit of doing one's daily duty. (Nadia Boulanger, 1973)

COMMUNICATION IS SO INTENSIVE now that differences are less, because artists go to teach and play in other countries and make a lot of recordings all over the world. Pupils come for masterclasses and go to study in other countries, so it is really mixing very much. In general the international standard is rising, but there was only one Mozart, and there was only one Bach, and great talents are and will be few. You cannot mass produce geniuses. (Irina Zaritskaya)

Conservatoires and universities

DURING THE EIGHTEENTH and nineteenth centuries well over 90 per cent of professional musicians learned their skills in the family, and it's really been only during this century that the music colleges have been producing people who then become professional performing musicians. Until even halfway through the century, the vast majority of music college graduates were women who became teachers, not performers. (Lucy Green)

WE WERE PREPARING A REPORT for the Gulbenkian Foundation, nearly twenty years ago. There were thirty-three university music departments in existence at that time and we were asking the question: 'Are there too many?' Well, if there were too many then, how many are there now? So it was a very pertinent question. Conservatoires in this country, of course, have remained a clutch, about eight or so. But they've all got better, I think, and that's the important thing. (John Manduell)

IT'S NOT ENTIRELY UNTRUE to say that in my youth the colleges produced performers who were superb as performers but could be near moronic as people, intellectually and culturally. On the other hand one could go to a university and never have to make music at all. One could do it entirely on paper. Now it's a very general thing that people are moving away from this. We all feel, in almost all universities, that this is a bad thing. (Wilfrid Mellers, 1972)

THE ESTABLISHMENT OF THE Faculty of Music at King's College, London, with Thurston Dart, I would see as a key turning point in a whole range of ways. One could identify other universities which between the 1950s and the 1970s evolved distinctive styles within their music departments and found ways for what was going on in the department to contribute to the life of the university and then, more broadly, to the life of the community. (Janet Ritterman)

IT USED TO BE LEFT to the universities to study not only history but everything beyond that, and to concentrate in the conservatoires on performance or on theory – so-called. Now the circumstances and balance have changed, partly of course out of sheer realistic response to employment needs. Years ago it was a lot gentler, it was a lot less realistic, and it was certainly a lot narrower. Young people today can see that career opportunities have to be much more diversified than they ever were in the old days. One of the greatly encouraging aspects of university life is that they've moved far more towards the practical, so that just as the conservatoires have moved towards understanding music better, so the universities have moved towards performing it to a higher standard. (John Manduell)

Current dangers: distraction

WE'VE BROUGHT IT ON OURSELVES, because of sitting watching TV at night. You sit and watch the television and the piano can't be practised. Extra-curricular work at school is the teachers' great grumble. They're really very depressed, and have been for about ten years. They can't get children to practise because there are far too many things at school. When I went to school, I studied music as an extra, but now there are so many options. Lunchtimes are awful. When they get home they might have their tea but then have to go back out again to do something else. And the worst thing, of course, is easy access to computers. So they play with those rather than practise. (Jean Harvey)

. . . synthesizers . . .

WHAT WORRIES ME about music made with synthesizers is that it is a single action that produces a variety of sounds. You press the knobs and dials and you press the same key and it produces one moment a harpsichord and another moment a piano and another moment a marimba. One of the most important things we were able to do in the 1950s, 1960s and 1970s was to engage children in classrooms with an enormous variety of sound-making possibilities. They learned without being told that if you bang a piece of wood you get a different noise from what you get if you bang a piece of glass or metal. If you scrape something the action produces one thing, and if you blow across or through something it produces another. Of course the synthesizer does all that for you, so you don't experience that. (John Paynter)

. . . decline of instrumental teaching . . .

SO MANY PEOPLE who have gone on to have significant careers in music, and to provide important musical leadership in this country and elsewhere over the last twenty or thirty years, would say that the way in which their musical opportunities began was through individual lessons made available to them in schools through peripatetic teaching, for those who mightn't otherwise get that opportunity. That is often a class thing. The musical opportunities that have enabled us to encourage many young people to go on and see whether music was for them may be being reduced or certainly distorted. (Janet Ritterman)

WE DID RESEARCH between 1994 and 1997, and we were horrified to find that 333,000 children were denied access to learning instruments. The government had to acknowledge this research, and they said, 'We will do another similar research in the year 2000' – which we're going to do, to see if the situation has changed at all. (Jean Harvey)

. . . a retreat from musical education?

WE'VE RECENTLY HAD David Blunkett's announcement on 'The Three Rs' – that we really have to concentrate on that – and Chris Woodhead's letter to the Inspectorate, saying to them that we won't look quite so hard at music and drama; we'll concentrate on the main things. Headteachers instantly took up that hint, and music is now dropping like flies, so our 'Make Music Live', the big thing that we do all day with the LSO at the Barbican, was sold out a year ago, but the in-service training course, which used to be absolutely full, was down 50 per cent, because after that statement all the teachers said to us, 'Headteachers are now entrenching.' (Richard McNicol)

THERE HAS TO BE A SITUATION in which there is recognition from government of how relatively little money is needed to do a powerful lot of good. We build a dome for hundreds of millions of pounds. If we just made that dome a little bit smaller, and hived off a small part of that, we would transform our arts provision in this country. That's a political statement, but I think it's also an incontrovertible one. (John Manduell)

THERE IS AN ENORMOUS AMOUNT that's going on which is wonderful, exciting and innovative, but we are eroding the infrastructure very fast indeed. We're taking the building apart. Within three or four years we will have that Meccano back in bits in a box unless we address the infrastructural issues immediately. That means setting up a new standards fund to rebuild the infrastructure of music support services, which would include in-service training for teachers, and it means putting all those things in place very rapidly. We have to do it in the next twelve months, or we will reach the point where the reconstruction process is going to take far too long. (Roger Durston)

. . . *or cause for optimism?*

Blunkett and Smith Strike a High Note for Music

Children in England are set to benefit from a £180 million boost for music . . . £150 million to support services provided by Local Education Authorities and £30 million to the Young Music trust. The money will support:

- instrumental music tuition
- in-service training
- supplying instruments and
- providing youth orchestras and bands

Mr Blunkett said, 'Music is a vital part of every child's education and plays an important role in this country's culture. Years of under-funding have left some children without access to musical instruments or the tuition they desperately need. The Government is determined to reverse that decline.' (*Department of Education and Employment News*, 27 January 1999)

MUSIC EDUCATION DURING this century has grown in breadth and depth. It's made valuable musical experiences available to an increasing number of children who might never have recognized that they were musical, and it's continued to expand into the twenty-first century, but I don't think we can look back now. (Lucy Green)

14 Music and the Masses

*If you are really creative . . . I don't think that you can
have an audience in mind.*

PIERRE BOULEZ

COMPOSERS IN FORMER CENTURIES, for the most part employed by
rulers, aristocrats or the Church, had a clear idea of who their
audiences were and what they wanted. For the modern composer,
especially one writing in a style that as yet has little popular appeal, the
question is either a much more difficult one or an irrelevance: composers may well feel that they cannot do otherwise than write the
music that they are inspired to write, regardless of whether the public
is ready to appreciate it. Those who go to concerts are in any case a
minority, for the most part middle class and middle aged; those who
go to concerts of new music a minority of that minority.

During the twentieth century some composers have tried to address
neither of those minorities but the majority, those who never go to
concerts. Paul Hindemith, credited (though he later denied it) with
inventing the term *Gebrauchsmusik* – 'music for use' – wrote that 'a
composer today should write only if he knows for what purpose he is
writing. The days of composing for its own sake are perhaps over.' The
motive was often a political one: to write a form of music that would
assist the struggle of the working class for power, to provide music that
would promote *esprit de corps* among members of a political group,
etc. But others, aware of the sustaining, inspiring and enriching role that

music played in their own lives, wished to make music more available and to remove barriers in the way of experiencing it. Composers wanting to write music that would appeal more widely than to the concert audience soon realized that they would need to change their idiom or at least make some stylistic compromise. This generally meant the adoption of elements from current popular music.

Some of these attempts to reach a broader public were hugely successful. Soon after its première in 1928 *The Threepenny Opera*, with text by Bertolt Brecht and music by Kurt Weill, was estimated by Weill's publisher to be playing in never fewer than ten theatres simultaneously; it received several thousand performances in its first year. But by that time (see also chapters 4 and 19) the media of broadcasting and recording had brought about a revolution in public access to music. In the year that *The Threepenny Opera* had several thousand performances the number of radio licences issued in Great Britain exceeded 4 million. The first recording to sell a million copies, a coupling of 'The Japanese Sandman' and 'Whispering' by Paul Whiteman and his Orchestra, was first issued in November 1920.

None of these examples of music reaching a mass audience was universally welcomed. The influential Belgian critic Paul Collaer said of Weill that he wrote 'in a way that appeals to the most uninformed tastes. His music is vulgar.' Arnold Schoenberg said of Weill that 'his is the only music in the world in which I can find no quality at all', and he was particularly angered by his pupil Hanns Eisler's use of elements of serial technique in popular-style works written for propaganda purposes. Weill emigrated to America after the Nazis' rise to power in Germany. He did not abandon his ideal of writing music that combined popular appeal with political awareness and social responsibility, but because his subsequent career was in the commercial world of the Broadway musical and Hollywood he was for a long while respected, in Europe and among serious critics, only for the works that he had written in Europe, mostly in collaboration with Brecht. That his musicals and Hollywood film scores were a continuation of that work, intended to address serious political and social issues for a broad public, was not widely recognized until some while after his death.

Eisler later became the composer laureate of the German Democratic Republic, but his reputation did not perish with his death or the decline of state communism. His combination of political engagement and high musical standards was an inspiration and a model, of course to left-wing musicians but also, together with Weill, to those (like the group of Austrian composers led by H. K. Gruber and Kurt Schwertsik) who sought to break down barriers between 'serious' and 'popular', and to whom the radical tradition of German and Austrian cabaret was important. Cornelius Cardew, a convert to Marxism after a period as a very influential composer of 'experimental' music, was an extreme but not an isolated example of those who condemned the modernist avant-garde (in his case in a book entitled *Stockhausen Serves Imperialism*) as fatally cut off from all but a narrow intellectual élite. Others have questioned the wisdom of concentrating the small amounts of money available to subsidize new music on officially approved modernist composers in whom the concert-going public persists in demonstrating very little interest.

Not long after the incorporation of the BBC, which gave it the right to charge a licence fee (of ten shillings – 50p – a year) to every owner of a radio, the London *Evening Standard* printed a letter from a listener complaining at being charged such an exorbitant sum when an evening's broadcasting was interrupted by twenty-five minutes of music by Bach and Mozart: 'As the majority of licence-holders are workpeople and others who require relaxation and amusement to lighten their burdens, they should not be expected to pay . . . for such programmes.' Sir Thomas Beecham (who later changed his mind on both subjects) virulently attacked both broadcasting and recording as crimes against music which would eventually empty the world's concert halls. When it was objected that people living far from those concert halls would not hear orchestral music except through broadcasts or recordings, he replied, 'If people cannot get decent musical food, that is no reason why you should give them poison. Rather than wireless or a gramophone, take prussic acid at once.'

Other and more thoughtful reservations about radio and recording have continued to be made, for example the objection that great art is devalued when it is available with no effort, at the turn of a switch, and that limitless availability encourages the passive overhearing of music rather than true listening. Attempts to spread knowledge and appreciation of music, through education and by making concerts and opera more generally accessible, have been less controversial. But those attempts were usually made by the educated classes, and could be paternalistic, patronizing and restricted in their definition of culture. The eminent composer Sir Arthur Bliss, the BBC's Director of Music from 1942 to 1944, proposed a separate channel for dance music and other light entertainment; he referred to it as 'the dirt track'.

The benefits of twentieth-century technology include the fact that more people than ever before have access to music of high quality, and access to a far broader repertoire of music than has ever before been the case. But there has been no comparable increase in public participation in musical performance, and there is a risk that for many people music will become a passive experience, received primarily or wholly through electronic means. Music from its very origins has been a social and participatory art. The objectives of those who sought to bring music to the masses have very largely been met. But taking part in music-making, hearing music live and engaging with performers and composers remain activities in which only a minority participate.

*

An élitist shudders

TODAY WE ARE WITNESSING the triumphs of a hyper-democracy, in which the mass acts directly outside the law, imposing its aspirations and its desires by means of material pressure. Grievously, the mass took it for granted that, after all, the minorities, in spite of their defects and weaknesses, understood a little more of public problems than it did itself. Now, on the other hand, the mass believes that it has the right to impose and to give force of law to notions born in the café. The characteristic of the hour is that the commonplace mind, knowing itself to be commonplace, has the assurance to proclaim the rights of the commonplace and impose them wherever it will. As they say in the United States, 'to be different is to be indecent'. The mass crushes beneath it everything that is different, everything that is excellent, individual, qualified and select. Anybody who is not like everybody, and does not think like everybody, runs the risk of being eliminated.

The mass is all that which sets no value on itself, good or ill, based on specific grounds, but which feels itself to be just like everybody, and nevertheless is not concerned about it. It is in fact quite happy to feel itself as one with everybody else. There is no doubt that the most radical division that it is possible to make of humanity is that which splits it into two classes of creatures. Those who make great demands on themselves, piling up difficulties and duties, and those who demand nothing special of themselves, but for whom to live is to be at every moment what they already are, without imposing on themselves any effort towards perfection. They are mere buoys that float on the waves. (José Ortega y Gasset, 1930)

The artist defies mediocrity

THE CONTEMPORARY COMPOSER expends an enormous amount of time and energy on the creation of a commodity that has little or no commodity value. He is, in essence, a vanity composer. The general public is largely unaware of and uninterested in his music. The majority of performers shun and resent it . . . Nor do I see why the situation should be otherwise. Why should the layman be other than bored and puzzled by what he is unable to understand – music or anything else? It is only the translation of this boredom and puzzlement into resentment and denunciation that seems to me indefensible. After all, the public does have its own music: music to eat by, to read by, to dance by, and to be impressed by. Why refuse to recognize the possibility that contemporary music has reached a stage long since attained by other forms of activity? I . . . suggest that the composer would do himself and his music an immediate and eventual service by total, resolute and voluntary withdrawal from this public world to one of private performance and electronic media, with its very real possibility of the complete elimination of the public and social aspects of musical composition. By so doing . . . the composer would be free to pursue a private life of professional achievement, as opposed to a public life of unprofessional compromise and exhibitionism. (Milton Babbitt, 1958)

WHY DOES THE BIG PUBLIC hate extreme artistic integrity? How can a great composer go forward at all in what looks like a voluntary cul-de-sac? Surely the matter is that the very big public masses together in a kind of dead passion of mediocrity, and that this blanket of mediocrity, whether communist or capitalist, is deeply offended by any living passion of the unusual, the rare, the rich, the exuberant, the heroic and the aristocratic in art, the art of a poet like Yeats. Why, it's clear from Yeats's life and writings that in this very passion of defiance, an artist can find both material for his art and vigour for his despised activity, but he may starve, because given our present disrelation between artist and public, it's obvious that patronage from one side, so to speak, from the public, and directed to satisfy the official taste, cannot for that reason be used honestly to satisfy the creative urges of a great artist. What alone has immortality, if there is to be such in any period, is the work of art, born from just this living passion of creation; the dead passion of mediocrity may kill the living artist and the nation's art, but it cannot project its own deadness beyond its own death. (Michael Tippett, 1954)

How did the artist become élitist?

I THINK IT'S POSSIBLE to put the issue in perspective if you look at this notion of artistic autonomy, something that's very much in discussion nowadays in music scholarship, and define it in three ways. There's a social aspect to autonomy, the status of the composer, and historically speaking that is a relatively recently won autonomy, whereby in the early nineteenth century the composer becomes a sort of freelance. There's aesthetic autonomy, how we actually approach works of art, the rise of the concert where we listen to music on its own terms, rather than it being part of a elaborate social function (whether state or religious or whatever). That kind of aesthetic autonomy is a development of the late eighteenth century. And then you might also talk about a kind of structural autonomy, whereby we stress the individuality of a piece of music as opposed to its fitting into some kind of standard format or genre.

Taking all these three things together – social, aesthetic and structural autonomy – we can see a development in the nineteenth century leading to the music of the turn of the century, where the composer is pretty much isolated. He (it's usually he) is composing music of incredible originality. No genres are being copied but each new work creates its own genre, and this music really has to be understood very much on its own terms. There are tendencies in this direction throughout the nineteenth century, but in the twentieth century autonomy is such that the composer is totally isolated. Very few people seem to want to have anything to do with his music, and would have trouble even if they did want to do so, because it's so unusual and original. (Stephen Hinton)

A gulf opens . . .

UP TO THE START of the century popular music included popular opera and all kinds of symphonic music and so on. Perhaps with the advent of recording, with the changes that came at the time of the First World War and the advent of broadcasting, there was a division between what might be called popular music and what might be called classical music, and that's where things started to drift apart. (Raymond Gubbay)

. . . and grows wider

CERTAINLY WHEN SCHOENBERG worked out his twelve-tone method in the early 1920s, he seemed to talk about the future quite a lot, and was rather disdainful of his younger colleagues who seemed to be composing for the present, so at that time in his life he certainly seemed to be composing music that his pupil Hanns Eisler termed 'for the bottom drawer' – for posterity. (Stephen Hinton)

IF YOU ARE REALLY CREATIVE, and you want to express what you wish to express, I don't think that you can have an audience in mind, or just very vaguely. How can you conceive the audience in thirty years, even? Either you are a kind of tailor making suits for people, or, as in the entertainment world, they have to have instant success, which is rewarded by money, and that's the core of their activity. But I think when you want to go further in expression of feelings, ideas and expressions of yourself, then you have to write what you want to express. (Pierre Boulez)

Mass and class

THE DIVISION OF SOCIETY into masses and select minorities is not a division into social classes and cannot coincide with the hierarchic separation of upper and lower classes. Within both these classes there are to be found mass and genuine minority. It is not rare to find today amongst working men, who before might be taken as the best example of what we are calling mass, nobly disciplined minds. (José Ortega y Gasset, 1930)

A new generation, post-1918

IT SEEMS TO BE that the First World War had an enormous impact on this generation, many of whom either came into the war very late or didn't serve at all because they were too young. Many values were overturned for them, and this period was also the time in which the new media, in which there really were possibilities for reaching the masses, were being developed.

What they usually did was revert to some kind of tonal language, the language that had been overturned by Schoenberg, initially in the direction of atonal music in the first decade of the twentieth century and then into twelve-tone music at the beginning of the 1920s. When Eisler studied with Schoenberg he wrote in an atonal way, and also used a fairly rudimentary form of twelve-tone music. Thereafter the music he composed – which seems as much as anything a protest against aspects of the Schoenbergian legacy – is in a rather mixed style, but when he was actually writing 'applied music' he'd have to write tonal music. In these compositions Eisler was very proud of the handicraft that he was using: various niceties of motivic manipulation and all sorts of rhythmic subtleties, and he still maintained that there was a type of tonal music that could have an effect on listeners, that would sort of dupe them. He wanted his listeners to remain alert. He felt, for example, that emphatic tonal closure might suggest that everything was nicely wrapped up, and so he tended to leave his cadences rather

open. You could say that in many ways he was applying an auto-
nomous aesthetic, expecting people to be listening very carefully,
whereas what was probably going on is that they were getting wrapped
up in the proceedings, but a lot of ink has been spilt by analysts who
want to draw a great distinction between Eisler's applied music and
regular pop music. (Stephen Hinton)

Useful music

OUR AIM IN CREATING a new useful music is not to compete with the
composer of hit tunes. It is simply to bring our music to the masses.
That can be attained only if our music is capable of expressing simple
human emotions and actions. It's not a question of renouncing the
intellectual ambition of a serious musician. Our hostile critics point
out that in our works the musical language is drastically simplified.
Nobody talks about tonal or atonal. Nobody's afraid of banality, but
it's true: our tunes sometimes sound quite like light music. But they fail
to notice that our music is not catchy but rousing. The intellectual
bearing is serious, bitter, accusatory or, at the very least, ironic. But,
above all, our poetry and music would not exist without the ethical
and social framework of the drama. (Kurt Weill, 1925)

The risks of addressing a new public

A PIECE OF AMATEUR MUSIC – written by Hindemith for example –
could be informed by the composer's desire to turn away from composing for the concert hall, to reach a rather different audience.
Ultimately Hindemith couldn't determine what that audience was, but
in trying to realize his goals, if he got caught up in the youth-music
movement – which he did – he might have become involved unwit-
tingly with various people who turned out to have right-wing interests.
I think this was certainly the case. There was a general trend towards
writing music in a simpler style, music written for amateurs, and the
amateurs could belong to communist organizations or to fascist organizations. All these things happened in the 1920s.

In the immediate post-Second World War period, the composers
who'd gone through the Nazi period seeing just where applied music
could go – which is down a very unpleasant road indeed – recoiled
from this notion of applied music. In a way, the social, aesthetic and
structural autonomy of the post-war period is even more acute than it
had been in the pre-Second World War period. If you look at the music
of the Darmstadt school of composers, for example, in many ways

that's as far removed from the mass songs of Hanns Eisler as one could possibly imagine. (Stephen Hinton)

The Arts Council: teaching new games

DON'T THINK OF THE Arts Council as a schoolmaster. Your enjoyment will be our first aim. We have but little money to spill, and it will be you yourselves who will, by your patronage, decide in the long run what you get. In so far as we instruct, it is a new game we are teaching you to play; to play and to watch. Our wartime experience has already led us to one clear discovery: the unsatisfied demand and the enormous public for serious and fine entertainment. This certainly didn't exist a few years ago. I don't believe that it's merely a wartime phenomenon. I fancy that the BBC has played a big part, the predominant part in creating this public demand, by bringing to everybody in the country the possibility of learning these new games, which only the few used to play, and by forming new tastes and habits and thus enlarging the desires of the listener and his capacity for enjoyment. (John Maynard Keynes, 1945)

INSTITUTIONS HAVE A VERY particular function. What they think they're there to do is to purify, to be the gatekeeper, to make judgements of value, and then to mediate and reproduce a particular view of what constitutes important music in our day. (Georgina Born)

Eisler's influence

FOR MANY OF THE STUDENTS in West Germany Hanns Eisler was an example of a composer who on the one hand took seriously the traditions that he had learned with Schoenberg, the traditions of German art music, but on the other hand developed a social consciousness. Composers such as Luigi Nono and Hans Werner Henze were very much in Eisler's debt, and enormously appreciated what he had done. They appreciated at the same time that they were working in rather different circumstances from Eisler and adjusted their creative efforts accordingly. (Stephen Hinton)

MANY PEOPLE THINK, since I'm a left-wing man, that I should now write for the workers exclusively. That is not at all necessary, and would be a little bit odd. I do write for workers. I write music for workers' singing groups and things like that when they ask me to do so, but it is much more important to fight for the working class to have enough leisure, time and self-assurance to understand that music belongs to them and not to the rich. (Hans Werner Henze)

The avant-garde under attack

YOU WILL ALWAYS HAVE the avant-garde. What we did, curiously, through this century, certainly the second half of it, through the funding system, was to say, 'Let's jump in with the avant-garde.' In pre-war days, when Schoenberg was the revolutionary, when Picasso was painting in the most extraordinarily iconoclastic way, they were challenging something: they were challenging officialdom and the Establishment. What has happened now is that the avant-garde has become the Establishment, and we've lost that ability to challenge it. (Gavin Henderson)

ONE DISTINCTIVE POINT we can talk about is what happens when you get the rise of the institutions, specialized institutions for the support of music education and of composers: the universities, the music colleges and conservatoires, and finally, the even more specialized institutions such as IRCAM or ZKN. What's interesting then is that this becomes a kind of aberrant moment. I'm not saying it's going to go away, though it may be under threat because of the continuous debate about public funding of the arts and about the place of music education, but in the long scheme of things, the rise of these dedicated institutions or dedicated spaces within subsidized institutions to support composers is exceptional. (Georgina Born)

ON THE SIMPLEST LEVEL we can say that any music is good that benefits the people, and this is a political criterion. Raising the level of consciousness of the people is a political task. Everything that music can do towards raising the level of consciousness of the people is part of this political task. The artist cannot ignore politics. To deny this is to cast yourself adrift in the realm of fantasy, and if you are an artist your work will be judged according to the political criterion first, and the artistic criterion second, and it will be seen notwithstanding any artistic merit it may have to be misleading the people, not raising their level of consciousness and hence supporting capitalism and serving to prolong its domination of the working oppressed people. (Cornelius Cardew, 1974)

Not one audience but many

CULTURALLY SPEAKING THERE ARE many publics, many audiences, and they are stratified. What I mean by that is that different parts of culture, different kinds of music, come with different degrees of status;

different degrees of economic backing – from different sources, public and private – and that they have different degrees of what we call, technically, 'legitimation', cultural value. There are arguments about their cultural worth, longevity, and so on. Therefore there are many publics consuming musics that come with no publicly recognized high status, no public funding, no arguments being made for their value and worth and longevity. Composers will torture themselves by reflecting on this too greatly. I think it can be productive, but I also think it can be deeply inhibiting. (Georgina Born)

The effect of broadcasting and recording

IN OUR DAY, when there seems a kind of law that the more seriously a composer applies himself to his art, the less public he can have at all, then the serious young composer may come to feel he can't start any-where, that his public must remain ever non-existent. Yet the truth of the matter may be that his public is just ones and twos, those few folk really interested in new things; and here it is that, through the radio, if his music can once be played, his public of ones and twos can be assembled, so to speak, without assembling. This is in fact what does happen. Most new music begins its real public life on the radio.

Nevertheless, radio hasn't changed our musical or social life so rad-ically that we go no more to concerts, because radio cannot reproduce all the real thing. And despite our new methods of communication by radio and television, the big public that wants to hear music in concert halls and see opera in theatres is still our idea of the music public. (Michael Tippett, 1954)

IT SEEMS TO ME that what happened during the greater part of this century was the emergence of broadcasting and recording, and the availability of superlative performance, which turned music into a commodity. It gave the composer a wonderful scope, because immedi-ately you could hear the work pretty well as the composer intended it to be, whereas formerly, for instance, even the Beethoven symphonies you'd had to learn in piano-duet arrangements or even perhaps through a brass band playing them. There was very little scope just to switch on and listen to Beethoven's Fifth Symphony. We take that for granted now; it's at our fingertips. And so what happened was that with the commercialization of music a heritage culture was immedi-ately established. Music had a shelf life; it was something you reached out for and switched on. The sense of making music, which everybody did to a greater or lesser extent, swiftly disappeared. The real dilemma is that music became something that could be so easily commercialized and so easily sold, and the cheaper it was to package and present the more it became in a sense popular culture, and people stopped making music themselves, because they had inhibitions suddenly about the kind of music, the way in which it was made. Far better for the publican to put on a record or put on a tape than have somebody singing round the piano. But previously we *did* sing round the pub piano, we sang in church, we danced on the village green – all those folky things. It was a true living culture, which got anaesthetized by recording and broadcasting. (Gavin Henderson)

IT WAS A SOCIALIST IDEA of the 1960s to make the best available but not for profit: that was not the prime objective; whereas now it would appear that we're faced with a late capitalist Utopia – the idea of everything being provided, with commercial and artistic values mixed up, and the whole thing over-expanded. Having music available on the BBC or Classic FM or whatever, having the run of the CD market, while very beneficial in some ways, also commercializes the whole structure of music listening and takes the emphasis away from musical literacy, by which I mean being able to read music and being able to play or sing it, however modestly. The fruit of over-availablity and democratization – what I'd call the wall-to-wall music that's now available – is passivity. The listener is no longer active but enfeebled and passive, and probably does something else while listening to music, and ultimately this makes music into Muzak. (Alexander Goehr)

Engaging with a living culture

IF ONE LOOKS AT the boom of what we call world music, what people feel that they are in touch with is a true sense of a living culture: they see cultures where people can make music. It's something you can reach out and feel and immediately engage with, and that's why the promotion of that sort of music has developed as rapidly as it has. However, what's perhaps more exciting in some respects is the experience I've had, for instance, at Dartington Summer School, where people used to come and sing in choirs for the great oratorios and masses, and they played chamber music of Mozart, Schubert, Beethoven and so forth. They are actually now much more wanting to engage with composers, and they want composers to write works that they can play and they can be part of – simply for the enjoyment of playing them, not because they're going to be performed, not because they're going to be recorded or broadcast, but because they want to make that music. The crisis of the twentieth century was the distinction that grew up between those who make and those who take, whereas previously the sense of living culture had been something where people had an appetite for the new work because they were going, probably, to have a chance to play and sing it, and be part of it. That was taken away from them, ironically by the super-access of broadcasting and recording. (Gavin Henderson)

I WOULD WANT TO ARGUE that music should still have very much to do with attachments between certain social groups, social categories, and this notion that we no longer live in a world in which there are social attachments but they're created out of musical tastes. This is a nightmare scenario. What is promised by the Internet or by the increasing reliance on the technological mediation of music is rather frightening, because what it can do is to break even more of these links between music and practice and a sense of social relatedness, and that's highly problematic. (Georgina Born)

WHAT HASN'T BEEN INVENTED YET is digital sex, and music at its most basic, from time immemorial, has been about mating and about bringing people together. Either they've come together to perform it, or it has been the thing that has brought them together. What the recording world has done, and to some extent broadcasting, is to sterilize that process. It's encouraged a kind of home-based take-away culture, but people are missing that rubbing shoulders, the smell and touch of being out there. Why do the Proms succeed where other concerts fail? It's because it's a smelly bearpit of people who are rubbing shoulders with each other: it is a social experience. That was true of the Victorian music-hall. It's no accident that the music-halls, the Italian opera houses, the Georgian theatres, were built round court-yard spaces, with the audience facing each other across the divide of the hall, not in beautifully designed, well-upholstered seats facing the stage. There was a very good reason for that: it wasn't because architects were stupid, and didn't think of perfect sightlines. It was that people wanted to gather, and the sense of gathering and being part of the performance, engaging with it, was very important. We lost that when the cinema came, and cinema architecture then influenced the building of other performance spaces, because so often those spaces had to be available for the showing of films, and so architects began to think of the perfect sightline, the well-groomed auditorium, the way in which you glide to your seat from your perfect parking place, and we lost that sense of rough and tumble which is engaging in performance.

What may be coming about now, through the Internet and through interactive technology, is a different kind of rough and tumble, but you still won't get the smell, the touch and the raw metabolism of it. (Gavin Henderson)

15 Music and the Mind

*One great relief of putting down a book of philosophy and listening
to a Beethoven quartet is that you've gone to something that doesn't
have a meaning: it's got something else.*

PETER KIVY

MUSIC IS RECEIVED by the ear, but conceived and perceived by the
mind. For centuries there have been enquiries into the nature,
value and function of music, examinations of musical aesthetics and
discussions of the differences between music and the other arts. The
fundamental questions of how music is conceived in the mind and
perceived by it, however, could not be seriously addressed until such
disciplines as psychology and neurology were developed. A pioneering
study into the physiology of the brain, concentrating on those of
distinguished scientists, was published by Rudolf Wagner in the early
1860s; his book bore the significant title *Preliminary Studies in the
Scientific Morphology and Physiology of the Human Brain as a
Spiritual Organ*. Later in the century and early in the twentieth, other
scientists made specific investigations of the brains of musicians, and
again the title of one of them is significant: S. Auerbach's *Contribution
on the Localization of Musical Talent in the Brain and Skull* was published serially between 1906 and 1913. Auerbach examined the brains
of several eminent musicians, including the conductors Felix Mottl and
Hans von Bülow, and suggested that certain areas of the brain were
particularly prominent in the musically gifted. His findings were

confirmed by studies of the phenomenon of amusia, the loss or impairment of musical ability, which can result from damage to the same areas of the brain that Auerbach had studied.

It is, however, much easier to recognize which parts of the brain affect musicality than to discover how they do so, and this area is still the subject of much research and speculation. But study is not confined to the laboratory and to the pages of scientific journals. Much can be learned or inferred by examining such 'normal' yet complex areas of musical experience and activity as composing, rehearsal, performance and listening. Further insights can be gained from observing the phenomenon of memory, as crucial to the perception and understanding of music as it is to performance. These perceptions enable us to consider whether music can be usefully described as 'a language', and in what sense it can be said to have meaning. Musicians may give one set of answers to such questions, but by examining them from quite different perspectives neurologists, brain scientists, psychologists and philosophers may valuably reply with others. Many of the answers given here are speculative, or suggest analogies for processes that are as yet imperfectly understood. But at the very least they offer a fresh approach to such questions as whether music can express anything (and if so what) and how inspiration may be defined.

Many of the earliest researchers into the anatomy of the brain were concerned with damage or malfunction and how they might be cured or alleviated. Another insight into the way that the brain responds to music is found in the developing field of music therapy, where music can at times not only 'minister to the mind diseased' but even ameliorate severe physical symptoms that do not respond to conventional medical treatment. Most of the chapters in this book are concerned with the factors that have formed music during the past century; in this one there seems to be a distinct sense of a new area of knowledge opening up whose vast possibilities will be fully understood only within the century that is now beginning.

*

Music: natural phenomenon or artificial illusion?

MUSIC IS A SUM TOTAL of scattered forces. You make an abstract ballad of them! I prefer the simple notes of an Egyptian shepherd's pipe; for he collaborates with the landscape and hears harmonies unknown to your treatises. Musicians listen only to the music written by cunning hands, never to that which is in nature's script. To see the sun rise is more profitable than to hear the 'Pastoral' Symphony. What is the use of your almost incomprehensible art? Ought you not to suppress all the parasitical complexities which make music as ingenious as the lock of a strong-box? You paw the ground because you only know music and submit to strange and barbarous laws. You are hailed with high-sounding praises, but you are merely cunning! Something between a monkey and a lackey. (Claude Debussy, 1901)

MUSIC IN A WAY is always a lie, because it's an artifice that passes itself off as nature. But one of the pleasures we take in music is our complicity in that lie. We believe its naturalness, we submit and accept its naturalness, and at the same time we know that it's all an illusion. (Nicholas Cook)

Models of the human mind

I REMEMBER A PHRASE of the great philosopher Schopenhauer: 'And the musical tones inhabit and form a universe of their own, and with the human mind have created the materials and reduced them to order.' (Igor Stravinsky)

PERHAPS THE EASIEST ANALOGY that springs to mind is the idea that each instrument or group of instruments is very similar to different regions of the brain. If you look at the brain, you know that very conspicuously there are very different types of brain structure that make it up; it's a hotchpotch that's developed over evolution. You have a cauliflower-shaped-looking structure at the back and a long straggly thing that extends from the spinal cord and so on. Anyone could point out different regions, just as anyone, even if they were tone deaf or a Martian, could point out the difference between a violin and a drum. Similarly, the fact that those instruments make different sounds is rather analogous to the effects of damage to these different brain regions, which manifest as different behavioural problems to greater or lesser extent. This is a rather simple analogy but one that holds, because just as we can't really say, when we hear a symphony, exactly what the contribution of a violin is (the whole being more than the sum of its parts) so it is with brain regions. We know the signature of each brain region, inferred from clinical data, just as we know the signature sound that an instrument might make, though of course the tunes will vary and their contribution to the symphony at any one moment will vary. So it is with brain regions. (Susan Greenfield)

WE'RE QUITE COMFORTABLE with the idea that our thoughts pass and change and go on and become something else. Susan Greenfield has an idea that the actual patterns of the cells of the brain are at the root of this process of the turnover of thought, so that the billions of flickering patterns that happen every second – we can't begin to even contemplate the speed at which our thoughts work and develop – are organized in hierarchies of patterns, one thought nested inside another thought inside another, and the way one 'firing pattern' gives way to another is the key to our ability to change what we're thinking about. Obviously, if you examine your own mind, you will know the times of day when you think slowly. When you get up out of bed you're not very aware, and you're not thinking of anything in particular. You could say that you're thinking rather slowly. At another time, when you perhaps are late for a train and you're looking at your watch and running along the street, you really feel that everything is going about five times faster than is comfortable. You're in a panic, so there's a very rapid turnover of your thoughts.

The cell assemblies and the speed of their turnover are key factors when we're thinking about how the brain works. Susan Greenfield thinks that these billions of firing patterns are organized by central focusing groups of cells which become relatively hard-wired and act as the hub of activity, and this hub grows from perhaps one impulse, which made an impression of some kind, and built connections wired from one part of the brain to another, from one idea to another. These focuses or epicentres become the centres of meaning, and how these epicentres are activated and stimulated is at the root of of our thought processes. It's the growth and the building and strengthening of these epicentres that's the key to the speed of turnover of thought. She even links it to the evolutionary concept of the survival of the fittest, so the strongest, most robust, most strongly wired epicentre then becomes the thought that dominates. (Julia Usher)

IF YOU ASK FOR A definition of the epicentre, metaphorically it's the thing that triggers off consciousness. It's like a stone dropped in a puddle or the bell ringing so that you pick up the phone. It's something that is the centre of your consciousness. In phenomenological terms, it would be worry, fear, hope: it's the thing that dominates your consciousness at that moment, and of course in us sophisticated humans it can be something internalized that's already there. In neurological terms, I don't think each of these things is represented by a single brain cell; we know that you don't have a single brain cell for hope any more than you have a gene for criminality or a chemical for pleasure. What you could have is a hub, a hard-wired hub of brain cells. This epicentre, or hub of brain cells, is a fairly enduring feature of the brain. It's what I call the mind, the personalization of the brain. (Susan Greenfield)

I DON'T THINK any cognitive psychologist except perhaps the most arrogant would claim to have built up a model of how the mind works. What we are coming to believe is that the mind is a set of partially separable machines doing very specific jobs, and the most that any one of us can hope to understand is how one bit of that machine works. There's talk about the mind being modular, so there's a module for language, a module for spatial behaviour, and there might well be a module for music.

Very often these things can operate independently of one another, or cross-talk, but sometimes the cross-talk isn't as much as one might think, so you get these extraordinary cases, for example, of people with brain damage who completely lose their ability to talk or understand speech, but can still play the piano or can still compose. I'm thinking of the case of Clive Wearing, who I had the privilege to know and to sing under. He was a professional musician: a pianist, an organist, and he ran choirs in London. Then in his mid-thirties, at the height of his powers, he was hit by a terrible viral disease, which knocked out half of his brain, and the result of that disease was that he had no memory of his former life. When taken to a piano and sat in front of it and asked to play, he said, 'Why are you taking me here? I don't play the piano. I've never seen this in my life.' But when actually sitting at the piano, he suddenly was able to play.

Data like that produced by Clive Wearing suggest that although we have a very strong sense as conscious beings of our mind being a unity, we're not really aware of the degree to which the various functions of our mind are quite separate, and separable. Consciousness almost misleads us into thinking that our mind is more orderly and unified than it actually is. (John Sloboda)

THE NATURE OF THE HUMAN MIND is the most difficult question nowadays, a question that my philosophy department spends most of its time on. I'm not a brain scientist or a philosopher of mind. I simply use a common-sense notion of what the mind does, the same notion that everybody has: that we have a memory, that we can perceive things, that when we perceive things we perceive them under certain descriptions. You don't just see visual blurs; you see a clock or you see a table. My approach to music is to consider what goes on in people's minds – in that perfectly ordinary sense of mind – when they listen to music, not what goes in their neurons. (Peter Kivy)

I HAVE A MODEL of how music goes through the human mind. I think that music has an immediacy, in the apprehension of tonally moving forms, but the way in which we respond to and even more the way in which we represent or articulate those forms is hugely determined by many social and cultural factors. Although music in some ways speaks directly to us, nevertheless the way that we represent it and the way we think and talk about it determine our experiencing of the sounds. That's something that we acquire as we grow up, as we talk with others, as we operate within society and particular institutions. All of these things impinge on our experience of music, and to that extent the social dimension is definitive of music as we experience it, as we live it.

The ways that responses to music have changed in history are one of the most sensitive indicators of the way individuals sense who they are, but also how they sense the society that they are part of. After all, what is society but the combination of different senses of what society is? In this context Beethoven's Ninth Symphony has acquired so many meanings, meanings that have changed and varied from place to place. Think of Beethoven's Ninth Symphony in Japan, in Communist China: it has acquired all sorts of meanings that were totally inconceivable at the time that Beethoven wrote it. What more dramatic and sensitive indicator of the changes in society and in people's sense of who they are within society could there be than the history of Beethoven's Ninth Symphony? (Nicholas Cook)

Memory and the mind

MEMORY IS VERY INTERESTING in relation to epicentres if you think, for example, of a particular tune that you heard when you got engaged. Before you got engaged to be married, you had heard that tune a few times, and it became the centre of a memory, but it was a pretty weak one among many other tunes that you knew. Now, suddenly, your husband proposed to you while that tune was playing. You were in a highly heightened state of excitement and emotion, and all of a sudden that incident and that event became very highly dramatized in your mind, and many connections were made to that epicentre, which then grew quite big. Now, every time during your life when you thought of lovely times, particularly focusing on that particular memory, it would be reanimated with very strong feeling and you might add new things to that memory. So the important thing about memory is not that there is some total recall of a fixed memory that never changes, but that every time it's called back you make new connections, and the epicentre grows or indeed wanes. (Julia Usher)

OTHER PARTS OF THE BRAIN are involved in the kind of memories that would be involved in sensory motor skills – playing the piano, for

example – where you're co-ordinating your senses with your movement. That kind of memory requires lots of practice, whereas other
memories you don't have to practise. You don't have to practise going
to the seaside with Auntie Flo: that's a one-off event that is frozen in
your memory.

With the so-called episodic memory, if you're remembering a simple
fact like the word for 'table' in French, it doesn't change: it doesn't get
upgraded or downgraded. Similarly, sensory motor skills will get better
with experience, but they're not dramatically transformed. The most
interesting memories, the kind that most of us mean when we talk
about memory, are memories for episodes, and of course they get
refreshed and changed and upgraded. The reason is that every memory
is nested in thousands of other memories and assumptions, and it's
predicated on a whole lot of cultural ideas, so that as these perceptions
change – which they inevitably do as we go through life – then of
course you'll see something in a different way. It's very different therefore from analogies with a computer in which a memory is an isolated
thing. (Susan Greenfield)

MEMORY IS ABSOLUTELY ESSENTIAL in listening to a piece of music,
that is, remembering to some extent what you've heard before. Of
course it takes a person with a musical mind like a Mozart to remember
every event in a piece. Mozart apparently could walk out of a performance and write down what he heard. Few of us have a memory like
that, but the great composer relies on our being able to remember the
things he did at the beginning, because then when he gets to another
point, maybe he's going to do them again but differently, or maybe he's
going to do something very different from what he did at the beginning. You won't recognize it as different unless you remember what
happened earlier.

There's another very important role that memory plays, in that
when you listen to a piece of music, what you hear is a function of all
of the other music you've heard in your lifetime. Composers know
that, and they certainly play with it in the way they react to the composers that came before them. Beethoven's First Symphony is very
familiar to concert-goers, and it's a very easy work for them, but it was
a very difficult work for Beethoven's contemporaries. One of the things
he did right at the beginning was start with a chord that would have
not been a permissible way to start a composition if one were Haydn
or Mozart. It shocked his listeners – and he meant it to – because they
remembered how a piece of music is supposed to start. So when you
listen to a piece of music even for the first time, you're not *really*

listening to it for the first time because you are acculturated in the style of that work. A composer of the kind we're talking about plays with surprise and expectation. Sometimes your expectations are fulfilled, sometimes not. (Peter Kivy)

LISTENING TO MUSIC in an engaged way is in some sense about keeping track; constantly, as we listen to music, we're trying to guess what's going to come next on the basis of our prior experience of music. The expectations that are built up in different musical cultures are different. They are a function of the particular way in which notes and rhythms and harmonies are put together in those cultures, and that's one of the reasons why many people find music of other cultures initially so baffling, because *everything* is unexpected. We can engage emotionally with music only when there's a balance between the expected and the unexpected. When we're listening to music in a language we don't understand, or from a culture we don't understand, everything is surprising (and therefore in a sense nothing is surprising), and our emotions begin to disengage. It has been said that that's one of the reasons why many people find it so hard to listen to atonal music, aleatoric music, etc.: there are no signposts. (John Sloboda)

FOR THE COMPOSER, memory works in different ways. In *Les noces* Stravinsky was writing a piece about a Russian peasant wedding, but there's a little musical fragment that came to him when he was in a train in Switzerland. One evening, two drunks got into the train and started singing. It's not a Russian tune at all, but when Stravinsky had a particular purpose in mind, he had no shame about taking what he wanted from wherever he could find it. He said that music that he loved he liked to steal and use himself, doing things to it in order to stamp his own identity on it. So you have this Swiss song appearing in a piece about a Russian wedding. Non-authentic memories or experiences might be pressed into the service of supposedly genuine memories. (Paul Webster)

How do we hear music?

WE HEAR MUSIC as sound events that we can describe to ourselves and to others, and it depends on the depth of our musical training how we perceive those sounds, under what descriptions. People born into a culture don't have to be taught to listen to music. If they're in an environment where music is played, they naturally become acculturated to that music, the same way that if you're born in France, you naturally speak French. What technical training or any kind of increase in your knowledge of what you're listening to does is make the object of your perception a larger object. The more you know, the more enjoyable it is. There are more and more things you perceive as part of the object of your perception, and the pleasure is the pleasure in perceiving those events. (Peter Kivy)

WHEN I PLAY *LES NOCES*, I'm telling my body to respond exactly to Stravinsky's rhythmic notation, which is presumably what he was feeling when he chose to notate it that way. He said that the acoustical reality was a biological reality for him, and that he needed to touch the sounds when he was composing. The extent to which the perversities (if you want to call them that) of his notation in *Les noces* are understood either consciously or subconsciously by the listener is a very debatable point, but it obviously fulfilled a necessary function for him as a composer. But there are lots of games that are played by a composer, or indeed any creative artist, in the process of creating that are private to themselves and they may well be processes that actually fuel the creative fire and don't have to be heard or understood by the audience. (Paul Webster)

Is music a language?

THE NOTION THAT MUSIC is a language is one of the most persistent that I know of. It's language-like in certain very obvious respects. Firstly it has something that's very analogous to a syntax. What it doesn't have in my view is a semantics. It doesn't have a dictionary – it doesn't have meaning in that sense. What it means to have meaning is a highly contested philosophical problem. In the sense in which a French sentence has a meaning, and you can translate it into English and then you can translate the English into German – if that's what you mean by meaning, music doesn't have it. One of the problems here is that people argue that either music has meaning or it's meaningless. If it's meaningless it can't be important. But it is important, therefore it must have a meaning. There's something wrong here: not everything in the world that's important has a meaning. It's a Western hang-up to think that everything has to have a meaning. One great relief of putting down a book of philosophy and listening to a Beethoven quartet is that you've gone to something that doesn't have a meaning: it's got something else. (Peter Kivy)

MEANING ARISES OUT OF PATTERNS of similarity, but to call all that a language is really taking the terminology far further than it will bear. But music is language-like; the metaphor of language is one of the main ways in which we grasp music. We've created academic studies in music in which the idea of music as text, of music as language, is the guiding metaphor through which a discourse has been created. It goes beyond that because the metaphor of music being a language has actually been built into some musical traditions themselves. There was first the tradition of seeing music's ability to persuade as a kind of rhetoric, and the idea of music as rhetoric makes a lot of sense applied not only to seventeenth-century opera but to present-day television commercials.

Equally, the idea of music as language has simply been a metaphor for talking about music's orderliness, its coherence. The idea that music should be coherent, an expression of some kind of unity, is enough to explain the values underlying the metaphor of language. But the metaphor has been applied, as metaphors always are, in a more literal way. Ideas of the language of music – ideas that Schoenberg probably thought about in developing the twelve-tone system – then got built into culture in way that was never supported by the aesthetic perception of listeners. The rift between the process of composition and the processes of listening is one of the most characteristic features of the story of music in the twentieth century. (Nicholas Cook)

ONE OF THE THINGS a language has to do is provide a common medium for communication, so that when you speak the other person understands what it is you're referring to. It's not clear at all that music has that function or is meant to have that function. If it did, it wouldn't be music, it would simply be another language, and the whole point about music is that it doesn't have that kind of specific referential meaning. There are certainly things that music can suggest to a listener. For example fast, loud music suggests the behaviour of an energetic or an angry person, and slow, soft music suggests the behaviour of a mournful and dejected person, because they share some sound characteristics with the kind of behaviour that would be produced by such a person. By these kinds of association routes we can get some sense that music is about something, but that doesn't mean it has meaning in the full sense of a language. (John Sloboda)

A VERY INTERESTING QUESTION is how language actually relates to music. The popular idea is this left brain/right brain business. People like to think that the right brain is the feely-touchy area, that it's emotional and sentimental and lacking in logic, and the left-hand side is the scientific side, concerned with language. More recent research suggests that that is a rather over-simplistic view of things. A much more interesting way of looking at it is to say that there are differences between the hemispheres, but they're differences of precision. So the right hemisphere gives you the background, the overview, the feel for something, whereas it's the fine tuning and the more precise manipulation that occurs in the left hemisphere.

There was an interesting study done with music students. Like most people they tended, before their training, to have a dominant right hemisphere while listening to music. When they were tested after their three-year period they had transferred to the left, showing that the left hemisphere has more to do with attitude and the amount of analysis you're bearing on something than the skills or the functions themselves. (Susan Greenfield)

Should we look for meaning in music?

THE GREAT ORIGINATOR of what is called formalism in music, Eduard Hanslick, published a little book called *The Beautiful in Music* around 1854. He said that of course music has a content. Its content is music and its content is its form. If you want to apply the word 'meaning' to that, you can, but I don't think it serves any useful purpose. There's an old story about a Cambridge or Oxford don who was elected Master of his college, and unfortunately he had a dog and dogs weren't allowed, so the college declared his dog a cat, and he got the job. If you want to say that music's meaning is its form, you've preserved the word the way that college preserved its rule, but I don't think it's very helpful. (Peter Kivy)

Can music express ideas?

THERE WAS AN IDEA that developed around the early part of the nineteenth century and has survived through a good deal of the twentieth that music in its most basic form is 'pure' music. That was never true. The time that words disappeared from the music itself, that words were excluded from the musical text, was also the time when the modern concert hall developed. More than that: the time when the modern programme note developed, so that the words that were excised from the music itself flooded back into its reception. I'd also take issue with the idea that there is any music that is not also extra-musical. Sonata form is, *par excellence*, pure music, about nothing but itself. But a sonata is in essence an imaginary drama between two protagonists represented by some combination of themes and a tonal structure: a kind of dramatic story of opposition and reconciliation. You can also think of it as a process of exploration, of movement away and a sense of homecoming: a kind of search narrative. (Nicholas Cook)

Music and the emotions

IF MUSIC SPEAKS DEEPLY to the emotions, I don't think that means that music is speaking from the voice of nature outside culture. If you think of particular pieces of music written in particular traditions, it's the qualities of the traditions and the whole culture from which they came that the music brings with it. It speaks deeply to your emotions because it comes as a complete bundle. You hear the music, but what is coming into your mind is all the associations with the music. Music naturalizes them.

There was a stage when talking about the emotional appeal of music was out of fashion. However, all sorts of things have come back on to the musical agenda that had disappeared from it: issues of meaning, of ideology, and of personal or emotional involvement are now very much at the centre of the more progressive musicological agenda. (Nicholas Cook)

ONE OF THE FAVOURITE and seemingly most apt ways of describing music, particularly if you're not using technical language, is in terms of emotions. Everyone agrees, pretty much, about which pieces of music are sad, which are happy. The philosophical question that has been tossed around for the last hundred years is: 'What are we saying when we describe music in emotive terms?' The general consensus today is that in a way that's not thoroughly understood music possesses emotions as perceptual properties. We have no problem, for example, in describing a piece of music as 'turbulent'. A 'tranquil' piece of music moves along calmly. Those properties are perceived in the music, and the most popular current notion among analytic philosophers is that those are emotive properties; some philosophers would call them 'emergent properties'. They 'supervene' on other properties in the music, so they're properties of the music, but they are not by any means the only important properties of the music, and they've been greatly over-rated. There's a lot more to talk about in music than the emotions. (Peter Kivy)

EMOTIONS, BY AND LARGE, come about because of surprise. Human beings are made to respond to surprise because it is very important in evolutionary terms for any animal to respond to a situation that is different from that expected. If things are going as you expect then you can behave as normal; if something happens that you don't expect it could be something dangerous, or it could be something advantageous. You have to interrupt what you're doing and attend to the new thing, and emotions are nature's way of interrupting normal activity and making us attend to something that might be dangerous or might be important.

Music engages those systems by being inherently patterned, and therefore creating expectations that are then either fulfilled or thwarted or delayed or whatever, and in the same way therefore we become emotionally aroused. The question of what emotion you feel is much more complicated, because that has a lot to do with how you're feeling when the music starts, what your associations to the music are, whether the people who are playing the music are people you know or care about – a whole range of idiosyncratic and cultural factors come into play, so it becomes very difficult to predict exactly what emotion a person is going to feel when they hear a particular piece of music. (John Sloboda)

AT THE MOMENT WE KNOW relatively little about emotions, physiologically, and this is because most brain scientists have been happier working with processes such as learning and memory, where you have a very clear output that you can measure. It's much harder to measure how much someone loves someone or how upset someone is. Moreover, and this is the thing that really sticks in the craw of many scientists, emotions are subjective. That notwithstanding, people are now trying to understand the basis of emotions. One route is by looking at drugs. We know that drugs modify emotions, and that they modify chemicals in the brain, and therefore by looking at chemicals in the brain and how they work, we're starting to understand a little bit about emotions.

With imaging techniques, where you can actually visualize someone's brain while they're awake, what you can see in depressed people is enhanced blood flow, more activity in the part of the brain called the pre-frontal cortex. Why that is the case, and how that brain region functions in concert with all the other brain regions to make someone feel depressed, is something that we don't know. But my own view of what emotions might be is a very simple form of consciousness. Emotional states are present in adults when they take drugs or when they put themselves in scenarios where they are being bombarded by their senses – let's say they're listening to music. When you're having those emotions, you're much more a passive recipient, you seem to have given up being self-conscious for a while. We should see emotions in the context of an ebb and flow, of our self-consciousness, of what we call our minds, of our preconceived connections, our memories and so on. It seems that at any one time there's a coalescence, where you have emotions there to some degree, your mind there to some degree.

There are extreme examples: when you're very depressed your mind is over-dominant. At other times – the rave, the orgasm, downhill skiing – you have literally blown your mind. In fact the word 'ecstasy' means to stand outside yourself.

Where does music come in? It is a very quick way of bringing that state about, where you are drowned in your senses. There's such an overpowering abstract stimulation of your senses that you no longer have to lock it into words. (Susan Greenfield)

How does the mind compose?

THE FUNCTION OF THE CREATIVE ARTIST consists in making laws, not in following laws ready made. He who follows such laws ceases to be a creator.

Creative power may be the more readily recognized the more it shakes itself loose from tradition. But an intentional avoidance of the rules cannot masquerade as creative power, and still less engender it.

The true creator strives, in reality, after perfection only. And through bringing this into harmony with his own individuality, a new law arises without premeditation. (Ferruccio Busoni, 1911)

OUR IDEAS OF HOW COMPOSERS compose have been largely affected by Beethoven. He bequeathed us an enormous repertoire of compositional sketches and other materials. It seems that he really didn't know what he thought until he saw what he'd written. He would write something, and then he would know what he was trying to write. He used paper to improvise, to fight against – letting the paper speak back to him – whereas other composers of the day and of today would often work at the keyboard, and the keyboard doesn't leave the same kind of traces that Beethoven's process did. Yet there's a flaw: we know so much about Beethoven because he composed in a way that nobody else did. (Nicholas Cook)

TO GET INSIDE the composer's mind, to try to understand what's going on when he produces music, is one of the most difficult challenges in the cognitive psychology of music. I don't think we've begun to grapple with it. The problem is that it's no use waiting until the composer is dead, or even until the piece of music has already been composed, because by then the crucial trails, the details of the cognitive processes, are forgotten. What you need to do is to be alongside the composer while he composes, so that as he writes a note down or tries something out on the piano, the investigator can say, 'Why did you do that? Why did you choose this note and not that? Tell me what you're thinking now.' It's a very rare composer who wishes to subject himself to that kind of scrutiny while composing. Composers feel that that kind of intrusion into the compositional process will disrupt the process itself. By intervening with human beings to study them, you're very often changing the nature of the activity, and we haven't solved that for composition. (John Sloboda)

NEUROSCIENTIFIC WORK ON CREATIVITY is still very much in the Dark Ages. None the less a common view is that a lot of stages go on before they reach consciousness. My own view is that throughout life one has assemblies of brain cells that are banding and disbanding, connections getting stronger and weaker as you have experiences that gather up other ones like blobs of mercury or like clouds forming. Given that they are doing this all the time, and given that the brain is a seething mass of activity and your brain cells are restless all the time, and that there are lots of internal factors that are imposing on them, like your endocrine and immune systems and your state of arousal and so on, it's not inconceivable that, in this banding and disbanding, new configurations occur rather as with chaos theory or complexity theory – these are mathematical models for embracing just those kinds of dynamic phenomena. And what happens, I would imagine, is that one might have a concept that has never occurred before. How it comes into consciousness is another issue. My own view is that consciousness comes by degrees; it will occur when you have a sufficiently large number of brain cells corralled up, so there's a lot of banding and disbanding going on, and eventually something literally links up, so you have bolted on a whole new population brought in as a kind of mass import, and then finally you have such a large seething mass that it will actually come into your consciousness, and you will see that as inspiration or a novel idea. (Susan Greenfield)

I DON'T KNOW WHERE inspiration comes from except that I like the idea of epicentres suddenly firing. That makes a lot of sense to me, as a composer who works with images all the time. I love setting words, so that I have very strong pictures in my head. That moment of inspiration can come as such a rapid spark and yet if you look at the idea, it's very often very small, very fuzzy or very global. You can see a vast landscape but you can't see any of the details. It's all fog and smoke, but it's so beautiful and wonderful, and carries all the possibilities which at that stage you can believe you'll actually be able to realize. It's the disappointment that comes later when you find out you can't fully realize that first inspiration, and yet how do you know you haven't realized it if you don't know what it is? This is a mystery. (Julia Usher)

THE NOTION ABOUT INSPIRATION is that what music is about is musical genius. It's astonishing that this idea is still around, because historians of science have been grappling with it in terms of scientists and what's called the 'Eureka moment'. Not that that isn't important, but what you're leaving out is the hard graft of years of training, of practice, of crumpling everything up in a ball and throwing it away. What you're doing is always trying to make things unique. (Penelope Gouk)

COMPOSERS CLEARLY DRAW ON the whole of their past experience, and one hypothesis about inspiration is that it's rather like reminiscence: you're reminiscing over the stockpile of all the things that you ever heard or thought of, and some of them come into consciousness at a particular time.

Inspiration is a reality, but a very misconstrued reality. A lot of people naïvely believe that compositional inspiration means a composition springing fully fledged into the composer's mind, as if by divine gift, and the composer's job is simply to write it down. That simply just doesn't happen, or if it does it happens very rarely. From composers' own accounts, what happens more likely is that a little germ – a little theme, an idea, a harmony, a couple of harmonies – springs into the composer's mind, and that's the root of the inspiration. Then, by a much more painstaking and conscious process, these materials are welded together, developed, turned around, played with, in the same way that a sculptor might chip away at a piece of stone. It's a much more conscious and work-like activity than most naïve observers would believe. (John Sloboda)

ONCE YOU'VE HAD the 'Eureka moment', then it has to be put into practice. If you suddenly have a vision of the music you then have to translate it into reality. Remember T. S. Eliot: 'Between the idea and the reality falls the shadow'? That's the problem: translating something, giving it a form, because sometimes you can have a concept, some abstract idea of how something might relate to something else, without necessarily knowing the best way to express it.

What we think might be happening in the brain is that there's an area called the pre-frontal cortex, which seems to be very special to us humans because it's twice the size it should be for a primate of our body weight; even compared to chimpanzees it's massive. There is a consensus that one thing the pre-frontal cortex does is to mediate working memory. Working memory is the ability to keep many things in mind at once, lots of assumptions, lots of premises, all the relevant factors that will dictate your action. So it's not too improbable a supposition to say that once you've had your idea, when you're trying to think of how to implement it, your pre-frontal cortex is working on overdrive. What it actually does, where it sends its signals, is another issue. Connected brain areas would be other parts of the cortex: the outer layer of the brain, the so-called association cortex. These areas aren't strictly related to senses coming in or movement coming out, but are related to the co-ordination of the two. (Susan Greenfield)

STRAVINSKY SAID THAT COMPOSERS and painters are not conceptual thinkers. The composer works through a perceptual, not a conceptual, process. One way of paraphrasing that is that a creative artist is digging to find material that already exists, rather than actually creating it. You can take your choice: they're both metaphors for the creative process. But I do warm to that view of creativity, that it's just waiting there to be found, and because there's an infinitely large amount of material to be discovered then there's room for all manner of composers and painters. (Paul Webster)

The mind in rehearsal and performance

A MANUSCRIPT SCORE is brought to a concertmaster, he is kindly disposed, he looks it over, and casually fastens on a passage: 'That's bad for the fiddles, it doesn't hang just right, write it like this, they will play it better.' But that one phrase is the germ of the whole thing. 'Never mind, it will fit the hand better this way, it will sound better.' My God! What has sound got to do with music? The waiter brings the only fresh egg he has, but the man at breakfast sends it back because it doesn't fit his egg cup. Why can't music go out in the same way it comes in to a man, without having to crawl over a fence of sounds, thoraxes, cat-guts, wire, wood, and brass? Consecutive fifths are as harmless as blue laws compared with the relentless tyranny of the 'media'. The instrument! – there is the perennial difficulty – there is music's limitations. Why must the scarecrow of the keyboard – the tyrant in terms of the mechanism (be it Caruso or a Jew's harp) – stare into every measure? Is it the composer's fault that man has only ten fingers? Why can't a musical thought be presented as it is born – perchance 'a bastard of the slums', or 'the daughter of a bishop' – and if it happens to go better later on a bass drum (than upon a harp) get a good bass-drummer. That music must be heard is not essential – what it sounds like may not be what it is. Perhaps the day is coming when music-believers will learn 'that silence is a solvent . . . that gives us leave to be universal' rather than personal. (Charles Ives, 1920)

WHEN A PIECE OF MUSIC is being rehearsed or learned, what's happening is that the learner is trying to discover all the various different ways in which the elements of the music connect together. In other words intelligent learning is about making connections: that this theme is similar to or different in certain respects from the previous occurrence, that there is a clear sectional structure, that this bit is more important than that and I can see where the main boundaries and the subsidiary boundaries are. It's like building up a rich and complex map of the musical structure, and in a sense there's no end to this, because a complex piece of music like a symphony or a sonata has so many layers and so many ways of being structured that you can never come to an end of understanding all the different ways in which these things can link together. That's why it's possible for a professional musician to live with a single piece throughout their lifetime, and yet still feel there are things in it undiscovered.

We have some evidence that the most effective learners, people who learn music the quickest and retain it the most effectively, are those who see structural elements in the music, and build up very consciously a sense of how the various parts of the music fit together. They are thinking structurally. The people who are not so good at doing the task are the memorizers by rote, who think the job is simply to start at note 1 and play through to note 1000, and then go back to the beginning and start again. (John Sloboda)

THE AUDIBLE PRESENTATION, the 'performance' of music, its emotional interpretation, derives from those free heights whence descended the Art itself. Where the art is threatened by earthliness, it is the part of interpretation to raise it and re-endow it with its primordial essence.

Notation, the writing out of compositions, is primarily an ingenious expedient for catching an inspiration, with the purpose of exploiting it later. But notation is to improvisation as the portrait to the living model. It is for the interpreter to resolve the rigidity of the signs into the primitive emotion.

But the law-givers require the interpreter to reproduce the rigidity of the signs; they consider his reproduction the nearer to perfection, the more closely it clings to the signs.

What the composer's inspiration necessarily loses through notation, his interpreter should restore by his own.

To the law-givers, the signs themselves are the most important matter, and are continually growing in their estimation; the new art of music is derived from the old signs – and these now stand for musical art itself.

If the law-givers had their way, any given composition would always be reproduced in precisely the same tempo, whensoever by whomsoever, and under whatsoever conditions it might be performed. But, it is not possible; the buoyant, expansive nature of the divine child rebels – it demands the opposite. Each day begins differently from the preceding, yet always with the flush of dawn. Great artists play their own works differently at each repetition, remodel them on the spur of the moment, accelerate and retard, in a way which they could not indicate by signs – and always according to the given conditions of that 'eternal harmony'. (Ferruccio Busoni, 1911)

MUSICAL PERFORMANCE IS an incredibly complex and multi-layered phenomenon. To carry off a Beethoven sonata requires so much that any one psychologist can study only one bit of it at a time. I've been particularly interested in the improvisatory aspect of performance, because even though the notes of a Beethoven sonata are specified, there is a great deal of freedom for the performer to interpret. Indeed if you just played a piece of classical music as written on the page it would be very dull. A great deal of the art of good performance is the added value that you give to the performance, and I've been trying to study whether there is a systematic way in which good performers add that value.

There are some very simple things that most effective performers add to their performance to make it come alive, and these are to do with communicating the structure of a piece of music. Most classical music, indeed most tonal music, is broken into phrases, and it's very helpful for the listener to get an orientation within the piece if he knows where one phrase ends and the next begins. Performers can help this process by subtle fluctuations in speed and dynamic, for instance, and we now know that effective performers within the tonal domain very often subtly and imperceptibly slow towards phrase ends, and speed up in phrase middles. These are small effects, and very often they're not consciously noticeable, but they do help listeners to work out the structure.

If you ask what the relationship is between what's going on in a performer's head and what's coming out of their fingers, that in a sense may be the wrong question. When you're at a very high level of expertise, there is no gap between thought and action. Thought *becomes* action, and one of the most intriguing things about high levels of skill is the sense the practitioner has that they're almost floating: there is no sense of effort between the conception and the action. It's a seamless activity. One talks to performers about what their experiences on the concert platform are like, and it's very clear that they have this sense of being inside the music, almost losing themselves, and sometimes losing bodily awareness. (John Sloboda)

WHEN YOU'RE PERFORMING, the area of the brain that would be figuring largely is the cauliflower-shaped structure on the back of the brain, the so-called little brain, the cerebellum. We know if that's damaged: people are very clumsy, they can't co-ordinate their sense with their movement very well. Some people are better than others at sensory motor co-ordination, and the more you practise at something your sense and your movement become very finely tuned. This is perhaps one reason why this area of the brain is the best known. It's often been modelled on a computer because it doesn't require consciousness. It's the very area of the brain that seems to function on auto-pilot, and is the most tractable to computer modelling because it's very much related to inputs coming in, experience-weighted multiplications and then responses out.

Other areas of the brain would also be involved in performing. This is where the emotional tone comes in, which is directed by something conscious. When people play well they're not playing subconsciously; they're concentrating on and aware of what they're doing. We don't know, of course, what makes one person a genius and another just a skilled musician. (Susan Greenfield)

What happens in the minds of the audience?

WHEN AN AUDIENCE HEARS a performance of Beethoven's Ninth Symphony, it is hearing an instance of the work. They are in the presence of the work when they are hearing a performance of it, even though when the performance ends the work doesn't cease to exist. A very great American philosopher, Nelson Goodman – the first philosopher I know of who ever tried to figure out what the logic of musical notation is – came up with a notion that was violently objected to by musicians. It was that there could be only one correct realization of the notation. One thing we would agree with Goodman about is that if you change enough things it will cease to be an instance of the work. If there are too many mistakes it will not be an instance of the work. Goodman drew the conclusion, which many people found preposterous, that if there were just one single mistake, even if nobody could hear it and it was just a brief mistake, it wouldn't be an instance of the work. This of course raises the question of how much you can do in a performance. Putting aside the obvious things like playing the wrong notes, how many alterations can you make to the way a musicologist might claim the composer intended the work to be performed? How many changes can you make without ceasing to be giving an instance of the work? Performers are usually allowed an enormous latitude, in the nineteenth century perhaps more than they are today, so that the notion of what the nature of the work is dovetails very beautifully into what the nature of the performance of the work is, and what leeway the performer has to do things that might not be approved of or mandated by the composer. (Peter Kivy)

ONE OF THE MOST interesting questions is what's going on inside the listener in a standard concert situation, where the listener's role is to sit quietly, not to tap his feet, not to sing along, not to behave in any way, but to remain totally silent. The question of what's actually going on inside his head at that point is a very difficult one. We can attempt to simulate some of the conditions of the concert hall in the laboratory, so for example in a series of studies that I've been engaged in recently we asked someone to come into the laboratory, sit and listen to a piece of music, and then react in certain ways while the music was going on. What we can get from this is two things. One is that there are commonalities of response. If you ask people to press a button or move a joystick to indicate when the music is very emotional and arousing or when not very much is happening, what you find is that most people agree; the form of emotional energy in the room will be common. But if you then go one stage further and ask people, 'What were you actually thinking or feeling at that point of high intensity?', then you get as many different answers to the question as there are people in the room. (John Sloboda)

ONE OF THE MOST characteristic things about music is its repetitiveness. Why is it repetitive? Why if something's worth saying does it need to be said twice, and then maybe several times again later in the piece? It's not that as you listen you suddenly think, 'Ah! I'm hearing this again!' Sometimes it articulates a sense of homecoming; sometimes you're conscious of the homecoming but not of the repetition that stimulated it. As well as this feeling of being where you were before, there's also a sense that there's something tangible about the music, something that's not just evanescent but in some way stops time in its tracks or folds time back on itself, a sense of some kind of mastery over time, of the construction of a object that persists through time through music. This paradoxical sense of creating the untimely out of the timely is one of the things that we value within our musical tradition, and almost all musical traditions are built on repetition.

It's obvious that the reproduction of music isn't just a reproduction but a recomposition. You can complain that today's musical culture has become almost entirely a culture of repetition of an almost static repertoire of masterworks, but the point is it's not a mere repetition, it's a repetition in which value is added, in which creativity is expressed, in which all that you might express from music is created around the texts of the received masterworks. A canon is a repertoire of texts that are so well known that when you listen to them, you can really focus your attention and respond to the performance that you hear, as against the horizon of expectations created by other performances. The extent to which we respond to, say, Beethoven's Third Symphony against the background of other performances of it seems to be an enormously important part of our musical culture. (Nicholas Cook)

Where does music exist – mind, score or performance?

THERE WAS A TIME when we thought of the work of music essentially as the score – if not the score as published then the score as the composer would have intended it. So the whole process of interpreting music, whether in performance or in critical interpretation, was seen as a question of sweeping away all the accreted layers of interpretation and misinterpretation so as to get back to the original. Increasingly that isn't how musicologists behave, for two reasons. In the first place the whole process by which people make meaning out of music, by which music is interpreted and misinterpreted, the way in which musical works handed on from the past have been continually reinvented in the light of our own purposes and changing social ideologies, increasingly seems the most interesting part of the entire enterprise.

But at the same time there's a second element. The idea of the original score or the score as the composer intended it increasingly seems problematic, because even deciding what the notes on paper should be, certainly deciding how to make sense of them, is itself an act of interpretation. Interpreters decide what there is to interpret in the first place, so the entire business of musicology is tied up with reception and is indeed an act of reception. (Nicholas Cook)

A PAINTING IS AN OBJECT: it hangs on a wall, there's only one of it, if you own it you hope it's the authentic one (since there may be very many copies of it) and it's locatable in space and time. Musical works don't exist in that way. Asking 'Where is Beethoven's Ninth Symphony located?' is a category mistake, like asking what colour Thursday is. Beethoven's Ninth isn't located anywhere, and that's what makes it a puzzling kind of object for philosophers. Its location is surely not the score – there can be many scores of Beethoven's Ninth Symphony – and if all the scores were destroyed and one person remembered Beethoven's Ninth, it would still exist. What philosophers tend to say about this is (and this language comes from the great American philosopher Charles Sanders Peirce) that at least one possible way of seeing a musical work is as what Peirce called a 'type', and the performances of the work he called 'tokens'. Each pound coin is a token of the type 'the pound coin'. So one way of looking at Beethoven's Ninth Symphony is that it is the type of which all the scores and all the performances are tokens or instances. (Peter Kivy)

I HAVE A QUITE CLEAR VIEW on the question 'Where is music?' or 'Where does music exist?' It exists in the mind. I believe that because I can actually imagine one of my favourite pieces of music. Without being at an instrument, without hearing it, I can run the whole thing in my head, and I think it is actually the appreciation of the way that music fits together inside a human mind that constitutes what music is. One doesn't need even a physical sound for that. Of course one needs the memory of sound, but music is inside one's mind. (John Sloboda)

WHEN I HEAR A PIECE of mine performed, there's the terror of performance, of course, but the most wonderful part of the experience usually is hearing what the performer brings to it that is not from me, where the performer has interpreted something I didn't know I'd written. Hearing the inside of your head becoming something that exists in the outside world is sometimes an incredible experience.

The ownership of the music changes. It floats somewhere out there, and is gone away from you. Does it exist at all when it isn't being sounded, when it's not being performed? It doesn't really exist on the paper. It does exist in your mind, but you really don't sit down playing your compositions in your head very often, so where does it exist? Really only in that moment of re-creation. (Julia Usher)

Music and mental health

THE RELATIONSHIP BETWEEN MUSIC and mania has remained constant. On the one hand there's a view that music calms or can help madness, but if you look at composers and poets it's fascinating to realize that they're interested in the expression of madness through music – especially when it comes to mad women. The other side of this is the romantic theory of artistic genius and creativity. In the twentieth century it's the notion of being on the edge – there's something very fashionable about being thought to be slightly mad, and of course this is not about really mad people, but about people who play at madness because that will give them somehow a higher power. There was a fashion for this around 1600, so you have John Dowland and the whole cult of melancholy. You have it again in the cult of Romanticism in the nineteenth century. I don't think it was fashionable in the eighteenth century, where order and balance were much more important. The most fascinating thing is that it's almost always been composers and artists that have laid the path to what doctors think human nature actually is. In the making of representations of madness most doctors have based them on a completely literary construct; it's not about reality at all. (Penelope Gouk)

IT IS CLEAR FROM SOME of our most recent research that people do use music deliberately to modulate their moods, and that they have pieces of music they know will reliably help them to be in a different mood. These can be very mundane domestic things: when you're doing the cleaning or the washing-up, which is a boring task, you want a piece of music that will help you get through that. But there are some more serious and profound uses of music. We have a lot of evidence of people who have used music in situations of great personal stress and distress, and the music has been the thing that has actually in some sense kept them sane.

Some very interesting work was done by a colleague of mine in Sweden, Alf Gabrielson. He did a very large national survey, through television, radio, etc., and he asked people to write to him on the question of what is the strongest experience that they'd ever had of music in their lives. A story that one of his participants told was of being committed to a mental institution with severe depression, and taking a particular piece of Rakhmaninov, playing it incessantly through this deep depression, and finding in it some consolation, some hope of healing, and in fact attributing healing from the depression to this particular piece of music. (John Sloboda)

MUSIC SEEMS TO ACCESS many different parts of the brain in what has often been likened to an orchestration of activity, and this orchestration brings together many differing impulses. So for people who have damaged brains or whose brains haven't developed to their full ability for whatever reason, music can bring together many things that wouldn't normally come together. There's very strong evidence that if you sing using words, you use more parts of the brain than if you just speak, so equally if you play an instrument and sing, you're going to use more parts than if you're just talking, and again this has very strong therapeutic implications. I have experience of a woman who was suffering from Parkinson's disease, and who had been a dancer and was now pretty well unable to move. We found that if we played music fairly slowly and very expressively – particularly Tchaikovsky ballet music – she was motivated, with some assistance, to rise to her feet and to lift her limbs and to move very slowly, and she would express in words that it felt lovely to her.

One of the things that we believe about music therapy is that it seems to be able to speak to that part which is undamaged in almost everyone, regardless of what the 'experience' has been. (Julia Usher)

16 Music and Musicians

I could play it more accurately, but I couldn't play it better.
ARTUR SCHNABEL, 1938

STANDARDS OF MUSICAL PERFORMANCE have, on the whole, risen immeasurably during the twentieth century. Solo passages from orchestral scores that were once considered almost unplayable (for example the famous bassoon solo that begins Stravinsky's *The Rite of Spring*) are now quite commonly used as audition material for young players, and the century's composers have made ever greater demands on orchestral musicians. Solo playing, too, has advanced considerably. Many violinists now play, for instance, Paganini's *Caprices*, works of consummate virtuosity that, it was once thought, could be played only by their composer.

Many critics and performers have expressed anxiety that the present level of technical excellence has sometimes been achieved at the cost of interpretative individuality. It has been suggested that performers of the past, though some of them had faulty techniques, were more individualistic than their present-day counterparts. Audiences have always responded to virtuosity, but the widespread availability of recordings, often more note perfect than a live performance could be, may have led to an expectation and an overvaluing of mechanical perfection. Recording has also contributed, along with developments in the design of instruments and the twentieth century's growing ease of travel – for audiences as well as performers – to a general homogenization of orchestral sound. At one time, as recently as less than half a century ago, French orchestras sounded unmistakably French, because of their use of particular types of instrument and because of national traditions of instrumental training. Much more recently, and for similar reasons, Russian orchestras sounded unmistakably Russian. These distinctions are now far less marked, where they still exist at all. The result, according to the most pessimistic observers, is that there is a growing tendency not only for all orchestras to sound similar, but for all violinists to do so, and all pianists. There is a certain nostalgia for an age when pianists as different as the scholarly Artur Schnabel, the lofty Ferruccio Busoni, the fascinatingly unpredictable Josef Hofmann and the soberly virtuoso Sergey Rakhmaninov might give concerts in the same city within days of each other.

Another factor contributing to the change, though, has been scholarship. A music-lover with a long memory might say that nowadays he finds it hard to distinguish performances by all but the greatest conductors or instrumentalists, whereas in a previous generation no one could confuse a Toscanini performance with one by Stokowski or mistake Cortot for Pachmann. But another might retort that musicians of earlier generations often stamped their personalities on music by taking liberties with it that no performer would contemplate nowadays. Quite aside from all other differences, Toscanini's account of Brahms's First Symphony can readily be distinguished from Stokowski's by the fact that the former adds rolling drums to the chorale at the end of the finale, while the latter, equally unjustifiably, plays it very slowly and smoothly. Cortot's Chopin had wrong notes; Pachmann's was rewritten to accommodate his flawed technique.

The latter half of the century saw a hugely expanding interest in authentic performance, with players and very soon entire specialist orchestras using period instruments or careful copies of them. For some this brought a further diminution of individuality, and it is true that some 'authentic' performances took more trouble over the minutiae of period phrasing and ornamentation than over forming and expressing any particular interpretative insight into the music. Other musicians, however, have found more freedom in the area of early music, or of classical and early romantic music played on authentic instruments, than they have experienced in modern orchestras; yet others have found that the enquiring approach needed when investigating the performing styles of the past brings a new freshness when they return to later music.

Contemporary music is a special problem for the performer, confronted on the one hand with an unfamiliar new score that may be difficult to play or even, initially, to read, and on the other with the need to grasp the music's essence and communicate it to the audience with great directness. Again, some performers find that contact with new music, with the mind and perhaps the person of a living composer, seeking points of contact between the new score and music that they already know, gives them new insights when they return to the familiar classics. Nearly all of today's performers have repertoires ranging over a much wider period than their predecessors. At worst this can lead to performances in which all music tends to sound much the same; at best it can give insights that were not available to musicians of earlier centuries.

*

Furtwängler: every performance different . . .

AFTER THE CONCERT in Hanover, we spoke among us colleagues: 'Oh, this was wonderful Brahms and he [Furtwängler] never can do this Brahms better', and then in Cologne was another First of Brahms, and a better one than which we did in Hanover! He improvised, you know. It was not uniform, the concert. He was a musician who couldn't do the same First Brahms on Saturday that he did on Sunday, and Sunday was another First Brahms. It was the same stuff, but – what shall I say? – his mind was other, his behaviour was other, there was improvised a new Brahms.

I was in the Chamber Orchestra of Edwin Fischer, and the cadenzas of his Mozart concertos, he was improvising them, and one day these cadenzas were terrible, and the other day he did wonderful cadenzas. You know, it was not uniform. It came over him, so to speak, and so it was with Furtwängler. He did rehearsals – well, it was so-so; but every concert was another concert. You could never say, 'This was bad.' Every concert was excellent, but sometimes we said, 'Well, that was the best.' And the next day was another best concert. (Fritz Peppermuller, 1964)

. . . but always sounding like Brahms?

THE PERFORMANCE WAS very good but not at all Stravinskian. I remember the rhythms were there, but very much mellowed. Very often with Furtwängler, everything sounded like Brahms, and so did Stravinsky in this case, to a certain degree. He went to New York for one season and did not have a very great success there, I remember. Toscanini's orchestra, as we know, was highly polished in those days, and Furtwängler, who always preferred to get a certain improvised, rugged sound from the players, could not really tackle that orchestra. I remember when he came back to Berlin he said, 'It is a good orchestra, the New York Philharmonic, but unpleasantly virtuoso.' We mustn't forget that Furtwängler improvised with the orchestra; his performances were always very spontaneous, and whilst they lasted, they took the audiences as well as the orchestra, of course, completely under their spell. When it was over, one very often realized that what one had heard was marvellous but wrong!

I played once in Berlin, with Furtwängler, the Fifth Brandenburg Concerto. He was a remarkable pianist but, if I may be frank, I was more impressed by his Brahms or Bruckner or Schumann or the symphonies of Beethoven than by his Bach. I remember after a performance of the *St John Passion*, I asked Hindemith, who attended the performance, 'How did you like Furtwängler's Bach?' He said, 'It was not very much Bach, but it was a great experience.' (Szymon Goldberg, 1964)

Stokowski rewrites Beethoven

WE'LL TAKE BBEETHOVEN. He has tremendous ideas, this man – extraordinary man he must have been. Now, to put what he hears within himself, to put that down on paper, he has to limit it down. Our system of writing music on paper is extremely limited. It's just factual. This is G, or G♯, or G♭, three possibilities. There is such a thing as G♯♯ and G♭♭ – five possibilities, but that's all. So you have to bring it down to little black marks on a piece of white paper. To bring that out, back to Beethoven's conception, is very difficult. (Leopold Stokowski, 1969)

A Russian-sounding orchestra . . .

HEARING THE LENINGRAD – now St Petersburg – Philharmonic Orchestra for the first time, conducted by Yevgeny Mravinsky in 1986, was quite a shocking experience. One knew that this was one of the great orchestras, the orchestra that people really wanted to hear. Coming as I did from the London music scene, where I used to revel in the sounds of the Philharmonia and the London Philharmonic or the London Symphony Orchestra and so on, going out there and hearing a Russian orchestra sounding so unhomogeneous was absolutely mind-boggling, and at first quite shocking, quite upsetting. But, after a while, when you came to appreciate what those musicians were attempting to achieve, and often surpassing what you thought was possible as orchestral musicians, it was something really jaw-dropping.

The whole impetus behind music-making in Russia is somewhat different from what we have here. Historically, they have no strong youth orchestra scene. Music education is very different over there, so young players' training is almost diametrically opposed to what we have here in that they don't get to play with other young musicians until they're actually quite senior young musicians. But what they do end up with, by the age of twenty, say, when they may be ready to enter into some professional work, is an extremely secure technique, a personal mode of expression that is very, very strong. You just have to look around international competitions, and you see that Soviet Russian young performers do tend to get lots of first prizes, and that's a wonderful thing. But when it comes to orchestral playing, they have less flexibility and less skill at sight-reading, less fluency in styles. There are very few great Russian performers of Mozart or Bach – of course there are some, but proportionally there are fewer – yet once you get your hands on these highly trained musicians in an orchestral context the things you can achieve are absolutely stupendous – given the time. They need more time. Things need to be learned at a different rate from the learning process that happens here. British musicians are so quick; the sight-reading is quite phenomenal. (Martyn Brabbins)

. . . is transformed within ten years

THE ST PETERSBURG PHILHARMONIC'S change over the last ten years has been something quite remarkable, because of the exposure to the West, exposure to foreign conductors and the demise of Yevgeny Mravinsky, who for fifty years was the personality of that orchestra. That's why the orchestra sounded as it did when I first heard them in 1986 when Mravinsky was still alive. (He died at the beginning of 1987.) That one single man actually totally dominated that orchestra's life and musicianship, and since his death the change has been quite phenomenal. If you were to be able to compare a recording, say, by Mariss Jansons of Rakhmaninov from last year or the year before with a twelve- or thirteen-year-old Mravinsky performance, they would sound like very different orchestras. I do feel that exposure to Western standards, Western values, call it what you like, the exposure to CD-making they've recently had to undertake, the touring they've undertaken, the obvious changeover of personnel, and introduction of different instruments – the use of American brass instruments, for instance, French woodwind instruments – these things have totally transformed the sound of that orchestra. I'm not saying by any means that now they're a bland Western-sounding orchestra, because patently they are not. They are still a very exciting, pulse-racing Russian orchestra, but the change in the last dozen years has been extremely rapid, whereas with other cultures the change has been a much more gradual process throughout the century. (Martyn Brabbins)

A Czech orchestra refuses to sound Czech

I DO FIND THE DISAPPEARANCE of national styles very sad. I suppose it's virtually inevitable. Now that you can find cornflakes and McDonalds on every street corner, it's hardly going to be different with music. But conducting the Czech Philharmonic the other day, I was quite shocked, really, by how American they sounded. I was doing Czech music with them, and I said, 'Can we make it a bit more Czech?' And they said, 'No, we like to do it like this.' I think that's very sad. (Roger Norrington)

The decline of personality?

WE HAVE MANY very fine violinists, and even pianists, and yet I can't think of anybody that has made history in violin-playing or piano-playing the way Paderewski did, or among violinists Ysaÿe, Kreisler, Heifetz, and if I may add my own name to it . . . None of the young people today have the personality, for some reason or other, or the individuality. They all play well, but it's very hard to distinguish one from another. Maybe it's the fault of the age in which we are living now. We are living in an age of collectivism, and this may have some kind of an effect. The reason those personalities made history is because they were different from each other; each one had something of his own which the other did not have. Today they all play on the same level, they all play technically very well, they all have a certain good sound, but they lack the repose, they lack the poetry – everything that in my opinion is necessary in art. I think that a good many of the younger artists are almost afraid to be considered a personality because they want to please the critics, and it's very necessary for them to have good notices in order that the managers should be able to procure engagements for them, and if they don't get the critics' approval of what they do, then they are out of luck. Now in my day, when I started, we also had people that criticized us; we used to get bad criticisms, but we were never afraid to stick to our convictions. I'm afraid that the younger generation is afraid of projecting that which they really feel. I've had many occasions to speak to the younger people, and I've asked them, 'Why do you do this, why do you do that?' 'Oh, because the moment I would play it *that* way, you know, I would be criticized for it.' Now, you see, he is not conscious of what he's doing; he's conscious only of what he's going to be criticized for. When I go out on the stage, I'm not concerned what the critic is going to say tomorrow about my playing; I'm only concerned with my interpretation, to do justice to what I feel towards the music, and not what the critic feels towards the music (if he feels at all). (Mischa Elman, 1961)

Four utterly different violinists

FROM THE VIOLIN POINT OF VIEW the four outstanding influences, shall I say, on my own emotions and thoughts on violin-playing were four utterly different types of players and temperaments and people and personalities. Eugène Ysaÿe, the Belgian, was dynamic and dramatic. He would stamp his foot and he would give a leonine performance; sometimes you heard only the bottom and the top note of a run, but it was thrilling and exciting, and his interpretation was always vivid and unforgettable, and he had the most exquisite *pianissimo*, I think, that I've ever heard. Then Fritz Kreisler: what a touch! He had these natural finger-pads: they gave a quality to his playing that went straight to your heart. You didn't stop to think, you only felt every note that he played. Sometimes he would not be as good as others, but it didn't matter because this pure personality and tone and exquisite emotion came right through every time: it never failed. Then there was Mischa Elman. He had perhaps the biggest and boldest and most thrilling tone of all, but he was too excitable to control it. He once played the Tchaikovsky Concerto, and at the end of one of his dramatic passages the bow left his hand and flew out into the audience, but it was picked up quite close to me and returned to him just in time for him to come into the next part. Then there was Carl Flesch. He was quite different. He was very calm. Some people thought he was cold, but his playing was silver pure, and I think his performance, once, of the Beethoven Concerto to me was perfection. I'll never forget it until I die. (Daisy Kennedy, 1960)

Perfection or freedom?

IT'S VERY EXTRAORDINARY when you go back and listen to Alfred Cortot, for example, who is one of my absolutely favourite artists of all time. He's someone I listen to all the time, and of course it's colossally inaccurate: there are wrong notes everywhere! But as someone so beautifully put it years ago, 'They were the wrong notes of a god.' Now you hear the right notes of a mediocrity quite often. I'd far rather hear the wrong notes of a god. His wrong notes were so much better than other people's right ones. And Cortot was by no means unique: there were others.

I think it's a question of what one's aim is in art, where your priorities are. What are you looking for? Are you looking for some sort of highly skilled typist to play the right notes, or are you going to sacrifice, perhaps, a degree of accuracy for an ultimate act of virtuosity in the Lisztian sense of creating atmosphere, character, the very innermost life and essence of a work? A greater expressive freedom in phrasing, in *rubato*, and a greater desire to probe to the very character of the composer? If I can give you a favourite example of mine – it's much quoted but I never tire of it – the luckless young producer who said to Artur Schnabel many years ago, when he was recording the Brahms D minor Concerto and the great big octave flourish in the first movement was a little inaccurate, 'Now there were some wrong notes there; we'll have to do that again.' And Schnabel said, 'Well, I could play it more accurately but I couldn't play it better.' I thought this was a very placing remark, the producer was more or less being told to sort himself out; I know exactly what Schnabel meant. (Bryce Morrison)

The journey and the destination

I THINK THAT THERE'S A DANGER that perhaps in the course of study we leave behind the reason for the study. In other words the goal at the end of it has become so important; it's become so important to get your career off the ground when you're eighteen, otherwise it'll be too late. Perhaps we don't take enough time to pause and reflect why we are doing something. We perhaps don't enjoy our journey enough; we're too busy trying to get somewhere, and maybe we lose the heart of things because of that. To grieve, to be sorrowful, to be happy, to love, to lose: all of these things are basically the bedrock of musical emotion. They are all necessary to be explored and thought about and experienced in order for a performer to be able to re-create this through the music. I think that it's true that as we live our lives, as we experience more of the difficulty and the joy of life, our music can become deeper and more meaningful. (Tasmin Little)

More than just music

I'M A GREAT BELIEVER in well-rounded people. I'm very tired of meeting music students who sound as if they've been shut in a cupboard for the last forty years and just practised scales all day, and have simply no notion that if you view music as the profoundest reflection of human experience you can think of, that practising scales is hardly an adequate notion of it. Music is related to life itself and how we think and feel. I think it's possible and important that the average student should know as much as possible about what they're doing. However, there are people, and always have been, who are rather like *idiots savants*, who know simply nothing at all and play the piano like a god. There are lots of those I could mention. That contradicts what I was saying, but generally speaking I think it's important that students, be they good, bad, indifferent or whatever, should know as much as they possibly can. More than just music. Of *course* you should know about literature that is related to the time, about painting . . . How can you, for example, look at something like the *Années de pèlerinage* of Liszt and not know that Liszt was totally absorbed in painting, and knew a lot about it, and read all of Dante and everything else? Well, he did it, so you should be doing it. In fact, many years ago, I had a long conversation with Horowitz, and he said, 'You know, the kids come to me now and they know this piano piece they're playing, but they don't know the other works around it.' He said, 'When I played a Brahms intermezzo, I knew all Brahms's *Lieder*, I really did; I played through them with singers. I knew the symphonies, I knew everything, and I hope that is reflected in my playing.' It does reflect in your playing: a largesse, a richness, some cultural context. You can't play a piece of music as if it just grew, like Topsy, somewhere. It's related to its environment. I always remember going many years ago to talk to Clifford Curzon. He was an avid reader, and he said, 'If you think of the Brontës, for example: there they are in Haworth, up on the Yorkshire moors, cut off from everything. You had to use your imagination in those days, nothing was done for you, and it meant you had a radically different sort of mentality.' I think one of the problems nowadays is that so much is available and done for you, and you now have American-style phrases like 'couch potato', meaning people sit around watching someone else do something or listening to someone else, and the cultivation of your own imaginative life has been traduced. I think this has profound significance in terms of a sort of stunted growth, perhaps not so much intellectually as imaginatively. People do your imagining for you now. (Bryce Morrison)

Recording: 'as much alive as possible'

WHEREVER I GO, I have my children, you know. And I love to play
with people like Daniel Barenboim and Pinchas Zukerman and with
Itzhak Perlman, with people who are very young, very fresh, and they
easily accept. Nobody teaches, no one at all. We just happen to feel the
essence of the music and have enough daring to do so. And sometimes
if I make a recording, I don't like splices, I don't like any falsehood, I
don't like perfection. I like the way it is, even if there are some mistakes of lesser importance. When the spirit is there, it's good enough
for me. It will never equal a live performance, but I think that right
now they do a lot of echo chambers, and they do a great many things.
I prefer to do it as much alive as possible. Some of those very few
recordings I did with Heifetz, we played through and went home.
(Gregor Piatigorsky, 1974)

The letter and the spirit

I MUST SAY I RATHER LIKE to have a certain freedom of interpretation,
because if everything's told to me about the way I should be playing it
then, in a sense, I'm almost redundant: I can't interpret, I can just
regurgitate something that's on paper. If I feel terribly confined then I
simply ignore it and just do my own thing anyway because, at the end
of the day, it's my interpretation of something: I am the performer, I
am the person with the instrument, and I have to play the music the
way it speaks to me. If I have been told that I must play a certain
passage, for instance, all slurred, and I feel that it doesn't come across
in the right way, then I have to say, 'I've now got to the stage where
I'll simply change it.' My composers are definitely not sacred. Apart
from Bach!

Certain styles of playing have changed, and they're no longer acceptable to our ear. There's a lot of *portamento* that Albert Sammons did
in the Elgar Violin Concerto, and I can't quite get to grips with it.
Obviously it's hard for us to say what Elgar would have thought of our
interpretations of his music today. He'd have probably thought they
were very slow. But I'm sure that what we do now is just as valid in
terms of re-creating a style that is of our time. I think that's exactly
what performers do; they are playing to people of that particular point
in time. Sammons was doing that when he was playing, and the audiences of those days were used to listening to a lot of *portamento*, a lot
of slides. That was how people played, and of course audiences loved

it. But nowadays you're not going to tell me that audiences would love it if I souped up every single note. There's no way that they would, it would be so foreign to people's ears.

It's interesting if you take a player such as Yehudi Menuhin: his style did change over the years. It's always him; you can always tell it's him, but he too was making allowances for the changes in fashion. That's really what we're talking about as far as performance is concerned: what is fashionable. I think that we are all influenced by what's going on in our own time. (Tasmin Little)

Before early music

SOMEHOW WE DIDN'T THINK of Handel as early music. That's the curious thing about it. The style of playing in the 1920s and 1930s was the style of that period. That's the point. It was Handel–Harty, turned into a nice, early twentieth-century, semi-romantic orchestral work. The Brandenburg Concertos were played with full strings, with perhaps Furtwängler, for example, playing a continuo on the piano. These works were turned into full-blown late nineteenth-century orchestral pieces. The string parts would be with long slurs, rapid detached playing would have been off the string at the heel, which is not idiomatic of the period. You would either have a continuo on the piano – the harpsichord was not loud enough in those days, so it was often the piano – or these works were performed without a continuo. In editions of Handel choral works the harmony was put in with wind arrangements, as in Mozart's editions of Handel, which were often used. But I must say this: audiences enjoyed listening to them. We are in great danger of saying, 'What a terrible way of performing!' But when you think that Mengelberg gave a performance of Bach's *St Matthew Passion* every year in Amsterdam, and it was one of the great experiences of people's lives, to go to hear it. So when we listen to it, and say, 'Tut tut! Oh dear!', what about the audiences? They enjoyed it.

There wasn't the scholarship, and anyway, there was the attitude – you could read it in plenty of books at the time – of saying, 'What a pity that Handel's orchestration was so inadequate. We, who have a much better understanding of these things with our magnificent orchestras, we can improve Handel and do it in the way that the music demands.' Toscanini, for example, performed the Second Brandenburg Concerto with clarinets instead of trumpets.

In the 1920s, when the *Neue Sachlichkeit*, the 'new objectivity' overwhelmed Germany, Klemperer was one of its prime exponents. Music was performed as written, and not in any other way, so

Klemperer gave his performances of Bach in the 1920s – and to a certain extent in the 1930s – with a rigid disregard of accentuation, phrasing, everything. It was just straight playing, as written. I sang in Fritz Busch's last performance at Glyndebourne in 1951: *Don Giovanni*. Now, Fritz Busch, when he came to Glyndebourne: no appoggiaturas, no cadenzas. Busch's Mozart is very much admired, because he had removed the excrescences of an earlier style. Busch was admired for the purity of his Mozart. But of course now we have rather more understanding and sympathy for the approach – which after all is documented clearly in Mozart's own handwriting – that cadenzas were quite regularly performed, and that he and other composers expected them, and of course the appoggiatura is now an accepted part of a vocal performance. There was shock initially, but then don't forget audiences are not scholars; audiences haven't got the text in front of them; audiences respond to what they hear. If they enjoy what they hear, they are not going to say to one another, 'Oh, Mozart didn't write a cadenza just there.' They don't think like that; they enjoy it or they don't. (Bernard Keeffe)

Two views of authenticity

OUT CAME THIS INCREDIBLY, searingly passionate music. None of the familiar vibrato or luxuriousness; it had no schmalz about it at all. It was just terrifyingly Purcell. (Roger Norrington)

WHAT IS AUTHENTICITY? I don't want to have a musicological discussion, but authentic will never be authentic because the performers themselves have gone through all the centuries before and they cannot go to the music of the eighteenth century without the habits taken progressively during the nineteenth and the twentieth century. For instance, what do we know about ensemble playing? Nothing at all. We have books, but nothing at all on what people considered to be together or not together. Intonation, for instance. We are now very demanding on intonation. What do we know exactly of the practice of the eighteenth century? Were they really asking for such accuracy as we ask now? We never know. We have indications on the speed of music, but was it really the speed in the eighteenth century? I don't contest research for authenticity, but I say there are many questions that will never be answered. (Pierre Boulez)

ONE HAD TO INVENT a way of singing Schütz, singing and playing it. We just had to discover what the music was like – because no one knew – and so the more we sang it, the more we discovered how dramatic it was, and how different it was from the music that came before – consciously different. There's this so-called *seconda prattica*, this dramatic personal view of the world which Monteverdi and Schütz have, whereas in Byrd and Palestrina it's all restrained and hidden inside some sort of mystical aura. This is much more modern music, much more music of the stage, in Monteverdi's case particularly. Those are the sort of things we discovered: how you had to accent notes and bring out the words strongly, and how powerful it could be. After ten years of doing Schütz and Monteverdi and so on, when we emerged towards Handel and Bach, it was habit by then to think, 'Now, what should Bach be like? Should it really be like the way we hear it nowadays, with a huge orchestra, and should Handel have a big orchestra and a large chorus and so on, or is there another way?'

A tremendous amount of room is left for you. What it does is to clear up the ground plan of the game that you're playing. Each music is a sort of a game, and each period has its own rules. When you just start from now and look back and play all the music the same, you're not realizing the various kinds of games that there are. That tended to be what happened when I was brought up in the 1940s and 1950s: you played all the music the same; you put it through the same mincing machine. And what we've tried to do is to is to go back and find out what the composers expected they would hear, which might have been thought a rather effete and boring thing to do, but the experiment seems to have proved itself to be an exciting one, because by going backwards and being old-fashioned, the music very often seems to me to sound newer and brighter and fresher. It's a strange anomaly, that, in a way.

Of course I do 90 per cent of my work with modern orchestras, and so my mission at the moment is just gently nudging modern orchestras towards that area, so they begin to think about those things as well. I can't do it all myself and I don't push them over the edge, but they really all want to know now. They all ring up and say, 'Can we go on to natural gas, please?' I sort of go round in my overall. (Roger Norrington)

Interpreting new music

IF AN AUDIENCE IS STRUGGLING to understand and it observes people on the stage struggling, then it's going to get the impression that something's mighty wrong, and the whole thing feels very awkward and uncomfortable. So what an audience wants to see is a performer appearing to be totally within the piece, understanding its hidden message and performing it with great aplomb. which therefore means showing its style. It's hugely important, I think. (Terry Edwards)

WHEN IT COMES TO DECIDING on a style with contemporary music, basically you just have to follow your instinct. I have no other way of getting myself into a piece of music other than my initial reaction to it, which actually is not such a bad thing, because if it's a new piece this is precisely how an audience is going to react to it. They are going to have their initial reaction, and in a sense it probably helps if my initial reaction is on their wavelength, because then I'm not trying to force a piece into a pigeon-hole to which it doesn't belong, and I hope I'm going to be able to put across some ideas that will reach my audience and also help them into the music. So other than just relying on my heart and on my ears and a little bit perhaps on what the composer might be guiding me towards, really it's just a question of playing it and trying to decipher the mood. I think that these moods can be quite easy to get to grips with because unless there's a very complicated idea behind a piece (which sometimes there is, in which case the composer will tell you about it), basically music is music, and it's going to be speaking to you, and it's going to be pulling you in a certain direction. (Tasmin Little)

I THINK THAT THE MUSIC we're hearing today has not been cut off from the past; it's just that the connections are very hard to see, but that's part of interpretation, that's part of finding our way, and part of an artist trying to find a voice. The problem is that our culture today wants newness all the time, it wants individuality, and in a way artists are trying to please, because after all the reaction is the audience. The more you know the style of a composer, the more music you know from a composer, the more you begin to see the links one after the other. It just takes time. Somehow the dust has to clear after the wind has blown. You begin to see the connections, those little lines going from one composer to the other. I think it'll take the twenty-first century to look back on us and begin to see that maybe there was revolution, maybe there was a lot happening, but somehow we have not lost our links. (Odaline de la Martinez)

I'VE COMMISSIONED THROUGH the London Sinfonietta and Electric Phoenix a vast number of pieces, and of course each composer has his own language, his own way of writing down the sounds he wants (which is one problem), and of course none of the pieces sounds like any of the others. I remember once someone saying, 'Why do you spend so much time learning one of these pieces that is so so difficult?'

And I used to say, 'Well, it's like climbing a mountain. You know, people climb the mountain because it's there, and we like to climb our mountain because it *isn't* there – until we've climbed it.' That's always had a fascination: to look at the impossibility on paper and produce a piece of music from it. We've had horrific problems sometimes actually deciphering what a composer wants and they've not really been practical in the way that they've put pen to paper. It has made it much more difficult to look at what they want and to arrive at the style. Whereas other people seem to have this facility to make a page look like it's going to sound, which makes it much simpler to get there.

I can remember a piece by Brian Ferneyhough, *Transit*, which looked quite impossible on paper, one of the things being that he was so keen to have every note performed in a certain way that as well as looking at the note – its length, its pitch – there were also four or five footnotes at the bottom of the page, and I spent a year photocopying the footnotes and sticking them in an appropriate place near the note in question, to try and see what he was after. I got to a stage where I really was in quite a panic that we would not get what he wanted. But then he himself said that what one did was to play the gesture. You looked at what you were being asked to do and then you had a go at it, using your intelligence and your musicianship and your technique and your voice, but you actually didn't let that get in the way of performance. I think it's much harder for singers than it is for players to do that. This is generalizing, but for players, because they are actually putting their fingers against the note and running from one to another, it's a much quicker thing to look at that on the page and do it than it is for a singer to actually feel it into the voice. So, particularly with that piece, I did have to encourage the singers to play the gesture and not to get held back by the fact that they couldn't get from one note to another. (Terry Edwards)

The burden of discovering the new

I THINK IT'S NO BURDEN. It's just the opposite: it's a pleasure. Whenever you come up with a piece of music, any piece of music, the first thing you want to know is: 'What is the composer trying to say to me?' And it's right there on that piece of paper with all the notes, and with your knowledge of what they're trying to say, and if it's something that's very distinctive, that you recognize has a bit from here and a bit from there, then you've got a lot of material to work with, so you feel at least that you're doing an authoritative performance. You know where you're coming from and where you're going. If you had to do the same kind of music all the time with the same kind of style it would be boring, and one of the most interesting things about the twentieth century is its infinite, enormous variety. (Odaline de la Martinez)

17 Music and Microphones

*Recording is the most dramatic thing that has happened in the
history of music since time began.*
BASIL TSCHAIKOV

BEFORE RADIO, RECORDING, film and television – all twentieth-
century inventions – the only ways of hearing music were to to go
to a public performance or to play it oneself at home. Neither option
was open to the poor. Except in the largest cities concerts and opera
performances were infrequent, and it has often been argued that people
listened more intensely as a consequence. Because of the greater accessibility of music through recordings and radio, music-making in the
home has greatly diminished; therefore a much smaller proportion of
listeners nowadays has any experience of performing.

But the electronic media have undoubtedly increased both the size
of the audience and, quite staggeringly, the amount of music to which
that audience has access. They have also fundamentally changed the
way in which music is experienced. In the early years of recording and
radio this change was obvious: the range of sounds that recording
could reproduce was so restricted that music was normally rescored in
order to eliminate instruments that the medium could not cope with;
only small groups of players could be used because of the necessity of
them all pointing their instruments towards the horn that collected the

The New Critics: 'The *pizzicato* for the double-basses in the coda seems to me to want body, Alf.' *Punch*,
10 February 1932

sound and directed it to the recording stylus; compositions were often cut in order to fit them on to a commercially viable number of sides. Until the invention of tape-recording, in the 1940s, recordings were made direct on to master discs, meaning that any work longer than a few minutes had to be recorded in numerous short sections, any mistake involving the re-recording of a complete side because editing was not possible. Radio too, for many years, had a restricted frequency range, so that very high and very low notes were inaudible and any instrument or voice whose character depended on the coloration of upper partials was distorted.

The invention, firstly, of electrical recording, then of tape and the long-playing record, with a far higher frequency response than the earlier 78 r.p.m. disc, produced results that were much more realistic. Tape made precise editing possible, and led to an expectation on the listener's part that any recorded performance would be note perfect, which few live performances are. Further advances have included stereophony, digital recording and the compact disc; at the same time VHF and digital broadcasting have similarly transformed radio. The result is that the home listener can now hear music with greater clarity and performed with greater precision than a concert-goer in the proverbial 'best seat in the house' (a phrase invented to advertise the advantages of high-quality audio equipment).

But the experience of listening at home is fundamentally different from that of live performance, and until very recent times all music was written with live performance in mind. No artist performs a work in the same way twice. It is continually growing in his or her imagination and is subject to the artist's development and mood, the acoustic of the hall, even at times to political or social events and the reactions of the audience to them. A recorded performance never changes. It can be said that a listener who knows Beethoven's 'Hammerklavier' Sonata very well, from repeated listening to a single fine recording, may in fact know it less well than a concert-goer who has heard only two performances of it, but strongly contrasting ones.

The 'best seat in the house' provided by a fine digital recording and audio equipment of high quality is in any case radically different from the experience of a concert. Most listeners to recordings and radio listen alone or with one or two others, experiencing little or nothing of the growing inspiration and excitement of a concert audience gradually realizing that the performance they are hearing is a great one, unrepeatable and different from any that they have heard before. A listener to a recording cannot experience the anticipation of a première or of a new operatic production or of a début. Nor is the sound emerging into a normal-sized room from pairs of loudspeakers a few feet apart in any way comparable, however 'high' the 'fidelity', to the sound of an orchestra in the environment the composer envisaged, a concert hall seating thousands of people, all of them participants in a unique occasion. In so far as radio broadcasts live events, whether from a studio or a public concert, it escapes the accusation levelled at recordings, that they are not performances but simulacra of performances, fossilized music.

The effects of this situation on live performance have been examined in chapter 16, and some ways in which recording might become a more creative medium are discussed in chapter 20. This chapter considers the history of the electronic media that particularly affect music and how audiences have reacted to them.

As the twentieth century neared its end the sheer vastness of the recorded repertoire was beginning to have an effect on the recording industry itself, no longer supplying an apparently insatiable public demand (which could be said to have been abundantly met by the simultaneous availability of over fifty recordings of many established classics), but seeking to create new demands by sometimes extravagant marketing ploys. At the same time the growth of the Internet, which could theoretically supply any consumer with a recording of any performance at which microphones were present, either in the form of a permanent copy or a single hearing, was seen by some as a new and optimistic revolution in listening, by others as perhaps the death of the recording industry.

There remains no doubt of the greatest change that the electronic media have wrought on the art of music: that nowadays most listeners face loudspeakers (or don headphones), not musicians.

*

Pre-technology: piano culture

IF YOU LOOK AT the music business in 1913, just before the First World War, professional musicians in large numbers were playing in public – in restaurants, in theatres, and so on – and the piano culture was still in place, meaning that lots of people had pianos in their homes. The piano was the norm in public entertainment and music publishing was based upon that norm. Music publishers sold and hired dots on the page. Now the American piano industry, by far the largest then in the world, was rapidly being taken over by automatic pianos, and the repertoire available on pianola rolls was becoming complete – not just piano repertoire but piano versions of all kinds of other works. But by 1913 two things had begun that were going to change everything: the silent cinema and recording. Both were given a great boost by the war. (Cyril Ehrlich)

Recording: a revolution in listening

I'VE NO DOUBT AT ALL that recording is the most dramatic thing that has happened in the history of music since time began. Until recording, a musician couldn't hear himself other than through his own body and his own ears, and the audience couldn't hear him unless they were in the same place as he was, so the relationship between the performer and the audience was one in which the performer held all the power. Now it's a small minority of people who listen to music in the same place as the people making it. The majority of people today are listening to the sound of the music more than they are listening to the music. (Basil Tschaikov)

The beginnings: acoustic recording

WHEN PEOPLE CAME to give a performance at the microphone in the first year or so of recording, they nearly short-circuited all the equipment, because they stood a foot away from the microphone and let rip, and deafened everybody who was listening. So a number of techniques were developed. The simplest one was that you made people stand a lot further away from the microphone, so that instead of standing close up, you stood six feet away, and the results were not quite so appalling. (Paddy Scannell)

Electrical recording arrives

NINETEEN TWENTY-SEVEN WAS a vital year. The arrival of the microphone had huge implications: practically overnight electrical recording defeated the old acoustic process. The acoustic process was so unsuccessful that you had to adapt seriously to get any kind of effect at all from a piano – an upright piano rather than a grand, virtually no pedalling, etc. Among the implications of that change for serious music is that the repertoire that could be successfully recorded became very much wider, piano music being the obvious example. (Cyril Ehrlich)

IN A MUCH MORE radical way the microphone began to redefine the resources of the human voice and of what could be communicated with it. In particular, instead of standing miles away from the microphone and bellowing, it was quickly perceived that you could stand close up to the microphone and that you could develop a far more intimate style of singing. You could whisper into the microphone, and this new style of singing, which was called crooning, which developed first in the United States but became enormously popular everywhere very rapidly – Bing Crosby and Frank Sinatra being key examples – was a style of singing that was particular to the use of the microphone. It transformed the nature of singing in public because it mediated intimacy in a public context in a way that was previously impossible. (Paddy Scannell)

The 78 r.p.m. record: stopping every four minutes

WE WOULD TRY TO GET some sort of a cadence where there was a logical pause, so that it wasn't just an abrupt stop, because as far as the artists were concerned, to stop in the middle of a phrase would have been impossible for them. They hated those side breaks. If you're in the process of giving a performance, and at a certain point you have to stop and start over again, and do that several times, and then try to go on in the same mood, the same atmosphere, the same musical texture that you ended up the previous side, it's very difficult.

Then test pressings were made, and it was always a wonderful process to set up a listening session to review them. In fact on the 52nd floor of the RCA building we had a fireplace and we had sofas for them to sit in, and we had access to cocktails to be served, and after putting them in the proper mood, we hoped to get their approval. I know that they were very sensitive to their own performance, whether it really represented what they felt they could do. Sometimes it had to do with their being very careful in a recording session because they didn't want to make wrong notes or play wrong phrases, and it *sounded* careful, and they just didn't want that to happen. 'I couldn't do it! I couldn't do it! I was too tense!' I've heard that phrase many times and in every language imaginable. So they would reject it out of hand and we would have to arrange to go back into the studio and re-record it. Until tape came in, of course, and then it was wonderful. (Jack Pfeiffer)

Tape recording arrives

THE NEXT BIG CHANGE was the tape-recorder. Up to then the recording industry had consolidated into big business: you needed a large professional studio, you needed a large factory, etc., to churn out 78s. But with the tape-recorder, in a sense you're back to Tom Edison's day. The tape-recorder being comparatively cheap, and of course very mobile, means that the recorder can go to the music. This tended to decentralize things, to allow small businesses to enter, etc., and people took recording machines off to the Continent to record all kinds of things that previously had been ignored or were not thought to be commercially feasible. (Cyril Ehrlich)

EVERYBODY THOUGHT THAT TAPE was going to make it much easier to make music. In fact it made it much easier to make records, and much harder to make music. One of the questions that I asked those who had done 78s and then subsequently tape (like myself) was whether they found it harder, whether there was more tension, etc. Of course they all said there was more tension when they did 78s than with tape, and since one wants a comfortable life one says, 'Oh yes, it's better.' But the fact of the matter is: can you have a great performance without tension? What does a great conductor do to an orchestra other than enable them to play better than they actually can? The double effect of spending much more time in the studio, and then the change from 78s to tape, meant that the sound was played back to you, so you were criticizing yourself all the time. It was as if you were looking in the mirror to see that every hair was in place. Now you might feel that when you'd got a beautiful parting and every hair was in place, that was how you wanted to look, but the thing that made you attractive for the girl you were in love with might be your dishevelled appearance. (Basil Tschaikov)

The long-playing record

IF WE TAKE THE 1950s as the first great long-playing boom, the most obvious feature of it from the serious-music angle is the huge and very rapid extension of repertoire: complete Mozart operas, Vivaldi. (*The Four Seasons* is a wonderful example, because that has enormous implications for the early-music revival.) The hardware for playing it was fairly cheap: for about ten pounds you could get a record-player as marketed by Decca, and you could plug that into the radio. The way in which those simple cheap players could reproduce a whole Mozart opera, say, in half-hour patches – that was so demonstrably superior to the earlier system that it was enough to create a market. It was a very exciting thing to have. (Cyril Ehrlich)

Performing to the microphone

SOUND RECORDING IS a different kind of art, closer to painting by an artist who does his work in private. It takes quite a lot of time, the recording sessions and the editing. When you have all those sets of different takes, you suddenly realize that a certain combination of phrases, which you would never even think of at a concert, can give a completely different emotional meaning to the piece, and that's why I sometimes even do my own first edits, in parallel with the engineer and the producer, just to try certain things, how they work. On several occasions I was quite pleased. (Nikolai Demidenko)

TECHNOLOGY SEEMS TO BE often thought of as something that comes between us and the person who's communicating to us. Actually in the twentieth century the most interesting technology has often had the effect of bringing us closer to that person. In cinema the example would be the close-up, but in music the electrical microphone allowed the intimate voice to be heard publicly: someone can sing softly and yet fill a hall. I think that has an effect on how we use our voices in everyday life. We learn from public uses of voices how voice and emotion go together. (Simon Frith)

THE PROCESS OF RECORDING does change our interpretation, partly because it makes you very self-conscious during the recording session. I know when I play in a concert there are many places in the music where my concentration switches from myself to my colleagues. If they have a leading melodic voice to play and I am accompanying them, then really I'm listening to them, and judging my own tone in relation to theirs. But when you do the same work in a recording session you can't do that, because you immediately realize on listening to the playback that in your own accompaniment there are lots of inaccuracies which you weren't really aware of because you were busy listening to your colleagues. That's how it should be, but when you hear it on the playback it makes you think that you must concentrate more on the detail of your own playing. For me that means that there's often a sort of bell-jar effect in a recording where I feel super-conscious of what I'm trying to do with my own part, and I'm afraid that if I let my concentration lapse and listen to my colleagues my own playing will become unacceptably unfocused. Therefore I try harder and harder with my own part, and I know that my colleagues feel the same. Quite often I feel that there's a sense of isolation in recording which sometimes goes further than that, to the point where you begin to resent your colleagues for the pressure that you are put under by each other in recording sessions, and of course that's absolutely antithetical to what chamber playing is supposed to be. (Susan Tomes)

FROM A VERY EARLY AGE, if you have a good teacher, you are deeply involved with what you are playing, and you also have some sort of outsider's view as well. Only if you can manage both attitudes, can you reasonably say what your performance was like: was it any good, or just completely awful? We hear the music inside us, and even when we play the instrument, a significant element of that which we hear is the music inside us, not what comes out of the instrument. The record producer is an outsider whom you trust. (Nikolai Demidenko)

Recording affects perception

I MADE A RECORDING of a performance of a Haydn piano sonata, and I used at the same time two recording techniques. One was recorded with modern stereo technique, with many microphones, up-to-date technology and so on. Simultaneously I used two old RCA microphones from the 1930s, and made a mono mix of it. To this mono mix I added a loop of surface noise from an old shellac disc, to give the feeling of an old recording. And then I presented these two versions to students. They had the opportunity to listen to each version many times, and I asked them just to evaluate the musical interpretation. Do you like the tempo? Was the style OK? And I found that a very big percentage – I thought it would be less, but it was a very big percentage – perceived the versions as two completely different interpretations. This was for me a kind of proof that the sound plays an inherent role in the perceiving of the musical message. (Gidi Boss)

Recording: reproduction or creative tool?

RATHER THAN TRYING to use technology in a somewhat deceptive sense, to claim that you were reproducing what already existed (which was the way in which the classical-music world tended, rather disingenuously, to talk about things like high fidelity: to pretend that they were giving you an exact account of a performance when they clearly weren't), the popular-music world was much more likely to think, 'What can we now do musically that we couldn't do before?' Therefore whatever else it did it added to the possibilities of how sound can be manipulated to give people aesthetic, pleasurable, political or whatever other sort of communication. It was as if this new technology became just a new tool for making music. People listening to classical music still tend to think that what they're hearing is a reproduction of a performance, and that therefore what they want from recording is to obscure what actually went into that performance – making you feel you really are in a concert hall, rather than making you think in different ways about how sound is put together. That's a symptom of the increasing gap between a backward-looking audience and a forward-looking composer. (Simon Frith)

Even more important than the microphone

BY FAR THE MOST IMPORTANT single thing that happened in 1927 was the arrival of the talkies. It was the end of the silent film, so that musicians were thrown out of employment for ever. During the silent-film period playing in silent cinemas was the main form of employment for musicians all over the world, and overnight that employment went. Now in the same way as talkies became the main form of public entertainment, in the home the radio took over, and it took over from the piano and from all other forms and became the norm of what people actually did at home. They had the family radio in the living room, and that was the centre of the home. (Cyril Ehrlich)

The influence of radio

IT WOULD BE FAIR to say that it was radio rather than the recording business that consolidated musical culture and musical life, and began to professionalize it and to set new standards. You can't talk of music as if it were some kind of generalizable or understood cultural category at the point when radio came along. You just had different kinds of musics that played to different kinds of socio-economic networks. In Britain there were élite concerts and élite concert-going publics, music was profusely available in cafés, at the seaside and in cinemas, and then there were the various forms of working-class music associated with the factory – the works choir or the works silver or brass band, legacies from Victorian musical culture. There wasn't a sense of music as something universally available and accessible to 'the public' at large, and that of course is what radio began to deliver. (Paddy Scannell)

Radio creates an orchestra . . .

THERE WASN'T SUCH A THING as a permanent orchestra in Great Britain. The principle of deputizing meant that for any concert you would have more or less a scratch team. You didn't have a group of professional dedicated musicians, who had rehearsed together as an ensemble, who had worked on a particular interpretation of whatever it was that they were playing. You just had a scratch team of people who knew how to play their individual instruments and somehow or other they got through it. The BBC Symphony Orchestra was the first in this country to give permanent full-time employment to orchestral players, and in their contracts it said that there should be no deputizing, so they couldn't work for anybody else. It established new norms about rehearsal, and of course the BBC had the resources, the time and the opportunity to do this, so that within two or three years under Sir Adrian Boult it became far and away the best orchestra in the country. People like Beecham railed and complained about it, but of course they all had to follow suit. (Paddy Scannell)

... an audience ...

PERCY SCHOLES IN 1923 said, 'Within five years the general music public will be treble or quadruple its present size', and that happened. People were aware of music. They might not have liked it, but they actually had heard it. You have to remember that Beethoven was considered very, very difficult at that time. There was a great incomprehension of Beethoven and Bach, and yet quite a high percentage of programmes was devoted to the avant-garde, and it wasn't necessarily the British avant-garde; it was Central European avant-garde. This came absolutely from Sir John Reith, who felt that one way to elevate the population was to get them to appreciate serious music. Reith's statement was: 'Give the people something better than they think they want.' It's Victorian middle-class values, and you find that not just in radio but in film as well; the film-documentary movement came absolutely from the same ethic, and it's interesting that John Reith came from a very Presbyterian Scottish background, and so did the leading figure in the film-documentary movement, John Grierson. They both took these new media and created something that was supposed to entertain, but more than that it was supposed to improve and educate. (Jenny Doctor)

... and a market ...

IN THE 1920S, most people heard bands. The territory bands in the 1920s and 1930s were how most people heard dance music or swing music, but as the national radio broadcast came into effect in America, you began to get broadcasts of the very best New York and Chicago bands, so that Benny Goodman and Count Basie or Duke Ellington replaced those local territory bands, and so while you probably lost some live music, more people were able to hear these terrific bands, because now, instead of having overlapping regional markets, you had one national market for swing music. (José Bowen)

... *but not an ideal listener*

THE ORIGINAL NOTION of the ideal listener to music on radio was somebody who could enjoy Henry Hall and Bach with equal enthusiasm. This of course is a nonsense and a chimera. All the evidence shows that the person who loves Henry Hall hates Bach and the person who loves Bach hates Henry Hall. This was borne in upon the BBC in two ways. Before they began to get feedback from listener research, most of the pressures on them came from the music profession, from players and composers, and there was a persistent chorus of complaint throughout the 1930s: 'Why aren't you playing British music? Why aren't you playing music by British composers? Why are you playing all this foreign rubbish? Why are you privileging foreign virtuoso performers and conductors at the expense of British performers and conductors?' That's a theme that repeats itself in a different way when you look at dance music. Secondly, when audience research began (and the Music Department did a great deal of what it called 'missionary work' to promote chamber music), the figures for audiences for chamber music were among the lowest of all categories. (Paddy Scannell)

Radio in wartime

EVERYTHING CHANGED WITH the Second World War. First of all, the BBC went down to one wavelength, so that the enemy wouldn't be able to locate the radio masts and bomb them. Then you got what was called the Forces Programme, which had the very specific role of keeping the forces entertained, but there was a lot of education on it as well. Then there was the Home Service, which was more like the pre-war broadcasts – it had speech and music – but it had very little contemporary music during the war. The idea of streamlining the programmes had already started taking shape in the 1930s, and there were various people who advocated it, but at that time they were a minority, and Reith strongly felt that it shouldn't happen and it didn't. But with the war they started to think about the function of the programmes. It wasn't just education *versus* entertainment; it had far more important implications. So you got *Music While You Work*, which was supposed to increase productivity, and there were other programmes that were simply to boost morale. (Jenny Doctor)

The wider community of radio

I THINK OF RADIO as the most important twentieth-century medium. Clearly the record industry depended on radio for its commercial growth, but radio used recordings in a context that was clearly public; it wasn't simply meeting private consumer needs or thinking purely in terms of markets. It was at the same time trying to put together some sort of sense of community, and I remain very suspicious of all the arguments about how in the twenty-first century we're going to have a world of economically rational individuals who choose exactly what television programme they're going to watch and read their own self-constructed Internet newspapers, etc. People are individuals, but always in the context of wanting to be part of something else. Radio to this day is a way of feeling part of a broader conversation, a wider community. The very fact that you don't know what is going to be played to you next on a good music programme, you literally don't know how it's going to fit with how you're feeling, means that you are having to think about what you're doing as a listener in the context of other people. Radio has done that much more significantly than any other medium. (Simon Frith)

WHAT CHANGED IN THE late twentieth century, and particularly since the 1960s (though it already began in the 1950s with the pop revolution) is that young people had money to spend and the freedom to spend it. The whole control of the family was shifting. One relevant technological change is the transistor radio, because as well as rapidly becoming cheap and efficient, the transistor radio was free of the family in the way that the valve radio never was, so the youngster could go up to his room with his transistor and have his own music. Since the 1960s the adolescent market has been the market leader rather than the follower, and that is arguably the biggest social revolution that music has ever experienced. (Cyril Ehrlich)

The effect of technology on performance

IF ONE WERE TO TAKE a survey at a Prom performance of, say, Beethoven's Ninth, and ask how many people in the audience already reckoned they knew this piece, I imagine a pretty high proportion would say they did. If you'd taken a similar survey at one of Henry Wood's Proms, I'm sure you would have got a very different answer. Even at a concert of the Vienna Philharmonic, though you might have had a highly cultured audience that reckoned it knew its music, it knew its music from going to concerts and from playing things on the piano at home as piano duets. I'm sure that in subtle ways that must have fed into the way people perform. If performers a hundred years ago were performing to an audience, their first duty was to put over what was happening in the music, to create a strong narrative. Inevitably nowadays performers tend to think that that's less important, that it's become the most important thing to put the text over, to do an accurate performance of the piece, and in a sense the narrative can take care of itself: it's clear there in the text and the audience does not need spoon-feeding. That's a shift that's observable on record, and it's probably quite a profound shift in attitude to what performance of a piece to an audience actually means. (Robert Philip)

The future

THERE IS A VERY BIG CRISIS. Just go to any big record shop and look at the amount of choice. People are bewildered. The market is saturated, and even the major recording companies have all kinds of marketing inventions, like for instance all these compilations, which, in my opinion, are acts of suicide. The record industry has run out of customers from the younger generation, who are buying different things. The major companies don't want to take risks, so they don't produce new things because they think no one will buy them. But if musical education from an early age was better there would be a demand for new things and a more interesting repertoire. Maybe the market would be less saturated, because at present the market is not saturated with Tippett but with Vivaldi. I'm very, very pessimistic. (Gidi Boss)

WE WILL HAVE new technology in the future which will allow more music to be delivered more easily. The CD was a new technology which brought more work for musicians initially because there had to be new digital recordings of everything, so we had this temporary blip, where everyone needed to replace their records. Now we're probably back to where we were in the 1960s and 1970s, when we were extremely pessimistic, as were some people in the 1930s and 1940s. But the new technology will mean that you can listen to things once, that in the future you'll be buying on a 'per-listen' basis, not owning a hard copy. And if you're paying for only one listen you can take a lot more chances. Today, when you buy a CD, you've got to decide whether you're going to listen to it again before you plonk down thirteen or fourteen pounds for it. But if you're paying only 20p to listen to it once, and then it's destroyed – it's no longer in your computer and you can't listen to it again – then you might listen to something you wouldn't buy because you're spending only 20p or 30p. That will encourage people not to listen to the same performer over and over again. I think it very unlikely that people will want to listen to Karajan's Beethoven over and over again when they have the choice of listening to lots of different orchestras and lots of different conductors doing the same piece in a new way every time. For serious listening, we'll want to hear the same pieces done differently every time. (José Bowen)

BENJAMIN BRITTEN WAS drawing attention to the dangers of music on tap decades ago, and at that stage the CD hadn't even arrived. So much great music was written for great occasions, where there was a great build up of anticipation before you even went to the concert or opera: it was a rare event. Inevitably, if you remove that rarity you make it commonplace, or you make a semblance of it commonplace. Put on a recording of the *St Matthew Passion* – you don't even have to dust it off – control it remotely, the telephone rings, you can temporarily stop it and then after your telephone conversation go back to the *St Matthew Passion*. But the roots of it have disappeared; the need for it, the occasion has disappeared, and the use of it has utterly changed. (Cyril Ehrlich)

YOU NEVER COMPLAIN that Tesco or Safeway have too much on offer, do you? Or would you ask them to limit the amount of products they sell to a very basic loaf of bread, bit of milk, maybe yoghurt for breakfast, some I Can't Believe It's Not Butter and a few other things and that's it? No, because you've got your tastes; I've got different ones. And the same thing is true of music. It's up to the individual to decide what he wants to listen to and what he doesn't. (Nikolai Demidenko)

_LE SACRE DU PRINTEMPS _ musique de Strawinsky
Danse sacrale de l'élue _
chorégraphie de
Nijinsky

18 The Rite's Century

I am the vessel through which Le sacre *passed.*
IGOR STRAVINSKY, 1960

NO WORK OF twentieth-century music has been more influential than Stravinsky's ballet *The Rite of Spring* (*Le sacre du printemps*), first heard at the Théâtre des Champs-Elysées in Paris on 29 May 1913. Its Russian title means something closer to 'Sacred Spring'; Stravinsky said that it would better be rendered into English as 'The Coronation of Spring'. Its subtitle, 'Scenes of Pagan Russia', suggests the nature of its plot: in prehistoric Russia a group of elders chooses from among the tribe a virgin who, at the end of the ballet, dances herself to death to propitiate the gods of spring and to ensure the end of winter.

Its first performance was greeted by scenes of violent protest. The melodic, harmonic and rhythmic aspects of the work were of such startling originality and opened up so many paths for other composers that its language has already been discussed in some detail in chapters 8, 9 and 10. Another aspect contributing to the ballet's riotous reception was its choreography, by Vaslav Nijinsky. Flatly contradicting the 'first position' of classical dance (heels touching, toes turned out at ninety degrees, body and head erect, arms held parallel to the body but not touching it), Nijinsky's basic position was toes together, heels turned out at ninety degrees, knees touching, body bent, arms hanging. To many his choreography reflected the shocking denial of all the 'rules' that they also heard in Stravinsky's music.

There seemed to be no precedent for *The Rite of Spring*, even in Stravinsky's own music. His first great success, *The Firebird* (commissioned, like *The Rite of Spring*, by Sergey Diaghilev for his Ballets Russes company) was a work recognizably in the tradition of Stravinsky's teacher Rimsky-Korsakov, and although its successor, *Petrushka*, was far more original, it prepared no one for the shock of *The Rite*. According to the composer the idea of it first occurred to him when he was completing *The Firebird*, but realizing that such a challenging work would require painstaking and probably protracted work, he decided to relax and gather his forces, composing in the interim what was planned as a relatively light-hearted *jeu d'esprit* for piano and orchestra. This, at the prompting of Diaghilev and with the assistance of the stage designer and art historian Alexandre Benois, soon became *Petrushka*. Stravinsky had already begun sketching *The Rite*, and with interruptions for *Petrushka* and other compositions he worked on it from August 1910 to early 1913, making final adjustments to the scoring in March of that year. He later said of one complex passage that he could play it at the piano before he could work out how to write it down.

The Rite of Spring immediately acquired the reputation of a mould-breaking work of profound and innovative originality. In recent years, thanks to the researches of Richard Taruskin and others, it has become apparent that many of its melodies are in fact based on folk tunes from published collections. (Stravinsky admitted to only one melody being of folk origin, and affected disdain of composers who used folk sources.) Researchers have also demonstrated that the melodic and harmonic language of *The Rite* is deeply indebted, however personal the use made of it, to a scale or mode that had been much used by earlier composers, especially by Rimsky-Korsakov. This mode, proceeding by alternating tones and semitones (the 'normal' major and minor scales are of irregularly distributed tones and semitones) has a number of intriguing properties. Starting on, say, C, it reaches another C – thus the sense of being 'in C' is not denied – but after eight steps, not the seven of the conventional major or minor scale; for this reason it is called the 'octatonic' scale. It is also possible, by choosing either a tone or a semitone as the first step, to create two quite different 'routes' from C to C. Using the octatonic scale beginning with a semitone many 'normal'-sounding harmonies can be produced, but this is not true of the scale beginning with a whole tone.

Rimsky-Korsakov investigated both forms of the octatonic scale and their potential uses with great thoroughness, and all his pupils used the scale to a greater or lesser degree. In *The Rite of Spring*

Stravinsky used it far more radically than his teacher but in so doing 'disguised' his use of it; in much the same way he modified some of the folk melodies that he quoted to such an extent that they are hardly recognizable. In later life he never mentioned the octatonic scale, which remained an important constituent of his music for many years, and went to great lengths to deny that Rimsky-Korsakov had an influence on his mature works.

Likewise, and presumably for similar motives of emphasizing his own originality, he minimized the contribution of Nikolay Roerich, well known for his knowledge of Russian prehistory, to the scenario of *The Rite*. In his earliest descriptions of the origins of the ballet he spoke of a 'fleeting vision' of its plot; he later said that it came to him 'in a dream'. His correspondence with Roerich, however, demonstrates that he was dependent on him for much more than ethnologically accurate detail. Indeed an interest in 'scenes of pagan Russia' was widespread among Diaghilev's circle.

Alongside its unparalleled dissonance the most obviously innovative feature of *The Rite of Spring* is its rhythmic asymmetry, bars of dissimilar length and metre often being juxtaposed. This was paralleled in the choreography, which the dancers found so difficult to learn that Nijinsky was obliged to call in Marie Rambert, then known for her studies of Dalcroze eurhythmics (a system of teaching music through bodily movement), to help him. The dancers had an extraordinary number of rehearsals (some reports say several hundred). The orchestra for the first performance had relatively few and Pierre Monteux, who conducted the première, made no reference in his correspondence with Stravinsky at the time to the score's difficulties. The riot that took place in the theatre was so noisy that the dancers could hardly hear the orchestra, and it may be that the uproar in the auditorium prevented anyone from noticing inaccuracies in the orchestra's playing. For many years the score was thought of as close to the very limits of playability. In recent years, as players have become used to *The Rite* and to still more extreme demands on their precision, it is no exaggeration to say that orchestras now find it relatively easy, indeed a useful score for showing off their virtuosity and that of conductors. Noticing this, Stravinsky jokingly said that the opening bassoon solo should be transposed up a semitone every few years in order to regain its sense of strangeness and precariousness.

The Rite of Spring was rarely heard in its earliest years. The original production in 1913, with Nijinsky's choreography, had only six performances, and Diaghilev was not able to revive it until 1920, when he commissioned new choreography from Leonide Massine. Concert performances were initially infrequent, due to the outbreak of the First World War, to the difficulty of the work and to the fact that the publication of an orchestral score was delayed. Stravinsky, however, prepared an arrangement for piano duet in 1913, for rehearsal purposes, and this circulated widely. As a single instance among many, Bartók was seen carrying a copy to all the rehearsals of his opera *Duke Bluebeard's Castle* in 1918, in the hope of persuading the Director of the Budapest Opera House to stage Stravinsky's ballet. Many musicians first encountered *The Rite* in this piano-duet form.

The influence of *The Rite of Spring* was widespread. Elements of its violent dissonance and rhythmic asymmetry were soon heard, often superficially imitated, in the works of Stravinsky's younger admirers, and there was perplexity among them, especially in Paris in the early 1920s, when he returned after the disruption of the First World War not with works that followed up the shock tactics of *The Rite* but with compositions that seemed to retreat from its extreme position. The 'neo-classical' ballet *Pulcinella*, based on melodies by Pergolesi and other eighteenth-century Italian composers, was found particularly perplexing and retrogressive. In fact, however, Stravinsky was continuing to move forward, with aspects of the language of *The Rite* being further developed in such works as the *Symphonies of Wind Instruments* written in memory of Debussy and in the ballet *Les noces*, as masterly a score as *The Rite* itself though using far more slender resources (voices, four pianos and percussion). The works of his neo-classical period and even of his late 'conversion' to Schoenbergian serialism, though both were seen at the time as violent changes of direction, often contain rhythmic devices that refer back to *The Rite of Spring*, and references to the octatonic scale occur as late as Stravinsky's last major work, the *Requiem Canticles*. For many other composers *The Rite of Spring* has been intensely liberating not only in its questioning of all the established 'rules', especially those of harmony, but in the profound originality of its rhythmic language and its use of simultaneity and juxtaposition. As these have become more deeply understood, and as the false 'Stravinsky *or* Schoenberg' antithesis has dissolved, the influence of *The Rite of Spring* has intensified rather than diminished in recent years.

As far as can be ascertained the first time that the complete work was heard by anyone other than the composer was when Stravinsky and Claude Debussy played it as a piano duet at the home of Debussy's friend the journalist Louis Laloy on 9 June 1912. Laloy wrote, 'We were dumbfounded, flattened by a hurricane from the depths of time, which had taken life by the roots.' In a fine performance that shattering impact can still be felt, and this 'classic' of the twentieth century can still sound shockingly new.

*

Russia before The Rite

THERE WAS DEFINITELY a feeling around 1900–1905, at the time leading up to the First Russian Revolution, that people wanted to go back to what they were fond of identifying as pagan roots, and those roots were expected to guarantee the primeval power of the Slavic peoples. They were also expected to reveal a link between the late Slav culture of the turn of the century and the East, which was vaguely identified with Indian culture, Mongolian traditions, and so on, often reinforced by escapades into archaeology, rediscovered religion, tourist expeditions into the Far East and Central Asia, the beginnings of Russian anthropology, the study of shamanic rites in Siberia. All this was part and parcel of the beginning of the century in Russian culture. You could say that it's just a development of the nineteenth-century love affair with the folk, with village culture and early Christian culture, which is already very familiar from the earlier operas of Rimsky-Korsakov, Borodin and Musorgsky. (Gerard McBurney)

Stravinsky before The Rite

STRAVINSKY CAME INTO CONTACT with a lot of musicians. For a start, his father was a singer at the Mariinsky Opera, a bass baritone. Many said that he was as good as Chaliapin. Stravinsky must have seen the standard repertoire, which would have included quite a lot of Russian operas that we don't know any more, like the works of Serov, as well as standard repertoire of the kind that we would be familiar with: Mozart, Verdi, and so forth. There's plenty of circumstantial evidence that he was a fairly regular attender at those things. And then, when he fell in with Rimsky-Korsakov, whom he first approached in 1902 and who started giving him some kind of lessons in 1903, he regularly attended musical evenings at Rimsky-Korsakov's and rehearsals of concerts. Rimsky-Korsakov was really the big noise in St Petersburg concert and operatic life in the early years of the century. (Stephen Walsh)

RIMSKY-KORSAKOV IS A VERY interesting composer, underrated today; not the greatest composer, not as great as Stravinsky, but very important indeed as a teacher, and also very important because he methodically came up with a harmonic language, which obeyed its own rules, based on modes and certain chords. One of the modes that he used, a mode that he particularly associated with all that was mysterious and macabre – the underworld, the sinister – was the octatonic scale. This scale was much used at the end of the nineteenth century: Rimsky used it, but you find it in Liszt, Musorgsky, etc., and Stravinsky made huge use of it. (George Benjamin)

YOU CAN DIVIDE UP the earlier works, pre-*Firebird*, into works that are very well-behaved student pieces, written more or less under Rimsky-Korsakov's supervision, and others which show more individuality and which there's no particular evidence that Rimsky-Korsakov supervised at all, like *Faun and Shepherdess* and of course the first act of *The Nightingale* and *Fireworks*, which Rimsky-Korsakov never saw. Those are more individual pieces, but still in a recognizable Russian tradition. That's still broadly true of *The Firebird*; it's a very eclectic piece, it's quite a mixture. It's only with *Petrushka* that you suddenly get a completely new approach, and that's probably the first thing Stravinsky wrote of which you could say, 'This is Stravinsky.' But really Stravinsky was a good Russian until Diaghilev came along. (Stephen Walsh)

The Diaghilev connection

IT WAS THE DIAGHILEV CONNECTION that really made Stravinsky interested in folklore. People from his social class and his urban surroundings felt far above folklore. Diaghilev and his associated painters had a very different attitude towards folklore from that of the Russian nationalist composers. It's something that the art historians have a word for: they call it 'neo-nationalism'. There was very little of it in music, but lots in the visual arts, where you would take peasant artefacts and imitate their style, rather than simply imitating the subject matter. It's very ironic that because Diaghilev had a genius for promotion he knew that the way in which Russia would conquer Western Europe artistically would be by being *extra* Russian, and 'extra Russian' meant being Asiatic and barbarian, and so of course he turned Stravinsky 180 degrees around. (Richard Taruskin)

The 'fleeting vision'

ONE DAY, WHEN I WAS FINISHING the last pages of *The Firebird* in St Petersburg, I had a fleeting vision which came to me as a complete surprise, my mind at the moment being full of other things. I saw in imagination a solemn pagan rite: wise elders, seated in a circle, watched a young girl dance herself to death. They were sacrificing her to propitiate the god of spring. Such was the theme of *The Rite of Spring*. I must confess that this vision made a deep impression on me, and I at once described it to my friend Nikolay Roerich, he being a painter who had specialized in pagan subjects. He welcomed my inspiration with enthusiasm, and became my collaborator in this creation. (Igor Stravinsky, 1933)

Roerich's contribution

ROERICH WAS THE CENTRAL FIGURE in the genesis of *The Rite of Spring*. I met Roerich's son, and his co-workers, and they contested Stravinsky's account. Roerich said, 'Stravinsky could have had a dream, but I was the scenarist of *Le sacre du printemps*', and the chronology he mentioned was that Stravinsky needed another ballet. He went to Diaghilev, and Diaghilev said, 'Go to Roerich. Roerich has two scenarios.' One was a Slavic ritual, and the other was a game of chess. He offered them both, and Stravinsky chose the ritual. (Kenneth Archer)

THE MOVEMENTS OF ANCIENT MAN are whole; his thoughts are strictly at one with his aims; his sense of measure and his impulse to adorn are keen. Strange, to think that perhaps what stands closest of all to what our times are seeking is the legacy of the kingdom of stone. (Nikolay Roerich, 1909)

THERE'S AN OPERA BY Alexander Serov called *Rogneda*, that has a scene of dancing around an idol and a human sacrifice. Of course there are plenty of other operas with human sacrifices: Stravinsky could have also seen Bellini's *Norma*. There are poems by a poet Stravinsky knew named Sergey Gorodetsky that duplicate some of that scenario: the hacking out of a idol from a birch tree to which a maiden has been tied, killing her in the process, and her blood fecundates the idol. That can be compared with the final dance from *The Rite of Spring*. The point is that Stravinsky had that one idea. He took it to Roerich, who had a very thorough knowledge of Russian antiquities and Russian folklore, and Roerich fleshed out this idea into the scenario that we know. Roerich had a far greater input than Stravinsky. Stravinsky's contribution was basically that final dance, which is the one part of it that is not ethnologically accurate: we don't really have any evidence of ritual human sacrifice among the ancient Slavs. (Richard Taruskin)

Nijinsky's revolution

WE HAD TO LEARN individual steps with vague countings, and listening to this strange music at the same time, building the thing up into a pattern. The groupings were divided, of course, and at times they met in terrific clashes. I found that this production of Nijinsky was fiddly. He'd used the rhythms too individually; they weren't spacious enough. Consequently the whole thing became vague to the dancers. Our trouble was, you see, that we couldn't hear ourselves count, and without counting that type of ballet you can't do it. (Lydia Sokolova, 1960)

THE DANCERS DID NOT LIKE this connection to the system of Emile-Jacques Dalcroze, of studying music through body movement. They thought it was like going back to school. But the truth was that they were struggling. Not because they weren't great rhythmic dancers, but because Nijinsky, following the clue from Stravinsky of the shifting accent, often in *The Rite* has people moving with one rhythm with the feet and another rhythm with either the head or the arms. This is fiendishly difficult to do if you cannot count on the accent of the rhythm. Never had a ballet audience been confronted with something so anti-classical, an affront really to the aesthetics that they were there to see, and as it was presented on the same programme with *Les sylphides* and *Le spectre de la rose*, it was framed in the most radical possible way. The figures – all of them, male, female, old and young – really could be carved from wood or stone. There is this feeling of old Slavic totems that were still in existence at the time, and which Roerich showed to Nijinsky.

The other thing that was very upsetting to people is that the head was not held straight on the shoulders. Much of the time the head is dropped to the side. It's a very vulnerable position: it expresses a sense of awe and subservience to the forces of nature that is in the choreography. It apparently upset people a lot, and that's what prompted this quip from somebody in the audience, calling for a doctor, and then somebody else – because the dancers had their hands on their cheeks with the head tilted – calling for a dentist. All these signs, not of impotence but subservience, giving way to the power of nature, were not what the audience at the Théâtre des Champs-Elysées expected. (Millicent Hodson)

THEN CAME THE GREAT FIRST NIGHT of *Sacre*, which is a historic first night, of course. As the music started playing: already a dreadful noise in the audience. We couldn't hear the music; we couldn't count.

Nijinsky was counting wildly in the wings; I was counting on the stage. We simply couldn't hear the music. And when, in the Second Tableau, the Chosen Virgin came on for her dance she had her hands folded under her cheeks, her feet turned in, and she was trembling, trembling, with her hands against her cheeks. Somebody from the gallery shouted, 'Un docteur! Un docteur!', and somebody else shouted, 'Un dentiste!' And it went on. A woman bent out of her box and slapped a man who was clapping. Other people were slapped because they were hissing. It was a most dreadful scandal! (Marie Rambert, 1966)

Critical reaction

THE MOST IMPORTANT DISTINCTION achieved by *The Rite of Spring* is its claim to be the most discordant composition ever written. Never has the cult of the wrong note been applied with such industry, zeal and ferocity. From the first bar to the last, whatever note one expects is never the one that comes, but the nearest one to it; whatever harmony is suggested by a preceding chord, it is always another chord that is heard; and this chord and this note are used deliberately to produce the sensation of acute and almost cruel dissonance. When two melodies are superimposed, far be it from the composer's mind to use those that fit together; quite to the contrary he selects them so that their superposition should produce the most irritating friction and squeaking that can be imagined. (Pierre Lalo, *Le Temps*, June 1913)

How good was the first performance?

IF YOU KNEW THE PIT of the Théâtre des Champs-Elysées you would see that it was probably a terrible performance, because it's a small pit, and in small pits the only thing you can do with a very large orchestra is reduce the number of strings. With *The Rite of Spring* you have to keep the quadruple winds, because they each have a part. So it was probably a very small string section, with people totally unfamiliar with the style, probably totally incapable of playing right, and a totally wrong balance. Maybe it was even more savage and wild than what we hear now, because of the playing! (Diego Masson)

The eclipse of The Rite . . .

IT HAD ITS BALLET PERFORMANCES in 1913 and 1914. A couple of conspicuous orchestral performances in 1914, especially the one in Paris by Monteux in May, made the work famous as a concert piece, but then of course came the war, and the orchestras were disbanded, and there were no more performances until the 1920s. The score wasn't published until 1921, which is something people might forget, so for seven or eight years the work was virtually unplayed. (Richard Taruskin)

DIAGHILEV KEPT THE SETS and costumes because they were very expensive, and in 1920 he staged the so-called 'Second *Sacre*' with choreography by Massine, and they were used again then. After that, after Diaghilev died, they were handed on to Colonel de Basil, and eventually they were sold at Sotheby's in 1969. Quite a few are in London in the Theatre Museum. Some were at Castle Howard near York, and they were sold some years ago. Some are in Stockholm, some are at Austin in Texas, and some are in private collections. Twenty per cent were lost. (Kenneth Archer)

. . . and its re-creation

WHEN DIAGHILEV PRODUCED the ballet again with choreography by Massine in Paris in December 1920, Stravinsky published interviews in which he claimed that the music had come first and was a purely formal construct and had no original connection with Russian prehistory, but that the plot was simply mapped on to the music because a scenario was needed for a stage piece. This change of posture, from what was a neo-primitive ballet of a *fin-de-siècle* kind into a sort of proto-neo-classical piece of a purely formalist variety with an abstract scenario, you can imagine being reflected in the way the piece was performed, leading maybe to Stravinsky's 1940 recording, which is very crisp and 'classical'. It's hard to make *The Rite of Spring* classical, but the performance has that clean-cut quality. (Stephen Walsh)

Not an icon in Russia . . .

IT WAS CERTAINLY NOT a repertoire piece in Russia, and although Stravinsky didn't disappear by any means from Russian concert programmes after 1917 (the whole idea of him as an enemy of the people is an invention of the late Stalinist period) the most surprising fact for a Westerner is how *The Rite* seems to recede in importance for Russians. It doesn't seem to be a key piece for them. *The Rite* very quickly became an icon in Western culture, a position it's never really occupied in Russian culture. (Gerard McBurney)

. . . but becomes one in Hollywood

SINCE I WAS A CHILD I've been trying to understand music, its potentialities, because those potentialities are limitless, like space is limitless.
I have tried to understand new possibilities in music, and I had the
idea – I still have the idea – that millions go to the movies, to cinema,
who never go to a concert hall. They have a kind of feeling that it's too
formal to go to a concert hall, and they would feel uncomfortable, and
they're even afraid of great music. And if they hear it in a cinema they
realize, 'This is very interesting, this music!' Walt Disney, in *Fantasia*,
wanted to show how this little world we live on began, in primitive
forms and primitive animals and gradually developed until we had
man, and he said, 'What would be good music for that?' And I said,
'Stravinsky. *Sacre du printemps* in my opinion would be good for that.'
(Leopold Stokowski, 1969)

I WAS TAKEN TO SEE the film *Fantasia* when I was a little boy. In
Fantasia there is for its day, the 1930s, the very daring inclusion of *The
Rite of Spring*, and at the age of seven I found this marvellous, mysterious tale of the beginning of the world, the dinosaurs and volcanoes,
rather frightening and completely enthralling. (George Benjamin)

The rhythmic language

CAME STRAVINSKY, AND INSTEAD OF having bars in threes or fours he
had these irregular bars – 5/16, 3/16, 2/16 – a constant change of time
signature. I conducted *The Rite of Spring* in Paris and London in 1920
and its first performance in Berlin in 1922, and I had to invent a new
technique! (Ernest Ansermet, 1969)

[I FIRST TOOK PART in a performance of *The Rite*] at the Paris Opéra,
with Boulez conducting and choreography by Maurice Béjart. Of
course it was extremely exciting, and not only exciting but very difficult at that time. In those days we really needed to have a conductor
who knew exactly what was going to happen and who was going to
show us, because by ourselves we couldn't do it. He split the orchestra
apart, because we couldn't understand what we were doing, what was
the complete rhythm of a phrase that each of us had only a part of.
Now you don't have to do that any more. People know this music;
it's part of their life. An orchestra could almost play it without a conductor nowadays. (Diego Masson)

ONE OF THE RADICAL MESSAGES of *The Rite of Spring* (there are so many of them!) is: 'Goodbye, the Western conception of pulse.' There had been intimations of this both in Stravinsky's music and in earlier Russian music: you find changing time signatures a lot in Musorgsky, for instance. But in certain passages in this work he really uses additive rhythm, little rhythmic cells that are defined by their instrumentation and their harmony. Particularly in the *Sacrificial Dance* at the end there are about four or five of these, and the cells are juxtaposed continuously, and at certain points one cell remains the same, another one contracts, another one expands, and the tension of the music is given by a constant give and take between these cells, juxtaposed with no long-term regular metre underneath the music. That regular metre had been the fundamental of Western music for two or three centuries, and performers found it impossible to play music without it. I've heard stories of people literally (it seems unthinkable to today's musicians) unable to play in 5/8, let alone 3/16, 4/16, 2/16, 5/16. They simply could not do it. (George Benjamin)

AS IT WAS RATHER DIFFICULT, the young conductors began to ask for lessons. And this method of teaching conducting in lessons was directing the attention of the conductor on the technique, not the music! And then came a second element, especially in North America: the conductors had to do with a public who was not educated in music, and so they had a certain role to play in order to convince, and they became showmen. And they began to give more importance to the gestures they were giving to the public than to the gestures they were giving the players. (Ernest Ansermet, 1969)

The Rite *becomes a repertoire piece*

ORCHESTRAS NOW TOSS OFF *The Rite of Spring* without turning a hair. It's no longer a difficult piece for professional orchestras. They sight-read too much, especially in Britain of course, and this means they get too good at tossing things off without really getting under the skin, so it's become one of those glitzy showcases, and that is certainly foreign to the original effect, which was one of a knife edge. Robert Craft, when he went to Moscow with Stravinsky and attended rehearsals (I think he may have even conducted rehearsals for that performance conducted by Stravinsky which was recorded and issued on disc), he commented on the way in which a lot of the percussion scoring especially sounded suddenly much more wild and frenzied, partly because the players were not perhaps quite so used to it, but partly because there was something in the Russian tradition, something coarse and unrefined, un-drawing-room-like, that had been lost in the Western tradition. (Stephen Walsh)

I ONCE WENT TO A performance of *The Rite of Spring* by Simon Rattle. It was to me a very exciting performance. I went out to dinner afterwards with one of the most famous of living British composers, who was with two friends of his, and he said (and they applauded him), 'The trouble with *The Rite of Spring* is that it's such a trivial piece. It's just a boring old folksong suite, which is treated by modern orchestras as a showstopper. I think we've all got past that now.' I was very surprised because I hadn't got past it, and I still haven't got past it, and I think one of the tremendous achievements of the many people who have studied this score has been the recovery of the source materials of the work, which tells us about how Stravinsky manipulated this material, how he took these tunes and what he did to them. (Gerard McBurney)

Recovering the sources

TO HIS FIRST BIOGRAPHER, André Schaeffner, he said that there was only one folk theme in *The Rite* – that's the first bassoon solo – and he even gave Schaeffner chapter and verse. He actually showed him the source. Many years later, Laurence Morton, his friend in California, had the idea of going back to that source and looking for other themes, and he came up with a handful, and then I was able to find even further ones because I looked at Stravinsky's sketchbook which was published in facsimile by Boosey and Hawkes in 1969. Two songs from Rimsky-Korsakov's anthology went in: they were used in the *Spring Rounds* in the First Tableau, and then there are a couple of folk tunes that I know were authentic folk tunes because they were copied out very meticulously in Stravinsky's sketchbook, but I haven't been able to identify them. Then there are the ones that are recognizably from generic repertoires. One of them, the one that went into the *Ritual Action of the Ancestors*, is what's known as a *vesnyanka*, a 'calling in the spring' song, which is obviously related to the scenario of the ballet. Another one is called a *naigrysh*, kind of ostinato variations of the type made famous by Glinka in *Kamarinskaya*, and the very same kind of ostinato variation structure is in the *Dance of the Earth* at the very end of the First Tableau. So there you have resonance not only with a folk genre, but also with a very specific model in nineteenth-century Russian music, namely Glinka's orchestral fantasy *Kamarinskaya*. (Richard Taruskin)

I WAS VERY SURPRISED at first to hear that most of the melodies were not by him, and I was very surprised and very intrigued to find that he'd written to his mother to send him a book of folk songs, and that basically every melody comes from another source. And yet there's one thing that is very interesting, and which does define the Stravinsky sound, and must have sounded so strange to people at the beginning, and that's a sort of rupture between the linear and the vertical. This intentionally 'flawed' harmonization was one of Stravinsky's most distinctive and original strokes and was most probably intuitively discovered on the piano. He takes a very simple diatonic white-note melody, and harmonizes it in the most dislocated way with the most harsh chords: we're talking about six- or seven-note dissonant chords, bitonal chords. (George Benjamin)

The harmonic style

THE HARMONIC STYLE has lots of antecedents, even in Rimsky-Korsakov's work. Rimsky-Korsakov noticed a scale in the works of Liszt that alternated semitones and tones. Rimsky-Korsakov called it the tone–semitone scale; his pupils called it the Korsakov scale, and the work of Rimsky himself and all of his pupils uses this device. Most of the harmonic innovations in *The Rite of Spring* can be shown to be innovations within this tradition of using the octatonic scale in conjunction with folk themes. What Stravinsky liked to do was take a diatonic Russian folk melody, usually based on what musicians call the minor tetrachord – a whole step, a half-step, a whole step (tone, semitone, tone) – which is a segment of the octatonic scale: that much they have in common. So if you take a Russian folk tune that uses the minor tetrachord, you can harmonize it using the octatonic scale, and produce all kinds of wonderful new harmonic effects, which is what *The Rite of Spring* is so full of. (Richard Taruskin)

IT'S AS IF, INSTEAD OF progressing from dissonance to consonance after the classical model, it does the opposite. The fact is, though, that you can still sense and hear the remnants, the ruins, of the consonance still there, overlaid by layers or strata of dissonant accretions. It's in that sense that the roles have been reversed, and what is most important of all is not just the reversal of roles, but the way that the effect of that is actually to intensify the dynamic power of the music. Stravinsky isn't just turning music upside-down; he is moving it forwards in a very positive and not a negative way. (Arnold Whittall)

THE DIFFERENCE FROM THE other composers who were composing

genuinely atonal music (if there is such a thing) in the years preceding *The Rite of Spring* is that *The Rite* is a pragmatic piece because of Stravinsky's habit of writing at the piano. He's looking for shapes and listening out for sonorities, and he's working with his hands on the keyboard. He was a pianist, so his hands tend to fall into shapes that are perfectly normal, and he then maybe moves his hands around to get combinations, but they stay in shapes that imply either chords that you might find in a tonal piece or something similar. He was very interested in sounds that clashed by an octave plus or minus a semitone, so that the very harsh sounds in *The Rite of Spring* are very often octaves gone wrong. They're not straight semitone clashes; often, they're octaves gone wrong. That's the characteristic sound of *The Rite of Spring*: it's a black note/white note thing. There's no dense chromatics going on there; it's just a simple juxtaposition of things that belong in slightly different universes. (Stephen Walsh)

OUTSIDE RUSSIA NOBODY really knew about the octatonic scale, and Stravinsky never let on. He had an idea about his techniques, that they were his trade secrets, and he didn't discuss them. Although, by the end of his life, Stravinsky described himself accurately as being in a perpetual state of interview, never once to an interviewer did he ever talk about the Rimsky-Korsakov scale. He was thought of as a complete original, and he did what he could to keep alive that thought. In my own work on Stravinsky, I've had to work very hard to resurrect the contributions of Benois to *Petrushka* and of Roerich to *The Rite of Spring*. Stravinsky tended to deny all of this. He was obsessed with originality. This is a neurotic symptom, but it's one that he shared with many composers at the time – with most of them. We're only coming out of that now, to the great benefit of music. (Richard Taruskin)

The Rite *becomes a source*

LISTEN TO THE BEGINNING OF *Amériques* by Edgard Varèse, or his *Arcana*: they're inconceivable without his having heard *The Rite of Spring*. The idea of starting with a solo instrument playing a modal melody, as does *Amériques*, the percussive and repetitive elements in his music, the brutality of it, it's completely from Stravinsky. Bartók was hugely influenced by this piece, in his way of treating folk tunes not in a nice, comfortable way, but rough and extreme. *The Rite* had a huge impact on Messiaen. The idea at the opening (which he used to think was a birdsong chorus) of taking lines and simply superimposing them on a complex harmonic background, the idea of just superimposing lines with no connection, a sort of 'poly-music': that was very important to him. He was very interested in the cellular rhythms that Stravinsky used. The polyrhythmic element had a big impact on many composers: the idea of delineating certain strands in the texture by a timbre and register, while above and below there are other groups of instruments doing other things which have no relation to that, giving the music a surreal perspective. (George Benjamin)

I THINK IN THE FIRST INSTANCE people were probably imitating the rather superficial character of the music, its sheer dynamism, the weight of the dissonance, the very strong contrasts that are embedded in it, and during Stravinsky's lifetime the influence of the work was of that kind. But since the 1970s and right up to the present, we find composers who, whether through an instinctive feeling for what is essential in the work or through close study of it, are influenced by it in a much more profound way, by its modernism. Two important composers come to mind: Elliott Carter and Harrison Birtwistle. In both cases, in their large-scale works in particular, they work with different strata of material which they superimpose without seeking to integrate in a traditional classical way, so if you take Carter's Concerto for Orchestra, or his Symphony of Three Orchestras, these are works in which there are constant juxtapositions and superimpositions. That is something that Stravinsky pioneered more than any other early twentieth-century composer. If you move to Birtwistle and his large-scale orchestral work *Earth Dances*, the title itself is a homage to Stravinsky, and so is the music. (Arnold Whittall)

The meaning of the sacrifice

ROERICH WAS USING RITUAL ACTIONS that were based on shamanism and northern Slavic rituals, which are really about cosmology. They're about the meaning of the individual in society, and the dancers want to know why the sacrifice is being made, and why they are going through this ordeal. Musicians working with us and watching curiously began to ask what these things meant. It really came to a kind of philosophical moment between the dancers and the musicians, where everybody stopped the rehearsal and some of the dancers started talking about what they were feeling at this moment. Some of them became quite emotional. It's extraordinary to see a six-foot-three male dancer with tears running down his face. It's actually quite moving in the rehearsal to see them identifying with the meaning of the piece. The core idea of a society that recognizes the need for sacrifice, the fact that there can be that kind of general and collective faith and concern, that people will align their lives around an idea – I think that means a lot to young dancers, and maybe would to musicians if we took time to talk about it. (Millicent Hodson)

19 Music's Monolith

An orchestra is exactly the mirror of the society.
PIERRE BOULEZ

WHAT WE KNOW as the symphony orchestra is an invention of the
eighteenth and especially the nineteenth centuries. So many masterpieces have been written for it that any major Western city (and these
days many non-Western ones as well) is likely to feel a need for orchestral concerts, perhaps for a resident orchestra, in much the same way
and for exactly the same reasons that it needs a gallery of paintings
and sculpture. Yet full-time, salaried symphony orchestras were comparatively uncommon until the present century. Many of the major
nineteenth-century European orchestras gave concerts only when they
were not engaged in their city or state opera house. London, with a
rich musical life throughout the eighteenth and nineteenth centuries,
did not have a permanent orchestra until the twentieth, nor a contract
orchestra whose members were paid an annual salary until the foundation of the BBC Symphony Orchestra in 1930. Until that point concerts in London were usually under-rehearsed and the standard of
playing inevitably not always high.

Whereas a chamber-music ensemble can be and generally is a co-
operative body, all its members taking part in musical decisions about
performance, a symphony orchestra, if only for the sake of efficiency
in rehearsal, needs a single directing hand. In the early nineteenth
century direction was often shared between a keyboard player and the

first violin, the latter using gestures of his bow to ensure rhythmic precision and unanimity of attack. But as orchestras grew larger and the music written for them more complex, the need for a single conductor soon became obvious. Nowadays many listeners would give two main reasons for going to a symphony concert: to hear great music played by a fine orchestra, and to hear that music interpreted by a major conductor. Along with the importance of its historic repertoire, one of the main reasons for the survival of the symphony orchestra has been the allure of the great conductor.

But the role of the conductor has also changed. Many orchestras are now self-governing, and themselves appoint their conductors. It is unlikely that even a great conductor could nowadays, as Sir Thomas Beecham did more than once, found and recruit an orchestra himself. Players nowadays are in less awe of autocratic conductors, and respond better to a more subtle and sympathetic approach. And very few conductors today are prepared, as most were in the past, to spend the greater part of each year with the same orchestra. Many present-day conductors hold simultaneous appointments with two or more orchestras, and many orchestras spend much of their time working with a succession of short-term guest conductors.

Until the early years of the twentieth century orchestras were still developing and still growing, with composers such as Richard Strauss and the young Arnold Schoenberg demanding larger and larger ensembles, often incorporating new or unusual instruments. Composers have continued to write for the standard symphony orchestra, in part as a response to the challenge of its existing repertoire, in part because the number of established orchestras means that a successful orchestral composition might achieve widespread performance. But in reaction against the past, in search of new musical styles and also because (not least for economic reasons) orchestras have on the whole been unwilling to play much new music, composers have increasingly turned to smaller ensembles. Many of the century's most successful and influential compositions have been written for forces other than the symphony orchestra, and some important composers have written little or nothing for it.

In more recent years there has also been a tendency to realize that the modern symphony orchestra, nineteenth-century in basic make up, but with many instruments modified by twentieth-century technological developments, is ill-equipped to perform the music of the eighteenth century. This interest in 'authentic' performance has now extended into the early nineteenth-century repertoire and beyond, to such an extent that many symphony orchestras and their conductors no longer perform Bach or Handel, and feel uncomfortable with Haydn, Mozart and even early Beethoven. Some chamber orchestras on the other hand (of which many have been founded since the 1930s) have felt perfectly at home combining a modern repertoire with classical and baroque music. There are also numerous ensembles of various sizes who specialize in contemporary music. Their success – and their popularity with composers and often with audiences – has tended to reduce the 'core repertoire' of the symphony orchestra still further, to the popular, larger-scale works of the mid- and late nineteenth century and the earlier years of the twentieth.

The sheer cost of maintaining a full-sized permanent symphony orchestra is now very great. There have been repeated suggestions, for example, that London cannot afford its five symphony orchestras, and although many European and American cities are aware of the prestige and sense of community that a fine orchestra can bring, not all of them are secure in their funding. Many orchestras face the problem that their audiences are predominantly middle-aged or older, and are thus likely to diminish, that their tastes are conservative (leading to a restricted repertoire) and that full houses can be guaranteed only by engaging celebrated conductors and soloists. Conductors who can attract audiences to unfamiliar repertoire are rare, and their services are in great demand. In circumstances like these many have asked, 'In what form can the orchestra survive?'

*

The ideal . . .

IN THIS VAST ORCHESTRA would dwell a wealth of harmony, a variety of tone qualities, a succession of contrasts which can compare to nothing hitherto achieved in Art; above all an incalculable melodic, expressive and rhythmic power, a penetrating force of unparalleled strength, a prodigious sensitiveness for gradations in aggregate and detail. Its repose would be as majestic as the slumber of oceans, its agitations would recall the tempest of the tropics.

It would be necessary to adopt a style of extraordinary breadth each time the entire mass was put into action, reserving the delicate effects, the light and rapid movements, for small bands which the composer could easily arrange, and make them discourse together in the midst of this musical multitude. (Hector Berlioz, *A Treatise on Modern Instrumentation*, 1843)

... and the reality

ONE REHEARSAL AND THE members of the orchestra not interested: they just want to play through, with not the smallest idea of style – a situation brought about by the continued uncertainty of a professional musician's income. If a management does give you a chance of three rehearsals for a concert, what do you invariably meet? A different personnel, especially among the strings, at each rehearsal, and only on the morning of the concert do you get the players that are going to take part in the concert. Of course, the public know nothing of this, and accept – poor devils – just what is given them. (Henry Wood, *About Conducting*, 1945)

SO LONG AS ONLY THE CRITICS lament the shocking condition of orchestral music in London they are accused of ignorance or malevolence. Shall we never get rid of our lazy national habit of trusting to muddling through? Obviously what we need is not three or four second- or third-rate orchestras, but one first-rate London orchestra. (Ernest Newman, *Sunday Times*, 1927)

A modest proposal

(a) A symphony orchestra of 114 to play full-size orchestral works.
(b) A symphony orchestra of 78 to play smaller symphonic works.
(c) A theatre orchestra of 36 to play dramatic programmes, musical comedy, etc.
(d) A light orchestra of 67 for light music and lighter symphony concerts.
(e) A popular orchestra of 47 for miscellaneous requirements.
(BBC internal memorandum, 1928, proposing the engagement of a contract orchestra of 114 players and its possible subdivisions)

FOR YEARS MUSICIANS have deplored that in this country there has been no possibility of establishing orchestras as good and as permanent as those on the Continent, where the State comes forward with a subsidy. And now, when the BBC is able to put down the money and offer our best players engagements of good value and duration, the cry goes up about abuse of power and monopoly ... We might as well get the fact into our heads once and for all that broadcast music is with us and has come to stay. (Neville Cardus, *Manchester Guardian*, 1930)

London orchestras improve

ORCHESTRAS HAVE IMPROVED out of recognition. There was a great move made when Toscanini first came with his orchestra from America, and when the Germans first started coming over here. It was a revelation to everybody here, when we'd had appalling orchestral playing. I say this with full meaning. I remember taking my first rehearsal at the Albert Hall for the *Egmont Overture*, and I was then going to do the Mass of Beethoven. The *Egmont Overture* was so appallingly played that I spent about three-quarters of an hour and hadn't got time really to finish the Mass. That does not obtain today. We know all about the reputations of the old days – they will tell you that Nikisch was so pleased with the London Symphony Orchestra that he only had one rehearsal. Actually, when Weingartner had the same experience, he told me on the quiet, 'I'd either got to have one or six, and as they wouldn't give me more than one I did it in one, and I just had to hope that what happened would happen to the best.' He conducted magnificently, and they played very well, but the standards were much, much lower. You've only got to listen to the old recordings and it's perfectly clear that's true. (Malcolm Sargent, 1965)

Conditions elsewhere

I DO KNOW THAT during the Depression years it was difficult for the Chicago Symphony Orchestra. In those years, however, one of the things that is true is that musicians were of course grossly underpaid, and fund-raising was much less an issue than it is today, and you relied a lot more on ticket sales. (Henry Fogel)

I STARTED WITH ninety marks a month! Ninety marks! I don't know what it is today, but at this time it was about a half or a third of the minimum existence level. And this for eight years! (Herbert von Karajan, 1987)

Manchester before Barbirolli

NOW, THERE IS ONE THING I want to emphasize about the orchestra and music in Manchester and social life generally in the days before the First World War so far as it affected music in that city. It was very largely a foreign affair. The Hallé Orchestra itself consisted of many foreigners, and those chiefly interested in the concerts – the running of the concerts, the attending of the concerts – were men and women of foreign extraction, largely German. There was one very pleasant feature about the Hallé Orchestra, or rather a pleasant feature in the attitude of the public of both Manchester and Liverpool towards the Hallé Orchestra. The regular audiences – the fans, in other words – knew the names of everyone. The distinguished players were looked upon as personal friends. All these men, as I say, were like friends to us, and it may be there are audiences somewhere that still look upon the principal players of an orchestra with the same esteem, regard and affection. I'm inclined to doubt it, or if they do, it really isn't quite the same thing as it was then, when they were looked upon almost as members of the family. (Thomas Beecham, 1953)

EVER SINCE HALLÉ formed the orchestra in 1858, the players had been engaged as a casual orchestra, that is to say engaged per concert. They were paid per concert, and things went more or less well until just before the Second World War when audiences fell off, and not only was it most unsatisfactory from our point of view, but the players were not earning a living wage. As soon as the war broke out, there was a tremendous demand from the public to hear orchestral music, and we were badgered with requests to play here, there and everywhere, and we couldn't do it because the orchestra was not ours; we only hired it back from the BBC. So the only thing to do was to take an enormous risk. The enormous risk was to decide then and there to establish a salaried orchestra. (Leonard Behrens, 1958)

I CAME HOME EXPECTING to find an orchestra with at least seventy players, but when I got home I found I had twenty-six players, and in the space of about five weeks I was supposed to start the season with a full symphony orchestra. Anybody who knows the difficulties under which I had to proceed – the whole country was mobilized, male and female – and we immediately announced auditions that lasted six, seven hours a day and I had to look for people which I would say were 'partially maimed' – that means that they couldn't get into the Services. But for instance a chap with flat feet might have very good fingers. Sometimes it was very depressing to go through a whole day and find nothing, and then there were days of rejoicing when the most remarkable talent came to light. (John Barbirolli, 1965)

Legge founds the Philharmonia

I INVESTED EVERY PENNY I'd ever saved or inherited, and decided to make an orchestra because I wanted for my work in the Gramophone Company to have the best possible instrument. It was one of the great orchestras of the world. [It was disbanded, nineteen years later, in 1964] first of all because Karajan had been appointed Director of the Berlin Philharmonic, and I knew he would have less time to work with the Philharmonia than he had previously. Secondly, the other orchestras had awakened to the fact that they might outbid me for certain key players. As a matter of fact the BBC did: they took Jock Sutcliffe, who was the best oboe player in the country at that time. They took one or two other players from me, and search the country as I did I could not find players of the quality to replace them. The colleges and the academies were simply not producing them; neither were the private teachers. I went to the Musicians' Union and asked if they would let me import players from abroad, because the double-bass situation in England was bad then. (It's bad now.) If I'd robbed, if I'd taken the first double-bass from all the orchestras in the country I still couldn't have got a group of bass players half as good as Karajan had in Berlin. Britain should have one national orchestra. (Walter Legge, 1970)

Economics and a change of attitude

IT SEEMS TO BE ECONOMIC FORCES, I think, that changed the general attitude. In fact you see this huge paraphernalia of the orchestra growing ever bigger up to 1914 and then economic circumstances mean that it's no longer valid to use that. It didn't stop Strauss – the *Alpine Symphony* continued to be written – but at the same time, in *Ariadne auf Naxos*, Strauss had already pioneered using a small orchestra. With Stravinsky you start with something like *The Soldier's Tale*, which was written purely for utilitarian reasons, just a small set-up, which influenced his whole thinking. (Colin Matthews)

MY INTENTION AT THAT TIME was to ask different composers to write short works for me for a small orchestra of about twenty performers. I had the impression that after Wagner and Richard Strauss the days of the big orchestras were over, and that it would be delightful to return to a small orchestra of well-chosen players and instruments. (Princesse de Polignac, 1966)

I KNEW IT ALREADY as a boy: I wanted to have my own orchestra, and I knew exactly what the aims of the orchestra would be. I wanted to play old music and, especially, modern works. You see, I think every-where in Europe at that time you had very important, large symphony orchestras, important concerts with classical and romantic music, but they played very rarely modern works, and they were not able to play music, let me say, before Mozart. (Paul Sacher, 1993)

PEOPLE MUST WITHDRAW as much as possible from the influence of Richard Wagner . . . Complete renunciation of any inner programme, intentional avoidance of large forces, limitation of the means of expression in favour of an intensification of the inner powers of expression, instinctive ties to the style of *a cappella* music and the pre-classicists, finally a nearly fanatical preference for chamber music. (from *Die Neue Oper* by Kurt Weill, translated by Kim Kowalke)

AT THE TIME SCHOENBERG was organizing his Society for Private Musical Performances, his own style of composition was at its most radical. Previously, in *Pelleas und Melisande* and in the *Gurrelieder*, he had written for the huge post-Wagnerian orchestra, but now he turned away from the kind of large expansive forms associated with it. In his First Chamber Symphony of 1906, he condensed the customary four movements of the symphony into a single, uninterrupted form, less than twenty minutes long, and reduced his orchestra to a mere fifteen players. With his chamber orchestra, Schoenberg established a totally new concept, which has now become standard practice. (Alexander Goehr, 1987)

Two Academies:

of St Martin in the Fields . . .

IT WAS THE BEGINNING of the long-playing record, the LP; it was also the beginning of an interest, I suppose, in seventeenth- and eighteenth-century instrumental music, and as soon as these records began to circulate, not only in England but through Europe and then eventually in America, they became quasi visiting cards and we would get invitations to play in exotic places, and because we had these invitations to have exposure in important cities, then the record companies became much more interested in us, and it was a snowball. (Neville Marriner, 1993)

. . . and of Ancient Music

BOTH IN VIENNA AND AMSTERDAM there were very intriguing groups of specialist players who were playing in effect museum instruments. The patronage of Gustav Leonhardt, of Nikolaus Harnoncourt, of Eduard Melkus and a few similar people abroad led one to think that this same job could be done in England. I'd run the Academy as basically an ensemble for trio sonatas for a long while, because I felt this was a branch of repertoire unfairly neglected and I wanted to explore it. By pooling a few more string players and by ringing round and finding a few wind players who were experimenting and also by a lucky meeting with Peter Wadland, who was a producer for Decca and had just been given the right to make new recordings under the old imprint of L'Oiseau-Lyre, we started talking about how to approach historical music with appropriate groups. (Christopher Hogwood)

The London Sinfonietta

THE SINFONIETTA REALLY BEGAN as partly, to be honest, a springboard for myself, but also it seemed that there was a need in London for some sort of organization that could play well the repertoire that falls into this sort of middle ground between chamber orchestras the size of the English Chamber Orchestra and small chamber groups. (David Atherton, 1973)

The primacy of the conductor

IF THE NINETEENTH CENTURY belonged to the composer, the twentieth century belongs to the conductor. The new enlarged orchestras and the expanded forms required by Wagner and his successors could not be managed with nothing more than one player starting and stopping the others and marking the cadence points. The ways of chamber music could no longer apply. A new silent performer, the conductor, had to be invented, and if he was not himself the composer, stood between composer, orchestra and audience. (Alexander Goehr, 1987)

Conductors old-style . . .

SIDONIE GOOSSENS: There used to be absolutely no contact at all, especially between rank-and-file players and the conductor. The conductor was way up, you know, on a pedestal, and the rank-and-file players were something quite different.

INTERVIEWER: Who built the pedestal, the conductor or the rank-and-file players?

GOOSSENS: I'm not quite sure; I should think the conductor.

COLIN BRADBURY: I saw Colin Davis the other day right in among the first violins having a heart-to-heart chat with about three of them, everybody joining in; this would have been unheard of years ago.

GOOSSENS: Well, it's more of an equality age. All our conductors when we were young, they were all very much older and, well, it was just something to talk to them!

COLIN BRADBURY: That's interesting, Sidonie . . .

GOOSSENS: I feel that's why we all had such a respect for the conductors of those days, and that we would never think of arguing with a conductor or saying, 'Well, I feel I want to play it like this.' I mean, we would never have dared do that.

INTERVIEWER: Did you ever have coffee with the conductor during the interval?

GOOSSENS: No!

COLIN BRADBURY: Nobody would dare think of anything other than 'Dr Walter'. Nowadays, most of us shout across the orchestra when asking a question to our permanent conductor, 'Colin, should it be so and so and so?' And this is accepted.

(Sidonie Goossens and Colin Bradbury in interview, 1969)

THIS PAINSTAKING AND meticulous method may perhaps be right and necessary with the more unsophisticated players of southern Europe. It was the early method of Toscanini, and of others of the greatest conductors of their time. But it is undeniable that it uses up an enormous amount of rehearsal time and is quite fatal for the quick rehearsing that so often is forced on us in this country by economic necessity. I personally would go far further, and say that besides wasting time it is, from the psychological standpoint, an absolutely wrong approach to Anglo-Saxon professionals, and I might add to northern Europeans generally, as far as my experience goes. We Britishers, if driven from the very first bar, through a series of three or four rehearsals, will certainly lose interest long before the concert, and find it very difficult to recapture our freshness and come up to concert pitch even when we see the audience in the hall or the red light in the studio. Our people like to be led, not driven, and if I may adopt a sporting analogy, I feel rather like the trainer of a team or a crew, and want to begin gently and easily, then increase the tension as we go along. Indeed, even the final rehearsal is still a preparation for the concert rather than a model of it. (Adrian Boult, 1960)

. . . and new

THE ORCHESTRA IS ALMOST the only thing except sports teams (which are nothing like as big), the only community endeavour where people actually have to sit down with their colleagues and attempt to work with such a fineness and sensibility. It is the one place where you needn't actually suffer from this desperate isolation. But it also poses this: the submergence of the individual, and this is of course what they can't bear, and it's because the conductor is telling them what to do when they themselves are trained musicians. It irks and irks, you cannot get rid of it. (Colin Davis, 1969)

I HAVE ENJOYED ALL THE WORK I've done in the orchestra, but looking back I'm beginning to get some reservations. I've enjoyed my life and I shall continue to enjoy it, but if you lead an honest life as a musician and really play music, you end up with very little except your memories. (Frederick Riddle, 1973)

YOU'VE GOT TO PLAY FATHER to all these people; you've got to be prepared to discuss anything with them, even their personal troubles, perhaps, or their relationships with their colleagues. I've had the most odd conversations with some of them. You've got to like people in order to do this, which I do; I'm very interested. There's nobody in this orchestra I could say I actually disliked, but some of them are a mystery to me: that's another matter! And you've got to be sympathetic, you've got to love other people, you've got to know, to understand that every human being is made up of the same ingredients. It may be a slightly different recipe, but there's nothing that another man can feel that you don't know about. (Colin Davis, 1969)

Toscanini

I REMEMBER WHEN Toscanini first came to the BBC orchestra, and he rehearsed Brahms's Fourth Symphony, which was a work we'd played many, many times. I say 'rehearsed' but it really was a performance, because he stopped hardly at all. He was very pleased – I say it as shouldn't, perhaps – but he was very pleased with the way the orchestra played it, and he went through the two middle movements of the symphony actually without stopping at all. I remember that very well, and afterwards I asked various members of the orchestra what had happened. I said, 'Of course you were playing it differently.' 'Yes,' I remember one girl saying. 'Yes, I know we were playing quite differently from the way we usually play that movement, but we just seemed to have to play it that way. He was willing us to do it and we did it.' (Adrian Boult, 1969)

Beecham

I'VE ALWAYS CONSIDERED Sir Thomas Beecham to be the greatest conductor in the world. When, after eight years of orchestral playing, I gave it up in 1948, I had played for most of the big international conductors of the time. For me, Sir Thomas stood far above them all.

This opinion of mine has been strengthened in later years, when, as a member of the audience, I heard Beecham conduct on every occasion I could. Unlike so many of the big names among conductors, he had the ability to make a player feel that what he was doing was really worthwhile. This was so refreshing after the attitude of some conductors who, in the knowledge that they had the management's full backing, almost challenged one to make the slightest slip, so that the threat of being sacked cast a continual gloom over one. I've so often sat in the orchestra feeling as if I were a criminal to even dare to play the instrument at all, but Sir Thomas's warm and human approach came as a ray of sunshine on a winter's day. (Malcolm Arnold, 1961)

AH, BEECHAM JUST HAD MAGIC! He just did things with his hands and he sang very badly, but he conveyed the message, by Jove! (John Kuchmy, 1975)

Barbirolli: a permanent conductor

I'M ONLY THE FOURTH permanent conductor of the Hallé in a hundred and seven years of history. A conductor can't leave anything behind him, like a composer; almost the only thing he can leave is an orchestra which has a real tradition and a style of playing. Now, you may like that, you may dislike it, but anybody who hears the Hallé when I'm conducting knows it's the Hallé, and there's very little of that today because of these semi-permanent conditions. We have an enormous repertoire, which always needs touching up in certain places, like a quartet that plays together. But if I have a great work to prepare, like a big new huge Mahler symphony, we always place it at a period when we play more or less standard repertoire. The orchestra's not let off rehearsals because of the standard repertoire; it's called for the same number of rehearsals, which are used for these works they're preparing. It keeps them busy, and gives them the incentive of preparing something they've never heard or played before. So you see this really permanent orchestra has tremendous advantages both musically and morally, I think. (John Barbirolli, 1965)

Karajan

IF, LET'S SAY, a solo wind player had a bit of bad luck in recording, and a passage repeated several times still wasn't quite right, Karajan would never worry him or pick him out in front of the orchestra; he'd not even look at him after two or three tries. I mean, obviously it wasn't his day, or a little accident in the instrument or something. Karajan would just say, 'Oh, another time', and then record totally another passage. About a week later, maybe, he'd come back to that, and of course it would be absolutely fine. He understood the psychology of recording, I should think, earlier than any other conductor, however pushed we were for time, for recording time in a session. Very rarely did we leave that studio less than six, seven minutes early. We left with that little workman's feeling, 'We're slightly ahead of the game.' Karajan knew the value of morale. (Hugh Bean, 1987)

IN A REHEARSAL, you have to be with a sort of microscopic mind, and a microscopic ear. You have to hear the faults which are played, and the less personal engagement you put in the better, because the fault will come out of itself. You see it's like if you jump, on horseback: you don't carry the horse over the obstacle, you place the horse in a position that it will do the natural thing and jump. If you try to help an orchestra in the rehearsal, they will rely on you to help them in a concert, and they should not, because this is a basic principle that I spent a good ten or fifteen years in conducting to learn: that if you, so to say, carry the thing, then they will be lazy. (Herbert von Karajan, 1987)

A problem for orchestral players?

I DO THINK THAT quite aside from the schism that is often cited between audiences and contemporary composers, the true schism is between the composer and the orchestral players. The symphony orchestra is in a certain danger from composers because they tend to write things in which the players of an orchestra cannot involve themselves. In many works – I think it would be invidious to suggest a specific name – but many fragmented works (and this is a very large proportion of contemporary music today) allow single instruments of an enormous orchestra sometimes only to put in single notes here, there and around the place, and this means that they cannot do more than act as sort of computers. In fact they do a job that computers could do much better, and from that angle I think the symphony orchestra is in a real danger of having to give way, literally, to mechanical or electronic devices. (Norman Del Mar, 1970)

. . . or a problem with the orchestra itself?

MY SUBMISSION WOULD BE that composers have always been writing things in which symphony orchestras as opposed to chamber groups could not fully involve themselves. We know this empirically from such instances as, shall we say, the sixty *Tristan* rehearsals in Vienna after which the performance was cancelled. The reason why it is far more difficult for an orchestra to involve itself musically in the performance of a new work than for a soloist or a chamber body is simply that orchestral playing comparatively is an unmusical occupation. Nowadays, when composers write far more for bands within the band, for soloists within the band, the manifest musicality of the player is improving, but it is improving in proportion as the symphony orchestra as we know it is disintegrating. (Hans Keller, 1970)

IT'S SOMETHING I'VE BEEN very conscious of, that orchestras are frightened of composers and composers frightened of orchestras, partly because they don't get together very often. It's not as in the past, where whatever they played would have been by living composers. This, as we know, has retreated so much that it's a rare event for both of them, and so there's a lot for both of them to learn. It's one of the reasons that I've tried quite hard to help with composer residencies, which the CBSO, for instance, has been incredibly positive about. (Colin Matthews)

The orchestra continues to expand

PERCUSSION HAS BECOME the explosion of the century, because in the first place rhythm became a hugely important element in music during the century, and percussion is the obvious way of articulating rhythm. I think it also stems from the composer's desire to expand the orchestra, and it's the only area in which expansion is really possible. You can see it in the players: there are still a few players left who grew up in the post-war years having to learn little more, once they'd mastered tim-pani, than to be able to play the bass drum, cymbals and triangle, and that would be more or less it – a few odd side-drums or so, a bit of xylophone, glockenspiel. Now the expansion has been so huge that percussion players have to concentrate on one aspect of technique, so that you will find specialist keyed percussion players. The whole range of percussion has grown hugely, and composers have also written more and more virtuosic parts for it. I think you get the feeling that percussion used to be the dumping ground for the not-so-good musician. Now it is one of the most demanding and telling sections of all. (Colin Matthews)

AN ORCHESTRA IS EXACTLY the mirror of the society, and as a mirror of the society you have people – of course a minority – who are very progressive and want to discover. It depends very much on the

instrument, on whether its existing repertoire is rich or if its new repertoire is more interesting. Take percussionists, for instance. There are so
many who are very interested in new music because that's their life,
practically. Just playing the triangle in a work of Liszt or Brahms is not
terribly exciting, but if you have a big part on a xylophone or vibraphone, that's much more interesting for them, and therefore they like
this repertoire. (Pierre Boulez, 1989)

I THINK THE PIANO has become a standard orchestral instrument for
the same reason as percussion, because it can add rhythmic impetus,
but it's also – I find myself – a great foundation instrument. It can be
used as part of the orchestra without dominating; it's a hugely useful
colouring instrument in many ways. (Colin Matthews)

Economics and principles

AT ONE TIME WE HAD the ideal way, in my opinion, of running an
orchestra. We had a completely contract orchestra, and pensions and
so forth. This is the way an orchestra, in my opinion, should be run,
and in the opinions of my predecessors too, and this is the way it was set
up. But there comes a time, unfortunately, when the pure economics
get in the way and this awful decision: do you stick by your principles
regardless of economics (which means your principles go to the wall
anyway) or do you say, 'The first principle and the first ideal is to keep
the LPO as a first-class orchestra'?

I don't think anybody would claim that a musician is particularly
badly paid; he's not well paid by the standards of other professions, in
my opinion, but the problem is he has to work much too hard to earn
that money. For instance, last year the orchestra worked 550 full three-
hour working sessions. Now, there isn't an orchestra in Europe or in
America that will cover that amount of work. (Ernest Bravington,
1973)

FROM THE AMERICAN PERSPECTIVE, playing in an orchestra's an
extremely good job. It's well paid, good security, good conditions – I'd
say far better conditions and pay than you find in London. Perhaps it's
too comfortable, frankly. (Tom Morris)

THE BBC DID NOT EXPECT, you know, to live on the box office, but
with American orchestras you have to live with the box office. (Pierre
Boulez, 1989)

The orchestra and its community

IT'S FAIRLY TRADITIONAL NOW in all American orchestras that the largest financial support comes from individuals. If you go back to the nineteenth and early twentieth century many of the business people and leaders that you're dealing with are European immigrants who came from countries and cities with a strong musical life, a strong musical heritage. As you get now into this point of the twentieth century, I think, number one, sure, it's the signal of a major metropolitan area. From a pragmatic point of view, it's a signal that helps to entice senior executives, senior management to want to live in the city. Then there's the funny, hard to describe but I think very real issue of community pride. Chicago – I've been here thirteen years now – has this very interesting, what they call 'second city' mentality. Our wonderful major comedy club called Second City that's been so famous around the world sort of underlines that. It is a part of the ethic of Chicago to prove that it is as important as the first city, so there's a great deal of community pride.

The Chicago Symphony Orchestra underwent a financial transformation after that first tour of Europe in 1971. At that stage of my life I was operating a small commercial classical-music radio station in Syracuse, upstate New York, and I remember reading the news reports off the wire of the ticker-tape parade down LaSalle Street that Mayor Daley threw for the Chicago Symphony when it came back from that triumphant first tour with Georg Solti, and it transformed the orchestra in the minds of Chicagoans into something different from what it was. I think it's a sad but real fact of America that many Americans have, I would say, a lack of self-confidence in their ability to judge what they see as a European art form. It validated what they had built in Chicago when critics in Vienna and London and Paris and Berlin said, 'My goodness, this is a great orchestra!' And if you go back and look at the financial records from the early 1970s you can see subscriptions started to go up, and contributions started to go up because suddenly this was a winner, and people do want to belong to a winner. (Henry Fogel)

IT'S REALLY THE HIGHLIGHT of Berlin, so to get more tourists and more taxes and so on, you need a ambassador to go out in the world and say, 'This is the Berlin Philharmonic Orchestra.' That brings us guests to the city, and is good publicity for Berlin as a city. (Cultural Officer, City of Berlin, 1979)

CAN WE BE MORE ADVENTUROUS and still keep our public? But the

Berlin Philharmonic public is in a very good situation in the sense that it is very very stable and trustful, and we have on the one hand to keep the interest and on the other hand we have to give new answers to the crisis which the concert life faces also here in Berlin, just as in London. (Elmar Weingarten, 1997)

A basic problem

EVEN THE GREATEST CONDUCTOR with the most standard repertoire does not have the popularity of, for instance, a boxing match. You have, for a football match, let's say two hundred thousand people and, even for a Beethoven symphony, you have only five thousand. (Pierre Boulez, 1989)

Proposals, and a gloomy prediction

ONCE YOU START selling concerts on the basis of stars, or once you start selling concerts on the basis of the greatest hits, you get totally boxed in; you can't do it any other way, and it limits choices. (Tom Morris)

AMERICAN AUDIENCES, VERY SIMILAR to their English counterparts, are now influenced by soundbites. We seem to have come to a point where the attention of a listener has been diminished and we also have a problem hearing pieces that seem to last longer than seven or eight minutes. This is mostly due to commercial considerations, of course. Also, within our own music, people are much more interested, say, to hear *Quiet City* of Aaron Copland than they are the entire Third Symphony, although that contains the *Fanfare for the Common Man* that we all know. (Leonard Slatkin)

ONCE YOU START to water down the programme to appeal to a broader or a more mass audience, I think audiences also sense that you are playing down to them, that you are not taking their musical intelligence seriously enough, and you simply become less interesting. I've watched that happen in too many other cities, and it is a no-win game. (Fergus McWilliam, 1997)

IN AMERICA I THINK there are simply too many symphony orchestras, and if you look at what's happening, you'll find that a lot of the what I call 'middle orchestras' are going out of business. There's a number of them that have gone bankrupt. You generally find that the very big ones are doing quite well. What happened in the go-go years of the late

1970s and 1980s is a lot of orchestras over-expanded, not unlike record companies, thinking that they could pursue the golden egg for ever, and what's happened is they've all expanded beyond the ability of the community market to sustain it. And they're in trouble. And there will be fewer orchestras in the future, I'm convinced of it. (Tom Morris)

London, the city of five orchestras

I THINK ALL OF US very fondly look back to the late 1960s and early 1970s when London was unquestionably the music capital of the entire world. There was such a liveliness to all of the programmes and musical institutions and such new repertoire being introduced all the time – not only new music but unusual music of the past. And then somehow, over the course of these years, all of these formulas of concert-giving became a great deal more predictable and of course there were also economic crises and other things that had to be dealt with. But I think now, across the board – I mean everyone, performers and administrators, government sponsors and private sponsors – all of us alike are looking forward to a more open adventurous period again. (Michael Tilson Thomas, 1985)

I HAPPEN TO HAVE a passionate interest and belief and love of orchestras, and a fascination not only with the repertoire, but also in how it is that they're created, what makes them tick, what keeps their standard up and what are the differing factors from city to city and country to country and period to period that have actually kept them going. Why it is that some orchestras seem more stable whatever the external factors, and what are the determining factors about the sort of work that they do? They're fascinating beasts. (Roger Wright)

Pointers to the future?

BECAUSE I POINTED the Academy of St Martin in the Fields, which was a small orchestra to begin with, in the direction of playing symphonic repertoire (and in fact as we are today we're involved in recording all the Tchaikovsky symphonies, all the Dvořák symphonies, the Elgar symphonies, all the major symphonic repertoire), I did not want them in any way to lose the original character. Also, it's again a fact of life that the Academy of twenty-five players directed by Iona Brown or by Kenneth Sillito, who is now a co-director, fills the houses, the German and European concert halls, just as quickly as an orchestra of ninety players conducted by me. The Academy as a sort of label is attractive. So we could either offer them the symphonic repertoire or the large choral repertoire conducted by me, or they can have the two chamber-orchestral things, twenty-five to thirty players directed by either Iona or by Kenneth Sillito, or they could have the chamber ensemble which is anything up to the Spohr Nonet or the Mendelssohn Octet, eight or nine players, which is also directed by Ken Sillito. And it gives everyone a chance really to have, again, the sort of exposure that I felt we were missing when I was part of a symphony orchestra, and I didn't want them to get lost in the sort of morass of a large group, so we try to encourage the smaller groups to work rather harder than the large group now. (Neville Marriner)

THE CONCEPT OF THE symphony orchestra in the twenty-first century could be a rather shrunk affair: struggling for money, a sort of museum number, just sometimes put together out of prime players to perform these gargantuan pieces from the nineteenth century. Or it could be seen – as it really is in many American cities – as the prime focus for musical thought, and the administration of the symphony orchestra could be seen eventually to cover many smaller activities.

One could devise many more interesting plans, I think, for the future of the symphony orchestra, which is much more endangered by seeing it as a potential umbrella to cover some of the smaller interests, which nevertheless need to be represented, because they are now seen as the prime exponents of areas that were once the territory of the symphony orchestra. So I think as the symphony orchestra becomes more precarious as a building, it can be propped up by putting in place those groups who make it their main business to play baroque music, early classical music, jazz, educational music, opera accompaniments, very avant-garde electronic and percussive music, and these can all be items within the overall menu served by a symphonic orchestra's adminis-tration. (Christopher Hogwood, 1993)

THE FUNDAMENTAL OBJECTIVE of an orchestra must be to lead taste, not follow taste, and where you find success and audiences that are not getting smaller but growing, where you find audiences that are getting not older but younger, are places that are committed to that kind of really quite aggressive leading of taste.

Orchestral music cannot merely survive through electronic repro-duction. There's no substitute for the live experience, and in the same way that there'll always be a gallery to go look at Rembrandts, there will always be, I think, a great symphony orchestra, and there must be, to perform Beethoven's Sixth Symphony. And the best way to do that, the most compelling way to do that, is in fact to have a great instrument to perform it, a great orchestra that is trained, nurtured, has an innate style, knows how to approach music: there's nothing better. So it will survive. (Tom Morris)

AN ORCHESTRA IS A very delicate thing: an orchestra consists of human beings who must make music at a given time, and I think for a conductor it is a very dedicated thing to handle this affair in the right way. (Bernard Haitink, 1973)

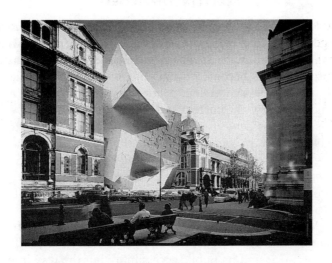

20 2000

I really don't think we'll ever know where music's going.
I think it's hovering.
JULIAN ANDERSON

THE WRITTEN RECORDS of the years 1899–1900 contain very few predictions of how music would develop in the twentieth century. A new century had begun (strictly speaking, of course, it would not begin until 1 January 1901) but a new era had not. That would have to wait until either 3 September 1912 (the first performance of Schoenberg's *Five Orchestral Pieces*, Op. 16) or 29 May 1913 (Stravinsky's *The Rite of Spring*). Which of those scores inaugurated the 'real' twentieth century was a matter for dispute for much of the rest of that century. Not even the most clairvoyant of commentators could have predicted either of them at the end of the nineteenth.

So many unpredictable events have taken place in music since that double shock nearly ninety years ago that musicians are wary of foretelling the future, despite widespread talk of the Millennium and a recognition that, after all, 2000 is a more resonant date than 1900. Only two or three decades ago assertions that the future of music lay on a line projected from Schoenberg through Webern seemed, if not universally welcome, quite probable. Now, although many composers feel grateful to Schoenberg's opening up of musical territory and have been influenced by the rigorous economy of his serial technique, few write in a style audibly dependent on him, while many have rejected him and his followers outright as an historical aberration. Instead of a 'historically necessary' main line of development, we now have, as previous chapters have made clear, a profusion of styles. It may be that this multiplicity has become normal and will continue, at least for a while. But very few would confidently predict this or, if it is not the case, which if any of the current styles will predominate.

As this book has demonstrated, the influences on twentieth-century music have not always been musical ones. Politics, commercial interests, technology (radio and recording above all) and a growing awareness of ancient and non-Western cultures have all affected the century's music profoundly. It has not always been possible, nor will it be in the future, to recognize and assess these influences while they were being exerted. It is only now becoming possible to speculate that some of those factors during the past century have not simply affected the language of music and its public accessibility but the way in which we perceive the art.

The recording industry, which has made vast amounts of music from every age and culture almost universally accessible, is itself changing as a direct consequence of that – some would say that it is in crisis – but how it is changing is uncertain, and how it should change is the subject of urgent discussion. Has our relation to music been fundamentally changed by the fact that we most often experience it though radio and recordings, and if so should we combat this effect or accept it? There is a widespread feeling that the traditional concert, devised in the nineteenth century, also needs to change, to take account of new (and rediscovered old) repertoire, changing listening habits and leisure patterns, and new audiences. If the concert is to change, clearly performers must also do so, and the places where concerts are given. But if these changes do take place will the music of the past that now seems so important to us become only one of a range of musics, perhaps a marginal one? Because of the high cost of live music, and the fact that it is paid for by those who do not benefit from it as well as those who do, an urgent need to find new audiences is widely felt. Will the art of music have to change to accommodate them? Is there a risk that music that does not appeal to that new audience will be seen as 'élitist' and therefore not to be valued?

While the audience has grown, and has indeed never been larger, the financing of the art remains precarious, as was shown in chapter 5, and still gives great cause for concern. Part of the difficulty of predicting what the twenty-first century will bring is due to this, with many music organizations having no long-term stable income. What is seen as government parsimony is exacerbated by a view among some politicians and

opinion-formers that what has in the past been termed, perhaps snob-
bishly, 'high culture' is only one area of a broader 'people's culture'
which embraces not only popular music (which many would welcome
and accept, as chapter 6 made clear) but television 'soap operas', sport,
fashion and all forms of leisure pursuit.

Nevertheless it can scarcely be doubted that music itself will still
exist at the end of the twenty-first century. What forms it will take cannot be foreseen; even to predict what sort of music will be composed
and in what circumstances it will be performed in ten years' time seems
both difficult and rash. The previous nineteen chapters have warned
the contributors to this one of the dangers of prophecy. But they are
not averse to learning from the past, warning of present dangers and
speculating about what might form the music of the future.

*

The pendulum of the twentieth century . . .

WHEN PEOPLE LOOK BACK on the century, what's going to stand out
more than anything else are the two world wars. Their significance,
culturally and musically, is going to be much greater in people's
explanations of what's happened in our century than it is in our explanations now. For instance, to understand what's happened since the
Second World War, it really does help quite a lot if you see it in terms
of huge, pendulum swings of reaction to the incalculable traumatic
shock of that event. The Darmstadt Festival and the whole movement
of trying to create a new kind of music that would eradicate the
composer and clear out all the romantic rhetoric that it was felt was
somehow complicit in the conditions that had made Nazism possible
and created the Second World War – that's very important. But it's
important also in the way that people who react against things tend to
mirror the things they react against. Darmstadt, with its lists of pre-
scribed and proscribed composers – another *Entartete Musik*, almost –
and its lists of dos and don'ts and its totalitarian approach to the way
that music could be manufactured in this will-less state, so strongly
resembles a parody of in some ways Nazism and in others the totalitarianism of Stalin, that it's almost comic to look at now. But it's
surprising how few people would have been able to understand it in
such terms then.

What sometimes worries me, looking at these huge pendulum
swings, is that all I hear is the sound of babies being thrown out
with the bathwater. There is a reaction going on against the kind of
modernism that appeared in the names of Schoenberg and Webern

after the war. How often does Schoenberg's name appear in a concert programme nowadays? Hardly ever. Yet he was *de rigueur* at one point in the 1960s. Of course there are so many things that I'm delighted to see the back of: Darmstadt modernism and total serialism. And yet the imagination finds ways of expressing itself in almost any technique that a human being can invent, and some of the things that were done by the great modernist figures that are now being turned into bogeymen were interesting – in spite of themselves, you could almost say. It's a shame that the reaction against something always goes too far, and you end up with another absurdity in place of the original one. (Stephen Johnson)

. . . and the unforeseeable twenty-first

THE TWENTIETH CENTURY has failed to produce a universally understood musical language, but simultaneously with that failure we have learned that the world is a much bigger place than we thought it was. It's been a century of enormous liberation, expressively and technically, and of discovering also the wonderful new constraints within which composers can work if they wish. It's also got composers out of their narrow little world and into the real world – I don't mean economically, but simply in terms of social reality. You cannot simply sit down and say, as Robert Simpson did in the 1950s, 'I'm going to write a big cycle of symphonies', without some irony or some awareness that you're a very odd creature indeed – unless you're making a specific point against writing other things. I feel as much a stranger to most of the Western tradition or as much of an amateur in it as I do in Japanese music. I really don't think we'll ever know where music's going. I think it's hovering, and I think it may simply continue to hover. It's inconceivable now that somebody like Pierre Boulez could say, as he did in the 1950s, 'This is the future of music.' No one aesthetic movement could possibly sweep the entire world now. (Julian Anderson)

SCHOENBERG IS A VERY, very difficult one, isn't he? He is unquestionably important in terms of what happened this century, and nothing is going to change that. But Meyerbeer was an important composer in terms of what happened in the nineteenth century. He was a huge influence on and through Verdi and Wagner and Musorgsky. If you had asked a music-lover in the earlier part of the last century who were the most important composers of the time you'd probably have found Meyerbeer, with Spohr and Spontini, high on the list. (And that strange Austrian composer Franz Schubert would have been nowhere –

he was a real connoisseur's composer.) I wonder if in the twenty-first century Schoenberg will be seen as Meyerbeer is now? I find it harder and harder to say why anybody should listen to the vast majority of the twelve-tone works of Arnold Schoenberg. (Stephen Johnson)

Recording: a crisis? . . .

THERE IS A MAJOR CRISIS over orchestras, and it's not just a crisis of funding. It's a crisis as to whether the whole idea of the concert is something that still has validity. That gives me a great deal of pause because I don't believe in recorded music: I don't believe in it as anything more than a record or an *aide-memoire* or a point of reference. Music to me depends on live performance. (John Drummond)

THE MUSIC PROFESSION has changed more in the last two or three years than I can ever remember it before, and that is because of the situation with recording. Everybody took it for granted that it would always be there. I'm not really convinced that it will be in the way that we knew it before. I don't think that's necessarily a pessimistic thing to say. It may make and in a way force musicians to be more creative. The future would appear to be in new music. Record companies and the public are going to want to hear new things, different things, and that's a great opportunity for contemporary composers. We're already living in an age when people are open to judge a new piece of music on its own terms. It doesn't matter what style it is, because we've experienced so many different styles over such a long period of time that people's ears are now more open to accepting something in its own style. (Julian Lloyd Webber)

. . . or a new creative medium?

CLASSICAL-MUSIC CDS HAVE TENDED to be based on one composer's work, very often one medium (string quartet or piano or whatever), with no mixing and matching of performers, and no cross-fading or editing: you play the piece and there's a five- or six-second gap before the next piece starts. It's very orderly and they're all of a similar length, seventy minutes long, and they sell at the same price. I think you've got to look at a CD as as much of a work of art as a specially commissioned piece, and then of course you start making all kinds of connections that you wouldn't normally make. Just as you might dream up this fabulous concert that involves musicians from different parts of the world, you could do the same with a CD: you wouldn't be frightened of making quite bold connections. Then barriers begin to fall down, because you're allowed to make connections between long-dead composers and living ones and with musicians from other parts of the world. There has to be a very strong philosophy behind it; you would take a very firm stance about why you're putting something on CD. Then of course you're looking at something that's a creative document in its own right, so it's not frozen in time, or an enemy of live performance in any way. (Joanna MacGregor)

THE WALKMAN IS COMMONLY ABUSED because it seems to subtract people from social life. Actually the experience of the Walkman, the intoxication of the Walkman, comes from the fact that for the user they're not withdrawn from the scene that they're walking through or the tube train that they're sitting in. The Walkman-user is often creating a kind of a chance collage between the sounds that are filtering through and are purely contingent and the organized sound that they're hearing. There is a sense, therefore, of the recorded sound, which is fixed and complete and perfect, being deliberately exposed to the chance of what might happen. In the Walkman we have a perfectly ordinary and very casual coming together of the impulse towards absolute technical perfection that we find in CD technology, in which what we hear has never really taken place in any here and now – it's a purely artificial sound – and the aesthetics of John Cage, who wanted music to be an exposure to the here and now, to the chances of what happens to happen; there is a great hunger for that contingency. We've become much better at making swift links and snatching at continuities than living with growing organic wholeness, but we've also become much better as listeners at tolerating openness and chance, and at living in a world of multiple stimuli. That's our world. (Steve Connor)

Changing the concert

I THINK THE COLLABORATIVE PROCESS could be between artists from different fields. I'm very troubled by the fact that classical music still, at the end of the century, is so out of touch with other art forms that the thought of combining, for example, computer technology, dance and visual arts with music is seen as attacking a bastion of culture. I've done combined-arts concerts that have been very carefully thought through and tastefully executed, and you'd think that I'd come on in the most garish outfit imaginable and danced naked around the piano. Some of the critics think that somehow I am attacking their values by doing this. To me this isn't really recognizing where audiences are.

Audiences are constantly one step ahead of mainstream thinking, and their everyday lives bring them into contact with many different art forms at once. I think we have to find a way of reflecting that. (Joanna MacGregor)

PEOPLE ALWAYS SEEM to be looking for some event. The best-attended concerts are usually parts of a series that somehow captures the imagination. But this can lead to what you see every summer now: open-air concerts, concerts with fireworks, proms in the park. It's highly debatable whether that is the right way to present classical music well. I know as a performer that to play the Elgar Cello Concerto outdoors is actually extremely difficult. You're completely reliant on the weather and the sound system, but people seem to want an event, and just to go to a 3000-seater concert hall and hear a standard overture–concerto –symphony programme will not, in thirty years' time, be something that will capture the imaginations of large numbers of people. In the future there will be more mixed concerts, and they won't be to everybody's liking. There'll be electronic music mixed with live orchestral music. The traditional symphony-concert formula will always be there, but in thirty years' time it won't be a regular thing. (Julian Lloyd Webber)

IT'S NO LONGER GOOD ENOUGH to present a season of concerts that are simply overture–concerto–interval–symphony, leave it at that and have no relationship with the audience at all. The London Sinfonietta, which is where I started, was the very first orchestra to develop an education programme in a significant way. Because this work has been going on for such a long time, there is a different atmosphere in the hall. Very often the musicians have a different attitude to the music because they've gone on a journey with it. They've attempted to communicate that music to other people in ways that go beyond simply performing it. They've worked with each other in a creative way because they've been involved perhaps in improvisation and composition, and they also have a relationship with the audience. There's nothing like going to an audience that is not the usual comfortable concert audience for throwing what you're doing into sharp relief. For example, we've taken operas into prisons. I remember one instance in Holloway Prison where we took a piece of Hindemith into a room crowded with a hundred and fifty women. It was a courtroom scene, and at one point the person playing the judge banged a gavel and sang, 'All stand', and the whole room stood up, because there wasn't the artifice, the barrier between the front of the platform and the audience. It was for real, and you wanted to say 'Stop! it's only an opera', but it was too late. (Gillian Moore)

Changing the performer

UNTIL RELATIVELY RECENTLY very little was asked of the classical performer. You were asked to learn a piece and play it brilliantly. That's not enough now. You have to communicate so much to the audience, and be part of the very important triangle composer–audience–performer. In some ways, also, those distinctions get blurred. You have to be a bit of a composer, a bit of a creative thinker, and know what it is to be in an audience as well. All these things come together and once you've acknowledged that, then the concerts themselves have to change quite radically. In terms of presenting contemporary music, the way to do it is to look constantly back to the past and to the roots of the living composer and find ways of linking the two. As soon as you put contemporary music into a context, not only are you taking the sting out of listening to something unknown, but you're allowing the audience to draw conclusions about how this composer relates to this particular time. There's nothing better than to play interesting juxtapositions. It almost replaces the pre-concert talk. (Joanna MacGregor)

I THINK THAT ORCHESTRAS and opera companies and traditional music institutions have come to realize in the last decade or so that they can be, in Pierre Boulez's words, 'an ensemble of possibilities'. They can break up into small chamber groups; they can be a kind of task force of three or four musicians working in a primary school. They can give a concert in a prison; they can work on deprived housing estates and in community centres with young people. There are orchestras who are working with Holocaust victims or having residencies in hospitals. They are redefining what performance means, and where it can take place, and who's allowed to come and see it. (Gillian Moore)

All kinds of audiences

I BELIEVE PASSIONATELY that we can make of opera, of an ensemble like English National Opera, a kind of motor to drive all kinds of work forward, and reach all kinds of audiences. You can do that in two different ways. You can take the work out and you can say, 'Here we are, in a place a long way away from the Coliseum. You, the audience today, don't necessarily want to come to the Coliseum; we don't think it's our duty to drag you in there. This is work for you: we're going to write, we're going to sing, we're going to play with the ideas, whether in an opera or in work that you do yourselves.' We use our talents and their latent talents to make something happen out there.

On the other hand, there is something that happens inside an opera house when you perform *The Magic Flute* or part of *The Ring* or whatever, that you could never possibly do other than inside that house. When you see a child or somebody who's never been before, or someone who's been part of a project that happened somewhere else and then comes to see you giving a highly professional opera performance in the theatre, it does something to the human spirit you could never replicate anywhere else. (Paul Daniel)

ONE PHENOMENON OF THE twentieth century is that music has become more abstract, perhaps more divorced from social function and from the ritualistic, the religious or the celebratory. None the less, from my experiences in working in extreme areas of society, taking what people might regard as very difficult music into areas such as prisons or schools, I believe that good art does speak. I hate the idea of a composer saying, for example, 'This is going to be performed in a school, so I'm going to write something very simple.' We've had the most extraordinary reactions to Ligeti, to Birtwistle – to composers that concert audiences often find too complex to listen to – from the innocent ear: from children who haven't heard any concert music at all, or from their parents who come up and talk to the musicians and make the most profound and perceptive comments about the music that has been performed. (Gillian Moore)

WHEN YOU WORK for an hour with some children or some members of our Hoxton Singers (who are people who live in Hackney and work with us in the ENO Works) – you discover they're not professionally perfect, they're not involved with the pursuit of perfection that goes into making a CD; they're involved with what their hearts do when they respond to an artistic idea which they have created themselves, and that is the highest possible art. At the end of that hour they have achieved the best they could achieve. Opera companies have simply been, for two or three centuries, repositories of accepted, complex, involved, professional music and words. The future lies in loosening that definition, understanding once and for all that big opera companies are supported by the roots of society. Much of English National Opera's money comes from the taxpayer at large, right across the country. It is our job to get back to those people. (Paul Daniel)

EVERYBODY'S INTERESTED IN MUSIC. It's important to people in every aspect of their lives: they need it for social occasions, for ritual and ceremony, for relaxation and for celebration. I think also that there are no boundaries to the types of music that people like. I'm very against the approach, for example, that you teach only pop music in schools because that's what the children are into. A far more exciting approach is to examine musical principles and get people excited about musical ideas across a wide range of styles. For example, I've seen a fantastic music teacher in an Inner London school talking about word-setting, and he was using as references not only rap but recitative from eighteenth-century opera and Schoenberg's *Pierrot lunaire*. (Gillian Moore)

Changing the concert hall

I'M VERY UPSET THAT there are still new concert halls being built that are completely inflexible. A very simple thing would be to have seating that could be removed. There's an absolutely marvellous hall in Manchester, the Bridgewater Hall, which is a wonderful design: light, airy, modern-looking . . . Unfortunately it has seating that you can't remove. It seems to me a very basic thing, to acknowledge that sometimes audiences want to sit down and sometimes they don't; sometimes they want to stand up, sometimes they want to dance around – similarly with staging that can be taken in and out. Looking at the buildings themselves tells you everything that you need to know about the minds behind the promotion and the running of the halls. Why constantly do concerts in buildings that were designed to be concert halls a hundred years ago or more? You absolutely have to take the music to the audience. You have to know who your audience is and where they are – and that might not be in a concert hall – and just take it to them. Of course you have to transport instruments and everything, but I'm more interested in going to where those people are, particularly where young people are. This is the audience of tomorrow, and if they're not coming into the concert halls, we've got to pursue them where they are, whether that's in clubs or gyms or arenas or shopping malls, wherever it is. The music will survive. Great masterpieces are like Shakespeare plays: you can do all kinds of things to them and they will still survive; they're very tough. (Joanna MacGregor)

Welcoming new technology

I'M VERY INTERESTED IN new technology, and in bringing it into classical music – not just brand-new music but older music. I don't see any anomaly in this at all. An example of this was a concert I did with a computer artist who threw up live computer images on to a screen while I was playing. The very first piece I played was by William Byrd, written around 1600, and the artist did a whole series of marvellous abstract designs which absolutely followed the structure of the music, so it was one obvious example of bringing together things that were ostensibly separated by four hundred years, but actually were very close, and it made the piece by Byrd appear what it is: a very modern piece of writing. It's almost like a jazz piece at one point: it improvises wildly and very imaginatively over a ground bass.

What I would like, though, is that sense of performance with different collaborative artists, so at a live event somebody is creating something while you're playing. That requires from the musician an element of improvisation, a very important skill that's gone out of classical music but that's coming back in, quite rapidly. Without that skill you can't collaborate with musicians from other fields, you simply can't get on stage with a jazz player or an Indian classical player or an African drummer. That global aspect to music-making requires of the performers a much wider range of skills. (Joanna MacGregor)

Finding links

THERE WERE POCKETS of the popular in which a certain kind of work of inquiry was done on behalf of serious music. Jazz has always performed that function, as the place where classically trained musicians went off and made discoveries in their lunch hours or in the evenings, and certain areas of rock music have also performed that function, so there will seem to be much more complicated links than we ever imagined there would be when we look back over the century. Certainly jazz, certainly some areas of rock music, some areas of improvisational music, and of course, most particularly in the last twenty or thirty years of the century, the influx of non-Western musics. (Steve Connor)

How WOULD I IDEALLY programme a big Messiaen piece? I'd be given a space to take over. I'd have a gamelan orchestra as the audience were walking in. Maybe I'd give a performance of the *Vingt regards sur l'enfant Jésus*, which lasts two and a half hours. Then perhaps we would have some Indian classical players coming on, who I could improvise with, so you would have that link of Messiaen's interest in Indian rhythms. I would also try and incorporate the prepared-piano world of John Cage: this is such a gamelan-influenced invention, and it uses such a lot of Indian ideas and philosophies, and you can, as I have done, improvise with a tabla player on the prepared piano. Of course with one bound you're getting out of this solely Western way of looking at Messiaen; you're showing all these different influences. You'd have to finish with a big jam session with all these musicians. I would do it in a space where people could sit down if they wanted to – of course this is a long gig we're talking about, so they'd have to be able to sit down, or even better lie down. I'd do it in a space that would be lit really interestingly, where you'd have a raised space so you could see where the performers were and what they were doing. You'd possibly have some video screens so people who weren't close to the performing space could still see and hear. Most importantly you could move around – you'd probably want to sit still for the Messiaen, but you could walk in and out. It's very interesting that in Indian classical concerts, which do go on for seven or eight hours, you sit still and you watch and you're very informed, but you can go out and then come back in again. (Joanna MacGregor)

I THINK THAT SERIOUS MUSICIANS have underestimated people like Gershwin. Dare I say Cole Porter? Dare I say *West Side Story* of Lennie Bernstein, which is a masterpiece by any standards? When hundreds of new operas were being put on, say in the 1810s and 1820s, all over Italy, most of them were probably forgotten immediately but opera was a very live form, opera must have been the equivalent to the audience then of musicals in our own century. We should and perhaps we even have a chance of getting through to a different kind of public, and when we look back on twentieth-century music, I think we will take a great deal more notice of people like Cole Porter and George Gershwin than we have done hitherto, and we will see that in their work they have a lot of pointers to the future. (Peter Maxwell Davies)

A CONCERT COMPOSER LIKE Toru Takemitsu has been very influenced, for example in his film scores, by the Japanese fascination with noise. Rock bands in Japan have had an abiding fascination with noise really for the last decade or so. It's as though these musicians have wanted to find, first of all, unsuspected passion and intensity and beauty in noise and, as it were, to encounter a kind of painfulness which music traditionally has had nothing to do with. Music has had to do with difficulty surmounted, and I think there's been an exposure to the sheer difficulty of absorbing what is painful in sound. The best example of a contemporary British musician working at this kind of interface and also crossing between concert music, tape music and the electro-acoustic tradition is John Wall, in works like his CD *Fraktur*, where there's a collage of sounds running from the grinding sounds of scratching vinyl all the way through to the very sweetest combinations

of sounds characteristic of the string quartet, and he creates a continuum, a vast sound palette, moving from one end to the other. (Steve
Connor)

Present discontents: high culture disdained . . .

THE FACT OF THE MATTER is that culture in the sense which I grew up
experiencing it isn't perceived publicly now, certainly not by our political masters; it's to do with the changing nature of politicians. When I
started, forty years ago, being aware of public life and of organizations
like the Arts Council, the people who made it up may have been a bit
stuffy and a bit old-fashioned, but at least they had an absolutely clear
view of what culture was, what its place in society was, and what the
aspiration towards self-improvement was. Everywhere you looked, in
Parliament, for instance, you would find people of culture on whatever
bench. On the Tory benches there were Edward Boyle, a magnificent
pianist and an extraordinarily fine and sensitive musician, and David
Eccles, who knew everything about Chinese ceramics. There was
Michael Foot, who knew more about the English novel than anybody,
and Jo Grimond, who knew more about Scottish history than anybody. Wherever you looked there were men of culture. I look around
the political arena now and I see a different kind of person. They have
skills, but they are not those of the traditional view of culture. Neither
the right-wing view ('it's what we put on our walls and what we own'),
nor the left-wing view ('it's what we aspire to and what we want to
share with other people less advantaged'). Now there is what I call 'the
revenge of the suburbs': an entirely consumer culture based on having
a larger car or a better hi-fi or a second holiday or a holiday home, and
I don't sense in the heart of government now any concept of culture as
someone like Maynard Keynes or Kenneth Clark or Isaiah Berlin or
Arnold Goodman (who were the men at whose feet I sat when I was
learning my trade) understood it. That seems to have gone. (John
Drummond)

ONE DOES GET VERY, VERY UPSET about the utter philistinism of
governments in their attitude towards music of the kind that interests
me. The Blair government doesn't seem to be doing all that much better
than its predecessor, and in some instances worse. (Peter Maxwell
Davies)

WE HAVE RIGHT IN THE heart of society very influential people like the
Prince of Wales or Peter Mandelson who go around saying that they
reject the culture of our time. Mandelson rejects classical music, says

it's finished and dead and doesn't need any help. The Prince of Wales rejects living architects and does great damage to individuals. People say, 'I don't like it; I don't understand it.' My education was: 'If I don't understand it or like it, it may well be my fault, so why not go and find out a bit more about it?' (John Drummond)

... banality exalted ...

AT THE MOMENT IT SEEMS as if (if this were literature) one gave the same respect and admiration to Jeffrey Archer's novels as one did to A. S. Byatt's novels or if one were confusing the poems of Patience Strong with those of T. S. Eliot. I feel very strongly that a lot of the stuff that is passed off these days as classical music, purveyed particularly by our friends on Classic FM, is background music, conversation music. It's a branch of the pop-music industry that happens to have long pieces on occasion. (Peter Maxwell Davies)

... overhearing, not listening ...

THERE IS A HUGE PROBLEM when there is so much music available. It has led very much to the denigration of listening. Going to dinner parties with intelligent people, who read a lot and are interested in other forms of cultural activity, I've said, 'Can we have something else instead of this music?', and several of them haven't even noticed that music was on, because a certain kind of low-level musical sound is part of their everyday continuum, like the throbbing of the heart in the womb. That's desperate. The downgrading of music is something that can be done very quickly, and it has happened very quickly.

A great deal of music, whether one is aware of it or not, in all kinds of genres, has a kind of sedative effect. It can take a very long time to recover from something like that. I don't hear anything that's being said by educationalists that seriously addresses the question of what listening is – not just analysis, not just being moved by a piece of music, but in some way having your life changed by it. It seems to me that vast numbers of people today are involved in the arts without being in any deep way engaged with them. It seems to me that we do need élitism, in whatever musical style. Imagine if in anything that matters you did *not* take a selective/élitist approach. (Stephen Johnson)

... head-count culture ...

I DON'T MIND THE IDEA that culture is also the way we dress or the way we eat – of course they are forms of culture – but I don't believe, I *know* that great music and poetry and drama and art have a reverberation that has gone on for a longer period than the Spice Girls. I find it deeply embarrassing that we have a Prime Minister who invites the Spice Girls to Number 10 but doesn't invite Simon Rattle. Beethoven is better than the Spice Girls – not different, better. I will go further and say 'more important'. We've got terribly nervous about making value judgements. The most dangerous thing that's happened to culture in our time is the head count, the idea that something matters only if it's appreciated by everybody. (John Drummond)

... artists subsidize art ...

IN THIS COUNTRY PARTICULARLY it's been the artists who have subsidized the work all the time. When I was younger, doing something like *Eight Songs for a Mad King*, nobody believed in that, and Harrison Birtwistle and I had to find money to put that and other things on. I found that I was paying for costumes, for rehearsal space, and I had no money to do it with. You might say, 'That's very good for a creative artist in the early stages of his or her life.' Yes, it can be, but forever fighting does become a bit galling, and it doesn't seem to change as I get older. One has to fight and fight and fight. (Peter Maxwell Davies)

... music education in decline ...

MUSIC EDUCATION IS NO LONGER a compulsory part of the National Curriculum. I was very fortunate to come from a musical family. Had I not had that, I don't know whether I'd have done music at all. Where would I have got my music from? From the school, and if music isn't considered a necessary part of young people's education, we're liable to lose a lot of talent in the classical-music field because some people will just never be exposed to music. The thing about music education is that people need it regularly. They need lessons once a week, not just some players from an orchestra to visit them once a term. We talk airily about how music is going to be in thirty years' time. It's not going to be there at all if the players aren't coming through. Of course the National Youth Orchestra is wonderful, the cream of the youth orchestras is still wonderful, but at the general level I detect that it's not quite as wonderful as it was. There are one or two 'difficult' instruments, like the bassoon for example, where you're not getting the level of players that you did twenty or thirty years ago. Looking ahead twenty or thirty years, goodness knows what that situation means. (Julian Lloyd Webber)

. . . opium and its antidote

THEY GO ON ABOUT CANNABIS and heroin and whatever, but the real drug, the real opium of the people, is neither cannabis nor heroin nor even religion. It's television! People sit in front of that damned thing and they switch off their minds and expect to be entertained on a very superficial level. It's not a question of élitism, it's a question of living intensely. You want to live every moment of your life as intensely as you can, and I can't imagine sitting in front of something like that and watching something banal and stupid. Life is too intense to spend like that. If you can only get out to them, if you ask the best of people they give it. If you are working, particularly with young people, and you present them with ideas that are shining and challenging, they understand. (Peter Maxwell Davies)

Views of the future:
Changing the nature of music

WHAT BEGAN AT THE BEGINNING of this century was recorded music. It began as a way of controlling, in a sense maintaining, music in its place. In its audiences and its modes of distribution recording has been largely a conservative force over this century. The phonographic revolution foreseen by Edison never took place because phonography became gramophony: it became the distribution of already recorded sounds. But as recording itself has become so much easier and recording technologies so much cheaper, that phonographic revolution is now taking hold. This means that music is not being produced in a number of defined and authoritative centres, and radiating out from them, but is being produced in lots of different places for lots of different occasions, and this means that the syntaxes of relationship between music and other kinds of social forms and activities are becoming much more diffuse: music is not taking place on the occasions and in the places where it has customarily taken place. Music is everywhere in contemporary mass culture, but the meanings of music are now under active and experimental investigation.

Take the interest of composers like John Zorn in this new genre, the imaginary film score, for example his *Spillane*, which seems to tell some wonderful disjointed story – a *film noir* but without any story and without any film. And there are other composers working along those lines: Roger Doyle is another example. So music, which has throughout this century known its place, is starting not to know its place. Music, which has settled into particular kinds of locations and occasions (notably, of course, when we're talking about serious or classical music, the concert hall), has begun to migrate to other places. Music has always been a matter of a convergence of techniques and materials and persons, but now it is undergoing a massive dispersal. It is appearing in different contexts, performing different functions, and this is fundamentally changing the character of music. Music has hitherto been thought of as an art defined on its own terms, an art with its own rules. The definition of music as the highest form of art because it doesn't refer to the world and refers only to itself is breaking down. (Steve Connor)

Understanding tradition

IF ONE TAKES A LITTLE BIT of care in thinking about what tradition is, about the thought processes, the metamorphoses that went on in the brain of a composer like Haydn or Mozart and made possible those large tonal structures, I think that those are so deeply ingrained in the way we think, the way we conceive – the way we move, even – that if we're going to think about large architectural forms, something using some of those principles is going to be absolutely essential.

I can't say dogmatically how it will be, but my own hunch is that this is a problem that has got to be faced, and it's a very fundamental problem to do with understanding what tradition really means because, my goodness, we need it! Not the superficialities, not just having common chords and making it nice for Joe Public in the first instance so that they have some kind of warm wash over them when they go to a concert and they hear a piece for the first time, but making a challenging structure which might last a long time, where you can actually feel the progress of the music going from one point to the next, where there is a logic in it, where you feel that the grammar and the syntax are actually working and communicating. They need not do this in exactly the old way, but there are certain archetypes in the unconscious, really deep down in us, that do demand certain conditions be fulfilled, but I can't say in words what those are. Perhaps I try in my larger pieces to grope towards what that might eventually be. (Peter Maxwell Davies)

ONE WORK I'VE ALWAYS REGARDED as extremely significant in terms of what happened in our century is Vaughan Williams's *Fantasia on a Theme of Thomas Tallis*, written as it was in the first decade of the century. It's about the rediscovery of a long-distant past and how a new sound defines itself in reaction to that past. Is it based on understanding? Is such understanding really possible? What does the oldness of this music signify for Vaughan Williams and for us listening to it? It's an extremely profound and very modern piece of music, but very rarely understood in such terms.

With recordings nowadays one has, as it were, a choice of parents that's absolutely terrifying – vertiginous – and yet from such a situation artists are going to have to learn new ways of defining themselves. But the same thing happened for painters, philosophers and writers in the Renaissance, when they rediscovered the Ancient Greeks and were revolutionized by that discovery and had to redefine themselves in terms of that discovery. Some very odd ideas grew up in the Renaissance, for instance the belief of the Florentine *Camerata* that they could re-create Greek drama in its artistic totality. But from that opera was born, and it could be that equally strange ideas will be born from our ferment and give birth to things that have a life of their own. It may be that they're here already and we can't see them yet. (Stephen Johnson)

Freedom at the margin

I'M GOING TO continue composing. They have no means of stopping me! If it means only writing pieces for one piano I will continue doing it. One of the wonderful things about new music is that economically it is completely marginal. It makes no profit, and it costs . . . something, yes, but in comparison to opera and so on, even an orchestral piece by a contemporary composer costs very little. So in the economic terms of the whole country – or any country in Europe, so far as I know – we're not a factor at all. We're completely on the margins, but isn't that wonderful? We're free to do what we want to do. (Julian Anderson)

Hearing ourselves: a rich variety

I DO LOVE THAT SAYING of Ernest Bloch: 'When we listen to music what we hear is ourselves.' Music is a language that enables us to hear ourselves in a way that nothing else does. It's extremely important that music's voice should be heard, particularly now, in this age of mind-numbing, soul-destroying commercialism. But I do hate the way the argument is polarized. Either everything has to appeal to the largest possible audience or the large audience is condemned as though it were the equivalent of a Nuremberg rally. I was at the first performance of Anthony Payne's completion of Elgar's Third Symphony, and I'm very glad I was part of that, just as I'm glad to have heard the first performances of several works by James Dillon as part of an audience of twenty, huddled together in a freezing church in London's East End. These are different kinds of experience, and they make you aware of how rich and varied the experience of creative listening can be. (Stephen Johnson)

List of Illustrations

Index

CD